The Theology of
JOHN CALVIN

The Theology of
JOHN CALVIN

Karl Barth

translated by
Geoffrey W. Bromiley

WILLIAM B. EERDMANS PUBLISHING COMPANY
GRAND RAPIDS, MICHIGAN / CAMBRIDGE, U.K.

First published 1922 as
Die Theologie Calvins
by Theologischer Verlag, Zürich

English translation © 1995 Wm. B. Eerdmans Publishing Co.
2140 Oak Industrial Drive N.E., Grand Rapids, Michigan 49505 /
P.O. Box 163, Cambridge CB3 9PU U.K.

Printed in the United States of America

00 99 98 97 96 95   7 6 5 4 3 2 1

Library of Congress Cataloging-in-Publication Data

Barth, Karl, 1886-1968.
[Theologie Calvins. English]
The theology of John Calvin / Karl Barth ; translated by Geoffrey W. Bromiley.
p.   cm.
Includes bibliographical references and indexes.
ISBN 978-0-8028-0696-3 (paper : alk. paper)
1. Calvin, Jean, 1509-1564. 2. Reformed Church —
Doctrines — History — 16th century. 3. Theology,
Doctrinal — History — 16th century.
BX9418.B15713 1995
230'.42'092'—dc20   95-33983
                                        CIP

Contents

Contents

Translator's Preface

Barth's Calvin lectures are naturally outdated. They are also incomplete and rather formless. Nevertheless, the wrestling of one theological giant with another can hardly fail to be exciting and instructive, no less and perhaps more so when they belong in general to the same theological and ecclesiastical tradition. Sooner or later, as pastor, preacher, expositor, and professor, Barth obviously and inevitably had to come to close grips with Calvin. Predictably, the impact when he did so would be decisive for himself, and in some way also for those with whom he might share the confrontation, as he does in the present lectures.

Barth's initial approach to Calvin, of course, had been gradual. His early theological interests had taken him in rather different directions, especially in Marburg. The pastorate in Geneva stirred his interest. It could hardly fail to do so when he found himself speaking from the very place where Calvin used to lecture. Among the commentaries he then used at Safenwil those of Calvin claimed a regular place. At one time he seems to have had a grandiose but nebulous idea of bringing the theology of Calvin into some kind of synthesis with that of Schleiermacher. His duty to teach Reformed studies at Göttingen, however, was what finally brought him face to face with the greatest of the Reformed fathers.

In the Calvin lectures one senses at first some reserve in the attitude to Calvin. In the staunch Lutheran center that was Göttingen, Barth could not escape the originality and vitality of the great first-generation reformer, Luther. We need only note the greater incidence of Luther quotations in what would eventually become *Church Dogmatics*, I/1 and 2. In comparison, a man of the second generation with its different tasks and problems seemed far less exciting and attractive. Calvin's own character appears also not to have made any immediate appeal to Barth's sympathy, and his theology had both formal and material features that could not command his wholehearted approval.

In the lectures, however, before devoting his attention to Calvin individually, Barth surveyed with extraordinary theological insight the relations between the Middle Ages and the Reformation on the one hand, and those between Luther, Zwingli, and Calvin on the other. Originally planned as the first two sections of an introductory chapter, these surveys expanded in a way that shattered the original program. But the loss was also gain, for theological analyses resulted from which all serious students of theology can still profit.

When Barth did at last come to Calvin, the intended brief introductory account of his life became a more detailed presentation that crowded out more specific discussion yet remained fragmentary. In this presentation it is noticeable that Calvin increasingly emerged as a dominant figure who knew what he believed and how to expound and defend it, and who also knew what he wanted and how to achieve and establish it. Barth never dealt with the culminating ministry in Geneva, the definitive *Institutes,* the discipline, the ecclesiastical influence. Nevertheless, by thorough discussion of the 1536 *Institutes,* the catechism, and the church constitution, along with the dispute with Bern and the lessons Calvin learned from the early experiences, Barth was still able to give what is in the last resort an appreciative as well as an insightful account of the essentials of Calvin as believer, theologian, commentator, pastor, and ecclesiastical statesman. One thing in particular to which he draws attention is the brilliant and consistent way in which Calvin both in theory and practice relates eternity and time without losing either one in the other.

If readers want a full-scale introduction to Calvin, this is not the work for them. Nor will they find here new detailed information. What we have instead is an exciting interaction that has all the freshness of the younger Barth, and that incidentally tells us a good deal about Barth himself and his own theological development, especially when read in conjunction with his contemporary letters to his friend Thurneysen. For these reasons no one with serious theological interest can afford to ignore these hastily composed lectures.

The translation follows the text scrupulously prepared from the difficult manuscript and typescript for the Swiss *Gesamtausgabe.* The few

Calvin quotations that Barth left in Latin or French, however, have been put into English. Many of the editorial notes have been shortened, some of the footnotes reworked, and datings adapted to the more familiar style of month first. Where the Swiss edition offers in the notes full Latin passages from Calvin, only the references are given. The structure of the work has been altered slightly in form to provide a more balanced presentation. Readers who wish to check Barth's analysis of the 1536 *Institutes* will find help in the translation (with introduction) which F. L. Battles published in 1975 under the title *Institution of the Christian Religion,* which uses the original 1536 Basel edition as well as CR and OS, and which usefully includes as well the 1532 Cop address and the 1534 placards.

We present this English version in the hope and confidence that it will make a significant contribution to the study and appreciation of both Calvin and Barth and that at the same time it will prove of personal interest and profit to all who read it.

Santa Barbara, Christmas 1992   GEOFFREY W. BROMILEY

Preface

Karl Barth and Calvin in 1922. Barth's interest in Calvin had first been kindled during his initial semester at Bern in the winter of 1904/5 when he attended his father's course on the history of the Reformation age. He referred to this influence in his own lectures.[1] He became interested on his own account in the fall of 1909 when he took his first post as auxiliary pastor to the German congregation in Geneva and when the great commemoration of Calvin's birth in 1509 was held there in the summer of 1909. The German congregation worshiped in the auditorium of St. Pierre where Calvin himself had once lectured. The idea of mounting the same rostrum as the reformer excited Barth, and during his Geneva years (up to 1911) he began to study the 1559 *Institutes* in depth. His letters from this period bear ample witness to this, as do his many markings in his copy of the *Institutes,* vol. II of the Corpus Reformatorum series. His lecture on the Christian faith and history (1910, published 1912) shows the impact of this reading, though Barth would say fifteen years later that it would have been better left unpublished.[2]

That Barth left Calvin's city with a real interest may be seen from the fact that he knew its local history so well and immersed himself in the study of the archives conducted under the Basel professor Paul

---

1. See 131.

2. For the former see *Vorträge und kleinere Arbeiten 1909-1914,* vol. III of *Gesamtausgabe* (Zurich, 1993), 149-212. See the autobiographical sketch in *Karl Barth-Rudolf Bultmann Letters 1922-1966* (Grand Rapids, 1981), 150ff.

Wernle.[3] More research remains to be done into Barth's early sermons to determine when, as he said,[4] he began to use Calvin's commentaries regularly in sermon preparation. By 1919 he had certainly read Kampschulte and Stähelin, whom he quotes so often in these lectures, and in his 1919 and 1922 *Romans* he constantly consulted Calvin's 1539 commentary. Intensive preoccupation with Calvin thus helped to form his theology even before his switch to an academic career.

When he accepted the call to Göttingen in 1921/22 to become honorary Professor of Reformed Theology, Barth saw it as his primary task to acquaint his students and himself with the classical documents of this theology.[5] The first winter he lectured two hours a week on the Heidelberg Catechism. The summer of 1922 he ventured on four hours a week on Calvin. He would then give courses on Zwingli, the Reformed confessions, and Schleiermacher.[6]

Calvin, then, was his first larger theme. The lectures show both diligent daily study of the material and fascination with it. We find both again, sometimes in language reminding us almost of contemporary Expressionism, in his letters to Thurneysen. Thus in a letter dated June 8, 1922, he calls Calvin a cataract, a primeval forest, something demonic, directly descending from the Himalayas, absolutely Chinese, marvelous, mythological. He saw no way of even receiving this phenomenon, let alone depicting it. Only a thin trickle passed into him, and he could pass on only a small portion of this. He could gladly spend the rest of his life with Calvin.[7]

Barth found himself forced at this time to gain his own understanding of the genuine Reformed tradition and to determine the specific character of what he called the second turn in the Reformation and therefore of the epochal significance of Zwingli and Calvin in relation and antithesis to Luther. He saw the historical mission of the Reformed version of the Reformation in its taking up again of what he took to be a common theme of the Middle Ages and the modern period, that of ethics, but now on the basis of the fundamental insight brought to light by Luther. We

3. See P. Wernle, *Calvin und Basel bis zum Tode des Myconius 1535-1552* (Basel, 1909), 107 n. 391.

4. See below, 392 n. 23.

5. Cf. Bw.Th. I, 357f., 360f.

6. The *Gesamtausgabe* plans publication of the first two courses, while the third is already available: *The Theology of Schleiermacher* (Grand Rapids, 1982).

7. Bw.Th. II, 80.

may set this underlying theme of the lectures in the context of Barth's own situation as an academic beginner and outsider on the Lutheran faculty at Göttingen. In the letter to Thurneysen dated May 22, 1992, he spoke with painful irony of the path he had to take in interpreting Calvin, beginning with the *Psychopannychia,* then going on to the sudden conversion, then to the Cop address.[8] He added that there would be constant allusion to ethics in contrast to the idle soul sleep of Lutheranism, naturally from the perspective of eternity, but in such a way as to dumbfound the Swiss[9] in particular. He was glad he had found what his ranking would be last fall.[10] It was essential that he be differentiated from Stange.[11] Distance must be kept.[12]

Text

For the summer semester 1922 Barth announced three hours a week on Calvin and three on Hebrews. But some months earlier he was very worried about this double load and in April he said a crisis had arisen that caused him to drop Hebrews and focus on four hours for Calvin.[13] He gave the classes from April 27 to July 28, with a week's break for Pentecost, lecturing from 7 to 8 A.M. on Mondays, Tuesdays, Thursdays, and Fridays to some thirty or forty students.[14] The original manuscript, now in the Barth Archive at Basel, is on both sides of 235 pages in black ink. The archive also has a typed copy from the same period possibly owed to his friend Rudolf Pestalozzi in Zurich. There are many mistakes in the copy, not surprising since the manuscript is so hard to read. Barth himself corrected some of these mistakes in his own hand. In the present edition we have compared the copy and the original and purged out most of the remaining errors.

---

8. See below, 146ff., 136ff., 141ff. See Bw.Th. II, 79.

9. The reference is to Swiss students in the class.

10. The reference is to the exposition of chs. 12ff. in the 2nd edition of Barth's *Romans,* in which he found a new approach to ethics in continuity with existing exposition.

11. Carl Stange (1870-1959) and Georg Wobbermin (1869-1943) were the professors of systematic theology at Göttingen.

12. Bw.Th. II, 79.

13. Ibid., 29, 65.

14. Ibid., 71.

Arrangement and Structure

Barth shared his original plan for the lectures with Thurneysen, but a month before the semester began he realized that he could not carry it out and that he must focus on Calvin's theology, especially his dogmatics. He would perhaps turn to the ethics in the winter semester, he wrote to his friend.[15] This scaling down did not affect his intention of laying a twofold foundation by surveying medieval theology and comparing Calvin to Luther and Zwingli.[16] These two sections, along with a sketch of Calvin's life, would make up the first chapter ("Presuppositions"). Four more chapters would follow with the emphasis on the last, that is, Calvin's preaching in ch. 2, exegesis in ch. 3, polemics in ch. 4, and finally theological system (1559 *Institutes*) in ch. 5. This is what he told the class the first hour,[17] and even on May 19, when he had spent more than three weeks on the first two sections of ch. 1 and was only just taking up Calvin's life, he still thought his plan was feasible, though he expressly regretted he could not adopt the better method his father had once used, namely, that of embodying the theology in a running account of the life.[18]

Even if we cannot track down in the manuscript the exact moment he changed his mind, he did indeed switch to the method he admired in his father. His breadth of outlook and pleasure in detail, however, meant that he could not by a long way reach the end of Calvin's life, but could cover it more fully only up to the summer of 1538 and then in the last three lectures give a mere summary of the Strassburg years (1538-1541) under three selected topics. Compared to the original plan, then, the course breaks off when Barth had completed only a small part of his first chapter, and he never even started the chapters that were to be the heart of the work.

If in dealing with Calvin's life Barth at first concealed this fact from himself, or at least from his audience, it came home to him with a shock in the Pentecost vacation. During these days he read all the Calvin material available at least to get some knowledge of the main part of the course which he would now never reach, having to remain stuck in the prolegomena. At best he would carry the life far enough, and give a genetic account

15. Ibid., 60.
16. Loc. cit.
17. See below, 9f.
18. See below, 131.

of the writings in such a way that he and the students would be introduced to the true theme. There could be no talk of the systematic treatment he had had in mind. He would need three further semesters for that.[19] On June 28 he complained that he would not finish by a long way and that the course was something of a monstrosity.[20]

Some compensation for the formal deficiency is to be found in the way in which Barth includes within the life an analysis of various early works of Calvin, especially the first edition of the *Institutes.* In looking at the texts and themes Barth deals with, and the actual structure of the fragment, those who know the material will note that even within these limitations Barth gives a materially good account of Calvin's theology. He does not see or present it fragmentarily but seizes on the essence and offers an integral account according to the nonpolemical content.

Barth was well aware of the oddness but also the advantages of his method, as also that he was skating all the time on rather thin ice. He described his monstrosity with a good deal of self-mockery as biography, theology, general history, exposition from the standpoint of eternity, and contemporary relevance, all wrapped up in a ball that rolls on very slowly. The real problem was the shortness of time for preparation. Each lecture he had to draw a deep breath and move on to something new. Often this was undoubtedly not very rewarding, and he made it tolerable for the class only by lecturing in a weighty and threatening voice.[21]

At a first glance chaotic, the structure proves on closer analysis to be good. The more detailed headings, partly supplied by Barth, partly added by the editor where it seemed appropriate, show that there is at least a fivefold hierarchy of division that is fairly easy to discern.

Reformation Sources

Barth had at his disposal the works and letters of Calvin and some minutes of the Genevan council in the relevant volumes of the Corpus Reformatorum (CR 29-68). His own references are constantly to this edition, though he does not specify this. When the notes give the detailed references they use CO for *Calvini opera* 1-59. As we know, there are many errors

---

19. Bw.Th. II, 80f.
20. Ibid., 86.
21. Ibid.

in this 19th-century edition. Four years after Barth's lectures his brother Peter, later aided by Wilhelm Niesel and Dora Scheuner, started a five-volume critical edition under the title *Opera selecta* (1926ff.). It is true that the first volume (OS I) did not quite measure up to the claims made for it, but we have followed here the method generally accepted in research today and used this edition (OS I-V) wherever possible. Since OS refers back to CO it is easy to compare the two. The same method is followed in listing the works and passages mentioned by Barth.

Similar principles apply when it comes to Barth's quotations from Luther and Zwingli. When he did not use secondary sources, his edition for Luther was the Erlangen edition and for Zwingli the Schuler and Schultess edition of 1828ff. The Luther references are not always exact, and we have added to them the corresponding references in the Weimar edition (WA), while in the case of Zwingli we have used the Corpus Reformatorum (CR LXXXVIIIff.).

A difficult editorial decision had to be made [in the case of the Swiss edition] as a result of Barth's different ways of handling firsthand material. Sometimes Barth stuck so closely to the original that he seemed to be giving a translation with interjected comments, and even when he adopted a freer approach it is always plain which sentences come from Calvin. This is the situation in the treatment of the 1536 *Institutes*.[22] The Swiss edition has in such cases given the original text in the notes so that readers can easily follow or check Barth's rendering. In other cases, for example, the two 1537 epistles or the answer to Sadolet,[23] Barth simply offers a summary of the contents and the notes offer no more than the up-to-date references. Since we cannot always fix the boundaries between the two methods with precision, the editors had to make judgment calls in many instances.

Barth had only limited access to German translations of Calvin. R. Schwarz had translated selected letters, and the biographies of Kampschulte and Stähelin contained some translated quotations. Barth used these when available, though with some freedom, but for the most part he used the Latin and French originals or made his own translations. If these are not always accurate — he once complained about his poor Latin with reference to this course — we do not indicate this in the notes unless the mistake affects interpretation of the text.[24]

22. See below, 157ff.
23. See below, 234ff., 402ff.
24. Bw.Th. II, 81. See below, 149 n. 16.

Finally, it should be pointed out that in quoting Calvin's French and Luther's German Barth modernizes the spelling. This edition accepts Barth's procedure without referring to the originals.

Barth's own distinctive style and spelling have been left untouched, though the punctuation has been quietly brought up to date, especially with the addition of commas, and any grammatically incomplete sentences have been completed in square brackets. Square brackets are also used when fuller biblical references are supplied. Barth's spelling of names like Occam, Eckhardt, and Butzer has been left intact in the Swiss text, though modern forms are used in the notes. A striking difference is the use of Stähelin for the author of one of the Calvin biographies. Though this is the name on the title page of the work, Barth, who knew many members of this old Basel family, always used Staehelin, no other form being thinkable in Basel.

Underlinings in color are reproduced in the form of italics, but pencil underlinings, which were simply to make oral delivery easier, are ignored. As he often did, Barth wrote long passages with no paragraph breaks, and to make reading easier the editor has followed the usual practice of the *Gesamtausgabe* and provided additional breaks.

Acknowledgments

The course on Calvin was one of the first texts to be assigned when the *Gesamtausgabe* was planned in 1970. The Basel church historian Max Geiger was put in charge. But when he died in 1978 no advance work on the project was found among his papers. The work was then assigned to me, but unfortunately I could not do much about it until finishing my term as rector at Wuppertal in 1985. That is why this important piece of the theological history of the 20th century is ready for the press only on its 70th birthday.

There is every reason to be delighted and thankful that it has now reached this stage. It could not have done so without the intensive help of many others. Thanks go especially to Hinrich Stoevesandt, who as director of the Barth Archive kindly gave supervision and assistance in some of the technical matters, who in letters and conversations also helped with the research, bibliography, and references, and who finally supplied the index of subjects, not to speak of the encouragement he gave to persevere at decisive moments.

I am also grateful to my former assistant Achim Reinstädtler, who stood by me so well when at difficult junctures not only industry but also élan and academic knowledge were needed. Work could hardly have begun in the late 1980s without his close cooperation both on the work itself and as professor and assistant at Wuppertal.

I am also indebted to the Wuppertal school and to the Rhineland Evangelical Church for practical help. In particular, the Wuppertal secretary, Christel Ebert, typed an essential part of the manuscript from the copy.

Work on the edition coincided with the introduction of computers, and Joachim Lenz, the Wuppertal assistant for development, deserves thanks for the technical help given on the notes with his computer. Carmen Birkholz and Martin Heimbucher helped with proofreading, and the former also supplied the index of scripture passages, the latter the index of names. All who read and use the book are in their debt.

Many others, colleagues, scholars, experts, and nonexperts, helped with information and references, and it is in gratitude to my contemporaries that I offer this volume to the world today. I do so in the conviction that these lectures are still important for three reasons even seventy years later.

First, this first great historical work of Barth is significant as a stage in his own theological development, bearing impressive testimony as it does to his ability to combine detailed study with a distinctive insight into epochal connections and also resolutely to bring together in his thinking, as well as to differentiate, time and eternity, as he then liked to say, or knowledge of God and knowledge of history.

Second, this almost improvised essay is not only astonishingly fresh and full of life as compared to the Calvin literature of the period, but even today it can be a gripping and reliable introduction to Calvin's work and theology, and it displays a sympathy with the Reformation cause, and a sensitivity to it, that are seldom reached in our century.

Finally, the lectures deserve to be evaluated in their secular context. On the basis of his own theology, so strikingly set forth in the second edition of his *Romans,* Barth opens himself to the impact of the person and thinking of the reformer, and brings this to expression in a way that gives readers of a later generation a feel for that age which manifested itself expressionistically in other theological and literary works of the day. "Absolutely Chinese, marvelous, mythological, demonic,"[25] this was how

25. See below, n. 25. See above, XIV.

Barth found Calvin, and so this 1922 account, though it may be rudimentary and something of an improvisation, meets us like, shall we say, Kafka's *Castle* of the same year.

Wuppertal, Summer 1992   HANS SCHOLL

Abbreviations

BI	Calvin's *Institution of the Christian Religion* (1536), ed. F. L. Battles (Atlanta, 1975)
BSLK	*Die Bekenntnisschriften der evangelisch-lutherischen Kirche* (Göttingen, 1930, 8th ed. 1979)
BSRK	*Die Bekenntnisschriften der evangelisch-reformierten Kirche,* ed. E. F. K. Müller (Leipzig, 1903; reprinted Zurich, 1987)
Bw.Th.	K. Barth and E. Thurneysen, *Briefwechsel,* ed. Thurneysen, *Karl Barth Gesamtausgabe,* V: *Gespräche,* vol. I: 1914-21 (Zurich, 1973); vol. II: 1921-30 (Zurich, 1974)
CD	K. Barth, *Church Dogmatics* (Edinburgh, 1956ff.)
CO	*Ioannis Calvini opera quae supersunt omnia,* ed. G. Braun, E. Cunitz, and E. Reuss (Braunschweig, 1963ff.) (= CR 29-87).
CR	Corpus Reformatorum (Halle, Braunschweig, Berlin, Zurich, 1834ff.)
CSEL	Corpus scriptorum ecclesiasticorum Latinorum (Vienna, 1866ff.)
CW	*Die Christliche Welt*
EA	M. Luther, *Sämtliche Werke* (Erlangen, 1826-57)
EOL	M. Luther, *Sämtliche Werke,* Opera Latina (Erlangen, 1826ff.)
EvTh	*Evangelische Theologie*
Inst.	J. Calvin, *Institutio Christianae religionis* (1559)

LCC	Library of Christian Classics
LW	Luther's Works
MPG	J. Migne, *Patrologiae cursus completus,* Series Graeca (Paris, 1857ff.)
OS	*Ioannis Calvini Opera selecta,* ed. P. Barth et al. (Munich, 1925ff.)
PhB	Philosophische Bibliothek
RE	*Realencyklopädie für protestantische Theologie und Kirche* (Gotha, 3rd ed. 1896-1913)
RGG	*Die Religion in Geschichte und Gegenwart* (Tübingen, 1st ed. 1909-13; 2nd, 1927-32; 3rd, 1956-65)
S. Th.	Thomas Aquinas, *Summa theologica*
Schaff	P. Schaff, *Creeds of Christendom,* vol. III (reprinted Grand Rapids, 1985)
ThB	Theologische Bücherei
WA	M. Luther, *Werke. Kritische Ausgabe* (Weimar, 1883ff.)
WA B	Luther's *Werke: Briefwechsel*
WA TR	Luther's *Werke: Tischreden*
Z	Huldreich Zwingli, *Sämtliche Werke* (Berlin and Zurich, 1905ff.) (= CR 88ff.).
ZKG	*Zeitschrift für Kirchengeschichte*

Introduction

In his exposition of Rom. 4:23 (49, 86) and the preface to his exposition of Acts (48, vii), Calvin quotes a saying from classical antiquity to the effect that history is life's teacher.[1] On this saying he made the interesting comment that if the telling of history can teach us so much about what we humans do and fail to do, and is worthy of so much praise, then how much more honor ought we to give to sacred history, the stories that not only help to make our external lives virtuous but also — which is far more important — show us how God had his church in view from the very first, how he is always present as a true Helper to those who rely upon his riches and protection, and how he grants grace and a hearing to poor sinners, so that as the stories teach us faith they also lift us up to heaven.[2]

A significant and fruitful principle of distinguishing between history and sacred history lies behind this statement. All history is morally instructive, said Calvin. But sacred history is instructive as regards our relation to God, or, more accurately, our relation to the salvation that comes from God. He found this history, of course, in biblical history, which was for him, first, at least a sphere of its own, and second, something sharply different from secular history. If we ponder this, we can hardly abandon this sharp distinction, contrast, and tension between the two histories. It is by no means obvious that history should be instructive not

1. CR 49, 86, and 48, VII, quoting Cicero, *De oratore* 2.36.
2. CR 48, VII.

1

merely in morals but also in relation to God. This is not something given. It has to take place. We have to agree with Calvin, too, that the Bible must be viewed as the great, unique proclamation of this event. But perhaps we have to make the distinction rather differently so as to bring out the fact that the biblical history only proclaims the sacred history, salvation history, the history of God, the history that is the meaning and content of all history, and that seeks to speak in and above and beyond all so-called secular history.

Calvin himself did not keep consistently to the line of distinction that he usually drew. Thus in his 73rd sermon on Job (34, 145f.) he expressly said that we must not only profit from what is contained in holy scripture but also have the wisdom, when we read what pagan writers have to tell us, to apply to ourselves what God did there.[3] As we see from the context, he had in mind only divine judgments on the ungodly; and in the many passages in which he ascribed to pagans some knowledge of the good, and indeed of eternal life and even of God himself, he always insisted that this served only to make them inexcusable. Yet he fully integrated world history into the history of God even though, unlike Zwingli,[4] he found salvation history, and the community of the elect, only in biblical history and the related history of the Christian era. The latter point involves breaking through the mythological biblicism that in Calvin — I have in mind especially his view of the relation between the OT and the NT — points everywhere beyond itself. In discussing his concept of holy scripture we shall have to speak expressly of the way in which he looked ahead in this regard.

But that is not now our concern. We are looking at the rule that history is life's teacher in the light of which Calvin could view secular history also as sacred history. For my part I would like to make this saying the methodological principle of all the semester's work. That we should learn from history Calvin argued at the end of sermon 79 on Deuteronomy (28, 682-83 [on 32:5-7]) on the simple ground that we humans are not oxen or asses that know only the present but have a reason that embraces things past and things to come.[5] We have, then, a sense of time. For Calvin this meant at once that we are able to "dispose of things ourselves."[6] Again,

---

3. CR 34, 145f.
4. Cf. Zwingli's *On Providence* (1530), Z 6, 3, 182, 15-16, and 224, 30.
5. CR 28, 682.
6. Ibid.

this meant immediately that we can see that "the whole redounds to the honor and glory of him who has given us this intelligence."[7] Looking at the past, we see how God has ruled the world and we thus arrive at ourselves and draw the necessary conclusions from the insight. Investigating the past, we should "contemplate the works of God that he might be glorified by us."[8] For Calvin that was the essence and purpose of historical study. As he said in sermon 31 on Job (33, 385 [on 8:7-13]),[9] history is "an ocean and abyss of wisdom." Naturally, he went on, mere pleasure in reading, mere historical interest in the past, would be a "kind of vanity." History must be for us a school in which we "learn to regulate our lives"[10] in the knowledge that from the creation of the world God has at all times ruled in his church. Even more important in this respect is a passage from sermon 1 on Ephesians (51, 250 [on 1:1]) in which Calvin comments on the words *tois hagiois tois ousin en Ephesō* that though the name of the city is given, the teaching is for all of us *(commune)*. God meant it to be used by us, and we should accept it as though Paul were alive among us. Indeed, we should not pay heed merely to Paul but to him who sent him. For Paul died when he had run his course, but the Spirit of God is immortal. If I may interject a brief word, in making Calvin the object of the semester's study, we shall not do violence to him if we look at him from the same standpoint as he did at Paul, or, I might add, as Paul did at Abraham: "Il est trespassé après avoir achevé sa course: mais cependant l'Esprit de Dieu est immortel."[11]

But what does the saying that history is life's teacher mean? I have given you an example of how I understand it. Three things it cannot mean. First, we cannot stop at establishing that four hundred years ago Calvin said this or that. We may have excellent documentation. We may argue the point cogently. What we establish may be interesting in itself. But to stop there would be to deny that history is life's teacher, and, I would add, it would be to deny the immortal Spirit of God whom Calvin heard speaking through Paul even though Paul was long dead. It may well be true and worth noting that Calvin said this or that, but if we are not taught by it then — I venture to say — his statements are not historical.

---

7. Ibid.
8. Ibid., 683.
9. CR 33, 385.
10. Ibid.
11. CR 51, 250.

The historical Calvin is the living Calvin who, as he did say this or that, wanted to say something specific, one thing, and who, insofar as his works are preserved, still wants to say it, perhaps in a way that he could not do in his lifetime and to earlier readers of the works. Historically the French and Latin words that only the editors of the Corpus Reformatorum can assure us are really Calvin's do not derive their force from the fact that they are in the Corpus but from the fact that their original didactic meaning leaps out from them with all the depth and breadth and vitality that Calvin did not just by chance put into them the moment he wrote them, but aimed to put into them with the full intention and intuition of his personality that these words are only one possible way of expressing; that he had indeed to put into them insofar as the whole Calvin himself with all his words is again only one possibility, one stage, in the march of the one eternal truth that, while we humans come and go, remains the same and yet is fresh each morning [Lam. 3:23]. Calvin's theology is historical because, through every transparency and means of communication, it is teaching by the immortal Spirit of God.

Second, we do not have teaching by repeating Calvin's words as our own or making his views ours. That would not be to make his words historical, that is, to give them life. Perhaps at times or to a large extent we do this. Why should we not adopt some of Calvin's formulations as they stand and make them our own? We may, but that is not the aim in studying Calvin. Be they never so devout and faithful, those who simply echo Calvin are not good Calvinists, that is, they are not really taught by Calvin. Being taught by Calvin means entering into dialogue with him, with Calvin as the teacher and ourselves as the students, he speaking, we doing our best to follow him and then — this is the crux of the matter — making our own response to what he says. If that does not happen we might just as well be listening to Chinese; the historical Calvin is not present. For that Calvin wants to teach and not just to say something that we will repeat. The aim, then, is a dialogue that may end with the taught saying something very different from what Calvin said but that they learned from or, better, through him. Calvin's doctrine is the teacher, and therefore history is when it kindles in us our own independent knowledge which basically makes that doctrine superfluous no matter how much or how little of the teacher's words we can directly make our own. For if a teacher is able, and students do their duty, then by the year's end they do not need the teacher. If they stay where they are, then that would be a terrible symptom that something is wrong. If as students they have really

4

found a good theological teacher, as I once did in Wilhelm Herrmann,[12] then they will surely know what I mean. We listen, we learn, and then we go our own way and in so doing we give evidence of respect, of doing the teacher justice.

Third, we cannot make Calvin say something other than what he said four hundred years ago. Like Paul, he is dead, and the deposit of what he said in his writings and recorded sermons is the only form in which he can speak to us today. If we want to know what he would say to us today, we must keep to what he tried to say then, and to what in some degree he did actually say, in all its historical necessity and also contingency, in all its limitation and uniqueness. We must pay our first and very serious attention to him, beginning our thinking with him, if we really have it in view to let ourselves be taught by him. It is an open possibility that he might have said then something different from what we with our best knowledge and conscience have to say today. In handling Reformation history we must be on guard against falling into the style of refined Roman Catholic hagiography and presenting the absolute — or what we regard as such — as though it were wandering on earth in the form of Luther, or, if we are Reformed, Zwingli or Calvin. In that way we can do justice neither to them nor to their opponents or critics, nor finally learn from them what is to be learned if we view impartially the way in which they were historically conditioned.

But I must issue a warning here. With any classic it is at any rate a bold venture to claim that he said something different from what we have to say when we seriously tackle the same subject even when the wording formally cries out aloud that he did say something different. It is a bold thing, and in most cases simply out of taste, to assume that, for example, Paul or Luther was mistaken, or, to put it bluntly, that they did not really know what we think we know with our more thorough discussion of the same subject. As a rule it is better to let the alien saying of such an author, for example, what Paul says about the powers that be in Rom. 13, at least put a question mark against our own ever so well-grounded opinion, or to set it in its own living context, throwing light upon it from other dicta of the same author, from his total thinking, or not least of all from the immanent logic of the matter itself, interpreting it and perhaps correcting

---

12. In the summer semester of 1908 and from November 1908 to August 1909 Barth was in Marburg and heard Herrmann on dogmatics. For statements about his relation to Herrmann cf. *Karl Barth-Rudolf Bultmann Letters 1922-1966* (Grand Rapids, 1981); and Barth, *Theology and Church* (New York, 1962), 157.

it, but not at all abandoning it, and in any case first seeking what seems to us to be wooden, banal, perverse, or meaningless in the text in our own view of it rather than in the text itself, which may be a little better than we suppose, even the objectionable feature being meant in a much more vivid way than first appears.

I cannot stress too strongly that you should always treat an author with a certain humility on the one side and on the other — and this is much the same thing — with a certain free and understanding humor, presuming that the author is probably always right in some sense even when wrong, so that our only task is to see how far this is always so, perhaps even unintentionally. Insofar as I know Calvin thus far, I would not dare in this respect to put him absolutely on a par with Paul and Luther, but in a modified sense I would still say the same about him. Hence we need not feel under any pressure when we read his words and thoughts as they are before us, but may do so quietly and if need be with a full inner freedom to hold aloof from what he says. At the same time we will not do violence to him by not entering into the dynamic of his thoughts, into what he wanted to say even if in some cases he was unable to do so. For we are aware ourselves that, being human, we can only to a limited extent say what we really want to say. If others want to understand us historically, they may not simply read what we have really said, or work on it, but must at least have the skill to detect what we wanted to say. Those who as readers of a historical source will not even to the very end think after and beyond the author's thoughts as he has expressed them are thinking just as unhistorically as those who believe they must inject their own thoughts into the author's. Obviously it is not easy, and indeed it is incredibly dangerous, to steer a golden path between this Scylla and Charybdis. But that does not alter the fact that we must at any rate seek it.

Since these methodological observations do not enjoy universal recognition, I must support them with some basic theses.

There is much talk of objectivity in historical research. But how far can history be just an object, a theme, something detached from the eyes that see it? As intellectual history at any rate — and when is history not intellectual history? — history is at least as much subject as object, at least as much here in my eyes as there in the sources. The historical Calvin is not a fixed, finished, dead entity imprisoned in the years 1509-1564 and unable to leave them. The 59 volumes of the Corpus Reformatorum that contain his works are not secretly his coffin. In Calvin studies we cannot keep Calvin to what he once said as though he had nothing more or new to say today! His work did not simply occur then; it still occurs today. In what he once said he still speaks, saying what he once wanted to say. We may not speak merely of Calvin's historical impact; Calvin himself has an ongoing history into which we insert ourselves when we deal with him, in which we have a part to his honor or dishonor and to our own good or ill. Is not the history of philosophy also the history of Plato? Is not the history of modern Germany also the history of Bismarck? Is not the history of Christian theology also the history of Paul? Is it not true that four hundred years after his own lifetime Paul not merely had an impact but did something really new for Augustine, and that eleven hundred years later he said something really new to Luther? Might it not be that Jesus of Nazareth said things in John's Gospel and the rule of St. Francis and Grünewald's "Crucifixion" and the novels of Dostoyevsky that he did not say in the Synoptic Gospels? Is history, or, more pointedly, the historical in history, only a thing of yesterday and the day before and not also of today and tomorrow?

What is in the *Institutes* was certainly decided when Calvin set his hand finally to the work in 1559. Yet it is decided again in a distinctive way in our own eyes as we read the *Institutes* today. Let us see in what way it is decided in us and for us. Calvin can run through our veins like electricity so that we become Calvinian and are set under extreme compulsion and for this reason are supremely free, citizens of heaven and hence also resolute citizens of the world, watching and therefore hastening [cf. 2 Pet. 3:12]. But there are those with whom Calvin can do nothing but put them in the fire, and Michael Servetus is not the only one to whom Calvin has done this. You can clearly hear the cries of the burning in more than one book about Calvin, even in books that are brilliant. In power or weakness, for good or evil, and probably both, the work of Calvin is done in us if we give ourselves to him, and it is a different work from what was done four hundred years ago, yet his own original and highly distinctive work. The variety of historical phenomena, the multiplicity of historical individuals, the fact that I am not Calvin nor Calvin I, is undoubtedly a problem that confronts us, very true and very enlightening in its own way, but only as a fact, not as a metaphysical reality. We all indeed come up against this apparently undeniable fact of the absolute distinction between the I and the Thou, and it is in our better and most fruitful moments that we do so, not merely those who in obedience to the commandment love their neighbor as themselves, or would like to do so [Mark 12:31 par.], not merely naive Bible students who in the words of a remote psalmist hear their own voice to their astonishment or judgment, but even the most objective investigators who in order to understand the text try in some measure to think its thoughts as their own.

As we certainly do not overlook the fact of variety, of individuality, no less certainly this fact obstinately and at every juncture points beyond itself. The angle from which we see what we are studying, and the presupposition of what we are studying, seems not to be multiplicity but unity. We come from that and return to it. It is the great "As if" with which we always work, whether wittingly or unwittingly. The God of Abraham? The God of Isaac? The God of Jacob? Yes, but not the God of the dead [Luke 20:37-38], of those who have been, of those who are lost here and there in the sea of time, of those who are isolated and limited, but the God of the living, *the* God in whom the multiplicity of our life is unity. *Pantes gar autō zōsin,* in him, the One, they all live, adds Luke, the pupil of Paul (Luke 20:38). And *poly planasthe* is Mark's word (12:27) to those who have *ears* to hear but not ears to *hear.* The problem of individuals, of ethics and history, will not leave us alone, because it implies unity, the unity of God. We see that the past is so important for us, not just true or interesting or profitable but vitally necessary, because it has present significance. We open books from the past in order to come to ourselves. The living, speaking, working past is the present.

All study of the past is thus done for its own sake. Historical study is itself historical action and passion; it is itself history. The past seeks to live again, to speak and work, to be the present. That this may happen can alone be its purpose, and that we may be open to its happening can be its only essential presupposition. This is not for me a postulate but a simple fact. All study of history is above all itself history, the living, speaking, and working past, and thus itself the present as well. No historian can be detached and not seriously seek and find himself or herself in history. Have you ever found a historical book that is not above all else a mirror of its author's soul? That image, history as a mirror, does not come from me but from Calvin, who liked to use it (33, 386; 34, 146).[13] Each time, then, one can only ask: Who is reflected in this mirror? What kind of present is it that studies the past there? Or what is the past living and speaking and working there? We are all hearing, but with what ears? We are all seeking, but what?

13. CR 33, 385f., on Job 8:9-10; also 34, 146 on 22:4-5.

When we consider how uncannily different are the answers to these questions, we have the solution to the riddle why the results of historical research, especially into the Reformation, are so uncannily different. With astonishing justice we reap what we sow in this study of history [cf. Gal. 6:7]. Or rather, history with astonishing justice gives to each his own *(suum cuique)*. It gives us what we are and therefore what we seek and find: anecdotes if we want anecdotes, dogmatics if we are dogmaticians, weapons if we are squabblers, a museum if we are antiquaries, beautiful lines of development if we are cultural philosophers, edification if we are devout, grounds for new skepticism if we are doubters. "If I know what I believe, I know what is in scripture, because scripture has in it no more than Christ and Christian faith" (Holl, *Luther,* I, 559).[14] It is also true, however, that those who are nothing and seek nothing will undoubtedly also find their own nothingness. To those who have will be given so that they are full, but from those who have not will be taken away even what they have [Matt. 13:12]. History confirms all of us in our openness or obduracy, in our honest seeking after truth or our erring and perhaps wanting to err, in our profound unrest or our illegitimate rest. We can only take our place in this regard and say to ourselves that this is how it must be. History will talk to us and we will then be shown who we are. To study history is to come under judgment. That carries with it a promise but also a threat, a threat but also a promise. For the verdict may be twofold. We do not have the possibility of approaching history without presuppositions, but we do have the possibility of reflecting on the presuppositions, on the final presupposition, of bowing under the judgment under which we stand, under the grace or lack of it, and of giving unremitting obedience to the command with which we are constantly released from that judgment. Perhaps a glance into this situation that is free from all illusions will best enable us to see and understand what has happened with relative calmness of vision and sureness of judgment. And perhaps this approach to our subject, the theology of Calvin, is particularly appropriate because it rests on the thought which describes his theology better than any other, that of the divine majesty and freedom before which we are nothing and which claims us totally.

I plan to begin my lectures with a chapter on the presuppositions of Calvin's theology, the relation of the Reformation to the Middle Ages,

---

14. K. Holl, *Gesammelte Aufsätze zur Kirchengeschichte,* vol. I, *Luther* (Tübingen, 2nd and 3rd ed. 1925), 559 n. 3, quoting WA 8, 236, 18-20.

Calvin's relation to Luther and Zwingli, and Calvin's life and personality. Then in three shorter chapters I will deal with Calvin's preaching, exegesis, and polemics. Finally, in a fifth and main chapter I will treat of Calvin's theological system on the basis of the *Institutes*. In my view we must first prepare the way for an understanding of the *Institutes* by getting a picture of what Calvin said extemporaneously when addressing the congregation, when he read and expounded the Bible with no set purpose, and when he fought with opponents now on the one front and now on the other. Little work has been done in this field, and I cannot promise to cut a wide swath through this almost unexplored territory. But the last great book on Calvin, that of Wernle,[15] has made it clear to me that I must at least venture to take this course.

I am quoting Calvin from the Corpus Reformatorum edition, vols. 29-87 (quoted as 1-59).[16] Tholuck has editions of the *Institutes* and the most important exegetical writings.[17] These editions may often be picked up, and I recommend you to buy them if you have the chance. E. F. K. Müller of Erlangen edited a German translation of the *Institutes* and most of the exegetical works, and Rudolf Schwarz translated a selection of the letters.[18] These are aids for which we must be grateful now that almost all of us do not read Latin as readily as our parents and grand-parents. Yet that does not mean that if we really want a thorough grasp of the subject we can do other than stick to the original text.

I will add further books for study as we come to each section.

---

15. P. Wernle, *Der evangelische Glaube nach den Hauptschriften der Reformatoren,* vol. III, *Calvin* (Tübingen, 1919).

16. See the editor's preface above.

17. *Johannis Calvini Institutio,* ed. A. Tholuck (Berlin, 1834-35); and *Johannes Calvini Commentarii in NT,* ed. A. Tholuck (Berlin, 1831-34).

18. E. F. K. Müller, *Johannes Calvin, Unterricht in der christlichen Religion* (Neukirchen, 1909) (translation incomplete) and *Johannes Calvins Auslegung der Heiligen Schrift in deutscher Übersetzung,* 14 vols. (Neukirchen, 1919ff.); R. Schwarz, *Johannes Calvins Lebenswerk in seinen Briefen: Eine Auswahl von Briefen Calvins in deutscher Übersetzung,* 2 vols. (Tübingen, 1909; 2nd ed. in 3 vols., Neukirchen, 1961-62).

PART I

PRESUPPOSITIONS

Reformation and Middle Ages

Loofs, *Leitfaden,* 4th ed., 601-62; Tschackert, *Entstehung der lutherischen und der reformierten Kirchenlehre,* 6-33; Seeberg, *Dogmengeschichte,* 2nd ed., IV, 1-55; Troeltsch, "Protestantisches Christentum und Kirche in der Neuzeit," in *Kultur der Gegenwart,* I/4, section 1; and on this Loofs, *Luthers Stellung zum Mittelalter und zur Neuzeit* (Halle, 1907); Troeltsch, *Soziallehren der christlichen Kirchen und Gruppen,* 427-512; Hermelink (in Krüger's *Handbuch der Kirchengeschichte*), 1-58.[1] No matter what our evaluation of them, it will be seen that the works of Troeltsch had the greatest influence on early 20th-century discussion.

In the first instance Calvin's theology naturally interests us in its historical context as an outstanding record of Reformation theology that historically and at times even legally has served as a basis of proclamation in modern Protestant churches. If it is of concern to us as Protestant theologians to be clear where we come from and where we are going as

---

1. F. Loofs, *Leitfaden zum Studium der Dogmengeschichte,* 4th ed. (1906; enlarged 7th ed. by K. Aland; Tübingen, 1968 [page numbers given in parentheses]); P. Tschackert, *Die Entstehung der lutherischen und der reformierten Kirchenlehre* (Göttingen, 1910); R. Seeberg, *Lehrbuch der Dogmengeschichte,* vol. IV (Leipzig, 1917; 4th ed.), §73, Prolegomena; E. Troeltsch, "Protestantisches Christentum und Kirche in der Neuzeit," in *Die Kultur der Gegenwart* (Berlin and Leipzig, 1906), 254-69; F. Loofs, *Luthers Stellung zum Mittelalter und zur Neuzeit . . .* (Halle, 1907); E. Troeltsch, *Die Soziallehren der christlichen Kirchen und Gruppen,* Gesammelte Schriften, vol. I (Tübingen, 1912); H. Hermelink, *Reformation und Gegenreformation,* part 3 of *Handbuch der Kirchengeschichte,* ed. G. Krüger (Tübingen, 1911).

such, then we have every reason to turn again and again to the question how far what we are and think and say does truly, and not merely according to the claim made or displayed on Reformation Days or similar occasions, correspond to what the founders of Protestant theology were and to what they thought and said about God and the world and humanity. And if beyond that perhaps it is also necessary that we should consider the justification of ourselves from a deeper angle, namely, as a question of truth, then we really have cause to be concerned why it was that Protestant theology came into existence as a newborn child, and how in that early period it put to itself and answered the question of truth.

Before we turn to Calvin in particular, we would do well to take our bearings in a brief survey of the relation of the complex of events that we usually call the Reformation to the age which preceded it and also more generally of what this complex meant, as a symptom, for the human situation as a whole. Naturally in this compass I cannot unfold the problem of the Middle Ages and the Reformation in all its breadth. Use the literature on the subject, but with caution. For nowhere is it so obvious how much the historical position of the historian affects the picture given, as we see in the controversies regarding this problem over the last fifteen years.[2] Finally, even though our knowledge of the sources be modest, it is better to try to see with our own eyes than to follow one of the grandiose hypotheses now current, stimulating though these might be in detail. Since Calvin's theology is our theme, I will limit myself to showing how to get a basic grasp of the relation between Reformation theology and that of the Middle Ages which preceded it. When I compare the thinking of the reformers to that of medieval theologians so far as I know them both, the following picture emerges.

§1 Connection

The first and most direct impression that the comparison gives us is of something strikingly new and different, especially in Luther. We find this man and his thinking moving in the reflection of a great and strange light that falls lightly upon him. We see him faced with an incomparable,

2. Barth had in view the thesis of Troeltsch that the Reformation belonged to the Middle Ages and the replies of Loofs and Seeberg. See below, 65f.

unheard-of question and then at once, in and with the question, in possession of an equally incomparable, unheard-of answer. The thoughts in which he tried to give an account of what he saw both to himself and to others are disturbingly and wildly contradictory. Only with difficulty could he put them together, and even then they largely exclude one another. No specific, or, at any rate, no systematic or planned deeper meaning rules in these thoughts; he would clearly have liked to say everything much more simply, but with great embarrassment he constantly ventured paradoxes that in their significance may be placed alongside the boldest insights of philosophical thinking and that in their immediate force put far in the shade the formulations of most philosophers. Even where he does not speak in paradoxes a light like that of the morning sun shines constantly over his trains of thought. They breathe like fresh air after a storm. Was he offering edification? Was he preaching? Was he thinking academically? Who would be so pedantic as to make a distinction? What do categories[3] mean here? In these thoughts something takes place, a decision, a breakthrough, an event. We have the feeling regarding them that the words are not just words. We witness a process of knowledge that we cannot distinguish from an act. And this act, the longer and more radically we let it speak to us in its own true sense, does it not significantly, but also with a claim, and erasing all the borders between here and there, thrust itself into our own existence? Can we escape this word, this act, or do we not feel, like those who heard Zwingli, that we are taken by the hair[4] when we really hear this voice? That is Reformation theology, not just in Luther but also in Zwingli and Calvin and the lesser lights around them, for what counts here is not the genius or originality of the individual thinker but the quality of what all of them were thinking with more or less force and depth.

But precisely when we take seriously our direct impression of this theology, precisely when we believe we have to do here with something new and wholly different, precisely when we are inclined to ascribe to the event that unfolds before our eyes a dignity and significance that a word

3. On the relation between edification, preaching, and academic lectures cf. Barth's *Ein Briefwechsel mit Adolf von Harnack* (1923), in *Theologische Fragen und Antworten, Gesammelte Vorträge*, vol. III (Zurich, 1957, 2nd ed. 1986), esp. 19f., and Harnack's reply, 30f.

4. According to Thomas Platter; see H. Boos, *Thomas und Felix Platter . . .* (Leipzig, 1878), 39. For an edition of Platter's work in modern German cf. *Thomas und Felix Platters und Theodor Agrippa d'Aubignes Lebensbeschreibung*, ed. O. Fischer (Munich, 1911), 64.

like "experience"[5] does not really cover even though we do experience something also, precisely then we must be careful in describing this as a new theology compared to the old. If we take the word "different" seriously, what does it mean to confront something totally different?[6] If we are not finally to be guilty of mere bombast, can the *totally* different be one thing in contrast to this or that other different thing? What do "new" and "old" mean when it is a matter of *this* new thing, when it is a matter of the knowledge of *God* in this theology? Who gives us the courage at once to divest the terms of their meaning again by excluding the poor Middle Ages, the old, from this new thing? Precisely when we sense somewhat the superiority of this theology, we must maintain its newness and difference on the plane of historical things only with reservation, only in a relative sense. On the plane of time one thing always and everywhere stands alongside another, certainly with significant differences, but in such a way that great differences often mean very little and little differences mean a great deal.

In assessing what we can see here, those who can only reckon, count, and measure run the risk of hardly being able to avoid serious confusion and mistakes. For the absolute is not directly visible on this world's stage. The great light in the reflection of which we see the reformers and their thoughts move is not itself a phenomenon; it does not become one thing among others. And what we see in the reformers, the reflection in which they stand, is only relatively and not absolutely different from what we see around them, in their predecessors and successors. It is a new and different thing, but not *the* new thing, *the* different thing. It is at every point in continuity with what came before and what came after. *The* new thing is not something that we can establish in the reformers, and *the* old

5. Experience was a basic theological and religious category early in the 20th century in the theology of Barth's teacher W. Herrmann, which Barth at first rated highly; cf. Herrmann's *Communion of the Christian with God* (1913); cf. also R. Otto, *The Idea of the Holy* (1923; German, 1917); and many other authors. For Barth's criticisms cf. his *Romans* passim and *Briefwechsel mit Adolf von Harnack*, 10.

6. For the wholly other cf. Otto, *Idea of the Holy.* How far Barth was dependent on Otto for his use of the term in the 2nd ed. of his *Romans* is contested by scholars. For his view of Otto cf. his letter to Thurneysen on 6.3.1919, in which he expressed his enjoyment of Otto's work in spite of its psychological orientation because it clearly points to the nonrational element in the numinous as the wholly other, the divine in God. He saw here the beginning of a fundamental overcoming of Ritschlianism. There is in it at least a pointer even if things did not go far enough because of the restrained role of the theologian as a spectator, which does not accord with the fairly good understanding of the object.

thing is not something that we can postulate of the scholastics and mystics preceding them. On both sides the old and the new confront one another on two fronts, first invisibly, never a perceptible phenomenon, as the distance and fellowship between God and us, eternity and time, infinity and finitude that is the point of the term "sacred history" which we discussed briefly at the outset — and then visibly, in a historically percep-tible way, as the historical dialectic of different human possibilities, higher and lower, better and worse, here stronger and there weaker, that point to the original hidden antithesis of old and new, yet never in such a way that a human possibility coincides directly with that which all human possi-bilities can only indicate, and never in such a way that a human possibility is totally meaningless relative to that hidden antithesis — and we have in mind here the whole range of what is usually called secular history. Always and everywhere that which we see as historical occurrence on the second front stands only in relation to its origin in the primal antithesis, but always and everywhere historical events do to some extent stand in relation to this their origin. Historical events that do so to a higher degree than others can do no more than make us aware that fundamentally even events that do so to a lesser degree do stand in the same relation.

The new thing that in Reformation theology makes on us the im-pression of something new and totally different is obviously *the* hidden new thing of the first front. We need not be surprised, then, that as we seriously follow up that direct impression, as we translate it from more or less contingent experience to knowledge, we come to see the relative degree of the distinction between the Reformation and the Middle Ages on the historical plane. Those who let themselves be taught by a study of the reformers what is in truth old and what is in truth new can hardly set up a fixed and more mythological antithesis between two ages and historical groups. They will appreciate the distinction, but they will really appreciate it, that is, value it, see its worth. That is, they will see its worth and meaning and point, and also its context, the deeper problematic of which all historical problematic is only a likeness. It will be impossible for them to point to this or that saying in Luther or Calvin, to this or that day in their lives, and to say that here the new and totally different thing was present or was spoken, as though those men could, for example, experience and express the new and totally different thing as others can experience and express what is beautiful. No, even what was there experienced and said is as such relative. It stands in continuity with the old that is so sharply different from it. Calvin and Sadolet were pieces on the same chessboard.

17

Only when we see what they experienced and said in this relation of earthly continuity can it take on significance for us in its difference within the relation. And it is then impossible for us to focus too tenaciously on this or that dubious feature of medieval theology and church life, as though that were really *the* old thing in contrast to the reformers and their position. No, no pope or scholastic was so diabolical as to be able to do or say *the* old thing absolutely, just as no reformer was so heavenly as to be able even for a moment to embody *the* new. Let us leave it to the Roman Catholic philosophy of history to place Protestantism under the category of apostasy, which is so freighted with meaning and for that reason, in the judgment of history, so empty of meaning. Let us not in any circumstances play the same game. What was experienced, thought, and said in the Catholic Middle Ages was also relative, relative, we may say, to the origin that things on the historical plane, be they ever so different, have in common. It stands with the Reformation counterposition in the one basic nexus of the first front where the antithesis is not that of Protestant and Roman Catholic but of God and humanity. Apart from that antithesis, which also means unity, the confessional antithesis was a tragedy in the 16th century and has now become a comedy.[7] If we are aware of the seriousness of the profound problematic of that antithesis, then we have to see the nonseriousness of the confessional antithesis on the second front between Protestantism and Roman Catholicism as historical forces. But one could also put it differently, namely, that the confessional antithesis on the second front can be really serious, important, and full of promise only when we are aware how nonserious it is in the last analysis.

You can check the truth of what I have just said if you reflect again on the direct impression of something new that we get from Luther's commentary on the Psalms or Zwingli's theses[8] so long as we have eyes in our heads. Must we not honestly admit that in these cases *the* new and wholly different thing that speaks forcefully to us confronts not only medieval and modern Catholicism but no less diametrically what we

7. Cf. K. Marx, *Der achtzehnte Brumaire des Louis Bonaparte,* in Marx and Engels, *Werke,* vol. VIII (Berlin, 1960), 115, in which Marx quoted Hegel's remark that all great historical persons and events come on the scene twice as it were, commenting that Hegel forgot to add that they do so the first time as a tragedy and the second as a farce.

8. For Luther Barth was thinking of the lectures on the Psalms of 1513-1516, WA 3, 11-652 and 4, 1-467. From 1922 he had these in the 2-vol. ed. of J. K. Seidemann (Dresden, 1880). For Zwingli cf. H. Zwingli, *Usslegen und grund der schlussreden* (1523), Z 2, 1-457.

ourselves think and feel? Can we fail to hear, then, the strong accusation that the writings of Luther and Calvin constantly bring against our so-called Lutheran and Reformed Christianity, church life, and theology, not simply because there has been declension from the Reformation, true though that is, but because the new and wholly different thing in the writings of Luther and Zwingli accusingly confronts all Christianity, church, life, and theology even when at their conceivable best? If we accept this judgment, if we recognize the antithesis that runs through the whole four hundred years of Protestant history, how then can the new and wholly other thing four hundred years ago simply be one thing among other historical entities, and how can it have been passed on to Protestant theologians to do with it as they like and with the possibility of handing it down to their successors? Is it not obvious that this new thing critically confronts the theology of the reformers themselves, being absolutely other than the old thing that in its relativity here also is part of the historical plane? And if that is so, must we not conclude that the antithesis between the true new and the true old runs also backward to the time before the Reformation, that what is old in time (i.e., medieval thinking) has its own share, as I see it, in what is eternally old, which is the situation and problem of all history, but that it also has, of course, its share in what is eternally new, the solution to the problem?[9]

So far as I can see, the reformers themselves had a much more restrained view of the epoch-making nature of their work than one might expect and than is often stated in later accounts in church history. It is clear that they had a strong sense of the unique importance of the historical moment in which they stood. Luther spoke again and again about the fact that, in contrast to the past, they were now once more in an age when God was sending forth his Word among us as the most precious of all his gifts. He liked to portray the Reformation under the image of a light that was now kindled and shining for a while.[10] He knew well — perhaps too well — his own personal significance for the process. Calvin, too, in his

9. Marginal note in pencil: "Chronik v. Bosshart 89." The reference is to *Die Chronik des Laurencius Bosshart von Winterthur 1185-1532,* ed. K. Hauser, *Quellen zur schweizerischen Reformationsgeschichte,* ed. Zwingliverein in Zurich, vol. III (Basel, 1905), 89, where it is noted that God revealed his Word through the Greek and Hebrew languages when Zwingli preached the gospel in Zurich, and that this was not of man's doing but God's.

10. Cf. Luther's admonition against revolt (1522), WA 8, 676, in which he says that it is of God's grace that the light of Christian truth has arisen again.

work against Pighius on the *Liberum Arbitrium* (6, 237) called the Reformation a miracle of supreme divine power, and in sermon 162 on Deuteronomy (28, 466) he could even call it a resurrection from the dead.[11] In his work *On the Need to Reform the Church* he expressly ascribed the same sending to the reformers as to the OT prophets who had to stir people out of the blindness of idolatry (6, 477).[12] In keeping was the eclecticism and the freedom that the reformers allowed themselves vis-à-vis the great theological authority of the early church. "Oh, the fathers were men as we are; we should consider this well and lay what they say on the scales, watching what they say," said Luther in his *Table Talk* (EA 62, 109) of the fathers, and of the scholastics he said that they had good heads but did not live in a time like ours (EA 62, 114).[13] As we know, apart from the Bible, the only strong authority for the whole Reformation was Augustine, but if I am right it was Augustine almost exclusively as the opponent of Pelagius and in such a way that Luther at least in his later years moved increasingly apart from this decisive teacher of his theological youth. It is also striking to me that Calvin in his relation to Scholasticism made no use of Anselm's doctrine of the atonement or proof of God as he might well have done in his own system, and that he had no links to Thomas Aquinas, so that there is no connection between the greatest Catholic and the greatest Protestant systematician, and how sparse in him are the references to the late Scholasticism of Duns Scotus, with whom we have the impression today that there would have been many positive points of contact.[14]

From all this we learn that the reformers were aware of standing at a decisive turning point in theological thinking when much that was old was perishing even if much was also at least quietly remaining. At all events, however, the reformers did not share the philosophy of history that we find in a saying of Schwenckfeld that Seeberg quotes and that he calls "monumental": "A new world is coming and the old dies away" (*Lehrbuch*, IV, 2). The Radicals and Humanists talked that way, that is, those specifi-

---

11. Cf. the defense of the orthodox doctrine of bondage and liberation against the calumnies of Pighius (1543), CR 6, 257. For sermon 162 see CR 28, 466.

12. CO 6, 477.

13. On the fathers see WA TR 4, 288, 25f. (no. 4387). On the scholastics, WA TR 3, 543, 18 (no. 3698).

14. So first A. Ritschl, "Geschichtliche Studien zur christlichen Lehre von Gott," in *Gesammelte Aufsätze*, vol. II (Freiburg, 1893), 67-89; and cf. Seeberg, *Lehrbuch*, IV, 575, on Calvin's doctrine of the divine will.

cally who had little awareness of the deeper antithesis that was being played out before them; but for all the zeal with which they, too, took part in the movement in their own way, they were interested for the most part only in what was taking place on the surface. Those who took part genuinely and radically, who saw what it was all about, felt differently, although they too, as we have seen, experienced powerfully enough the historical antithesis between the old and the new.

At least in Luther, however, a more powerful feeling than that of experiencing the dawn of a new age and being its strongest agents and heralds was that of the continuity of the divine work, his reverence for all that had come into being and was now there — a reverence that rested, of course, not merely on insight but also on nature and setting. It was as a monk and in the context of medieval theology that Luther came to his reforming thoughts that snatched him finally out of that context. We know how unwillingly, in obedience to the need,[15] he resolved to build a new church. As long as he lived, his heart still clung to the concept of the one holy catholic church in a way that for reasons deeply rooted in his specific situation was not the case with Calvin.

The fervor of the new age and world, of the new spirit and work, was something that we know again to some extent in our own postwar present. We perhaps find it best among the reformers in Zwingli, it being typically alien to Calvin, although, as I have said, with less sentimental emphasis than Luther, Calvin agreed with the latter that the concept of antiquity was most important for Protestant theology. In the epistle in which he dedicated the *Institutes* to Francis I he could not protest too strongly that what he and those like-minded with him in France were advocating was not something new.[16] He adduced a long list of witnesses from the church's past in which he thought he saw what he called the gospel, and in the *Institutes* itself he was at great pains to prove his agreement with the authorities of the early church. We have said already how eclectic his procedure was, but that does not alter the intention. For him as for Luther, if with an essential difference of mood, the break with the Christianity of the past was not felt to be one of principle. In Luther an example of this is the relatively friendly way in which Bonaventura is treated among the medieval fathers, and in Calvin we note the warmth

15. Cf. Schiller's *Braut von Messina*, V, 1: "Der Not gehorchend, nicht dem eignen Trieb."

16. OS 1, 25, also 27.

21

even with which he speaks of Bernard of Clairvaux.[17] Both were in their different ways typical representatives of what the reformers zealously combated as papism.

An even more striking example is the way in which both Luther and Calvin avoided the man in whom they must have recognized, even if he was not then the most widely read author, and whom they ought to have fought as their most dangerous opponent, the true genius of the Catholic Middle Ages. I refer to Thomas Aquinas. We have in his case a demonstration how often even the greatest among us, precisely in fulfilling their deepest intentions, often do not know what they are doing. The reformers engaged in close combat with late scholastics of the age of decline, about whom we say nothing today, when all the time behind these, and biding his time, stood their main adversary Thomas, in whom all modern Roman Catholicism has come to see more and more definitely its true classic; and apart from a few inconsequential complaints by Luther,[18] they left him in peace, apparently not realizing that their real attack was not on those straw figures but on the spirit of the *Summa,* on the Gothic cathedral and the world of Dante. How could it be possible that in the first half of the 17th century a Lutheran theologian from Strassburg could write a book entitled *Thomas Aquinas, veritatis evangelicae confessor!* (Loofs, 690).[19] All this shows strikingly, however, that the reformers did not see their work in the context of a great philosophy of history but in a fairly relative pragmatic context. Perhaps it is precisely the manner of truly creative people to take this view.

If we ask positively in what they saw the importance of their work, Luther's reply, so far as I can see, would be a sober reference to the fact that the Word of God was again being preached loudly and purely. Thus in a Coburg letter to the elector on May 20, 1530, he described the grace that God gives each of us as follows: "For, of course, your Grace's lands have the most and the very best of good pastors and preachers, more than any other land in all the world, and they teach so faithfully and purely, and help to keep the peace so well. There are thus growing up among us

17. For Luther on Bonaventura see WA TR 1, 330, 1 (no. 683): "Bonaventura the best of the scholastic doctors." Cf. 1, 435, 25f. (no. 871), and 3, 294, 35f. (no. 3370a); also WA 7, 774, 13ff.; and 8, 127, 19. For Calvin on Bernard of Clairvaux see CO 23.63; 31.540; 49.357; also the many quotations from Bernard in the *Institutes,* e.g., II, 3, 5; III, 2, 25; III, 12, 3; III, 15, 2.

18. Seeberg, *Lehrbuch,* 74 and n. 2.

19. Loofs, *Leitfaden,* 690 n. 3, quotes the title in this short form. The work was by J. G. Dorsche and was published at Frankfurt in 1656.

tender young people, boys and girls, who are taught the catechism and scripture so well that it does my heart good as I see how young boys and girls can pray and believe and talk about God and Christ more than all the foundations and monasteries and schools could do or still can" (EA 54, 148).[20] In face of these happy descriptions, no matter what we think of the catechetical success, we cannot possibly say that Luther made great claims for the breadth of his reformation.

There is a similar passage in Calvin. In his work on the need for church reform he described as follows what the reformers had done and achieved: "They aroused the world out of the profound darkness of ignorance to a reading of scripture; they worked hard at a purer understanding and were able successfully to expound certain important concepts of Christian doctrine, whereas formerly foolish fables and no less unnecessary definitions were heard in sermons, the universities echoed with the strife of words, scripture was hardly mentioned, and the clergy had an eye only to money" (6, 473).[21] Calvin did add, of course, that these were improvements that their foes ought to have acknowledged as made, but it is typical that he was content with this rather dry academic description of the significance of the new epoch.

We may note in addition that Luther used the expression "Word of God" both in the absolute and eternal sense that was naturally primary for him and in a relative sense as the Word that takes its course, that comes and goes, that falls like a shower, now here and now there, that can also be chased away and extinguished.[22] It is plain that the latter is the Word of God whose blessings he can extol so eloquently to the elector. For him it is to this category that his own reforming work belongs. It is part of the new thing in the second and relative sense. It is not for him *the* new thing. It is not even as new as appears in most of our historical accounts today, the theological at least. Nevertheless, it is something new, something very new, of course, even if he has to recognize its limits and end: "I am concerned that the light will not last and shine very long, for God's Word has always had its specific course" (57, 19).[23] This looking ahead to the

20. WA B 5, 325, 37-326, 44.
21. CO 6, 473.
22. Cf. Luther's plea for Christian schools (1524), WA 15, 32, 6-8, in which he says that you know God's Word and grace is a passing shower that does not come again where it has once been; cf. also WA 17/II, 179, 28-33.
23. Ibid., 4, 151, 11f. (no. 4123).

end of the new time, often stated in a bitter and threatening way, is not uncommon in Luther.

Luther could also say once (57, 17) that God's Word comes down always on the same time. I would comment that in its sober but very profound sense this statement is much more monumental than the dictum of Schwenckfeld that a new world was dawning. The context is as follows: "The world now faces God's Word exactly as it did two thousand years ago. God's Word comes down always on the same time. The world is still the world, the devil's bride."[24] The meaning, then, is primarily negative and pessimistic, as was befitting the mood of the older Luther. But be that as it may, the saying embodies the thesis that there are no different times in relation to God, or, as I would put it, that there is no progress in world history. The Word of God, when it makes itself heard, confronts the same world reality in the same tension even when the situation in world reality is supremely critical and significant and God's Word makes itself heard with great power. Indeed, Luther could go so far as to say that at all times from the beginning of the world, when God's Word is purely taught and preached, people are most offended and sins are at their worst and most horrible (57, 22).[25]

Finally, this highly relevant situation had for Luther a positive reverse side. If the world is always the world and even God's Word in history is transitory in its presence and limited in its effects, it is also true that God is always God even when his Word would seem to be lost in history. "God has preserved his Word," Luther can say most unexpectedly, and it is plain that he is not now speaking of a relative and transitory Word: "God has preserved his Word and Christ's kingdom has remained in the world under the papacy" (57, 53). Naturally the fact that this is so, he adds, "is the greatest miracle of our Lord God," but he does count on this miracle.[26] That was the radicalism of Luther's philosophy of history, and it was much greater than that of people of the stamp of Schwenckfeld with their jubilant shouting about the dawn of a new era. The threads of the kingdom of Christ and of God on the one side snap no more than do those of the world on the other, no matter what may be the specific course of God's Word. If it is true that in the so-called new age the old is truly present for the first time, it is also true, and even more true, that the new was also

---

24. Ibid., 3, 500, 2-5 (no. 3663).
25. Ibid., 3, 6-8 (no. 2806b).
26. Ibid., 3, 6-8 (no. 2806b).

present in the so-called old age. If any had the right to see the old and the new not merely in the light of the kingdom of God but also historically in harsh antithesis, it was the reformers themselves who were engaged in a violent battle in which everything was at stake, life or death. Yet they did not see it that way. They paradoxically left it to those who were further from the fray to view absolutely and mythologically the historical processes of which they were the heroes.

They themselves confirmed the insight that we gained last time by more basic discussion, namely, that nothing really new came into history with the Reformation, that its significance is to be sought instead in a survey of the connection. We must now pursue this insight both negatively and positively.

§2 Contrast

Let us look first at the relation between the Reformation and the Middle Ages as that of opposites, realizing that while the antithesis is great, important, and significant, it cannot in any case be clear-cut or absolute. The spirit of the Middle Ages is hard to grasp and especially to judge. Incredibly often and easily on the Protestant side (even the learned Protestant side; cf. Loofs, 498-99!),[1] efforts are made to characterize the essence of Scholasticism. Terms, highly critical terms, such as "formalism," "pedantry," "credulity," "artificial reconciliation of reason and revelation," and the like,[2] come almost automatically into our minds and on our lips when we hear the word "scholastic." Though there is naturally some truth in them, they are polemically crude, reminding us with some aptness of the foxes who could not get at the grapes.[3] We can hardly complain of formalism if we ourselves have no form at all, nor of pedantry if we want to establish our supposedly better truth no less perspicaciously or simply than the scholastics could do, nor of credulous submission to authority if we are not to ignore the serious problem of authority but be willing to think it out to the end, nor of the way of combining reason and revelation

---

1. Cf. Loofs, *Leitfaden,* 498f. (7th ed., 402), for the charge of formalism.
2. For this evaluation cf. G. Ficker and H. Hermelink, *Handbuch der Kirchengeschichte,* vol. II, *Das Mittelalter* (Tübingen, 1911), 186; also p. 185 on Occam.
3. Cf. Aesop's *Fables* 33.

unless we have better counsel to offer on the relation. We have here presuppositions that in general are missing among modern Protestants. Semler was right when he once observed that the poor scholastics have laid themselves open to too much derision, often on the part of those who cannot use them (Hagenbach, 297).[4] Those older theologians had the ability to think and they took pleasure in thinking. They had dialectical courage and consistency. Their academic tradition has had four hundred years of vitality. Once the reformers were no longer present, Protestant theology could do no better than adopt that tradition, and yet comparatively quickly it came to grief, while the older branch from Trent to our own time entered upon a second period of remarkable fruitfulness. All these are things that ought above all to give us respect for medieval theology if we do not already have it. The situation is the same with Scholasticism as with the Roman Catholic church in general. Those who do not admire them, those who are not in danger of becoming scholastics themselves, simply have no inner right to pass judgment on them. We cannot dismiss historical entities of this power by simply tossing around catchwords.

If we are to catch the essence of Scholasticism I would like to propose that we first pursue the direct impression one gets of it when speaking about it unconfused by modern preconceptions. If you ask me how and where to get this direct impression, I would suggest the following indirect way. Go to Cologne cathedral and study it well. Then from a good compendium of the history of philosophy acquaint yourselves with what Aristotle had in mind. Then by means of Dante's *Divine Comedy* learn to know poetically the path of the medievals, as taught by Thomas Aquinas, from hell through purgatory to paradise. You may then take up a dogmatic presentation such as that of Seeberg or Loofs, though I would advise you that in so doing you should check the sources of all the quotations — a history of dogma that consists almost entirely of quotations is that of Hagenbach, 1888.[5] Then perhaps you may try to read a work from the great age of Scholasticism like Bonaventura's *Breviloquium* (ed. Hefele, 1845), supplementing this on the right hand with an ascetic work like the *Analecta* on the history of Francis of Assisi (ed. Boehmer, 1904), and on

---

4. K. R. Hagenbach, *Lehrbuch der Dogmengeschichte,* rev. K. Benrath (Leipzig, 1888).

5. See ibid. Barth commended this work in a circular letter dated 3.26.1922 because the author modestly did not intrude himself but gave many well-chosen and instructive quotations from the sources. He found Loofs less rewarding for his purpose.

the left hand with a mystical work like the sermons of Meister Eckhardt (Diederichs, 1911).[6]

The impression that I have gained of medieval theology may be summed up in a phrase coined, I believe, by Luther at the 1518 Heidelberg Disputation: it is a theology of glory.[7] It attempts and achieves a knowledge of God in his glory, purity, and majesty. In the word of the Bible and the theology of the church it does not simply find denoted and described the mystery as such but signposts marking a dialectical path to the heart of the mystery, so that for those who take this path there is no longer any mystery. It recognizes no barrier, no command that it should stop at the object intended in the word of the Bible or in dogma. In the difficulty and obscurity that first conceal the object it simply hears a challenge in some way, notwithstanding the problems, to lay hold of the object. It is venturesome in the way in which it sets its goals and tries to reach them. It is youthfully fresh and healthy and robust and sparkling in all that it does. As readers we feel that we are in the hands of guides who with absolute certainty and confidence know what they want.

Some kind of unequivocal and direct communication of the depths of deity, and perhaps a well-arranged system of such depths, is in any case the goal of our journey if we entrust ourselves to them. In these theologians there is no place for banalities, generalities, or obscurities. Nor is there any place for the basic uncertainty, which oppresses many other theologies, whether theology itself is necessary or useful, nor for the related teeth-chattering question whether and how far theology is a science. Thomas teaches us that *esse* is *intellegere* (to be is to know), that God's essence is his knowledge, that the universal and absolute epitome of all that is known, of all being, is actuality, the first cause in all things.[8] To a lesser degree

---

6. Barth used Bonaventura's *Breviloquium* in the edition of C. J. Hefele (Tübingen, 1845). In a circular letter dated 4.2.1922 he said that he was reading this work so as not to know the Middle Ages only from excerpts. A note in P. Tschackert's *Die Entstehung der lutherischen und der reformierten Kirchenlehre* (Göttingen, 1910), 21, to the effect that the *Breviloquium* represented the church teaching of the time perhaps led Barth to engage in an intensive study of the work, though there are no visible fruits of the study in the lectures. On Francis see *Analekten zur Geschichte des Franciscus von Assisi,* ed. H. Boehmer (Tübingen and Leipzig, 1904). On Eckhardt see *Meister Eckeharts Schriften und Predigten,* tr. and ed. H. Büttner, 2 vols. (Jena, 1909f.).

7. WA 1, 362, 15 and 21.

8. Cf. Loofs, 535 (437). The quotations are from *S.Th.* I, q. 14 a. 8 i.c., a. 4 i.c., a. 13 i.c.; q. 44 a. 3 i.c. They may be found in Hagenbach, 340 and 354, though in part in incorrect form.

angels, and to an even lesser degree humans, have a share in this eternal knowledge of God.[9] That is theology. How can it not be a science when it is participation in the knowledge of God,[10] in the a priori of all science? And how can it not be necessary? It is the one thing necessary; it is our blessedness.[11] We have to read the descriptions of heaven that this theology gives[12] if we are to understand what it meant for the people of the Middle Ages.

At this point the academic theology of all the schools is at one with both orthodox mystics and heretical, pantheistic sects. "To have life is to see life," said Peter Lombard.[13] Two hundred years later Tauler, whom Luther greatly honored, said the same thing even more clearly: "Those who see the glory of God, that is paradise" (Hagenbach, 445).[14] According to the *Elucidarium,* an eschatological work of the 12th century, there is a triple heaven: the visible, which is the firmament; the spiritual, where saints and angels dwell; and the intellectual, where the blessed enjoy the vision of the triune God, drink from the fount of God's wisdom, and have knowledge of all things, simply all things and all relations (Hagenbach, 444, 447).[15] Listen to the way Heinrich Seuse, a contemporary of Tauler, puts it: "Look up to the ninth heaven, which is much more than a hundred thousand times bigger than the whole earth, and there is another heaven above, the *Coelum empyreum,* the fiery heaven, not called this because of fire, but because of the immeasurably sparkling clarity that it has by nature, unmovable and unchangeable, the glorious court where the heavenly Lord dwells and the stars praise God together and all God's children rejoice. See around you the countless throng, how they drink from the living, murmuring fountain to their hearts' desire; see how they fix their gaze on

---

9. For angelic knowledge in Thomas cf. Hagenbach, 258; and for human knowledge, 331; cf. *S.Th.* I, q. 12 a. 12 i.c.

10. Cf. *S.Th.* I, q. 1 a. 2 i.c.

11. Loofs, 534 (436), points out that since God is our goal and the goal has to be known, but perfect knowledge of God consists of eternal beatitude and is beyond the grasp of human reason — there has to be revelation and revealed knowledge; he gives citations from *S.Th.* I, q. 1 a. 4 i.c. and a. 1 i.c.

12. Cf. Hagenbach, 444f.: topography (heaven, hell, and intermediate states).

13. Peter Lombard, *Libri quattuor sententiarum,* lib. IV, dist. 49A, quoted by Hagenbach, 447.

14. Good Friday Sermon in Tauler, *Predigten,* vol. I (Leipzig, 1826), 291f.

15. Hagenbach, 436-50. For the second part of Barth's statement cf. *Elucidarium,* ch. 79, in Hagenbach, 447.

the pure and clear reflection of naked deity, on the mirror in which all things are open and manifest" (Hagenbach, 447ff.).[16] Or read the classic description in the final song of Dante's *Paradise:*

> Such keenness from the luring ray I met
> That if mine eyes had turned away, methinks,
> I had been lost, and so emboldened, on
> I passed, as I remember, till my view
> Hover'd the brink of dread infinitude.
> O grace, unenvying of thy boon! that gavest
> Boldness to fix so earnestly my ken
> On the everlasting splendour, that I look'd
> While sight was unconsumed, and in that depth
>
> Saw in one volume clasp'd of love, whate'er
> The universe unfolds, all properties
> Of substance and of accident, and beheld
> Confounded, yet one individual light
> The whole.
>   It may not be
> That one who looks upon that light
> Can turn to other object, willingly, his view
> For all the good, that will may covet, there
> Is summ'd, and all, elsewhere defective, found
> Complete.[17]

That is what Thomas calls the fruition of God and Eckhardt the supraforming of the soul with God, or even the birth of God in the soul.[18] That is the theology of glory, the fiery living heart, the essence of medieval theology. On this vision of God from face to face [1 Cor. 13:12] — and think of the ecstatic portrayal of the faces of the blessed as you surely know it from pre-Renaissance art — that theology counted as on an unheard-of possibility to which it had access by a steep but direct path. Here is the essence of celestial bliss, and for that reason all the medievals, or at least

---

16. Hagenbach quotes from H. Seuse, *Von der unmässigen Freude des Himmelreiches* in his *Leben und Schriften,* ed. M. Diepenbrock (Regensburg, 1840), 205.

17. Dante Alighieri, *The Divine Comedy,* Harvard Classics, vol. 20, tr. H. F. Cary, "Paradise," canto XXXIII.

all the more free and profound among them, never spoke of it except with a certain awe and restraint. But it was also part of our human essence, the supreme possibility of the human soul, which in exact parallel to the idea of a triple heaven is depicted in three divisions, as sensuality with the capacity for cogitation, as reason with a capacity for meditation, and finally and supremely as simple intelligence with the capacity for contemplation. This is how Gerson saw it at the beginning of the 15th century and Hugh of St. Victor three hundred years before him.[19]

This basic view of the fundamental accessibility of the mystery and glory *(doxa)* of God is what stamps medieval theology. It changes, of course, in keeping with the teaching of the later schools of Duns Scotus and William of Occam, and especially that of Eckhardt and his followers. Access became extraordinarily difficult,[20] but all the difficulties with which it was seen to be surrounded simply made it higher and more precious and caused it to be lauded more fervently. In a disturbing parallel the cathedral pillars became improbably more lofty and the naked eye had reason to fear they might not ever meet. Yet with unerring certainty they converge in the Gothic arch, even if only in the semidarkness of the vault. The basic concept of the theology remains intact. It is the serious and final thing in all medieval thoughts about God and the world. It does not rule out sharp antitheses. On the contrary, it evokes them. Triunity as the solution of all puzzles, how can that not be the source of all theses and antitheses? But it also embraces the antitheses. It is always also a synthesis. It stands on both this side and the far side of the tensions of intuitive and dialectical thinking, of world denial and world affirmation, of Aristotelianism and Augustinian Neoplatonism, of devotion and skepticism. It contains all these within itself, ejects them all, and takes back again that which is developed into a unity. For Thomas evil was a lack of good, a corruption of the good, which in the long run could only increase perfection.[21]

---

18. For Thomas cf. Loofs, 537 (439), and the text of *S. Th. Suppl.,* q. 96 a. 1 i.ci in Hagenbach, 447 (with some deviation). For Eckhardt see the bull *In agro dominico,* 10, quoted in Hagenbach, 398, with reference to Eckehart, *Predigten,* vol. II, ed. F. Pfeiffer (Leipzig, 1857), 103, 11ff., quoted in Loofs, 628 (521).

19. Hagenbach, 361, refers to Gerson's (*Considerationes de theologia mystics,* X-XXV) concept of the two basic powers of the soul, the cognitive and affective, and his arrangement of the former as simple intelligence, reason, and sensuality corresponding to contemplation, meditation, and cogitation. For Hugh of St. Victor see Hagenbach, 361 (no examples).

20. Hagenbach, 330f.

21. *S. Th.* I, q. 14 a. 10 i.c.

The theology includes various individual thinkers and groups of thinkers, an Anselm and an Abelard, and later the Dominican and Franciscan schools, and later still the *via antiqua* and *via moderna,* but all in an invisible discipline and fellowship that only seldom needed the corrective hand of church authority and in relation to which one had to be an outsider like Amalrich of Bena (d. 1205)[22] to be really a heretic, that is, not to be able finally to think the most extreme thoughts under the protection of the same vault along with less radical investigators. Most of the 15th- and 16th-century Humanists saw no good reason to leave that shelter. What nonsense to assume that only the outward, rigid concept of the authority of church dogma had the power to set in motion this host of youthfully fresh seekers and thinkers in its defense, and for half a millennium to keep it in step. It was the basic thought of open and direct access to the final mystery, the conviction as to the necessity and possibility of immediate knowledge of God, that made that possible, and the concept of church authority was simply an outgrowth of the basic perception, and for that reason was not felt to be an alien body that fettered thought.

That this theology was a theology of glory, a bold and confident theology sensing victory, is what we have to remember when we look at the decisions it reached on the individual problems that gave it its characteristic features and over against which the basic contradiction of the Reformation revolted (but only revolted!). If we adopt the same approach as that with which the scholastics tackled these problems, seeing and feeling them in all their unequivocal seriousness and beauty, then we cannot really be surprised that their decisions were so Catholic, but we can also see that the transition from the Middle Ages to the Reformation was not in truth as simple and self-evident as it might often seem if we look only at the polemical positions and counterpositions of individual thinkers and their adversaries.

In the light of that basic concept it was natural that the relation of God, the world, and humanity should be seen at every point as a graded structure of possibilities that are clearly different yet no less clearly in continuity, all leading up to the final possibility of a pure vision of God,

---

22. Hagenbach quotes two passages from Amalrich of Bena, who was condemned posthumously in 1210, to the effect that we are members of Christ by bearing his sufferings on the cross (388) and that having the knowledge of God we have paradise in ourselves, but that if we commit mortal sin we have hell in ourselves like a rotten tooth in the mouth (446f.).

and all experiencing their relative consecration and dignity from that supreme pinnacle and in virtue of their continuous connection with it. It was thus that the relation between reason and revelation was fundamentally regulated. They could not really contradict one another. They flowed from the same source, namely, the wisdom of God. So said John Scotus Erigena in the 9th century.[23] On the eve of the Reformation age, as though time had stood still, the Humanist Pico della Mirandola could say similarly: "Philosophy seeks the truth, theology finds it."[24] Between them, of course, lay a whole ocean of possibilities stretching the bow to the very limit. In any case one has to see two sides, not just one, even though one might be called William of Occam, who went as far as is humanly possible in exploring the problems of theology.[25] There was no serious or sharp opposing of reason to revelation or revelation to reason. All along the line the result was a kind of pyramid, the possibility, no matter how paradoxical, of striding across from the one to the other, the supplementing of reason by revelation, the understanding of revelation by means of reason.

Nor could there be any real antithesis between the authority of the Bible and that of the church, problematic though their unity might often appear to be. The authority of the church embodied the idea of the theology of glory, the unbroken possibility of a path to God. No medieval teacher contested the truth that the church's authority rests on that of the biblical revelation, but in the scales against this they all set the dictum of Augustine: "I would not believe the gospel if the authority of the church did not move me to do so,"[26] a saying that caused endless difficulties for his faithful followers, the reformers. Unlike the reformers, the medievals really saw no antithesis between a greater and lesser or a more distant and more immediate authority. Reconciliation was always possible.

In the knowledge of God, too, we have the bold ascent from the demonstrable existence of God to his essence, which is accessible to us humans only by revelation, though in the very same movement from us to God. In mystical terms we have here the movement from the finite to

---

23. John Scotus Erigena, *De divisione naturae,* I, ch. 68, p. 38, in Hagenbach, 320.

24. Pico della Mirandola, *Epistola ad Aldum Manutium,* Opera, Basel ed., p. 243, quoted in Hagenbach, 319.

25. Cf. R. Seeberg, *Lehrbuch der Dogmengeschichte,* vol. III (Leipzig, 1913; 2nd and 3rd ed.), 604-21.

26. Augustine, *Contra epistolam quam vocant fundamenti,* 5, 6 (CSEL 25/I, 197, 22f.).

rest in the infinitude of the ground of the soul that is one and the same as God. Either way the step that can be taught and taken is bold but also one that can be envisioned methodically. Thus in the doctrine of God and the world we find the brave thesis that God as first cause is present in second causes, a thesis that leaves the possibility of miracle open but also makes it basically superfluous.

Similary we have the ingenious and meaningful doctrinal structure of the first estate, the fall, original sin, freedom, grace, and justification, a structure which I cannot in this context depict in detail but relative to which, before we dismiss it with the catchword semi-Pelagianism,[27] we need to consider its basic and helpful and consistently observed practical aim of showing there really is a path from earth to heaven, of giving visibility to eternal paradoxical truth, expounded in time and basically divested of its paradoxical character. Those who want this — and where are the Protestant theologians who are sure they can really do without it? — must at least examine closely the minute scholastic distinctions to see whether they contain just what they seek, or whether, if they despise them, they can truly do without a new and probably much worse semi-Pelagianism. For the Catholic doctrine of the appropriation of grace is truly remarkable in the way it considers all the elements, neglecting none and exaggerating none: nature and grace, humanity and God, freedom and dependence, a justifiable sense of self and humility before God, doing and receiving, meriting and being given, time and eternity. The later Reformation doctrine of salvation hardly contains anything that does not somewhere find a place in scholastic teaching in a heavily emphasized and underlined way.

At the same time there is nowhere any one-sidedness, any ultimate either/or. We always find the way, the possibility, the method, the theology of glory, which knows no final difficulty and is never at a loss vis-à-vis the object before which it stands. Human innocence before the fall consists of a sure combination, free of all friction, between sensuality, understanding, and reason with its vision. Original sin is the absence of righteousness; we have been dealt a wound that is in need of healing. But we can become healthy — that is the famous freedom of the will *(liberum arbitrium);* we can be redeemed if are diligently concerned, and when love from above,

---

27. Loofs, 539 (443), where he points out that to accuse even later Scholasticism of Pelagianism or semi-Pelagianism needs elucidation, though he himself on pp. 613f. (507ff.) describes Nominalism as "the crassest semi-Pelagianism."

gratia gratis data, as Goethe said wholly in the spirit of the Middle Ages, plays its part in us.[28] For grace can make what we do meritorious, or, according to Duns Scotus, God in his grace can accept what we humans do as meritorious.[29] If this happens, then the prior grace that aids and disposes us becomes *gratia gratum faciens* or *infusa,* which is wholly God's work in us but is even so a wholly real and objective event, for grace does not abolish nature but perfects it (Scotus).[30] By it human nature becomes capable of faith, which is *infusa* in terms of its origin and *implicita* in terms of its scope: it orients itself wittingly or unwittingly to what the authority of the church commands us to believe, being formed by love *(caritate formata)* in order that there should be no question as to its efficacy or merit. For the justification of sinners is real *factio iustitiae* (Thomas).[31] It coincides with the infusion of grace.[32] From the work of Christ on the cross that procures forgiveness of sins an unbroken chain of equations leads to the love that is the work of the Spirit of grace. Or, as Eckhardt put it, the conceiving of God in the soul, that triumph of the theology of glory, is the blossom that contains within itself, and will never fail to do so, the action of Martha, the desire and love of virtue, producing them out of itself.[33] I ask again where in Protestant theology we find all this described in a way that is better or more illuminating or credible?

For this reason, too, the church in the Middle Ages was a real saving institution in which something was set up and achieved. As we have seen, the knowledge of God that marked the community of the elect was as such a possessing of God. This community not only had something to

---

28. J. W. von Goethe, *Faust,* II, lines 11934-11941. On the phrase *gratia gratis data* cf. Hagenbach, 395f. This grace effects our first estate of original righteousness, while *gratia gratum faciens* has an effect oriented directly to justification.

29. Loofs, 596 (490): For Duns merit is only by divine acceptation. Cf. Seeberg, III, 587.

30. Hagenbach, 396, states that for Duns there was more human cooperation than for Thomas; cf. *Sent.,* lib. III, dist. 34, 5. We have not to think of grace being infused into us as fire is into a piece of wood, i.e., as if grace were destroying nature.

31. *S. Th.* Ia, IIae, q. 100 a. 12, in Hagenbach, 395.

32. Hagenbach, 395, says that by justification Thomas understood not only remission of guilt but at the same time the infusion of grace by which God gives us a share in his own life.

33. See n. 18 above; also Eckhardt's sermon on Mary and Martha at Luke 10:38 in *Schriften und Predigten,* ed. H. Büttner (Jena, 1909), vol. II, 119f., where it is shown that the double mention of Martha's name indicates first her perfection in temporal works and then what is needed for eternal salvation, that she might not lack this also.

show but something to give. In virtue of the infinite merit of Christ's sacrificial death which was its basis, it was the place where grace is present and is dispensed, and outside it was no salvation.[34] We cannot contest this concept by urging against it the usual slogans. It was a bold and titanic concept, significant in its titanism. To overcome it we have to understand it. It explains the dominant position of the sacraments in that church. The sacraments were the visible form of invisible grace,[35] but as Scholasticism laid down with increasing decisiveness and consistency, they were not just signs. As signs they were the thing signified. They were not just signs of power but direct, real, sanctifying power. That is the difference between OT circumcision and NT baptism, taught Peter Lombard and Thomas Aquinas. The one merely signifies and takes its course with faith on the part of the recipient. The other, in the new covenant, has sacramental force *(virtus sacramenti)* by which the recipients are irresistibly given *(ex opere operato)* a sacramental character.[36]

We can see precisely from a study of the doctrine of the Lord's Supper how the principle of a theology of glory gradually established itself in this field that is so important in practice, first in the ideas of Gregory the Great, then in the debates focused on Radbert in the 9th century and Berengar in the 11th, then in the as yet uncertain definitions of Anselm, Hugh of St. Victor, and Peter Lombard, and finally in the full and unequivocal doctrine of transubstantiation proclaimed by Lateran IV in 1215. Later thinkers like Durandus of St. Pourçain, William of Occam, or Peter d'Ailly might express the victorious principle, in this case the equation of bread and wine with Christ's body and blood, in new forms, but in no instance did they question the principle itself.[37] The principle is that of our immediacy to God. That is what triumphed no less in the scholastic doctrine of the Lord's Supper than in Dominican mysticism, and any who are concerned about this principle should ask whether it does not really find

---

34. Cf. Cyprian, *Epistolae,* 73, 21 (CSEL 2/II, 795, 3f.) and Augustine, *De baptismo contra donatistas,* 4, 17, 24 (CSEL 51, 250, 25).

35. Augustine, *Epistolae,* 105, 3, 12 (CSEL 34/II, 604, 12f.).

36. Lombard, *Sententiarum,* IV, 1E, in Hagenbach, 408: The OT sacraments promise grace, the NT sacraments give it; cf. also Thomas, *S. Th.* III, q. 62 a. 6 i.c., in Hagenbach, 408. Hagenbach, 409, found the phrase *ex opere operato* in Gabriel Biel, *Collectorium circa quattuor libros Sententiarum,* IV, dist. 1, q. 3.

37. On the medieval dogma of the Lord's Supper cf. Hagenbach, 413-23; for Occam and Durandus of St. Pourçain §196, 425-27, divergent views being noted on 426. For Pierre d'Ailly cf. Loofs, 618 (511), directly after Occam.

justice done to it in the best and most appropriate way in the Roman Catholic church.

In the history of the sacrament of penance again the valleys were filled in and the hills laid low [cf. Isa. 40:4] as obligatory confession developed out of a pious monastic practice, as priestly absolution, which was originally intended to recognize and crown preceding works of satisfaction, became a means of liberation from guilt and of reconciliation to God, to be followed by imposed duties that would make satisfaction and free from sin's penalties, whether in this life or under purgatorial stress in the next life. Irritation at the well-known indulgence system that was meant to soften and regulate the later penitential exercises should not blind us to the intention underlying the whole doctrine. Here again we have something that is often regarded as specifically evangelical, namely, the making of a simple and direct way to God, the principle of immediacy. What Scotus would finally proclaim as the essence of this sacrament was precisely the exclusion of preceding works of merit, even a meritorious heart's attrition, and the immediate relation of the soul to God by grace, the only point being that we have to be *aliqualiter attriti*, that we must not put anything in the way of grace, that we have to receive it. For that reason it could be said of this sacrament — the most personal and incisive, we have to say — that no other way is as simple or as sure.[38] It would not be too hard to express this concept of penance in the language of a modern philosophy of immediacy, the only point being that the scholastics had at the outset the foresight to link the counterweight of works to be done after penance to the boldness of laying hold of what is immediate with such assurance of salvation.

If we try to listen to the whole of medieval theology from which I have selected a few typical details, we are surprised again and again by the great harmony, the mixture of boldness and sagacity, of profundity and common sense, that we find there. It is the harmony of the monastery garden with its rows of cherry trees and its splashing fountains and its surrounding walls that remind us of the world with its joy and grief[39] but also shut it out. Or again, this is the harmony of the Gothic cathedral with its high altar, its soaring pillars, its roomy transepts, its hidden

38. Duns Scotus, *Opus Oxoniense,* 4, 17, q. un. no. 13f., XVIII, 510f. in Loofs, 600 (493).

39. Cf. the beginning of the third strophe of J. F. von Eichendorff's *Morgengebet: "Die Welt mit ihrem Gram und Glücke. . . ."*

penitential stools, its eternal light, the dark glow of the windows of the choir — the cathedral where sinners and saints, worldlings and penitents, may all join together in common reconciling worship, where the last and deepest things may take place, where the donkey of Palm Sunday and the laughter of Easter are not out of place, where earth and heaven do indeed seem to touch. A "complex of opposites" is what Harnack called this church,[40] and that is also true of its theology.

Let us come back with a few general characteristics to the direct impression that it makes. We are astonished at the certainty about life that the authors display and spread abroad in spite of opposing symptoms. They stand with both feet on the earth precisely because they stride on up to the world above, for that world is also for them a wonderful but attainable possibility. It is only a step between the kingdom of the world and the kingdom of God, between the trivial and the ecstatic, and good care is taken to see that balance is constantly achieved between the two extremes. Even the most broken of these people seem to be able to take the step from below to above and to put the two worlds together. We are astonished at the completeness and subtlety with which this theology handles all its problems no less carefully than radically. What a waltz it dances in its investigations out from the center to every side! Everything is important, everything has to be elucidated and discussed, everything has to be at least prepared for further treatment by means of meaningful divisions and subdivisions in which the numbers three, four, and seven are particular favorites. The question of the hierarchical ranking of angels and the question what happens to Christ's body if the host is accidentally eaten by a mouse come under discussion with equal seriousness.[41]

We come away with the happy impression that we have really heard everything that we might want. We are also astonished at the definite way in which we are told about things regarding which we might at first ask with surprise how the authors can possibly know about them, but then have to admit shamefacedly that they have simply expounded to us in a meaningful and often very poetic way a dialectical possibility that is by no means obvious. Thomas, for example, assures us that the blessed ones in heaven are adorned with a golden crown *(corona aurea),* which, being

40. Cf. A. von Harnack's *What Is Christianity?* (New York, 1912), 264.

41. Cf. Hagenbach, 257, 357f., on the hierarchy of angels. Cf. also Seeberg, III, 201 n. 1, on the problem whether a mouse eating the host receives Christ's body (with many examples). Cf. also the reference to *S. Th.* III, q. 80, a. 3 ad 3 on p. 468 of Seeberg.

both golden and circular, signifies the perfection of the *fruitio Dei* in the contemplation and love of which they share. Superadded for martyrs and saints, however, and especially for monks and nuns, is an *aureola* (diminutive of *aurea*) because that essential thing cannot be transcended by anything greater but only by something less.[42] Or listen to what Heinrich Seuse has the damned in hell say about their punishment being eternal: "Woe on us, we did not want anything but this; if a millstone were so broad that it covered the whole earth, and if in the beginning it were so big that it even touched heaven, and if a little bird came every 100,000 years and bit out of it as much as the tenth part of a little millet seed, we wretches would wish nothing more than that when the stone was gone our eternal torment would have an end, and that cannot be."[43]

We are surely barren thinkers if we cannot see what insight is everywhere concealed in the imagery, yet we are no less astounded by the confidence with which these authors translate their insights into imagery that may often be striking. We must also be astounded at the remarkable peace that breathes over their discussions. It is true that here and there, for example, in Abelard or in scholastics of the age of the gathering 14th- and 15th-century storm, we detect highly existential inner conflicts and a hard struggle for composure before things can be as certain and unequivocal on paper as they now are. No doubt Scholasticism is renowned for its controversies and even conflicts. But what distinguishes it is the obvious rule that people spoke only when they were clear about things, only when what they had to say was ripe, so that there was no need to air abroad inner problems or unsolved questions or doubts, only at most to give an account of conflicts that had been ended. Hence, bitter though the quarrels between school and school might be, they took place within the same fellowship and on the same basic premises. The anger and tone of voice that we find in Reformation battles were alien to the Middle Ages. As we have to admit, Reformation contests were like peasant brawls compared to the elegant fencing of the scholastics. As I said yesterday, one could then make very radical assertions unhindered without going over the line or really getting out of step. When getting out of step finally began to

---

42. Hagenbach, 446f., on the *corona aurea* and the *aureola* for martyrs and saints, monks and nuns, a superadded prize in *S.Th. Suppl.*, q. 96, a. 1 i.c., according to Hagenbach, 447.

43. H. Seuse, *Büchlein von der Weisheit*, ch. XI, on the never-ending pains of hell; Hagenbach, 450.

happen, when a Bradwardine or Wycliffe or Huss began to say really bad things to others, the Middle Ages were at an end. In the best classical age, that was not done, and the stake did not come into action as a theological argument.

But we must stop and ask what all this meant compared to Reformation theology. In relation to Scholasticism, as we have generally described it, that theology was obviously something "wholly other," if we may again put it thus, though we are agreed that there was no real breach of historical continuity. Within the continuity, however, we find first the emergence of a totally new style, the outbreak of a total restlessness, we must say, for along with the intellectual *habitus* that medieval theology had developed, and in contrast with it, the theological attitude of the Reformation, so long as it was in flux as a true countermovement, was so as a deliberate and angry rejection of that *habitus*, as a wild and elemental event at the heart of a cultivated land. The harmony of the monastery garden was broken and instead we seem to be in the virgin wilderness of mountain forests, if not in the terrors of the Wolfsschlucht.[44] The harmony of the Gothic cathedral was at an end. The parallel lines to which we referred yesterday no longer intersected in the finite sphere no matter how high they might reach. No, they now relentlessly strove upward to a point of unity and rest in the infinite, the result being that the vault was broken open and heaven's daylight shone in from above. All was sober, nondevout, secular. The glory of God itself brought disaster to the theology of glory.

In saying this we have already disclosed the secret of the new theology. It made the discovery that theology has to do with *God*. It made the great and shattering discovery of the real theme of all theology. The secret was simply this, that it took this theme seriously in all its distinctiveness, that it names God God, that it lets God be God, the one object that by no bold human grasping or inquiry or approach can be simply one object among many others. God *is*. *He* lives. *He* judges and blesses. *He* slays and makes alive [cf. 1 Sam. 2:6]. *He* is the Creator and Redeemer and Lord. The Reformation did not really engender any new thoughts about God. It did the simple thing of underlining the *He*. And that put an end to the Middle Ages. For all the building stone by stone, all the mounting up step by step, all the moving from conclusion to conclusion, all this action in which the Middle Ages found its answers, had to become a question when it was underlined and understood that *He,* God, is the point of the whole

44. An allusion to act 2 of Weber's opera *Der Freischütz* (1821).

enterprise. The basic Reformation view is God *himself* and God *alone, He* the way, *He* the possibility; and therefore all our action, even though oriented to God, is vain even in the very best life;[45] all humanity, the whole world, even in its supreme possibilities, is guilty, lost, but still justified, yet saved only by sheer mercy. The Reformation, too, knew of the glory of God and could speak about it. But it said: To God alone be the glory! That put an end to the theology of glory.

Let us find out first, however, what the emergence of this insight had to involve externally relative to our final survey of the Middle Ages. What are we to say in this regard precisely when we have taken pains to do justice impartially to Scholasticism, precisely when we have learned to like the medieval thinkers, precisely when we have perhaps recognized in them our own deepest longings and desires? May it not be that much of what we have thus far regarded as our supremely modern striving, our whole modern style of religion even with its Christian coloring, is at its deepest level medieval? Who is Goethe closer to, Dante or Luther? That is a question we may at least raise. Where do we belong with our Romanticism, with our drive for immediacy, with our urgent concern to be shown a path that we can tread? Can we stay on those heights on which the reformers ventured, no, on which they were set against their own wishes or expectations, and where an immovable barrier arrests all striving for immediacy, where steps are possible but no path opens up before us, where we can live but only as the dying [cf. 2 Cor. 6:9]? Would we not do better to turn back? Instead of Calvin might we not take Thomas as the one we can really understand better?[46]

If we want the security that we find in the scholastics, then it might be as well for us not to turn to the reformers. Certainty about God, indeed, we may expect that here, but a certainty that entails a supreme lack of security, that makes of life a problem, a question, a task, a need, that makes of the Christian life an unceasing battle: a battle for existence itself in which we constantly confront the impossible and the intolerable that Scholasticism, at least in its teaching, could always adroitly sidestep; a battle in which in truth God wills to be and can be the only helper.

We may well ask whether we are wise to leave the solid Catholic ground of balance and to launch out on the wild sea of Reformation thinking. Even the symmetrical completeness of subtle responses to all

---

45. From strophe 2 of Luther's *Aus tiefer Not* (1524).
46. Cf. Goethe's *Faust,* I, lines 512f.

that we might want to know is something we cannot seek in Reformation theology. That theology is an emergency structure, not a well-appointed house. It offers no answers at all, or only incidental answers, to many interesting questions. The symmetry of the numbers three, four, and seven, the ladder to heaven that gives us confidence, the theological interplay, the highly intellectual feast — we find none of these things. The only concern in thinking here is to be serious and to keep the real theme in view. What a pile of ruins we have in Melanchthon's *Loci,* what a dark and threatening forest in Calvin's *Institutes!* Not everyone surely can have to tread these desolate places.

Nor may we seek in the reformers what is at least in part such reassuring and profound information about invisible things of which I gave you a couple of examples. The reformers were astonishingly eloquent on those relations between God and us about which one can speak, but astonishingly silent when it came to matters about which one can only be imaginative. They did not deny the possibility of speaking about such things but used the possibility sparingly.

And as for the peacefulness and decorum and good manners that might allow for disagreement but not quarreling, I have told you already that we cannot see these in the reformers. In them we do find quarreling. All the evil spirits of discord seem to have come to life. All the possibilities of quiet academic discussion between one view and another seem to have been excluded. Everything is so much a matter of principle, everything is in such deadly earnest, everything is so angry. Last things are always at issue. Innermost feelings are always exposed. Attacks on opponents are always pressed to the uttermost. For this reason the more delicate like Erasmus who found this hard stayed clear of the tumult so far as possible. Even Calvin would rather have passed his days as a private scholar than as a reformer, and he knew why. As a reformer, he found his life filled with conflicts on every hand concerning which we today can only with difficulty, if at all, convince ourselves that they had to be fought, or had to be fought in the way they were. Lovers of peace cannot possibly approve of this kind of life and this kind of theology in which there was constant hewing and stabbing on all sides. Is that really what the Reformation age involves? we might ask. But we do better to ask why it was that it had to be so and could not be otherwise in this new age.

The slogan that Luther used in the theses of the Heidelberg Disputation to distinguish his own theology from that of the scholastics was "theology of the cross." In what he said then, and in a similar situation and on the same front in his Disputation against Scholastic Theology a year earlier (EOL V, Arg. 1, 315ff., 387ff.),[47] we can see how it was that the reformers did not just cause an incidental disturbance but attacked the basic view of the Middle Ages. In essence we find two trains of thought in the records of Luther's initial attack on medieval theology, the first more apparent in the earlier Wittenberg Disputation (1517), the latter more so in the later Heidelberg Disputation (1518), but both deeply involved in one another and both pointing to one another.

The first is a negation, a protest, a sharp offensive. It contains what seemed to those outside the surprising and scandalous theses of the nexus of thought with which the reformers broke out of the circle of medieval possibilities. At Wittenberg we are told that once a person becomes a bad tree then that person can will and do only what is bad (4); or that by nature we cannot will that God be God but will always will that we be God and God not God (17); or that on our part there is no preceding disposition for grace but only the opposite, or even rebellion against grace (30); or that nature knows no righteous command or goodwill (34); or that by nature we cannot overcome our ignorance of God, of ourselves, or of the doing of the good (36); or that we cannot become theologians unless we do so without Aristotle (44); or that the law and the will are two foes that cannot be reconciled apart from grace (72); or that every work done according to the law is outwardly good but inwardly sin (77); or that love for God cannot coexist with love, even the highest love, for the creature (94).[48] Then from the Heidelberg Disputation of 1518 we read that human works, no matter what worth they have or how good they seem, are to be judged as mortal sins (3), or that arrogance is unavoidable, and true hope impossible, if in every human work the sentence of condemnation (God's) is not feared (11).[49] For, as Luther said in explanation, it is not possible to hope in God if one does not despair of all creatures.[50] We read again that those who do what they can to attain to grace heap up sin upon sin and become doubly guilty.[51]

So much from the first and negative train of thought. What is

47. WA 1, 224ff., 353ff.

48. Respectively, ibid., 224, 13f.; 225f.; 225, 29f.; 225, 37; 226f.; 226, 16; 227, 26; 227, 35f.; 228, 28.

49. Ibid., 353, 19f.; 354, 1f.

50. Ibid., 359, 20f.

51. Ibid., 354, 11f.

typically and decisively nonmedieval here is not the content in detail but the harsh one-sidedness with which Luther pursued the thought that in all circumstances we stand under judgment. He left no place for an "also" or a "but" or a "nevertheless." He did not look ahead to any higher stage of the way or any further possibility. The last and supreme possibility is that we are sinners. This was not an expression of humility before the eternal God. The Middle Ages knew that, too. By rudely stopping at such humility, Luther's thinking was an assault upon Scholasticism, upon its very heart. What was questioned was not just an aberration or subsidiary teaching of a Thomas, a Dante, or an Eckhardt, but what was best and highest and most inward and vital in them, if Luther's protest was right.

The second train of thought in the Luther of that period was positive, a proclamation or affirmation about God. And what a one it was, of course! Its content is that we live by the grace of God. In itself this is not surprising. It is no more new than the negation. Scholasticism was in truth aware of it, too. But it was suspect and dangerous and even more non-Catholic than the first line of thinking because of its association with the negation, namely, because here the grace of God is taken seriously, with bitter yet saving seriousness, only in connection with that radical protest against us humans as sinners. Set in that context, the proclamation of the mercy of God became the heart of the new Reformation theology.

Listen to Luther himself. At Wittenberg in 1517 he said that the best and infallible preparation for grace, the only disposition for it, is God's eternal election and predestination (29), that the presence of grace is enough to make works meritorious, yet grace is not idly present but present as a living, moving active spirit (54f.), that blessed are those who do the works of grace (81), that the good and life-giving law is the love of God shed abroad in our hearts by the Holy Spirit (85), and that to love God is to hate self and to know nothing outside him (95).[52]

Then at Heidelberg in 1518 he said that the works of God, no matter how hidden they are or how evil they might seem to be, are in truth immortal benefits ("merits").[53] In explanation Luther gave the following important exposition. The Lord humbles and terrifies us by the law and the sight of our sins, so that to others and to ourselves we seem to be empty, foolish, and evil, and truly are so. When we see and confess this, we have no form nor comeliness but live in the hidden God, in the

52. Respectively, ibid., 225, 27f.; 226, 32-227, 2; 228, 4; 228, 11f.; 228, 29.
53. Ibid., 353, 21f.

43

concealment of God, that is, in naked trust in his mercy; and in and of ourselves we can appeal to nothing but sin, folly, death, and hell according to the apostolic saying in 2 Cor. 6 [vv. 9-10]: As sorrowful, but always rejoicing, as dying, and behold we live. That is what Isa. 28 [v. 21] calls God's *opus alienum,* his strange work, for his work has to take place (in us), that is, he humbles us in ourselves by reducing us to despair in order to exalt us in virtue of his mercy, and by bringing us hope, as Hab. 3 [v. 2] says: When you chide, you remember your mercy. When this happens to us, we have no pleasure in ourselves and see no beauty in us but only deformity. Indeed, we do outwardly what must seem foolish and perverted to others.[54] Human existence of this kind under humility and the fear of God is what Luther calls the work of God that is eternally beneficial ("meritorious") in spite of appearances. (It need hardly be said that Luther's use of the category of merit here casts a special light.) We then read that this kind of talk is no reason for despair but is a reason for humility and a spur to the seeking of the grace of Christ (17).[55] For, says Luther in explanation, it is hope and not despair that is preached when the preaching is that we are sinners.[56] Nevertheless, we have to despair of ourselves if we are to be able to receive the grace of Christ (18).[57] For, the explanation adds, if we do not, we still rely on doing what we can, and we remain presumptuous.[58] The good theologian is the one who sees in the cross and passion the visible side of God that is turned to us and does not look directly at the invisible things of God, his majesty and glory, by way of profound spiritual vision.[59]

To support this thesis Luther argues that it helps no one to see God in his glory and majesty if he is not seen in the lowliness and shame of the cross.[60] Along the lines of a theology of glory Philip in John 14 [v. 8] says: "Lord, show us the Father," and he receives the answer: "Philip, whoever sees me sees also my Father." True theology and the true knowledge of God lie, then, in the crucified Christ.[61] A theologian of glory calls evil good and good evil, but the theologian of the cross calls things by

54. Ibid., 356, 37-357, 17.
55. Ibid., 354, 13f.
56. Ibid., 361, 12f.
57. Ibid., 354, 15f.
58. Ibid., 361, 28-30.
59. Ibid., 354, 17-20.
60. Ibid., 362, 11f.
61. Ibid., 362, 15-19.

their right names (21).[62] For, Luther explains, the theologian of glory does not see God hidden in the passion and thus prefers works to suffering, glory to the cross, power to weakness, wisdom to folly; in sum, evil to good. Such are enemies of Christ's cross.[63] Friends of the cross, however, call the cross good and works evil. For the cross demolishes works, and Adam, who is built up by works, is crucified.[64] The wisdom that would know the invisible glory of God by the way of human works puffs up, blinds, and hardens (22).[65] In itself, of course, it is not bad, but without the theology of the cross we make the best worst by ascribing wisdom and works to ourselves (24).[66] We are not righteous by doing much, but by believing much in Christ without works (25).[67] The law says, "Do this," and nothing happens. Grace says, "Believe in him," and all is done already (26).[68] The love of God does not find its object present but creates it (28).[69] For the love of God that is alive in us loves sinners, the wicked, the foolish, the weak, to make them righteous, good, wise, and strong. It overflows and lavishes good on them. Sinners are good, then, because they are loved; they are not loved because they are good.[70]

What we have in these theses of Luther is truly and literally a theology of the cross. Luther, too, sees a horizontal line before him,[71] our human striving, knowing, willing, and doing. The theology of glory thinks that somewhere on an extension of this line it will reach the goal of infinity, the invisible things of God. Its slogan is that grace does not destroy nature but perfects it.[72] Luther does not deny that there is this wisdom, this beatific vision, much, much further along that line. His objection is that one thing is overlooked, namely, that at the center, where each of us stands, we willing and knowing humans with our works, there is a break that throws everything into question.[73] To say human is to say sin, rebellion

---

62. Ibid., 354, 21f.
63. Ibid., 362, 23-26.
64. Ibid., 362, 29f.
65. Ibid., 354, 23f.
66. Ibid., 354, 27f.
67. Ibid., 354, 29f.
68. Ibid., 354, 31f.
69. Ibid., 354, 35f.
70. Ibid., 365, 8-12.
71. Barth has a graph in the margin here.
72. Thomas, *S. Th.* I, q. 1 a. 8 ad 2; cf. n. 30 above.
73. Barth has a graph in the margin here.

against grace, invincible ignorance of God, irreconcilable hostility to his law. What is radically set in question by this break in the middle of the line is not simply our banal everyday willing and doing, but just as much what we regard as our love of God, not simply our "sensuality" and reason but just as much our "simple intelligence," as Gerson would put it, at the heart of which, sunk in contemplation, we see God face-to-face.[74]

The theology of glory boldly pushes on beyond the gap that makes all this problematical. It storms ahead without a halt on the horizontal line toward the invisible things of God, not considering how seriously it is threatened in the rear and how much it increases the damage with its striving. In contrast Luther tries to draw attention to the vacuum, to the fact that passion (suffering) stands at the heart of life and speaks of sin and folly, death and hell. These fearful visible things of God, his strange work, the crucified Christ — these are the theme of true theology. A preaching of despair? No, of hope! For what does that break in the center mean? Who is the God hidden in the passion with his strange work, and what does he desire? Explaining Heidelberg Thesis 16, Luther pointed out that the strange work leads on to the proper work, that God makes us sinners in order to make us righteous.[75] The gap in the horizontal line, the disaster of our own striving, is the point at which God's vertical line intersects our lives,[76] where God wills to be gracious. Here where our finitude is recognized is true contact with infinity. He who judges us is he who shows mercy to us, he who slays us is he who makes us live, he who leads us into hell is he who leads us into heaven. Only sinners are righteous, only the sad are blessed, only the dying live. But sinners *are* righteous, the sad *are* blessed, the dying *do* live. The God hidden in the passion is the living God who loves us, sinful, wicked, foolish, and weak as we are, in order to make us righteous, good, wise, and strong. It is because the strange work leads to the proper work that there can be no theology of glory, that we must halt at the sharply severed edges of the broken horizontal line where what we find is despair, humility, the fear of God. For despair is hope, humility is exaltation, fear of God is love of God, and nothing else. The center of this theology, then, is the demand for faith as naked trust that casts itself into the arms of God's mercy; faith that is the last word that can be humanly said about the possibility of justification before God;

74. J. Gerson, *Considerationes de theologia mystica*, X, quoted in Hagenbach, 324.
75. WA 1, 361, 4f.
76. Barth has a graph in the margin here.

46

a faith that is sure of its object — God — because here there is resolute renunciation of the given character of scholastic faith (infused, implicit, and formed) as an element of uncertainty; faith viewed not as itself a human work but as an integral part of God's strange work, sharing in the whole paradox of it.

We see now why this theology was so basically polemical and militant. Without a constant critical debate with the infinitely attractive tendency, represented with such virtuosity by the scholastics, to press on to the goal, with the help of grace, by works, by "high-flying thoughts" (57, 208),[77] the demand for faith cannot possibly be made. Hence a second focal point of this theology was a constantly repeated reference to Christ as God's visible word and work in contrast to the lofty invisible things of the theology of glory. Luther admonished and warned us all to leave off speculating and not to float too high but to stay here below by the cradle and diaper in which Christ lies, in whom dwells all the fullness of the deity bodily (57, 211).[78] This reference to Christ is truly necessary here, grounded in the matter itself, for here Christ does not simply bring grace as a second thing, so that we can then go on without him, as mysticism in particular has blabbed, but he is himself grace, the proper work of God, the promise of the mercy of God that is grasped in faith, the one God who makes us righteous, even as he is the Crucified, the scandal, the strange work of God, which threatens our works at their very root, the same God who makes us sinners in order to make us righteous.

It was this theology of the cross as a theology of the justification of sinners that Luther rediscovered in Romans and the Psalms, and Augustine as the word which finally routs completely even the true longings of mysticism and Nominalist Scholasticism. That this word should be loudly proclaimed and thoroughly heard was for him the Reformation once he became aware that with this concept a reformation of Christendom, the church, and theology had in fact begun. Initially Luther had no other concern than to refer to the forgotten cross at the beginning of our human way, or rather, this one concern basically included all others, though pursuing them could not be for him a matter of incisive or decisive importance. We are forced to say that this one concern in all its one-sidedness is indeed the true essence of the Reformation. Where people have

77. WA TR 6, 38 (no. 6558) refers to high-flying thoughts in the attempt to get to heaven without the ladder of Christ's humanity.
78. WA TR 1, 108 (no. 257).

this concern, there is Protestantism; where they do not, or have moved on past it, there is a prolongation of the Middle Ages!

From all this we derive two insights. First, we see why there had to be the sharp clash between the Reformation and the Middle Ages that I have just intentionally depicted for you with almost futuristic vividness. Schwenckfeld was right when he said that two worlds dash against one another here.[79] We cannot both believe with Luther and also engage in mysticism with its devotional excesses, even though it be the finest and most insightful mysticism of an Eckhardt and his school. Medieval mysticism seeks with all its powers to move away from what Luther called God, though it could certainly speak a great deal about the cross and darkness and Christ. Luther turned his back with increasing resoluteness on what mysticism called God, although at first he thought he found his own outlook in the glorious little book of the *German Theology* and in Tauler.[80] We will come back to the connection, which was undoubtedly there. But at the very point where it is there we see clearly that a choice has to be made: Luther or Eckhardt. Once we realize that the Middle Ages also knew the vertical line but lived wholly and utterly on the horizontal, whereas Luther also knew the horizontal but lived wholly and utterly on the vertical, or, more accurately, at the point of the intersecting of the vertical by the horizontal, we need no longer be surprised by the harsh either-or that had to arise there, nor by the shattering of security that the Reformation entailed, nor by the incomplete and fissured nature of its theological presentations, nor by the paucity of its metaphysics, nor by the atmosphere of anger that lay over the whole of the first half of the 16th century and that began to dissipate only when the spirit of the Reformation also fled, nor by the much-noted coarseness of Luther, nor by the cold virulence of Calvin, nor indeed by Ignatius Loyola and the pyres of the Counter-Reformation. When the theology of the cross really becomes part of the theological problem, when theologians begin really to note what is the true theme of their generally peaceful vocation, it is inevitable that something primal, wild, undomesticated, and demonic in religion will be aroused as between friend and foe. It had to be so then, and it might be that if the Creator Spirit brings on the stage another theology of the cross it will have to be so again. Insight into the ineluctability of these consequences will keep us straight when we assess certain

79. See above, 20f.
80. Cf. Loofs, 701, 709 (524).

secondary phenomena of Reformation history with which we might have little sympathy. It will also keep us from looking for the essence of the Reformation in these secondary phenomena when we might well be in sympathy with them, as can happen.

The second insight clearly arises out of our account of Luther's starting point, where we have to look for what is problematic in the Reformation itself. We obviously turn to the horizontal line of human thought and action in time that is so sharply broken by the vertical line of the knowledge of God in Christ. The problem of human life and striving as the Middle Ages unbrokenly pursued it cannot be simply cut off by being put under the shadow of its finitude, that is, in the light of its origin. What does the attack of the vertical mean for what takes place horizontally? What becomes of all that we will and work here below on the line of death that is suddenly made visible,[81] that we have to will and work because as people in time we are always here below on that line of death? What becomes of all this when we confront the absolute beyond that meets the present world in a way that crushes it but is also full of promise, when we arrive at the sharp edges of despair, humility, and fear of God which, as we saw yesterday, still have their positive side, when we face God the Judge who all the same is none other than the merciful God? The Middle Ages died with Luther's discovery, but their problem, the problem of the active life, of ethics in the broadest sense, did not die with them. Nor can it be put to death. From the very first Luther was aware of this problem in his theology of the cross. Remember Thesis 55 at Wittenberg in 1517: Grace is not idle but a living, moving, active spirit.[82] On innumerable occasions he tried with great seriousness to solve the problem. Simply to make Luther a Quietist is an illegitimate simplifying of the situation. We may at least say that this question was not primarily *his* question. Luther's great concern was for the pure content and free course of the Word, no matter what might become of works. Here, however, in the matter of establishing the positive relation between the vertical and horizontal lines — the cross has to be left open in Luther[83] — we find the point at which the second turn in the Reformation, the Reformed theology of Zwingli and Calvin, had to enter and did in fact do so.

---

81. The expression "line of death" was an important one for Barth at this period; cf. *Romans*.

82. See above, n. 52.

83. Barth has a graph in the margin here.

§3 Common Features

What I have said raises the question of features common to the Middle Ages and the Reformation despite the sharpness of their differences. At the beginning of the section I argued that the new thing in the Reformation in the serious sense is something eternally new, and closer investigation confirmed the insight that the new thing then discovered was something so great that it is a priori impossible to assume that it was simply not present at all previously; conversely, the old thing that the reformers vanquished was so all-encompassing and universally human that it could not possibly disappear completely.

The Reformation was the expression of a crisis that secretly ran through all the Middle Ages. I have referred already to the tensions and contradictions that the medieval church was able to reconcile, but in truth the tensions were serious. The Middle Ages were in self-contradiction long before Luther came along and made the contradiction irreconcilable. But the Middle Ages could always find a way victoriously through the tensions to the triumph of the theology of glory. They did not finally accept their own self-contradiction. In spite of every shock, they could always restore equilibrium. We see the existence of that crisis of the medieval spirit at the most varied points.

In this regard we recall especially the problem of monasticism that was always present in the church from Benedict of Nursia by way of the Cluny[1] reform to Francis of Assisi. Originally we had here a real protest of the first order against the theology of glory even though later precisely the Franciscans and Dominicans became that theology's most brilliant champions. Initially monasticism questioned and even attacked a self-assured and worldly Christianity. It was an uplifted finger to remind people that we cannot have the kingdom of God so cheaply. The world took notice and caused the finger to drop. It made a place for asceticism. It offered this hard and dangerous function to the brave who were ready for it. It celebrated a new triumph by putting this possibility too, this highest level of human action, on the church's horizontal line. Thus the ascetics, though often with great pain, as in the case of a Francis, became protagonists of the triumphing world church instead of protesting against it. That does not alter the fact, however, that the Reformation was at least also an extension of the monastic line. The question of true penitence that brought the theology of the cross to the fore was a

---

1. The MS by mistake had Clugny.

variation on a typically monastic question. Monasticism now mounted its most powerful offensive. With full seriousness and with no holding back it now broke out of the cloister and became a universal matter. It would now question the world, not as before from outside, but from inside, not in the form of the ascetic lifestyle of the few, but in that of a cross lifted up in the life of all. It achieved perhaps its greatest victory in the man in whom it finally went bankrupt.

To do justice to the new thing that was already concealed in the old we must also look at the innumerable traces that Augustine left in the Western church, and along with Augustine examine Paul's epistles and the philosophy of Plato.[2] Wherever Augustine made an impact, no matter how faintly, there still glowed under the ashes some recollection of the vertical line. In almost every century during the Middle Ages Augustine won over some resolute disciples for himself, and if they were strong enough, also for his own teachers, Paul and Plato. As regards the transcendental knowledge of God, John Scotus Erigena followed in his steps in the 9th century, Anselm in the 11th, Bonaventura in the 13th, and Eckhardt in the 14th. As regards predestination, we find an echo of his teaching in Isidore of Seville in the 7th century, an extreme and defiant proponent in Gottschalk in the 9th, a renaissance in the 14th century in Bradwardine (the profound doctor, who wanted to defend it as "the cause of God" against a Christian world that had fallen into Pelagianism, Elijah against the 450 priests of Baal), and also in Gregory of Rimini, in whose formulas some have sought a source of the theology of Luther.[3] Again, at least as a restraining force, Augustine played a decisive part in the development of the scholastic doctrine of the appropriation of salvation. If at this point the doctrines of free will, of the possibility of earning merit, of infused grace and making righteous were hemmed about by so many distinctions that even in typical representatives of Scholasticism one might at a pinch expound them in better part along Reformation lines, or at least find in them a starting point for Luther's revolution, then unmistakably this was due, if not to the spirit, at least to the shadow, of Augustine.

2. For Barth's evaluating of Plato along with Paul cf. Barth's *Epistle to the Romans* (Oxford, 1933), p. 111; also his essay "The Christian's Place in Society," in *The Word of God and the Word of Man* (reprinted New York, 1957), 272-327; and *Romans*.

3. On Bradwardine cf. Hagenbach, 393f.; and Bradwardine, *De causa dei contra Pelagium*, Praefatio, according to Tschackert, 27 n. 1. On the influence of Gregory of Rimini on Luther's view of concupiscence and original sin cf., e.g., Tschackert, 38f.

Augustine's spiritual emphasis played a similar role in eucharistic teaching, though here the last powerful opposition to the theology of glory, that of Berengar of Tours, was broken already in the 11th century.[4] Finally medieval theology took over from Augustine something that it found congenial, his mystical devotion and his attachment to the church, while quietly ignoring his less congenial Platonism and Paulinism. Nevertheless, it could no more prevent the latter elements than the former from retaining their vitality. Those latter elements had only to be reasserted, which is precisely what happened with great force.

Along with monasticism and Augustinianism, a third Reformation element in the Middle Ages was undoubtedly the anti-Thomistic theology of Duns Scotus (d. 1308) and the so-called modern way of William of Occam (d. 1349), which had a similar orientation but went even further. With special reference to Calvin we must devote a few moments to these two British thinkers. A first distinctive feature in both was the questioning of the unity of the path of knowledge, of the stairway from reason to revelation. Not metaphysically but methodologically the statements of reason and revelation were for them irreconcilable. We are unable to mount up from reason to revelation. Theology is a practical, not a speculative, discipline, said Duns,[5] and Occam agreed that we cannot know God's existence, essence, or reality intuitively from ourselves or from the things of nature. God cannot be an object for us.[6] Occam went further, however, when he showed that our reason not only cannot prove dogma but might make it appear absurd.[7] Reality consists only of individual things, said Duns, and again Occam went further with his even sharper thesis that this is the reality originating in the idea of God, whereas the terms or names or concepts out of which reason constructs science exist only in the soul of the knowing subjects, so that logic is the only real science.[8] This thesis

---

4. Cf. Hagenbach, 416f.; Loofs, *Leitfaden*, 500-503 (7th ed. 403ff.).

5. For Duns see Loofs, 591 (486).

6. William of Occam, *Super IV libros Sententiarum*, sent. 1, dist. 3, qu. 2, in Hagenbach, 332.

7. Cf. Seeberg, III, 609-21.

8. Ibid., 569, in which it is pointed out that for Duns *individualitas* is a reality, the individual entity that constitutes the individual, *haecceitas* as the later expression has it (*Duns metaph.* VII, q. 13, 9). See Ficker and Hermelink, *Das Mittelalter*, 187f., with reference to Occam's agnosticism and Nominalism, or, better, Terminism (the individual thing originating in the idea of God produces a *terminus* in the soul of those who know it, and this is then universalized).

explains the historical use of the term Nominalism for the Occamist school, though the name by no means exhausts the significance of the school.

Something like the gap in the middle to which we referred in connection with Luther was undoubtedly the result of this agnosticism, and it seems to me totally out of the question that Luther, who could call himself an Occamist,[9] was not methodologically influenced at this point. But the difference comes to light at once when we note to what end the Nominalists made the rent. Unfortunately, at least so far as we can detect their theological purpose, they did not seek like Luther to humble us humans and to make way for the unique self-glory of God. Instead, as apologetics likes to do in every age when it is very refined, they were aiming to bring about a total subjection to all church doctrines, even though these might be as contrary to reason as they are! Occam expressly advocated implicit faith,[10] and their purpose was to make this seem to be the only possible means of rescue from the sea of doubt. If, as they believed, there was no direct path to the theology of glory by way of reason, they would attain to it by the sacrifice of reason.

This maneuver is certainly not the same as Luther's theology of the cross, which simply bids us halt before God himself and appeal to his mercy. We should not fail to see, of course, how insightful and significant it still was from a formal standpoint. We need only look at a saying like that of Occam to the effect that faith is a free gift by which the mind believes on account of God and against itself (Tschackert, 36).[11] Were it not for the fatal knowledge that this believing against the intellect does not lead to pure negation and hence to a true transcendental grounding of natural knowledge, but to the paradoxical superstructure of an additional supranatural knowledge that is not in pure antithesis to the natural; were it not for the knowledge that this believing is simply a secret understanding of a higher type, its object not being the origin of all that may be known, not the crucified Christ, but the hinterland of church dogma that is accepted for all the skepticism, one might say that here an insight into the relation to infinity that takes place precisely in an awareness of human finitude as such (the mind against itself), an insight into the

---

9. Luther, WA 6, 600, 11f., in his 1520 work against the papal bull.

10. Seeberg, III, 614, a reference to Occam's *De sacr. alt.* 1.16; quodl. IV, g 35; and cf. 616f.; also Ficker and Hermelink, *Das Mittelalter,* 188.

11. Tschackert, 36, ascribes this statement to the Occamist Pierre d'Ailly; cf. *Gersonii opera,* I, 68 A.

freedom of this relation from any discursive basis ("on account of God"), an insight into its origin by creation ("free gift"), had been wonderfully achieved.

That fundamentally nonmedieval insight did hover before those thinkers even though they did not develop it but were encysted and incapable of the grim seriousness with which Luther proceeded at this point. To see how it hovered before them we need look only at their distinctive doctrine of God.[12] Over against the whole system of causal necessity that we call the world God stands contingently as himself an indeterminate first cause, as free will in the absolute, as will that has its norm only in itself. In virtue of the absolute power of this will the whole world might have been different. In fact, of course, God simply acts in accordance with his plan that aims at the saving of the elect, in accordance with his ordained power. He thus wills everything as it actually is. Nevertheless, and this is the decisive point, the possibility remains, and has to be considered, that God might have willed and acted differently. God is not a prisoner of his own plan that we see worked out in the church, or of the logical and moral orders in which he executes the plan. It might happen, said Duns, that people attain to glory that do not receive the grace, the knowledge of God, that Scotists and Occamists, like other scholastics, think of as infused faith (Seeberg, III, 578). It might be, Occam ventured to say, that God could have made the morally good other than it is in fact, that hatred of God, theft, and adultery could be meritorious, had not God's command ordained the opposite (Loofs, 612).[13] In both the religious and the moral sphere we thus have to consider that things are pleasing to God only because of his acceptance of them on the basis of his free will (Tschackert, 36), and that when we speak of God in the forms of the age, when we speak of what he did, does, or will do, the now of eternity that we mean is the truth of what we say.[14] Only God's own essence is the proper object of his will. To all else he stands in a basically contingent relation; he is free relative to it (Loofs, 593-94).[15] Even Christ's passion is meritorious only by God's "acceptation." An angel or another

12. For what follows cf. Seeberg, III, 577ff.

13. Occam, *Super IV Libros Sententiarum*, 2, q., 9 litt. O, quoted in Loofs, 612 n. 2 (507).

14. Duns Scotus, *Opus Oxoniense*, I, dist. 9, q. unica no. 6, quoted in Loofs, 594 (488).

15. Ibid., I, dist. 39, q. unica no. 22; Loofs, 594 n. 2 (489).

human might have made reconciliation for the world just as well (Hagenbach, 387).[16] On this path that leads to Luther Occam put out such powerful ideas as that forgiveness of sins is not a making righteous but nonimputation.[17]

Most church historians and histories of doctrine tell us that the God of Duns and Occam was a capricious God,[18] but I believe with Seeberg that this view is wrong. As these theologians studied and deepened the concept of power, their unsettling reminder of God's absolute power was meant to anchor the more firmly the authority of the truth that holds good by God's ordained power.[19] They knew very well that one cannot establish a thing better or more effectively than by taking it back to its premise by the sharpest criticism of the way it is. The premise of all that God has ordained, however, is deity, God's freedom and majesty. What good is all our zeal toward God, or with God, or even for God, if we do not consider at all who and what God is, if there is no basic interruption of our zeal by the recollection that God's thoughts are not our thoughts nor his ways ours [cf. Isa. 55:8]?

To give a sure place to that recollection Duns and Occam introduced into theology a final uncertainty as to God's will and work. They did so for the very same reason — and this is why I deal with the point so fully — as that which would later lead Calvin to think he had found in the doctrine of double predestination the core and lodestar of the doctrine of God. Against the concept of God in Duns and Occam we are not to bring the charge of arbitrariness that has equally wrongly been made against Calvin, but rather — and this is what produced the misunderstanding — that of a charming and playful intellectualism, the lack of seriousness with which, unlike Calvin, they handled these necessary but dangerous ideas. They had no intention at all of using the critical principle of absolute power that they had discovered to call into question the given factor of the church that rests on the ordained power, to subject the church to this

16. Ibid., III, dist. 19, quoted in Hagenbach, 387, with the comment that Duns undercuts Anselm, for if Christ suffered only according to his human nature, an angel or another man might have suffered just as well.

17. Occam, *Super quattuor libros sententiarum*, IV, q. 8, according to Loofs, 620 (513).

18. Cf. the judgment of Loofs, 594 n. 2 (with a reference to F. C. Baur, *Lehre von der Dreieinigkeit*, II, 654f.); also 689 (409, 504); and Ficker and Hermelink, 187f.; Tschackert, 35.

19. Seeberg, III, 578f., in express opposition (in a note) to Baur, *Lehre*, II, 654ff.

critical insight, and in this way actually to destroy the whole theology of glory. Instead they used the insight as a paradoxical means to make a free path for scholastic dogmatics, ethics, and mysticism, for the whole titanic striving of the Middle Ages of immediacy. With this great caveat of the divine freedom they established the validity of such distinctive medieval ideas as infused and implicit faith, free will, merit, grace as habitus, justification as infusion, *opus operatum* in sacramental administration, eucharistic transubstantiation, and penance as a sure and easy path. They could advocate all these things precisely in a more vital way, and by reason of the piquant critical background in a more ingenious way, than the earlier and in the last resort naiver scholastics. Occam was the most important medieval advocate of the inspiration of the Bible and Duns Scotus was the hero of his Franciscan order as the highly regarded pioneering defender of the immaculate conception of Mary.[20]

That matters could take this course naturally forces the word "treason" upon our lips. We recall with shame and anger how 19th-century theologians sat at the feet of Kant in order that with the help of his critique of reason they might justify instead of challenge modern Christianity. Theologians have always been adept at ingeniously toying with the most radical and dangerous thoughts and feelings and then devaluing them in an attempt to justify and confirm contemporary religious thoughts and feelings. But who are we to complain in this regard? It makes no sense to doubt the personal sincerity of those who acted thus in the 14th and 19th centuries. Who among us do not have to complain of ourselves in this regard? Nominalism was a great theological possibility. If for a moment we look beyond the confusing interrelation of excellent intention and lamentable execution, in spite of everything we cannot fail to see how hopeful this theology was. It rendered its historical reforming service and is definitely part of the new thing in the old to the extent that it had a destructive effect on the proud structure of Scholasticism and at least greatly undermined the towers that it was neither able nor willing to overthrow. It is not in vain that we think the thought of God's freedom and majesty, the great and solemn thought of the critical negation of everything given, even though we take the thought no more seriously than did Duns and Occam. If the thought cannot work as a remedy, then it works as a poison. If it does not lay a foundation, then it creates uncertainty. If it does not equip theology for rethinking and renewal, then it

20. Loofs, 596f. (490f.)

56

results in culpable obduracy. If the Reformation found theology in a state of disarray and uncertainty, of poisoning and hardening; if it found its way easier as a result; if it could succeed in doing what an Anselm or Bonaventura or Thomas perhaps could not do, then that is the tragic merit of Duns, to whom contemporaries gave the honorary title of the subtle doctor, while the frank but crude Gottfried Arnold (*Kirchengeschichte,* I, 421) called him the foremost eccentric,[21] and perhaps he was both. This was also the tragic merit of Occam, whose contemporary honorary title of venerable inceptor was no less ambivalent. Luther called himself an adherent of this school.[22] Calvin, and perhaps also Zwingli,[23] studied in Paris, its main center, and must have been greatly stimulated by it. Yet as an Occamist neither could have become a reformer.

As a fourth line leading to the Reformation we may cite mysticism. You will have noted in the last hours that I regard mysticism only as one factor among others on the soil of the basic common view of the relation of God to us in the Middle Ages, and that I thus see it along with Scholasticism as the latter's finest flower, so that of almost no medieval theologian can we say where the scholastic leaves off and the mystic begins. All of them were to some extent both. We may rightly count many of them as mystics in the narrower sense and then trace a line from Hugh of St. Victor and Bernard of Clairvaux in the 12th century to Bonaventura in the 13th, Meister Eckhardt and his school, Tauler, Seuse, and the author of the *German Theology* in the 14th, and if one will Thomas à Kempis in the 15th.

Yet we should not lose sight of the scholastic element in these mystics, or of the mystical element in the other scholastics, or of the medieval problem common to both. The common factor in medieval mysticism, the human striving for immediacy, Luther was already calling the theology of glory in his 1516 lectures on Romans at the very time when he was also speaking in friendly terms about mysticism and had come into contact especially with German mysticism. He both knew it and rejected it as the

---

21. G. Arnold, *Unpartheyische Kirchen- und Ketzer-historie . . .,* parts 1 and 2 (Frankfort, 1729), 421.

22. See n. 9 above.

23. The reference to Zwingli studying in Paris is based on a note of his friend Gregorius Mangold. It was possible in the years 1499-1500, but a saying of Zwingli's quoted by H. Bullinger refutes the idea. Cf. on the whole question G. W. Locher, *Die Zwinglische Reformation im Rahmen der europäischen Kirchengeschichte* (Göttingen, 1979), 61f.

theology of glory. He said in the lectures that mystics wish "to hear and contemplate only the uncreated Word Himself, not having first been justified and purged in the eyes of the heart by the incarnate Word" (Tschackert, 41).[24] Remember what we were speaking of yesterday.[25] By the "uncreated Word" understand the invisible things of God that the enemies of the cross, as Luther calls them, contemplate, by justification of "the eyes of the heart" understand the strange work of God in which is hidden the proper work of his mercy, and by the "incarnate Word" understand the crucified Christ. Then this critical saying will make sense to you.

Our present task, however, is to trace the positive relations of mysticism to the Reformation. We face the fact that in spite of that and similar sayings Luther did speak in very favorable tones about mysticism, in tones that he never used for Nominalists, and elsewhere only for Augustine and the Bible. He drew from the same source as Bonaventura and Eckhardt, namely, Augustine, and historically the element in Augustine that had the most influence in the Middle Ages was his Neoplatonic mysticism. In later life Luther once expressly confessed that for a long time, and to his hurt, he had been occupied with the mystical theology of Dionysius the Areopagite (Loofs, 724).[26] In the middle of 1516, as we see from the Romans lectures, he was acquainted with Tauler and the *German Theology*, and he was deeply influenced by them, so that a modern scholar could speak of an "acute mystification" of Luther's theology at this time.[27] But what kind of union could there be between the Reformation and mysticism when it obviously could not include what is most striking in mysticism, its striving for immediacy, which Luther here at once perceived and attacked as an enemy? I think I see the unity of the two at three points.

1. It is understandable that Luther should at first unconcernedly greet mysticism as a precious treasure of knowledge even though he was unsympathetic from the outset with its striving for immediacy, its desire to hear and contemplate the uncreated Word. For this desire, this fundamental desire of the Middle Ages, contained within itself a problem that could not be

24. WA 56, 300, 1ff.

25. See above, 43ff.

26. *Disputatio prima contra Antinomos (1537)*, WA 39 I, 390, 3-390, quoted in Loofs, 714 n. 2.

27. Cf. Tschackert, 39f. For a first reference to Tauler cf. the 1516 Romans lectures, WA 56, 378, 13f.; LW 25, 368. Cf. A. W. Hunzinger, "Luther und die deutsche Mystik," *Neue kirchliche Zeitschrift* 19 (1908), 972-88, quoted in Tschackert, 40.

dismissed out of hand even though the desire might be viewed critically. Certainly Bernard of Clairvaux and innumerable followers of his depicted the union of the soul with God in the far too vivid similitude of the union of the bridegroom and the bride in the Song of Songs, and Eckhardt spoke of the ground of the soul in us where we are one with God, or of the birth of God in the soul, just as he also plainly translated the Trinity into the various aspects of the religious process in the soul, or made it our goal to become by grace what God is by nature.[28] What we find in these statements as they stand is the spirit of a religious shamelessness that takes what does not belong to it. We have to see, however, that the more perspicacious of the mystics recognized the danger and warned against the misunderstanding to which the statements can so easily give rise.

Seuse once spoke sharply about the mystic who in his flourishing rationality wanted to see in himself and in all things a part of the eternal, uncreated rationality: "He hurriedly addresses the matter in an unseasonable way, he blossoms out in his mind like fermenting fruit that even so is not yet ripe."[29] We are not to take literally the exaggerated way in which the mystics speak. It is evident that they speak in this way, using extreme and audacious similes and comparisons, because they face the difficulty of wanting to say things that cannot be said even in the strongest terms, and yet are calling out to be said: the actualizing, the taking place, the coming into being, and the actual being of the relation between us and God. The problem that oppresses the mystics is that of dealing seriously with the known truth of God, of the actuality of the revelation of God to us. For all their sharper insight into the difficulty of this problem, the British Nominalists did not feel it or live it out as existentially as the German mystics. If the former were the head of the later Middle Ages, the latter were the heart.

Luther was closer to the heart than to the head. He saw that the problem of the Middle Ages could not be solved with German exaggeration, Roman rationalism, or British skepticism and ingenuity. But he derived from the first of these the great sense of urgency, the profound and heartfelt seriousness, that underlay the whole medieval concern. The word that defied speech had to be spoken. The impossible possibility had to become an event. The very thing that had never been present,[30] that

28. On the former see Loofs, 522 (425). On the latter see ibid., 628-30 (521f.)
29. Hagenbach, 334.
30. Cf. the last lines of F. von Schiller's *An die Freunde* (1802).

as a human thought or action could be described only as mad folly, that very thing had to come into our lives as the thought and action of God. The Reformation did not ignore the underlying difficulty and hope but for the first time gave it the sharpest expression. It totally rejected and reversed the concern in its existing form, but in reality it still took it quite seriously. Yes, was Luther's reply to the medieval question embedded in mysticism, yes indeed, immediacy, but God's immediacy to us and not vice versa. Yes, life in God, but in the power of his creative Word, not of what is creative in us. Yes, God and the soul, the soul and its God,[31] but *God*, or else it is all error and idolatry. Luther heard what the school of Eckhardt was saying. He understood it. It was alive in him. But because he heard and understood it, he turned aside from the path of Eckhardt as such. There can be no success along that path in terms of the theology of glory, but there is success a hundredfold in terms of the theology of the cross for those who have ears to hear what medieval mystics must surely grasp when they let themselves be taught.

2. Mysticism differs from Scholasticism by stressing the historical person of Jesus. There is, of course, a strange paradox here. None made it more clear than the mystics that the Middle Ages at root did not know what to do with Christ. From the days of Bernard of Clairvaux they anticipated the modern Protestant cult of the gentle, humble, mild, and merciful man Jesus of Nazareth, adorned with all the virtues that they themselves highly rated, and Bernard has often been praised precisely on this account because something particularly evangelical has been seen in it.[32] Neither Bernard, Tauler, nor Thomas à Kempis could really get beyond the picture of Jesus as the model of our seeking of God and as the invisible head of all those like-minded with him. It is obvious that at this point, as the Reformation saw it, a misunderstanding had to be set aside. The ideal of medieval piety that mysticism equated with Christ, and that it enthusiastically used schematically in its spiritual direction, could not coexist with the theology of the cross, which summoned precisely this ideal of piety to judgment and sought to bring freedom from preoccupation with the self.

---

31. Cf. A. von Harnack, *What Is Christianity?* (New York, 1902), 61, where it is argued that if religious individualism, "God and the soul, the soul and its God," and subjectivism, if all such things are Greek, then Jesus was in the context of Greek development.

32. Loofs, 528 (427).

But a problem still remained at this point, in short, the problem of the historical element in Christianity, of revelation. The one and only historical Jesus had become important for medieval believers precisely because they came up against historicity, individuality, and uniqueness in their striving for immediacy. They suspected that this was the category under which alone they could grasp the revelation they sought. They ran up hard against the limits of their own individuality within which they finally could not find revelation. They sensed that they could find it precisely where they could not reach, namely, in the historicity, individuality, and uniqueness of the other. The other is the one in whom is revelation, and only as the other speaks directly to me and ceases to be the other, only as[33] he becomes an I, can I have a part in revelation. This other is Jesus Christ as the quintessence of the historical, the individual, and the unique, and therefore as the bearer of revelation. The Bible responds to the search for immediacy, when this seeks clarity about itself, with the wonderful message: The Word became flesh [John 1:14]. Revelation *took place* in the other, in Jesus Christ. The intersecting of the human horizontal line by the divine vertical line *is* a fact. Time *is* related to eternity, this world to the next, I to Thou.

The Middle Ages, too, heard this message. At first, of course, they misheard it — when and by whom is it not misheard? What they heard was that the Word became a pious man, and this went well with their basic view. But the Word that was truly sought and meant was not that. How can a pious man be revelation to me, set me before God, speak directly to me, cease to be another to me? He is and remains a he, the more so the more pious he is. He can demand that I imitate him, but if I try to do that I admit that my supposed finding has again become a seeking. He can be to me only a companion in my striving for immediacy. But he cannot bring this to completion by himself achieving immediacy.

In contrast to the medieval picture of Jesus, the Christ of Luther is not the pious man but the man who is set in the ranks of sinners under judgment, in the shadow of hell and death, the crucified Christ. Not the crucified Christ of edification, who kindles our admiration as a martyr and hero, whom we are to imitate in his submission to the will of God, whom we can depict and tolerate in his tragic beauty, but the nonedifying crucified Christ of Grünewald, who, when painted, proclaims the strange work of God; who has no form nor comeliness [cf. Isa. 53:2]; in face of

---

33. The MS had *dass* here, changed by the editor to *indem*.

whom love, the affection lavished so remarkably freely on this Savior in his piety, becomes an offering that we no longer resolve so easily to make; in whose lostness and mortal plight we are forced to see a pointer to God himself and his demand for saving despair, humility, and fear of God. This incarnate Word, the Crucified, can speak directly to me. In him the barrier that makes him another is torn down. In him, if I bow under his judgment, I can see myself, be set before God, be cast into the arms of sheer mercy. Here it is not at all a matter of imitation but of faith, not of a further search for immediacy but of revelation. Here it really happens that a hole is made in the Gothic vault, and God's heaven is seen high above. He who sees me sees the Father [John 14:9].

This incarnate Word then, and not, as we are sometimes told, the so-called historical Jesus, is what Luther rediscovered. Rediscovered? Yes, he was always there. He does not have to come and go with the shifts in understanding or nonunderstanding to which he is subject in the course of history. We hear at least, whether we understand or not; the problem of the human situation as such bears witness to him. This Word is known even when not known. Mystics, too, had no other Christ in view even though they almost always spoke about another. Their love of Jesus, which in the last resort was no other than a special form of their pressing on to the event, was something that Luther could let speak to him. It perhaps spoke more strongly in him than in all of them, and if in him, and in the Reformation in general, the rather thin water of the imitation of Christ with its poetry of blood and wounds became the strong wine of the message of judgment and forgiveness, we simply have here further testimony how seriously what was at issue was the new thing that was also already the old.

3. The third point of contact between Reformation thinking and that of medieval mysticism was the methodological principle of mysticism that we might sum up under the term "abnegation." In infinite variations the mystics tried to describe the outworking of this principle. They spoke of the need for separation, resignation, quiet isolation, simplicity of heart, calm, obedience that gives up all that is one's own, or conversely of entry into the inner ground that is the least we have (Eckhardt), of denying oneself, of imitating the passion of Christ with patient suffering and loving humility, of pressing oneself into this (Tauler), of surrender to God as a captive, of making the transition from creatures to God, of seeking God in pious ignorance and mental darkness (Luther),[34] of laying aside all that

34. On Eckhardt see F. Pfeiffer, *Meister Eckhart, Deutsche Mystiker des 14. Jahr-*

62

is created, I-ness, selfhood, every "me," "to me," or "mine," of not wanting to be something but nothing, and so on.

We can take all that these expressions denote in two ways. First, we might see them as the description of a temporal process that takes place, or ought to take place, in individuals, and that consists of the achieving — no matter how we think of it — of the greatest possible passivity of the conscious soul with the aim of effecting the souls' union with the deity represented as an event in time. Or, second, we might see them as the description of a timeless transcendental relation of the life of the soul, whether conscious or unconscious, active or passive, to its origin in God. In the first case abnegation is a pastoral injunction, a recipe, a method, a proposal how to proceed. In the second case, in the form of a psychological direction, it is a demand for contemplation or recollection of the truth that is the truth quite apart from any possible or impossible processes in the soul. We need hardly say that the first interpretation is more natural and closer to the text, as it were, than the second. If we read the works of Seuse, for example,[35] we see at once that this man fashioned his whole life upon a constant following of the recipe of abnegation, and with more or less strictness and success almost all mystics did in fact view abnegation as a definite and specific practice. Insofar as mystical abnegation is no more than practice of this kind, it has naturally nothing whatever to do with the Reformation. Instead, it is the supreme and most refined form of what the Reformation combated as works righteousness. How can one more distinctively pursue a theology of glory than by going beyond striving for it and making the negation of all striving itself a striving? (Cf. Gogarten, *Offenbarung und Mystik*.)[36]

We might see here a parallel to the way in which Duns Scotus and Occam made the dangerous dynamite of the doctrine of absolute power a smooth stone in the foundation of church dogmatics. At this third point, however, I think we do mysticism an injustice if we do not look beyond the historical kernel and note how once again it points ahead of itself. Here again dynamite is always dynamite. Note how Eckhardt in his sermons unequivocally negates not just position after position but ultimately negation itself, that is, the psychological path to which he himself

---

hunderts, vol. II (Leipzig, 1857), 155, 21f., quoted in Loofs, 629 (522). See Tauler's sermon on Luke 10:23, quoted in Hagenbach, 388. See Luther's Romans lectures, WA 56, 413, 18f.; LW 25, 404; Barth was using Tschackert, 41.

35. Barth had Seuse's *Deutsche Schriften,* ed. W. Lehmann, 2 vols. (Jena, 1911).
36. Cf. Gogarten's essay in *Die religiöse Entscheidung* (Jena, 1921), 65ff.

previously pointed. Note how he finally seeks a resignation that is not psychological resignation or passivity as a way of life any longer, but that is just as well, or even better as he often says, an active manner of life, so that paradoxically Martha, the busy one, is set above Mary, who sat at the Lord's feet.[37] This means, however, that he sees the transcendental character of the principle of mystical abnegation that is truly meant. He does not cease to be a theologian of glory. He uses the thought of death in the sense of Plato's *Phaedon* (chs. 9–13), which says of the philosopher that at root his only aim is to die and be dead, his work being no other than that of detaching and separating the soul from the body.[38] In my view abnegation for Eckhardt was in the last resort simply Platonic purification, the strongest critical means of clarifying the relation between God and us in which the greatest distance is precisely the greatest proximity. We must insist on this if we are to do full justice to mysticism. In this regard we cannot uphold an absolute antithesis between Luther and Eckhardt, between revelation and mysticism. Luther must have found something related, instructive, and illuminating when he recommended Tauler and the *German Theology;* while Calvin, even though in the latter work seeing and repudiating only medieval spiritualizing,[39] could not refrain, under pressure of the logic of the matter, from himself at a decisive point in the *Institutes* (III, 7-8) depicting the Christian life from the mystical standpoint of self-denial and bearing the cross.

As a fifth force preparing the way for the Reformation, along with monasticism, Augustinianism, Nominalism, and mysticism, we must finally refer, of course, to the 15th- and 16th-century Renaissance. Its positive relation to the Reformation is naturally on a different level from that of the other factors. From the latter, as we have seen, a straight if for long stretches broken line leads to Luther's view of the vertical intersecting the horizontal, to the theology of the cross. We certainly cannot say that of the Renaissance, though technically and formally the new interest in antiquity meant among other things that the original text of the Bible and Augustine, and through Augustine Plato, came into focus and played a part in the Reformation. The result of this rediscovery, especially in Luther,

---

37. See n. 33 on 34.

38. See esp. *Phaedon* 67de.

39. On Tauler see n. 27; and on the *German Theology* see Luther's prefaces to his 1516 and 1518 editions, WA 1, 153, 378f. Cf. Calvin's letter to the French refugee congregation in Frankfort, 2.23.1559, CO 17, 441f. in which he notes in the *German Theology,* if no major errors, at any rate an obscuring of the simplicity of the gospel. See 85 below.

was not intended, however, by the Renaissance, nor was it integral to its own logic. The theologically most interested champions of the Renaissance, those great lovers, editors, and expositors of the Bible, Erasmus and Lefèvre d'Etaples (Faber Stapulensis), were completely terrified by the spirits they conjured up,[40] by the bondage of the will and the break with church tradition, and they gave approval and support to the Reformation in neither its Lutheran nor its Reformed manifestation. The interest of the Renaissance was wholly in the direction of the horizontal. It continued the basic classical medieval view, or perhaps translated and reformulated it into the basic classical modern view, which for all the differences has more in common with the Middle Ages than with the Reformation. Common to the Middle Ages and the modern period is the idea of aiming at a goal in step-by-step progress. The goal for both is on the horizontal line. It is a goal of human willing and knowing. The concept alone stood in need of translation. The Middle Ages located the goal somewhere in one of the real or imagined upper worlds, in the so-called hereafter. It sought to mount up to paradise. It wanted to look upon pure deity, as Tauler put it.[41] It wanted ecstasy, as we might put it rationalistically today. Our own age thinks it is much cleverer by not shooting the arrow of longing too far. Impartially we might say: It is more weary and resigned. With a skepticism that is partly more questioning and partly more dogmatic it halts at the gates of the upper worlds. For some centuries the spiritual world has been unknown territory on the suspicion of being unreal. The gaze has been all the keener for what can be perceived directly in time and space, for what is called this world. With the same absoluteness and emphasis the goal is set in nature as we know it and history as we know it. The enthusiasm of pressing on to the immediate that once created the Gothic vault has changed into the enthusiasm for the concrete, for what has come into being, for what can be measured and controlled, for the colorful world of visible things that we can happily attain to without scholastic profundity or mystical abnegation. Goethe once gave classical formulation to the distinction and the common factor when he said that if we want to stride on into the infinite we must simply go on in the finite on every hand.[42] But in my view the difference between the two methods

---

40. Cf. Goethe's *Der Zauberlehrling* (1797), V, 91f.

41. Barth recalls here the quotation from Seuse in Hagenbach, 448, which he used earlier; cf. 29 n. 16.

42. Cf. Goethe's *Gott, Gemüt und Welt* (1815), V, vv. 29f.

is usually overrated. In the modern age we simply have the Middle Ages now become clever and also weary. The sleep has become half sleep, and who knows, perhaps we might put it the other way round. The Middle Ages could throw back at the modern age the charge of excessive enthusiasm, for the modern age with its rationalism is simply enthusiastic to the point of excess on a different level. The modern age can throw back at the Middle Ages the charge of intellectualism, for the Middle Ages were truly intellectualistic, but on a higher level. The two levels are steps on the same ladder. In principle the distinction in both cases is from the Reformation insight, from Plato and Paul, and therefore from the medieval trends that point back to Plato and Paul and forward to the Reformation.[43] The Reformation and all that is part of it in the Middle Ages and the modern period are both antimodern and antimedieval. The Reformation front cuts right across the opposite contrasting fronts of these two opponents.

This is an insight that I do not find clearly in Troeltsch, Loofs, or Seeberg.[44] In the Renaissance, at first in the form of a rebirth of the rationalism of antiquity, the modern spirit of an emphatic this-worldliness was born and took its first steps. There came to life a strong interest in nature, in the social and political order, in history, in the nation as such, and last but by no means least in the individual human personality. Outstanding Renaissance figures along with Erasmus, the first modern theologian, were Paracelsus, the student of medicine, for whom God did miracles but only human miracles through humans; Machiavelli, who has been called the scientist of the state; Giordano Bruno, who by equating God and the form and matter of the world challenged the reality of the upper world of the Middle Ages,[45] and who was one of the first and rare martyrs of the modern spirit. At root the Renaissance did not take part in Luther's Reformation. Its controversy with the Middle Ages completely bypassed that Reformation. To the degree that it hailed it as a comrade, it misunderstood it. Due to the same misunderstanding the spiritualistic Enthusiasts combined the Reformation with Renaissance aspirations. For all the apparently great contradictions, the Roman Catholic Counter-Reformation was better able to adopt, use, and amalgamate the Renais-

---

43. See above, 51 n. 2.

44. See 13 nn. 1 and 2 above.

45. Seeberg, IV, 12, who quotes Paracelsus but does not give the source. On Machiavelli see Seeberg ad loc. On Bruno cf. K. Vorländer, *Geschichte der Philosophie,* vol. I, PhB 105 (Leipzig, 2nd ed. 1908), 301.

sance with itself than the young Protestantism that opposed it. The positive significance of the Renaissance for the Reformation was that apart from it, and even against it, it put to it the fateful question: What, in spite of everything, did the Lutheran vertical mean for the horizontal, the theology of the cross for unavoidable human striving? The Renaissance with its most emphatic this-worldliness was needed to put this question to the Reformation, and in this way to bring the crisis to a head, to close the circle of the Reformation movement.

From what has been said it is clear, however, that through the voice of the Reformation the Middle Ages were also calling for a new answer to their own distinctive problem, the problem of ethics, of lifestyle, of the way. With the posing of this fateful question the second turn in the Reformation came that eventually, by a higher curve in the path, would lead back to the beginning and tragically enough, though in a way that is historically understandable, would lead it back onto a newly repaired stretch of the old horizontal highway, to the Christian secularity from which it had once broken free. But those who put the question were not spectators like Erasmus, but Zwingli and Calvin, children of the Renaissance, who, whether dependently or independently, shared the insight of Luther, the born scholastic and mystic. This second development and completion of the Reformation movement in its subsequent controversy with the newly arrived spirit of the modern age as we find that controversy in the theology of Calvin, the man who was both totally the reformer and totally the Renaissance man, which we cannot say of either Luther or Zwingli, will be the main theme, quiet but yet explicit, of our present lectures.

As a sixth group of advocates of the new thing in the old we must finally, for the sake of completeness, mention the Catholic reforming theologians of the 14th and 15th centuries, Bradwardine, Wycliffe, Huss, Gerson, J. Goch, J. von Wesel, Wessel Gansfort, and Savonarola being the best known. There is a book by C. Ullmann, *Reformatoren vor der Reformation* (1st ed. 1841, 2nd ed. 1866), whose title aroused lively opposition especially from Ritschl and his disciples.[46] Those who honor such men with the name of pre-reformers are not uninfluenced — and this is no disgrace — by the heroic, the tragic, and the sympathetic aspects of their stories. These men were fighters for an insight whose time had not yet

46. Ullmann's work was printed in two volumes (Hamburg, 1841 and 1842; 2nd ed. Gotha, 1866). See A. Ritschl, *Die christliche Lehre von der Rechtfertigung und Versöhnung*, vol. I, 4th ed. (Bonn, 1909), 129, 132. Cf. Loofs, 634 (527f.); and Seeberg, III, 640f.

come. By their work they did in fact stir up the unrest that became a movement at the Reformation. All of them, with more or less energy and insight, stood at one of the points mentioned from which the prospect of the Reformation insight was a possibility, Bradwardine, for example, as a Neo-Augustinian, Gerson as the champion of a noble and modified mysticism, Savonarola as a proponent of ancient monastic ideals, and Wycliffe as the forerunner of an attempted Christian renaissance, and precisely for that reason the most problematical of all these figures. Nevertheless, these pre-reformers have relatively less systematic interest as we try to elucidate the Reformation than do an Occam or an Eckhardt, for, so far as I can judge, none of them can be hailed as a classical advocate of one of the forward-looking possibilities. The medieval period with its possibilities was inwardly exhausted. The Reformation had not yet come. Why did Bradwardine or Gerson not become a Luther, Savonarola a Zwingli, Wycliffe a Calvin? Why did not the whole Reformation come a hundred years earlier? Who can say? The elements of Reformation were present at the time of the pre-reformers. But their presence alone was not enough. Passionate emphasizing of this or that new approach, passionate negation of the old that was perishing, clever and devout conservation and combination of the balance between the two, but without the will or the power to force through a decision, these were the possibilities for which the pre-reformers worked and suffered. Such possibilities were relative, very relative even within the great relativity of history. The pre-reformers were children of an age of transition, as perhaps we ourselves are again today.[47] A feature of such ages, at least in the judgment of history, is that they cannot achieve more than honorary results. The reformers could always speak of the pre-reformers with respect and admiration, but without owing them anything. This fact gives us cause to reflect, perhaps to our own comfort, that in history bridges of this kind, and not only those that carry it forward, may not be famous but are still of value. And value is the only thing we may strive for at the forum of history, the only thing we can be concerned about. The rest is neither a goal nor a task but grace.

47. Cf. Barth's letter to Thurneysen and other friends dated 1.22.1922 (Bw.Th., II, 30), in which he spoke of being in the corner between Nominalism, Augustinianism, mysticism, Wycliffe, etc., which was not itself the Reformation but from which the Reformation sprang, and then asked whether this was not their own place, in the shadow cast ahead by the Reformation, where there is still no assurance of salvation, no evangelical freedom, etc.

2

Calvin, Luther, and Zwingli

Loofs, *Leitfaden,* 684ff., 792ff., 875ff.; Seeberg, *Dogmengeschichte,* IV, 55ff., 355ff., 551ff.; Tschackert, *Lutherische und reformierte Kirchenlehre,* 33ff., 228ff., 381ff.; Troeltsch, "Protestantisches Christentum und Kirche in der Neuzeit," B; idem, *Social Teaching,* vol. II (Louisville, 1992), 515ff., 576ff.; Hermelink, *Kirchengeschichte,* 60ff., 85ff., 158ff.; W. Dilthey, "Das natürliche System der Geisteswissenschaften im 17. Jahrhundert," *Archiv für Geschichte der Philosophie* (1893); normative for Luther: Holl, *Kirchengeschichtliche Aufsätze,* vol. I (1921) (correcting Troeltsch's view of Luther). On Reformed theology in general the following is not yet outdated: A. Schweizer, *Glaubenslehre der evangelisch reformierten Kirche,* vol. I (1844), 1-79. Normative for Zwingli is E. Staehelin, *Huldreich Zwingli* (1895). On Calvin see H. Bauke, *Die Probleme der Theologie Calvins* (1922); K. Fröhlich, *Die Reichsgottesidee Calvins* (1922) (both to be used with caution). Finally, see P. Wernle, *Luther, Zwingli, Calvin* (1918-1919).[1]

---

1. Loofs, *Leitfaden,* 684ff., ch. I; 792ff., ch. II, §81; 875ff., ch. III, §88; Seeberg, *Dogmengeschichte,* 55ff., §74; 355ff., §87; 381ff., §88; Tschackert, *Kirchenlehre,* 33ff.: part 1, section 1, ch. 2; 228ff.: part 2; 381ff.: part 4, sections 1 and 2; Troeltsch, in *Die Kultur der Gegenwart* (Berlin and Leipzig, 1906), 229ff.; Troeltsch, *Soziallehren,* 512ff., 605ff.; Hermelink, *Reformation und Gegenreformation,* 60ff., §§8-11; 85ff., §14; 158ff., §§31-33; W. Dilthey, "Das natürliche System der Geisteswissenschaften im 17. Jahrhundert," in *Archiv für Geschichte der Philosophie,* vol. V (Berlin, 1892), 60ff., 225f. 347ff., 509ff., reprinted in *Gesammelte Schriften,* vol. II (Göttingen, 1957), 90ff.; Holl, *Gesammelte Aufsätze zur Kirchengeschichte,* vol. I (Tübingen, 1921); A. Schweizer, *Die Glaubenslehre der evangelisch reformierten Kirche . . . ,* 2 vols. (Zurich, 1844 and 1847);

Whether it makes any sense to single out Calvin from among all the reformers we shall see only as we complete the work of the semester. It is possible, however, and is part of our task, that we may find the direction in which we have to travel by comparing Calvin with Luther and Zwingli. In this way we can perhaps fix the place where Calvin stands in the Reformation as a whole. The decisive and representative figures by which to define and assess phenomena of this period, apart from Calvin himself, are Luther and Zwingli. Men like Erasmus, Sebastian Franck, and Martin Bucer are by no means as significant, important though they are to fill out the picture.

§4 Luther

The man who thought out first, and with most originality and force, the basic antimedieval and, as we saw last time, the basic antimodern thought of the Reformation, that of the theology of the cross, was neither Zwingli nor Calvin but Luther. Both Zwingli and Calvin learned from Luther, not without at once contradicting him, not without giving their own shape to what they learned, yet learning from him at the decisive point. Luther's Reformation was not the whole Reformation. It was not even the source or place of origin of the whole Reformation. Nevertheless, it initiated the movement which characterizes the whole and of which the Reformation of Zwingli and Calvin was primarily a repetition, even though a second turn was given to the Reformation in and with the repetition. That turn took place, as I said yesterday, in wrestling with the medieval and modern problem of ethics, which for Luther seemed to be suspended for a second between the times,[2] but then, in a wholly normal way, to call for fresh treatment.

A good member of the Reformed communion must begin by simply

R. Staehelin, *Huldreich Zwingli . . .*, 2 vols. (Basel, 1895 and 1897); H. Bauke, *Die Probleme der Theologie Calvins* (Leipzig, 1922); K. Fröhlich, *Die Reichsgottesidee Calvins* (Munich, 1922); P. Wernle, *Der evangelische Glaube nach den Hauptschriften der Reformatoren,* vol. I: *Luther;* vol. II: *Zwingli;* vol. III: *Calvin* (Tübingen, 1918 and 1919).

2. An allusion to the title of G. Gogarten's essay "Zwischen den Zeiten" (1919), which then became the title of the journal founded in 1922 with Barth and his circle as contributors and G. Merz as editor.

recognizing Luther's unique position in the Reformation, not moving away from or forsaking Luther, nor, in following the hints of Zwingli and Calvin, feeling compelled to go a step beyond him; but instead, while consciously following those hints, constantly coming back to him. At the outset we distinguish ourselves from Lutherans in this way. As disciples of the most loyal disciples of Luther, we do not detract from Luther any more than Lutherans do, whereas they for their part can never manage to promote regard for Luther without open or concealed polemics against Zwingli and Calvin.

In respect of discipleship of Zwingli and Calvin rather than Luther, we have to proceed with caution. What is a disciple? A loyal disciple? Is it the one who with the urge to be the self, yet also no ability to go beyond the self, sits at the feet of another, and, more or less successfully overcoming the resultant conflicts, seeks to say what the master has said? If so, Luther's loyal disciple was Melanchthon. But was he really a loyal disciple? In the hands of the loyal communicator Melanchthon, just because he was able to mediate Luther's legacy so loyally and painfully, did not the Lutheran Reformation become something alien to Luther himself?

A disciple might also be — you may recall what I said about this in the first hour — a person who can be and say something individual but who has also the ability to let something be said to him or her by another, which means achieving from the other agreement about oneself, so that this person, in whom is both productivity and receptivity, never ceases more or less successfully to appropriate what is heard, to say it, too, when it is heard, but to say it as something individual. Zwingli and Calvin were loyal disciples of Luther in this sense. Students complete their course when they cease to be students. They become masters when they take a step beyond their own master, whether the latter likes it or not. How remarkably obscure it all is when we are assured in the sense and tone of disparagement and superiority that Zwingli was only a disciple of Luther and that Calvin, as we read in Ritschl and Loofs,[3] was only an *epigonos* of Luther. It is surely as clear as daylight, and has simply been confirmed by continued polemics up to our own day, that disciples in the sense of slavish followers, *epigonoi* of Luther, are not to be found, at least in Zurich or Geneva.

We will first try to fix and understand more precisely the point at

3. A. Ritschl, *Geschichtliche Studien zur Lehre von Gott*, vol. II of *Gesammelte Aufsätze* (Freiburg, 1896), 97; Loofs, 876.

which students cease to be students and become teachers themselves, that is, the point at which the step was taken that took Zwingli and Calvin beyond Luther. When I read the works of especially the younger Luther up to about 1520, I get the picture of a curtain, thick in some places, thin in others, behind which a big, bright flame is burning. I see this flame flickering through the curtain. It is coming closer. The flickering becomes stronger. Every moment we expect the flame to engulf and consume the curtain that conceals it, so that only a blazing fire will be before us. It will be dangerous, it will be terrible, but it has to be. Something great and impossible and unheard-of will happen — and then? We dare not think beyond that. We do not know whether we ought to be terrified or to rejoice. Yet what we expect does not happen. The flame does not stop advancing but the curtain remains intact. It is as if at the last moment something invisible separates it from the flame. All we have is possibility, even probability, expectation, fear, and hope. All we have is — shall we say terrible or shall we even say intolerable? — tension. It is perhaps both.

I do not get this impression at all, however, when I read Zwingli's *Shepherd* or Calvin's *Catechism*.[4] Here again we must use a figure of speech. The fire has blazed up, it has burned a hole in the curtain, the great thing has taken place. The fire is still glimmering and flickering, but a thick pall of smoke now covers everything. The great thing has taken place, but it is not the impossible or unheard-of thing. The curtain as a whole is still intact. The fire is not spreading. For the moment the great flame flared up it began to die down, and the remaining sparks are not strong enough to burn up the whole. Something did happen, but obviously not what was really meant to happen. The approaching thing has become a static thing at a distance, the expectation has become a quiet survey of possibilities that are already to some extent known. Fear can be laid to rest and hope may to some extent be disappointed. The tension is no longer so terrible or unbearable.

Or should we not rather state with admiration and gratitude that at least something *was* achieved and *did* take place? We may put it either way. Note well that it was the flame of the knowledge of eternal judgment and eternal mercy, of the vertical line, of the twofold work of God, that Luther, and after him and with him Zwingli and Calvin, understood to be the beginning and end of all we humans do. The curtain is human life

4. Zwingli, *Der Hirt* (1524), Z 3, 68; Calvin, *Geneva Catechism* (1545), OS II, 72ff.; cf. *Tracts and Treatises*, II, 37ff. (Grand Rapids, 1958).

in time in its whole range, our good and bad works from the very least to the very greatest, the horizontal line on which the Middle Ages once sought the infinite and the modern age with the same fervor seeks the finite, the strange central stretch that is at least also there between the clearly perceived beginning and end. For so it is! That is how Luther himself once put it: Our human being and nature cannot for a moment be without action or inaction, suffering or flight, for life never rests (Tschackert, 97).[5] The horizontal did not vanish when struck by the vertical. We move every moment on that horizontal line. The world does not perish because the kingdom of heaven has drawn near [Matt. 4:17]. No, we live in the world, and not for a moment can we forget it. Action does not cease because we assert its radical questionability. No, we work no matter what, even if it is by sinking into the passivity of a Buddhist monk. But the fire that might have been kindled when the flame touched the curtain, and perhaps was kindled, obviously means that the vertical really intersects the horizontal; that the cross is really visible in our life; that time and eternity, God and humans, are not in metaphysical antithesis but indissoluble relation; that the power of the next world is the power of this world, as Troeltsch might put it.[6] In other words, the problem of so-called dogmatics is the problem of so-called ethics.

What do life and time and the world and human existence and nature look like if what Luther heard is true, namely, God's Word to the effect that God alone is the Lord and none other [cf. Isa. 45:5]? I referred yesterday to the fateful question that the Renaissance put to the Reformation. It would have had to be put in any case even if there had been no Renaissance. It was unavoidable. The dialectic of the matter demanded it. But the remarkable contemporaneity of the Reformation with this movement — which at the very same time as the former in its opposition to the Middle Ages discovered the vertical, emphasized the horizontal with a new sharpness and consistency such as the Middle Ages had never achieved — can hardly be an accident. To the Reformation answer in terms of eternity, pressed by the final problematic of human existence, it had to

5. M. Luther, *Von den guten Werken* (1520), WA 6, 212, 32ff., quoted with modernized spelling in Tschackert, 97.

6. Cf. Troeltsch, *Social Teaching*, vol. II (Louisville, 1992), 1006: "Das Jenseits ist die Kraft des Diesseits," quoted also by Barth in the same inaccurate version in "The Christian's Place in Society" (1919), in *The Word of God and the Word of Man* (London, 1928), 272ff.

pose the counterquestion of time,[7] now that in opposition to the medieval answer in terms of time there had been posed the question of eternity. The closely intertwined antagonists of the old and the new were ultimately in *one* hand. On this fateful question the ways of the Lutheran and Reformed reformation parted company, and fundamentally they are still apart today. The flame that approached but did not blaze up is Lutheranism. Its tragedy is that though the kingdom of heaven was here so close in the world, nothing happened, and the imminent kingdom of heaven is thus a dubious entity. The great fire that flares up yet fails to blaze, and finally dies down, stands for the Reformed. Their tragedy is that something, something truly great, did take place in the world, but in the process the kingdom of heaven moved further away, so that even that great event is a dubious entity. Lutherans and Reformed really have no cause to attack one another with correction and accusation. Normally they can only bear together that which is in different ways their common embarrassment and promise.

I realize, however, that this account of the problem is schematic and does not do justice to the full historical reality. It must be noted, then, that in this way we are simply describing general tendencies. If we are to go to the starting point of the movement, we must not make of Luther a Quietist who fixed his thoughts solely on justification by faith alone and had no feeling at all for the problem of ethics. He did have an awareness of this problem and wrestled with it all his life. K. Holl ("Die neue Sittlichkeit") has shown in what is for me a convincing manner that Troeltsch did violence to Luther when he roundly ascribed to him the sharp dualism of a double morality based partly on the Sermon on the Mount and partly on natural law, an ethics of love on the one side, a secular ethics on the other.[8] Though Luther was definitely not a man of the Renaissance, but a monk who then emerged into the world, he saw the link between gospel and law, the need for good works, the task of giving a Christian shape to both individual life and life in society, and he made genuine efforts to put these insights into practice. With increasing definiteness, of course, but from the very outset, he related the question of the gracious God to that of the obedience of the recipients of grace in

---

7. The MS had *entgegengeworfen* here, altered by the editor to *entgegenwerfen*.

8. K. Holl, "Der Neubau der Sittlichkeit," in *Gesammelte Aufsätze zur Kirchengeschichte*, I, 2nd and 3rd ed. (Tübingen, 1929), 281f.; cf. Troeltsch, *Social Teaching*, II, 973f.

the world, the forgiveness of sins to the new life, redemption to our existence in God's creation as the children of God, so that no one of these things can arise without at once bringing the other with it. Luther was not, as the Reformed can easily suppose if they do not look properly, a man who stood on one leg looking up to heaven. In the logic of his own innermost thoughts there had to be hoping and striving for the kindling of fire on earth. For "when the soul is pure through faith and loves God, it also wants all things to be pure, first its own body, and that everyone should love and praise God with it," he stated in 1520 (27, 189), and in the same context he lamented that "though the Christian life is so noble, unfortunately it not only does not exist anywhere in the world, but it is neither confessed nor preached" (27, 196).9 The first saying expresses Calvin's thought of the glory of God, for the sake of which we cannot ignore the relation between faith and life, while in the second we find Zwingli's concept of the reforming of life that must flow naturally, as it were, from faith if that faith is authentic. Luther thought both these thoughts frequently, seriously, and radically.

Nevertheless, we may and must say that these thoughts were not natural or intrinsic to Luther. They were implications that he made resolutely but secondarily. The whole relation between the vertical line and the horizontal, or rather the outworking of this relation, was for him, strongly though he emphasized it, of secondary and not primary importance. We often detect indeed how he gives himself a push to turn back from faith, his real concern, to works, which were not in the full sense his concern. We also detect at this point a deficiency. He is not by a long way so original or effective in this field. Above all we detect a constant looking back from the second concern to his real concern. Read again from this angle his 1520 *Freedom of a Christian* or his *Sermon of Good Works* from the same year.10 Read these writings that are so decisive for our problem with the question: What was really on Luther's heart? What did he really want to say to us? That we must do good works to please God and help our neighbor, or that good works can issue only from faith, and that without faith they are dead and in themselves at least neither good, demanded, nor necessary? Undoubtedly both. But you will clearly find that Luther's real interest is in the second point and not the first, not in the step into life and the doing of works, but in the fact that when they

9. WA 7, 30, 36–31, 2; 36, 8ff.
10. WA 7, 3-38; 6, 202-76.

are done they are done in faith. Rather maliciously we might compare Luther's ethical writings to the Echternach spring procession[11] in which there is one step backward for every two steps forward, so pitilessly upon the resolve to do good works does the weight lie that we must not think that in this way we can get to heaven, so unceasing here are reservations and limitations of every kind. Hardly anything is commanded that goes beyond the first commandment.

As we read, there seem to hover before our eyes reminders that call everything into question, the reminders that good works have value only for Christ's sake, and when done in faith. This is no real dishonor to Luther. The dialectic with which he made play so brilliantly is the dialectic of the matter itself. He cannot get away from it because he takes so seriously the need to ground action in transcendental freedom.[12] As we note also in Zwingli and Calvin themselves, there is a need constantly to go back again from what is plainly the Reformed ethical approach to a line where we speak as Luther did, in a way that is broken and dialectical and that refers back again and again to the commandments of the first table. But however that may be, it is a historical fact that Luther's heart concern was with the basis of works and not the will for them, with fighting *against* papist works and not fighting *for* works of the Spirit and love, remarkable and vital though what he said about these might be. It is surely no accident that the second half of his *Freedom of a Christian*,[13] the active part of Lutheran ethics that presses forward, was not the more effective part but the halting and hesitant part.

To see what it looks like when a theologian really stresses and unites both parts, when the fight *for* works of the Spirit is also self-evident and a heart's concern, we may turn in comparison to the beginning of Calvin's Geneva Catechism. In the closest connection we find here the question of the chief end of human life and the knowledge of God as this end.[14] For God created us and put us in the world in order to be glorified by us. Since he is the origin of our life, it is right that we should place this life in the service of his glory. That this should take place is our supreme good. Should it not, we are in sorrier state than animals. Nothing worse can happen to us than not living our lives for God. And here again we have

---

11. Cf. "Echternach," *RGG,* 3rd ed., II, 301f.
12. Cf. Kant's *Critique of Practical Reason* (New York, 1950), 43ff.
13. WA 7, 29, 31–38, 15.
14. OS 75, 3f., *Tracts and Treatises,* II, 37.

true knowledge of God in which we know him as we come to awareness of the honor we owe him. But the way in which to pay this honor that we owe is fourfold, (1) by putting our whole trust in him, (2) by seeking to serve him with our whole lives and doing his will, (3) by calling upon him in need and seeking salvation and every good thing in him, and finally (4) by recognizing him with heart and mouth as the "sole author" of all good. These four points are the basis of Calvin's whole presentation of Christainity. This, mark you, is what I would call a definite and unequivocal approach to ethics in contrast to Luther's. Calvin, too, realizes that faith alone justifies us and that good works can spring only from faith, but from the very first this insight regarding God is for him a significant and dynamic part of life as its chief and final end. In Luther the cross often seems to be open or only loosely related, but in Calvin it is related to the real cross.[15] His concern is not just that faith should be pure and fixed on God alone, but that this faith which is pure and fixed on God alone should be the final end of human life.[16] For him justice must also be done to the need to live out this faith before God and for God on the horizontal line. Calvin's whole Christianity is built on the need that to God's glory something must take place in faith, just as we might sum up Zwingli's whole Christianity in a saying from his letters: "For God's sake, do something brave!" (5.11.22).[17]

This relating to the horizontal, this unity of faith and life, dogmatics and ethics, this attempt to answer the question of human striving and willing that Luther's discovery had for a moment pushed into the background, was distinctive, natural, and original in the Reformed. In the self-evident way in which they make this step from Luther's basic view, the step into life, they are more original than Luther. What was Luther's own emphasized intuition occurs naturally, powerfully, and with a necessary basis in them. Though they never lose sight of the vertical, and just because they keep it in view, their concern is with the whole of the Christian life, something we could never say of Luther even though we recognize his desire to deal with ethics. The Reformed were also aware that by the Holy Spirit the work of God in Christ is the origin and goal of the Christian life. They, too, genuinely speak about despair, humility,

15. In the margin Barth has a diagram here.

16. See n. 9 above.

17. Cf. Zwingli's letter to the mayor and council of Zurich from the Kappel camp dated 6.16.1529, Z 10, 169, 4ff. (no. 858).

and the fear of God[18] as the first and last thing that is possible for us vis-à-vis God, and about the paradox of the sheer trust with which in that situation we have to fling ourselves into the arms of God. The unheard-of thing of this primary event to us and in us, in both judgment and grace, is constantly before them. No less than Luther they have before their eyes the lightning flash in the tower at Wittenberg, the bolt at Luther's feet: "The just shall live by faith" (Rom. 1:17),[19] though they were definitely not monks who had been happily freed from the basic conception of the Middle Ages but Renaissance men who had been converted to God. In neither Zwingli nor Calvin will we find even a single line in which they deal lightly with such matters as the bondage of the will, imputed righteousness, or the nonmeritorious nature of good works. On the contrary we find, especially in Calvin, systematically the clearer of the two, a stress on this side of his theology, even if with a certain nervous tension that we see in Luther only in his debate with Erasmus. As a Lutheran Calvin felt a need to work out consistently and to champion relentlessly the doctrine of double predestination, that sharpest of all the formulations of the concept of the vertical. He rightly perceived — and if we understand this we have already grasped the main point of his theology — that everything would be lost for Reformed theology if at this point, too, it let itself be robbed by just one jot of its well-considered definitions of the paradox of grace. The nervous tension with which he stressed and underlined this is undoubtedly an indication that here was the threatened point of this theology.

But in Luther's theology, too, there was a threatened point at which we see in him the same nervous tension. It was and is a dangerous undertaking to think through to the very end the thought that God's eternal judgment and eternal mercy immediately and unceasingly relate to real people living in this world in time, just as dangerous as thinking through the other thought that at every moment in time, over against every possibility in the world, these are always and unceasingly God's acts. If the Calvinistic thought might yield to the view that our seeking of perfection in this world in time is in itself the goal of our existence and a fulfillment of the will of God, we might infer from the Lutheran thought that our action in this world in time is hermetically sealed off against God,

18. See above, 46f.
19. Cf. what Luther says about himself in the preface to vol. I of the Latin works in the Wittenberg ed. (1545), WA 54, 186, 3ff.

78

follows its own laws, and is justified in itself by its relation to the eternal God. In practice we have here one and the same thing. If "the just lives *by faith*" was under threat in Calvin, "the just *lives* by faith" was under threat in Luther.

The result in both cases would be that we who live in this world in time are, as it were, secured against the claim and threat and promise that confront us as the righteousness of God. The medieval and modern concept of the triumphant horizontal line would then have gained the victory, in the one case by thoughtless emphasizing of the ethical significance of the knowledge of God, in the other by its thoughtless neglect. Luther naturally feared that victory no less than Calvin, and each was quick to detect the special danger and to counteract it. On the one hand, Luther had to show that his knowledge of God was ethically intended, and hence he could not do enough to assure us that the children of God can and must do good works of love in the world, in their callings, within the orders of creation, and even in questionable situations, for example, at times when it might mean cursing and slaying. On the other hand, Calvin had to show that his ethics was intended as knowledge of God, and hence, in paradoxical contradiction of the obedience that he required of our human will for God, he could not exalt too highly the majesty and sovereignty of this God even to the point of an almost unbearable concept of the unrestrictedly free divine good pleasure that rules over things almost like natural fate, and concerning the basis of which we can say nothing, or nothing other than that God himself wills it.[20] Here, then, we have self-corrections that are so vigorously made that they themselves by no means arbitrarily kindle the need for their own correction. These self-corrections are externally the most striking features of Calvinistic theology on the one side and Lutheran on the other. But we must not judge either of these theologies by these features. We must judge them by the opposing tendencies that in both cases, as these features show, had to be protected against misunderstandings.

If we inquire into the tendency that stands opposed to the most striking feature of Calvinist theology, the doctrine of predestination, and which was meant to be protected in its purity by that doctrine, we obviously come up against the strong desire to shape the world, or at least to do work in it. Here we have the basic tendency of this theology and of

---

20. *Inst.* III, 21, 1: "Then only do we acknowledge that God of his mere good pleasure saves whom he will and does not pay any reward, since he owes none."

Reformed theology in general. Naturally, the world was to be shaped and work done in it to the glory of God and under the strong urge to carry through the intersecting of the horizontal by the vertical, that is, to relate each to the other; yet the stress is on shaping, on work, on taking in hand, on doing something brave, as distinct from hesitation, holding back, passivity, letting things take their course, or basically giving autonomy to the course of things in this world. Of Luther, it is true, one may fairly say that there is only a certain hesitation and embarrassment about the fact of the ethical task, for he was at one with the Reformed in rejecting passivity or any recognition of the autonomy of worldly things. Yet the Reformed showed much less hesitation than he did.

Reformed theology, as we see especially when we study book III of Calvin's *Institutes,* is a bold attempt to overcome the whole distinction of first and second, of there and here, of orientation to God and orientation to the world, and to grasp as a unity the forgiveness of sins and sanctification, faith and obedience, but also divine and human action. Think of the well-known opening of book I of the *Institutes* in which Calvin points to knowledge of God and ourselves as the sum of human wisdom.[21] The two "parts" of knowledge are so closely related that it is hard to say which precedes the other or results from the other. The content of knowledge, as knowledge of God and ourselves, is in both cases the same:[22] knowledge of the infinite wisdom and goodness of God, and in contrast thereto, knowledge of our own nothingness, so that Calvin does not help us much in ranking the one standpoint above the other, and indeed at the end of ch. 1 he says that it is only the order of right teaching *(ordo recte docendi)* that requires us to discuss the knowledge of God first.[23]

If Calvin had really succeeded in carrying through the systematic idea that he obviously had in mind, that is, in truly and literally presenting a theology of the cross, of the vertical and the horizontal, of the point of intersection; in really leaving unseparated the knowledge of God and ourselves, the free imputation of righteousness and the sanctity of real life, whose inseparability he maintained (III, 3, 1);[24] in so relating dogmatics and ethics that each dogmatic statement would also be an ethical statement and vice versa; in ceaselessly depicting faith as obedience and obedience

21. OS III, 31, 6-8.
22. The editor corrected here the *dieselbe* of the MS to *derselbe.*
23. OS III, 33, 38ff.
24. OS IV, 55, 8ff.

as faith; in achieving on his side the unity that Luther also sought on his, though he did not achieve it — if, I say, Calvin had succeeded in carrying through this program that does not merely supplement Luther but goes beyond him, unquestionably we would have had to say that the work of the pupil was greater than that of the teacher. For clearly the aim of all theology is no longer to say first and second but to say the one thing that is the whole. Only those who can say this and the whole do a work that strictly deserves to be called *theo-logia,* talk about God, but such a work would deserve it.

As we shall see, however, Calvin did not succeed in carrying through the program any more than any other theologians either before or after him. In the very first sentence, by speaking about two parts *(duabus partibus)* of wisdom, he betrayed the fact that the unity he had in mind was breaking apart in his hands, so that he could only point urgently to the inseparability and interrelatedness of the two parts, and then the deliberations in book III involve an endless dialectic of the two stand-points[25] from which it is clear that Calvin was aware of the original unity, but could assert it only by tirelessly playing off each side against the other and thus expounding the duality that the unity entails.

As I told you last time, however, Luther's theology also moves within this dialectic of the two standpoints. Calvin failed to press on further toward unity, toward one word. He simply came at it — and this is his independence as a teacher — from the other side, namely, as a Renaissance man, from the side of ethics. His heart's concern was to proclaim the glory of God as the only worthy, the only real power over real people living in this world in time, or, to put it the other way round, to call rebellious people to submission to the will of the only wise and good God. Just as Luther, when he spoke about the new life of obedience, constantly came back with confusing zeal to faith, the Spirit, and the person and work of God, in a word, to the source of the new life, so Calvin, in all his depictions of this source, constantly jumped ahead to the demand for humility, for worship, for active obedience, for subjection to God's holy commands. "The just lives *by faith,*" says Luther. Yes, indeed, says Calvin, and he says exactly the same thing, but he makes it a major instead of a minor third, putting the stress at the end in the Latin form: Justus ex fide *vivit* ("The just *lives* by faith"). The third possibility, that of saying one word, seems at all times to have been for theology a squaring of the circle, an impossible

25. The editor here corrected the *erschöpft* of the MS to *erschöpfen.*

possibility that God has reserved strictly for himself alone to proclaim. I at least know of no theologian, not even those of the Bible, who succeeded in doing what Luther and Calvin failed to do and speaking this word. The things we know are simply pointers to the fact that Christ *is* this Word, the Logos, pointers that are not themselves *the* Word, but *a* word, tilting sometimes more to the one side and sometimes more to the other.

I would thus see in the theology of Calvin a word on one side, a one-sided word, and not a theological panacea. Its value is that as a converted Renaissance man he felt and saw more sharply than Luther, the liberated monk, the problem of ethics that the problem of God does not eliminate but truly poses for the first time. But this value of Calvin's theology is also a source of danger. Those who emphasize so strongly obedience and working for the glory of God can easily lose sight of the independent weight of the question of God. Calvin sees the danger, and the weapon with which he tries to repel it is his remarkably sharp understanding precisely of the concept of God. The interrelating of the true ethical tendency of his theology with the self-correction in the Lutheran sense with which he permits it to take effect results in the inner problematic of his theology, although outwardly, as distinct from Luther, it is characterized, generally speaking, by that ethical tendency. Those who as Reformed theologians have the task of making clear what is distinctive about their Reformed Christianity must direct their attention above all to the inner problematic of Calvinistic theology due to that self-correction in the Lutheran sense. Those who as Lutheran theologians see that Luther's theology needs to be supplemented must realize how its supplementing by Calvin powerfully develops the possibilities offered by Luther but also brings to light the difficulties of Lutheranism. We all of us see ourselves confronted by a grandiose human effort and yet also by the limitation of all human efforts, by the need to undertake such efforts seriously and yet also by the need to accept the seriousness of other efforts than those that we ourselves venture. If anything is calculated to make us seriously zealous and yet also seriously tolerant, it is the study of the history of the church and dogmas, especially as it relates to the Reformation period.

Before going further I want to try to give you an illustration of one part of the problem and my understanding of it. I have in mind the attitude of Luther and the Reformed to the questions raised by the Enthusiasts. It seems to me that at this point especially we see clearly the presupposition of all that has been presented, namely, that for Luther the ethical problem was properly and from the very outset a secondary concern and that his ever so intensive preoccupation with it was to some extent a shift to another genre. I view Reformation Radicalism, including spiritualizers like Sebastian Franck, as not merely an attempt to have the vertical line of the knowledge of God intersect the horizontal line of life in this world, serving merely as an occasion for ethical reflection on God's commands and the ensuing ethical obedience, but as an attempt to depict the vertical line directly, to have justification by faith tread the world's stage in person and without concealment, avoiding ethics and relying solely on inspiration and the power of the Spirit. What we have, then, is a brilliantly shortsighted simplification of the problem. The kingdom of heaven has drawn near [Matt. 4:17]. *It,* It, the great It, has been given openly and is possible and stands ready. We have simply to let it happen, whether in act or suffering. We have simply to set it forth in palpable reality, whether by a very holy or a very free private life, whether by the gathering of holy communities or by the replacing of all the orders of state and church and society by new and this time holy orders.

Am I mistaken if I say that Luther was intrinsically closer to this brilliantly shortsighted attempt than Zwingli or Calvin? He soon found reasons not in fact to take this path, but the rejection was primary and more natural and self-evident for Zwingli and Calvin than for Luther. For the Reformed this path was never a temptation. When they began to pen their first theological works any attempt along such lines, if it had ever been of interest to them, was at an end. They were convinced from the very first that we live in the world and not in heaven, that the commands of God are directions for living in the world and not in heaven, and that no human work, even the most holy, is in itself justified by faith. The justified here are in the first instance citizens of Zurich or Geneva with all that that involves. As such they are, of course, subject to God's commands, but only as such. The divine commands are not just norms of what is required of us but also norms of what is possible and attainable for us, even if in weakness and with no merit. There is no thought of leaving the world to achieve greater perfection, of a life's endeavor outside the existing orders whose continued existence is simply confirmed by God's commands.

Naturally Luther himself powerfully developed this repudiation, and it quickly enough found expression. But it seems to me that among the Reformed the "naturally" was a good deal more natural than in Luther. For Luther enthusiasm was a temptation that he had overcome. Who was it who read the *German Theology* twice with all the marks of affinity and enthusiasm and agreement, placing it directly side by side with the Bible and Augustine?[26] This little book was later the Magna Carta of all spirituals. Calvin, with an appeal to all that *he* understood as the Word of God, called it twaddle that the devil had produced to confuse the simple gospel and that was deadly poison for the church (17, 442; cf. 16, 592, and Farel, 16, 549).[27] Again, spirits like Carlstadt and Thomas Münzer and Sebastian Franck and Caspar Schwenckfeld flourished in the atmosphere of the Lutheran Reformation. From the very outset Zwingli and Calvin kept their distance from such people when they came within their orbit. They might spring up in Zurich or Geneva, but they could not possibly prosper there, and therefore the battle against them plays a relatively subordinate role.

Again, can we really say that the appeal of the revolutionary peasants to the gospel of Luther made no sense and is not understandable, and in contrast can we think there could ever even be any question of a similar appeal to Calvin's *Institutes?* The very force with which the pendulum later swung to the other side in Luther, the antiradical, antispiritualist, antirevolutionary zeal with which he later put the Reformed reformers in the shade, and with which, as we know, he even turned against Zwingli himself, is simply a sign that at this point he had to fight something that he knew only too well, just as the surprising emphasis with which he then argued that a Christian life that is pleasing to God is possible within the relations and orders of this world is a sign that at this point he had to convince himself of something. The Reformed were in a position to look more calmly and objectively at the problems that the task of living a secular life in obedience to God poses. They did not try to maintain so frenziedly against the Radicals that which we are not to maintain, namely, that marrying and vocation and war and public office may be works of Christian love. From the very first, unlike Luther, they stood on the ground that all such things rest on the natural law that the commands of God confirm, not precisely as works of love — for real ethicists are more sparing in their use of the term "love" than Luther was — but as works that we may not avoid in the context of the

26. Cf. Luther's "Vorrede zur Theologia Deutsch" (1518), WA 1, 378, 21ff. He published the work with prefaces in Dec. 1516 and June 1518, WA 1, 153 and 378f.

27. Cf. Calvin's letter to French refugees in Frankfort dated 2.23.1559. See above, n. 39, on 64. Cf. the two letters of Farel to Bullinger dated 7.28 and 8.31.1557 in reaction (along the same lines as Calvin) to Castellio's Latin translation of the *German Theology* (1557).

total action that God requires of us. More frequently and more beautifully than they, Luther spoke of the way in which the children of God, adapting themselves to the orders and necessities of this world, may and must live in it, consoled by their faith, always in need of forgiveness, yet joyfully doing their duty as housewives, servants, artisans, soldiers, councilors, or preachers.[28] But he spoke suspiciously loudly and zealously along these lines, and no less suspiciously made cautious practical use of this turning to the world. The Reformed spoke more softly and with more restraint, but they lived more calmly and with more self-assurance in the sense that Luther really intended.

I must offer some examples. In no work did Calvin try to prove that soldiers, too, can live in a state of grace.[29] Nor did Zwingli. On the contrary, Calvin often stated most definitely that those who resort to arms should do so with regret and should consider that this enormity has its root only in human malice; that the one who kills even in the most just of wars is soiled *(souillé)*[30] by the fact that it is done with guilt and not innocence; that such a one is expressly a *homicide* (26, 325; 27, 543). He could say this even though he cold-bloodedly drew up orders for the artillery that would defend the walls of Geneva against its wicked Savoy neighbors,[31] and even though Zwingli, as we know, died on the battlefield and his weapons may be seen in the Zurich museum, offering indisputable traces that he was not there simply as a military chaplain. We may say with some confidence that if the German Protestants had entered the Schmalkald War with the theology of Zwingli or Calvin, the outcome might well have been very different. We do not say this to slight Luther. What it shows is that he was not as convinced by his own arguments as might appear.

Again, Luther made some strong and confident and one-sided statements about the natural order of sexuality and the fact that marriage is pleasing to God. But how did he view his own marriage to Katharina von Bora except as an extraordinary act of defiance against the devil and the pope!32 In spite of everything, how unexpected was this step even to the

28. Cf. Luther's *Von weltlicher Obrigkeit . . .* (1523), WA 11, 258, 5-8.

29. Cf. Luther's *Ob Kriegsleute auch in seligem Stande sein können* (1526), WA, 19, 623ff.

30. Sermon on Deut. 19:1-7, CO 27, 543. On Deut. 5:17, CO 26, 325: God will pardon killing in a just cause; nevertheless "c'est une macule, l'homme est souillé."

31. Cf. CO 10/I, 126ff.

32. E.g., WA TR 6, 275, 15f. (no. 6928), where Luther says he took a wife to defy the devil and to put to shame papal harlotry.

loyal Melanchthon,[33] who, if anyone, ought to have understood his mentor! About the sexual problem, as about the military, Calvin was much more skeptical than Luther. For him the little heaven of fathers, mothers, and children lay much more under the shadow of original sin (24, 312; 26, 342; 28, 159; 46, 417; 49, 406).[34] But when the question of marriage arose for himself, he dealt with it very quietly as a self-evident matter, with no illusions at all but also with no reservations at all. The only problem for him was finding the right wife, and in the main he left this to his friends.[35] With both feet Calvin stood on the earth on which marriage is a divine order to guard against greater ills. He did not first have to make a leap onto the earth.

As one who was trained in law, Calvin also described the function of the state unromantically as that of doing police work on God's commission, a primary task being that of caring for the church of God on earth. So far as I can see, calling the work of government a work of love, or similarly explaining or spiritualizing something that as things are is necessary and commanded, finds no place either in the famous concluding chapter of the *Institutes* (IV, 20) or in other writings in which he speaks about the state and law and order (e.g., 27, 455 and 688; 29, 660; 49, 248ff.).[36] Calvin was so convinced that the political function is necessary and commanded, that the natural law of equity on which civil order rests is simply confirmed by the moral law of God ([*Inst.*] IV, 20, 16),[37] that even as a minister of the divine Word he never hesitated to act personally as a statesman. It was he who in his last decade actually shaped the foreign policy of the free state of Geneva, and in truth this was no more simple matter than if it had been a matter of the policy of electoral Saxony. It

33. Cf. Melanchthon's letter to I. Camerarius dated 7.21.1525, CR 1, 754 (no. 344).

34. Cf. the sermon on Lev. 12:1ff., CO 24, 312; also on Deut. 5:18, CO 26, 342; on Deut. 24:1ff., CO 28, 159; and on Luke 2:36-39, CO 46, 417; and the commentary on 1 Cor. 7:6, CO 49, 406. Calvin points out that apart from the fall marriage would have been perfect, but it is now an aid against a dissolute life to those who cannot abstain and who enter into it after prayer.

35. Cf. Calvin's letter to Farel dated 5.19.1539, CO 10/II, 348 (no. 172). With Bucer's help he married Idelette de Bure in August 1540.

36. For the *Institutes,* see "On Political Administration," OS V, 471-502. Other writings include the sermon on Deut. 17:12, CO 27, 455; also on Deut. 21:18-21 (on 21b), CO 27, 688; also on 1 Sam. 11:7, CO 29, 660; and the commentary on Romans at 13:1ff., CO 49, 248-54.

37. OS V, 488, 3ff.

was he who in 1541 revised the civil as well as the ecclesiastical laws of Geneva (10 [I], 128ff., 132ff.).[38] It was he, too, whom the Geneva council would approach in 1557 (Kampschulte, II, 380)[39] with the request that he should investigate a new and supposedly cheaper system of heating. As I see it, in Luther a relatively much stronger emphasis on Christian vocation and the justification of government, based on the thought of love, is accompanied in practice by a broad gap between the parsonage and the council chamber, and political activity is something rather compromising at least for preachers of the gospel — but if so, why not for all other Christians?

In saying all these things, I am not reproaching Luther. The dubious element in Calvin's approach, as we see from the examples given, is clear enough, and there were good reasons for the more hesitant approach of Luther. I am simply saying that when Luther had to make the step from faith to ethics concretely and not just theoretically he hesitated, whereas in the mind of Calvin, no matter what we think of it, faith and ethics were in practice coincident. The rejection of enthusiasm; the establishment of ethics, that is, of a practical goal which might well be a broken one due to a sense of the ultimate questionability of all human willing and doing, but which could be embraced all the more firmly and cheerfully precisely because of that sense, resting as it did on affirmation of the divine order that God has set up in the world to guard against greater harm; the insight that It, It, the great It of the kingdom of heaven, of the Holy Spirit, cannot be given or put into effect in any possibility of human action, and that therefore, in practice, it can be seriously seen only in broken form, in the form of the command of God that is appropriate to this world — of all these things Luther was well aware and would often speak most profoundly. But it was the Reformed, the Reformed Lutherans, one might say, who really put them into practice, and in so doing, I might add, accepted the new ambivalence and difficulty of which I spoke yesterday. It was indeed necessary by way of compensation, and to guard against a new righteousness of the scribes and Pharisees [cf. Matt. 5:20], that the doctrine of double predestination should be given the emphasis that Calvin gave it. Again, I might add, Calvin's great stress on the hope of the hereafter, on

38. CO 10/I, 125-46, where the editors have assembled fragments on civil and political legislation, on a police code, and on civil procedure.

39. F. W. Kampschulte, *Johann Calvin . . .*, vol. I (Leipzig, 1869), and vol. II, ed. W. Goetz (Leipzig, 1899).

meditating on the future life,[40] or something similar, was necessary as compensation if Reformed theology were not to take on the appearance of Christian Pharisaism, of which we have plenty of examples in America, England, Holland, and Switzerland even to our own day.

But let us stay with our thesis that in Zwingli and Calvin, in contrast to Luther, action in the world, faith's attack and defense on the soil of reality with all that is fitting and unfitting there, the translation of the absoluteness of faith into the relativity of the new obedience, is identical with the Christian life of faith. Here, then, the last trace has been lost of the monastic reaching and striving for perfection whose echo we catch in the ideals of the Radicals and from which — not without reason, we may say — Luther could not completely break free. With the eternal decree of God behind them, the law of the will of God above them, and future life ahead of them, Reformed Christians stood with both feet on the earth. That is either the completion of the Reformation or its end, or both at the same time. At any rate, the intersection of the two lines was made, the second turn in the Reformation had come, the theology of the cross had taken on its second sense.

In this regard at least, no matter how we interpret it, Zwingli and Calvin were not students but teachers, independent of Luther, rejected by Luther himself with the famous saying that they had a different spirit[41] there at the painful hour of division at Marburg that we might equally well call an hour of birth, for the eucharistic controversy was only an important but in itself indifferent battleground on which the first and second meanings of the theology of the cross collided. The debate whether Luther or the Reformed reformers were greater makes no sense so long as we measure Zwingli and Calvin by Luther's faith or Luther by the ethics of Zwingli and Calvin, for then it is clear that one may easily gain a confessional triumph for either side. What we need to do is to try to find the strength of both parties at very different levels and to see that the strength of neither lies at both levels. I would argue this even against K. Holl's account of Luther.[42] When we see that, we will stop playing off the significance of one level against that of the other, faith against ethics and ethics against faith. We will stop trying to

40. *Inst.* III, 9: "Meditation on the Future Life."

41. According to Osiander's account of the Marburg Colloquy of 1529 (WA 30/III, 150, 51ff.) Luther said it was obvious "das wir nicht ainerley gaist haben," nor can we when God's Word is simply believed in one place, but at another believing it is censured (with reference to "this is my body").

42. Barth had in view here Holl's "Der Neubau . . .," in *Gesammelte Aufsätze zur Kirchengeschichte*, I, 155ff.; and "Was verstand Luther unter Religion?" in ibid., 1ff., esp. 95ff.

decide the historical debate with the most inadvisable help of a premise taken from philosophical dogmatics. Instead, with fear and trembling [cf. Phil. 2:12], we will think of the one hand in which the two are one, of the unity over against which the figures of history are always in the wrong with their one-sidedness. Similarly, the artificial product of a theological and ecclesiastical union will then be irrelevant, and powerfully and resolutely developed distinctiveness on both sides will be a possibility, once Reformed and Lutherans find one another in a union of objectivity, of being right only by being wrong.

I thus understand the Lutheran Reformation as the characteristic opening up of the way, the first turn of the Reformation. To do justice to Luther in terms of his faith we must not speak of him as an academic or churchman or politician or German citizen, though naturally he was all those things as well, but as the monk who cut the Gordian knot of the monastic problem and thus destroyed the medieval view, when, as innocently as a child, he blabbed abroad his new insight into the *Deus absconditus* who is revealed in Christ, into the forgiveness of sins and the church of the elect, not knowing what he was really doing, not suspecting what enemies he would make or false friends he would attract, not suspecting or concerned what would be the fate or impact of the word that he thus placed in the world, concerned only that it should be kept pure, pure of the old leaven [cf. 1 Cor. 5:7], of the horizontal path, of reason and good works. What he then said, without the negative gestures of the Enthusiasts, whose ephemeral brilliance and tragic vehemence he could never understand because he understood them too well, without the frenetic attempt not to be a monk any more, but seeking only to proclaim directly to housewives, servants, princes, and soldiers the forgiveness of sins, simply trying to tell things as he saw them in Romans and the Psalms, no matter what the outcome might be in the empire of Charles V — that was Luther, the reformer of the first turn, and I would not hesitate to concede that in this regard Zwingli and Calvin, though they, too, knew what he knew, are not to be compared even remotely with him.

I would go on to say, however, that once the ethical problem came on the stage, the age with its questions and tasks, Zwingli and Calvin spoke more cautiously, confidently, consistently, and credibly than Luther did, notable though the insights and sudden flashes of Luther might be in this field, too. The Reformed version is the no less characteristic continuation and conclusion of the movement. The Reformed made this second turn in the Reformation much better than Luther did. Calvin, not

Luther, made the Reformation capable of dealing with the world and history when he hammered the faith of Luther into obedience. Calvin was the guiding spirit in the great defense against the developing Counter-Reformation around the mid-16th century. Calvin was the creator of a new Christian sociology that was so shaped as to be able to interact fruitfully with the different social principles of the new age inaugurated by the Renaissance, and to play a decisive role in their birth and development. Calvin was also the creator of a theological system that in virtue of a certain congeniality was inwardly adapted from the outset for debate with the unequivocally rational worldview of the modern period that was now arising. Reformed theologians were the ones who had sympathy with the first great philosopher of the modern period, Descartes, whether they agreed with him or rejected him.[43] It was to Calvin's system that later the historically most successful attempt to restate Protestant theology in the spirit of the modern period, that of Schleiermacher, attached itself.

The ambivalence of Calvin in this second field, that of history, as is clear from the example just given, is due to the ambivalence of the field itself. History is the field on which we have to live out Christianity but on which we have to compromise in order to fulfill our vocation through its movements of advance and decline, in order to be witnesses to that other kingdom which can never be moved [cf. Heb. 12:28]. Calvinism represents the historical success of the Reformation because it is its ethos. But to say success here is to say failure, inner loss, secularization. To say ethos is to stride off from God into the world; it is to turn one's back on God. We have to see both sides, the need to take this step, but also the need for renewed reflection and conversion. But when we see that, we see the need for both Luther *and* Calvin, both Calvin *and* Luther.

§5 ZWINGLI

In taking Calvin as the specifically and typically Reformed reformer as distinct from Luther, what I have in mind is that because of Zwingli's early

---

43. Among Dutch Reformed defenders and promoters of theological Cartesianism in the 17th century cf. A. Heidanus (1597-1678), L. Wolzogen (1633-1690), and C. Wittich (1625-1687). Opponents were G. Voetius (1589-1676), M. Leydecker (1678-1716), and P. van Mastricht (1677-1706).

death we have only Calvin's and not Zwingli's Reformed theology before us in developed systematic form, and it was Calvin, not Zwingli, who in large part left his imprint on the Reformed world. For a proper understanding of Calvin, however, we must not overlook the fact that the so-to-speak classical representative of the Reformed possibility was Zwingli. In a pure, one-sided, not too cautious, and very exposed form, the Reformed trend is much more prominent in him than in Calvin, who worked out much more sharply the dialectical relation to Lutheranism and thus took some of the edge off the antithesis. In the relation Zwingli was a pure type like the younger Luther. But the pure, or relatively pure, is not always historically the most powerful, and Zwingli's theology could no more establish itself than that of the younger Luther. Since the gods did not love Luther enough to grant him an early death, his early theology was given a historically viable form by the later Luther, then above all by Melanchthon.[1] In Zwingli's case, however, the death of its author, the lack of an executor of Melanchthon's stature, and above all the superior competition of the system of Calvin, which better met the general situation, did not allow his theology, or spared it, that type of conservation. We thus have to compare Luther and Zwingli but then compare both with Calvin as a new and third force if we are to see how the latter, having the experience of both behind him, uniting the possibilities they chose in some sense in himself, and even pressing them to their final logic, proclaimed perhaps a higher synthesis of the two, and perhaps spoke the last and ripest word of the Reformation. We can then see that in Calvin we have the harvest time but certainly also the melancholy late summer of the Reformation. We can then see how he is — as I simply indicated earlier — the truly tragic and the most profoundly problematic figure of the Reformation age.

First, however, we must see what linked Zwingli and Calvin together. I have referred to the resolutely taken step from the knowledge of God into the real world. These two were the prophets of the new Christian ethos. On three sides they spoke words that sounded very much the same.

1. The advocates of a moderate reform of the Catholic church had already throughout the 15th century and even earlier laid down the postulate of a renewal of Christian life according to the laws of God. The early 16th-century religious Humanists, of whom we have already spoken, powerfully took up their message. The new thing in Reformed activism

---

1. Cf. Plautus, *Bacchides*, IV, 7, 18, on the basis of a verse from Menander, *Fragments*, 125. Cf. Melanchthon's *Loci Communes* in the 1521, 1535, and 1542 editions.

as compared with the good and pious ideals of those sincere friends of progress was its unconditional nature. Earlier the postulate of a "reformation of both head and members"[2] had been a possibility; on the lips of Zwingli and Calvin it was a "Notwithstanding," a moral imperative with an estranging otherworldly emphasis because it was paradoxically related to a break with belief in our natural human goodness such as we never find in Wycliffe or a hundred years later in Erasmus, and because it was grounded in a concept of God such as they had never envisioned. The OT was discovered, and in it the majesty of God, and therewith the shattering seriousness of the problem of a real Christian life in the world. The Reformed started out with the thought of the divine providence that encompasses all things.[3] They viewed the Bible as simply the divine confirmation of the natural law that is written in the conscience.[4] These ideas naturally sounded congenial to Humanist ears. But the resultant ardor for the glory of God, with its bitter Mosaic taste, was accepted by none of those enlightened thinkers, to whom nothing could be more alien than the strange zeal for God that their converted colleagues represented.

2. The Enthusiasts too, whether along the lines of a free, mystically based individualism or along more moral, legal, and ascetic lines, demanded a reconstruction of life by the Holy Spirit, about whom they read in the Bible and on whose presence they thought they might count. There was certainly a link, though not a direct one, between the Reformed glory of God and the radical offensive launched by such circles. Martin Bucer sympathized with them, and Bucer's Christianity seems to have influenced Calvin. But if we look more closely we see that the attacks were different on the two fronts. The Anabaptists were separated from the Reformed by the same thing as the Humanists, namely, by the optimism with which they believed that a little of the Spirit and love would bring about a transformation of life. But then — and this is even more important — they encountered in the Reformed the soberness, or, let us openly say, the rationalism with which the latter asserted the unconditional nature of the divine command in which the Anabaptists also believed. The new

---

2. The demand for reform in head and members was a common one at Constance in 1414-1418, and we find it in the council decrees; cf. H. Jedin, ed., *Handbuch der Kirchengeschichte*, vol. III, 2 (Freiburg, Basel, and Vienna, 1968), 551f.; H. Bettenson, *Documents of the Christian Church* (London, 1975), 135.

3. First found in the *Sermon on Providence;* cf. Z 6/III, 64ff.

4. See n. 37 above on 86.

knowledge of the grace of God in Christ did not give the Reformed any cause to leave the solid ground of this world's reality and to lose themselves to God's glory in the boundlessness of religious feeling. Instead, it gave them every reason to set themselves for the first time firmly on that solid ground, and there — where else? — to do to God's glory, not the impossible, but all that they could do within the limits of the possible. They grasped the thought and took it to its logical conclusion, that the God of creation is one and the same God as the God of redemption, that his providence rules over the kingdom of nature as well as that of grace, and that even though our knowledge of it has been obscured by the fall, the natural law that underlies the written and unwritten laws of family, society, and the state is simply confirmed by the law revealed in the Bible. Again it was the OT that rendered the decisive service at this point, by marking out at least the bridge between that natural law and the demands of, for example, the Sermon on the Mount. Living according to the law and living according to the gospel are just as surely one and the same thing as the God of Moses and the Father of Jesus Christ are one and the same.

3. Luther was also on the scene. He, too, had something to say about ethics. He, too, was enthusiastically hailed by friends of light of every type, including Radicals on the extreme left. The new thing in the Reformed as compared to Luther was not something really new, as we have seen already. It was simply that they were in a position to take what Luther said more seriously than he did himself: without his separation of law and gospel, of the kingdom of the world and the kingdom of God, by which he had quickly alienated the hearts of both Humanists and Enthusiasts; without the slight hesitation of the former monk face-to-face with the need truly and unconditionally to accept things as they are in the world with all that that acceptance entails; yet also without the romantic explanations with which, basically alien to the world, he artfully evaded things as they are; in short, without the zigzags that betray his great uncertainty in this area. The NT with a similar earthly comprehensibility and applicability as the OT; the apostles of Jesus Christ with the same total ruthlessness as Moses or Elijah; a message of divine mercy sounding forth like the blast of a trumpet; a Christianity equipped for action and armed to the teeth, stripped of the most beautiful illusions and prepared for the worst eventualities — there we have the new thing in the Reformed as compared to Luther. Something involving decisive renewal was undoubtedly here, something incomparably more important than the new thing that the Humanists and Anabaptists thought they found in Luther,

but also something incomparably more dangerous. For precisely in the hesitant uncertainty of Luther face-to-face with the ethical problem lies the primary meaning and vitality of the Reformation, which at all events cries out for a second turn to complete it, but not for a step that will betray and surrender the new knowledge and return to the harlot reason[5] and the ungodliness of the papacy, as Luther might put it.

Two things could happen when the Reformation took leave of Luther's hesitation and emerged unequivocally as an ethical Reformation. It might, as we have said, lose its primary meaning and basis, spread itself abroad without power or worth, and merge into the cultural and political movements of the age. Or, with all the power and worth of its primary meaning and basis, it might take the form of the most radical and principled movement of all, surpassing and absorbing all the other movements, advancing into every area of human existence in the power of the knowledge of God, in an act of self-reflection and conversion on the part of Western humanity with unimaginable consequences, in short, in an event of almost eschatological breadth — though naturally we say "almost," for *last* things do not take place on earth, and yet why should not *little* things and even *great* things do so? Why should we not be allowed to believe that great things may also take place in history? Zwingli believed this, naively, firmly, confidently, more consistently than Calvin. That was his greatness and his problem. Luther also had this belief that great things are possible in history. Why not? It is almost impossible to think that he, too, did not dream the bold dream of a renewal of human life in the West, at least in the years 1517-1520. He knew, however, why he hesitated to take the great step in this direction, why he was so cautious. He recognized the greatness of the undertaking, of attempting this transformation of a purely religious movement with all the power of its origins. He was aware of the immeasurable danger that threatened, namely, that the transformation might be successful but the incomparable and priceless origins might be lost. Can we ever say how it came about that Luther's holy fear for the cause of God finally overcame his hope? We can only accept the result. Luther decided against that breakthrough into the world for the sake of the purity of what had to break through. He devoted his whole concern to guarding the priceless treasure, the noble Word of God, to keeping the gospel free of any admixture of nature, law, or reason.

5. Cf. Luther's *Wider die himmlischen Propheten* . . . (1525), WA 18, 164, 25-27: "die vernunfft des teuffels heurer."

It was for this reason that of all his opponents, with an antipathy surprising even in him, Luther called "den Zwingel," as he named him, a non-Christian, who did not teach the Christian faith correctly in any point, and who was seven times worse than if he had been a papist (30, 225).[6] He saw in Zwingli the man who in the most open way conceivable did the opposite of what he himself regarded as right in the interests of the cause of God. His heartfelt difficulty with Zwingli finds especially clear expression in a passage in the *Table Talk* (61, 16) under the heading "Enthusiasts Are Presumptuous and Foolhardy":

> The presumption and foolhardiness of the Enthusiasts is very harmful, for by it they fall and plunge themselves into trouble and distress. Listen to Zwingli's call: "Nothing can stop us, let us break through, in three years you will see that Spain, France, England, and all Germany will come to the gospel and accept it." They are so certain of this, only reluctantly praying our Lord God even once that his name be hallowed, etc., but let us break through, he said. With this fabled triumph and victory, however, he harmed himself, gave the gospel a bad name so that it was blasphemed, and strengthened the papacy. (How sad, all the Swiss have gone over to the papacy and built churches and altars, etc., except Zurich, Bern, and Basel, and unfortunately they will not hold out long.) This is what they have done with their *perrumpamus,* their breaking through; they are proud, presumptuous, and rely on their own good cause. And even if they had a truly good cause (which they have not), they should pray to God for success and blessing. For what is more right than the gospel! Yet we must always pray: Hallowed be thy name! Righteousness and progress and good fortune and good counsel must kiss each other. And the fools, even though in truth they are uncertain of their teaching, still do not pray.[7]

Luther's complaint against Zwingli was that with too great self-confidence, especially without praying the first petition of the Lord's Prayer, he wanted to lead the gospel to triumph in the world under the slogan *perrumpamus* or breakthrough, thus doing the greatest possible harm to it and bringing himself to ruin. How heartfelt was this complaint may be seen from the fact that he not only pursued Zwingli when alive with all conceivable

---

6. Cf. Luther's *Vom Abendmahl Christi, Bekenntnis* (1528), WA 26, 342, 21ff.
7. WA TR, 3, 56, 11ff. (no. 2891b).

invective, but even after his death spoke of his fate with pitiless and sanctimonious narrow-mindedness: "I could wish from my heart that Zwingli were saved, but I must fear the contrary, for Christ commands us to judge and decide as follows, that God will not know those who deny him and do not know him, or those who deny him and give the lie to him for the people. Those who do not believe are condemned already" (62, 15).[8]

We have to admit that Luther could think of Zwingli in no other way. Zwingli was indeed reckless. He could not understand, let alone even in the slightest share, Luther's concern for the purity of the gospel. He could not take this into account. He knew no restraint. Probably the idea that sheer movement might lead to the loss of the origins and goal never entered his head. He was the overconfident one who seemed to know only one question: How do we do it? That the whole Zwingli is described with that *perrumpamus* and a total forgetting of the first petition of the Lord's Prayer, and that there is no little corner for him in heaven, is a judgment that rests on Luther's nearsighted perspective, but how else could Luther see and depict him? It is not from Luther but from modern Lutherans that we should demand that Zwingli be finally treated with rather more objectivity and respect than is still the case. Eternally repeating Luther's narrow-mindedness does not really give credibility to the ongoing spirit and work of Luther.

At that time there could be no reconciling the antithesis. The two were both peasant sons. They both had sound but incorrigibly stubborn minds. They both had the same urge. They were both deeply claimed by the problems of the great movement of the age of which they were representatives and spearheads. Both were thus born leaders. For the rest, they were totally different. On the one hand was a heavy-blooded and troubled Thuringian, on the other hand an awakened and orderly and not easily overturned East Swiss such as one may still find in St. Gall canton, who would not let recollection of the last things in any way disturb his initiatives for the present, not in the least! Luther the North German was full of respectful regard for the system of divinely willed realities and dependencies, so that he was most incensed that Zwingli had supposedly once said that a window is as easily seen through as a pious prince (59, 248).[9] Zwingli had no fundamental reverence or regard for anything

8. Ibid., 1, 436, 27ff. (no. 875).
9. Ibid., 3, 572, 3ff. (no. 3729).

smacking of mediatorship, intermediate rule, or provisional authority —
a quality I must beg you to take into account today if you want to
understand us Swiss. The one was the child of a politically and culturally
rather backward zone, the other was at the heart of what was then the
blossoming urban culture of the German South. In the Reformation period
there were Zwinglians in East Friesland, and there was a Lutheran party
in Switzerland, especially Basel and Bern, from the early 1530s; indeed,
Lutheran thinking and sentiments are not uncommon in Switzerland even
to our own time, the proof being that today Ritschlian theology, as we
may calmly admit, is the dominant theology among us.[10]

The decisive difference between Luther and Zwingli was the difference between the hesitation of the one with its basis in faith and the
perrumpamus of the other with its basis in ethos. It is easy enough constantly to see Zwingli through Luther's spectacles and then, like Loofs and
Tschackert and others before them,[11] to offer the caricature that associates
Zwingli with the Anabaptist Enthusiasts as a former Humanist who could
not properly differentiate religion and culture, Christianity and politics.
It is equally easy, as we see especially in Ragaz in modern Switzerland, to
detest Luther, accusing him of being the great Quietist and the father of
an exclusive focus on divine grace that results in reaction.[12] In my view
both these evaluations are impermissible simplifications of the historical
truth, and a judicious Lutheran or Reformed theologian will have to come
beseechingly into the midst and ask above all else for a little calm and
justice on both sides. We must not tear apart the unity of the problem
that links Luther and Zwingli even though we must strongly emphasize
the difference between them within this context.

---

10. In East Friesland cf. esp. the work of John à Lasco (1499-1560) and his reforms
as superintendent in Emden from 1543 to 1549. On the work of Lutheran-minded pastors
in Bern and the Lutheran party there and in Basel from 1522 to 1540, cf. C. B. Hundeshagen, *Die Conflikte des Zwinglianismus, Lutherthums, und Calvinismus in der Bernischen
Landeskirche von 1532-1558* (Bern, 1842), 59ff. Cf. K. Barth, "Die kirchlichen Zustände
in der Schweiz" (1922), in *Vorträge und kleinere Arbeiten 1922-1925*, ed. H. Finze, vol.
III of *Gesamtausgabe* (Zurich, 1990), 35.

11. Loofs, *Leitfaden*, 800f.; and Tschackert, 257, who thinks Zwingli was closer
politically to Savonarola than Luther.

12. Cf. L. Ragaz, "Von den letzten Voraussetzungen der schweizerischen Neutrali-
tät," in *Die geistige Unabhängigkeit der Schweiz* (Zurich, 1916), 44, accusing Lutheranism
of being Quietist and of accepting even the worst of earthly rulers under God's supreme
rule. Cf. also M. Mattmüller, *Leonhard Ragaz und der religiöse Sozialismus: Eine Biographie*,
vol. II (Zurich, 1968), 82.

Since ethics, the turning to life with all that it involves, was Luther's problem too, inadequate though his solution might be, we must again underline this fact. Yet we must also say that Zwingli was undoubtedly a *total* Humanist, a *total* man of the Reformation, a *total* politician, a *total* Swiss. He was all these things totally, astonishingly, and often annoyingly, unrestrainedly, unbrokenly, and one-sidedly. But if the monasticism from which Luther came, and which gave him a tendency toward resignation, proves nothing against his ethical seriousness, the Humanism from which Zwingli came, and which gave him a tendency toward activism, proves nothing against the seriousness of his faith. Nor can we say that the antithesis of Saxon or Swiss, of reverence or lack of it, of being a man of spirituality or of reform, of being born with the mind of a subject or with a sense of political democracy in the kingdom of God, played any decisive role. Luther too, in his creatureliness, was what he was *totally* in a way no less annoying and questionable than that of Zwingli. If we do not see this in the haze that surrounds Luther, I can only assure you that it is so when we look at him more clearly from a greater distance. We must demand that on both sides regard should be had not to what is creaturely but to the sign preceding what is creaturely. We miss the main point in characterizing Zwingli if we do not go on to say: Yes indeed, a Humanist, a man of the Reformation, a politician, a Swiss, but also a converted Humanist, man of the Reformation, politician, and Swiss, who in intention at least had his basis in God, in the God of Luther and Paul. Were not all the creaturely elements that we see in him, and also in Luther, possibilities — no more, yet possibilities, equally good and bad in both cases? And who gives whom the right as a historian to call into question the purity of Zwingli's intention to a higher degree than anything that is human?

Certainly there was something secular and worldly and daylight-clear about Zwingli's style. In him we look in vain for the half-light, the obscurity, and the mystical bent of the German mind. In the eucharistic controversy the deep-rooted instinct of Luther that some mediation of salvation is needed collided with the equally deep-rooted instinct of Zwingli that salvation is only from God, from the *one* God. Mediation came for him when the voice of the heavenly Captain was heard and his banner was perceived on earth.[13] There is nothing soulful about that. Yet

---

13. Cf., e.g., Zwingli's *Usslegen und gründ der schlussreden oder artiklen* (1523), thesis 6; Z 2, 52, 2-4; also Z 5, 307, 20ff.; and G. W. Locher, "Christus unser Hauptmann," in *Huldrych Zwingli in neuer Sicht* (Zurich, 1969), 55ff.

the first turn in the Reformation did not come in Luther's German mind but in his faith. In comparison with the German mind Zwingli's Swiss and urban activism is not at any rate a nuance in the colorful array of legitimate human possibilities that necessarily means exclusion from the kingdom of heaven. In worth and significance the zeal for monotheism is at least on a par with the zeal for the thought of mediation.

We can indubitably describe as rationalism Zwingli's stubborn fight for the purely intellectual nature of Christianity that historically and in principle was his starting point and at least historically the point at which he parted company with Luther. But no matter how much or how little he had in common with what we call the Humanism of the time, we must ponder the fact that Erasmus at all events rejected Zwingli no less than he did Luther.[14] We then have to realize that this rationalism was paradoxically the same as the exclusive belief in revelation that so sharply opposed any transposition of the this-worldly into the otherworldly because it so emphasized the transposition of the otherworldly into the this-worldly, the glory of God in the world. This rationalism is the essence of what I have called the second turn in the Reformation. Are we to say that rationalism is a possibility for which there is no place in the kingdom of God? Are Plato and Kant divided from Christ because they were decided rationalists? Is the rationalisitic spirit of antiquity and of the modern period less capable of a conversion, of a resurrection from the dead, than the irrationalistic spirit of the Middle Ages? Does not everything depend upon the preceding sign? Those who are justified by faith alone must give glory *alone,* give *glory,* to the Justifier. To this urgent concern everything mystical, sacramental, and cultic, everything that is an image of deity, cannot but appear to be a hindrance and disruption. The *ratio* of the justification that is grasped in faith has to be at once the *ratio* of moral action. What is ruled out is the ambivalence of a religious world that comes between an equally resolutely affirmed otherworldly and this-worldly. For Zwingli religion was the knowledge of God and obedience, not a third thing. Christ does not give his people anything passive (4, 152).[15] That is what seemed to the Lutherans to be so secular in Zwingli, the rationalistic element.

14. Cf. Erasmus on Luther in a letter to Zwingli dated 8.31.1523, Z 8, 118, 2ff. (no. 315). As regards his attitude to Zwingli cf. his letter to him dated 9.8.1522, Z 7, 582, 1ff. (no. 236).

15. Z 2, 542, 4, from *The Education of Youth;* cf. LCC, XXIV, 107: "Confidence in Christ does not make us idle."

In spite of his Christian rationalism, no, because of it, Zwingli opened up the abyss of the fall, original sin, justification, and faith no less profoundly than Luther. His view, reminiscent of Abelard, that original sin is not guilt but *morbus,* a *Prästen,* was certainly not meant to excuse the *philautia* (self-love) of which the *Prästen* consists, but to show that we have here a plight that is so great that the moral term "guilt" cannot cover it, so great that there is only one answer to it, namely, the grace and election of God.[16] Again, the elect pagans with whom Zwingli peopled heaven, Hercules to Seneca,[17] were not an indication that he took any the less seriously our lost estate. Instead, they indicate that he did not see the division between heaven and hell, between Christ and unredeemed humanity, as directly dependent upon the presence or absence of Christian means of grace in the church, but wanted to anchor the Christianity or otherwise of individuals in the freedom of the redeeming God — a thought that is simply unavoidable if we think through strictly the concept of grace and take seriously the redemption effected in Christ, but that has nothing whatever to do with any glorifying or even saving of what we are by nature.[18] "We as little know what God is as the scarabeus knows what a human being is" (*On True and False Religion,* 1, 157).[19]

Like Luther, Zwingli called the Spirit of God who brings us self-knowledge, and assures us of forgiveness, an alien power or force (1, 192).[20] He expressly adopted the central thesis of Luther that the whole of the Christian life must be penitence (1, 194).[21] He was indeed an optimist and enthusiast, but we find in him not the slightest trace of optimism regarding our nature and situation apart from the grace of God, nor of any enthusiastic overrating of our human possibilities apart from the divine possibility. He recognized the full paradox of the relation between God

---

16. For Abelard's doctrine of original sin cf. Hagenbach, 368, who notes stress on sin as willing act and on motivation. Cf. Zwingli's *Usslegen und gründ* . . . on article 5; also *Züricher Einleitung* (1523), BSRK 8, 5, 21f.; 9, 9, 17; 13, 23; 51, 21, 23f.; also Hagenbach, 514; and Loofs, 805f.

17. *Exposition of the Faith,* LCC, XXIV, 275. Seneca is not listed here, but there are many references to him; cf. 106.

18. The view rejected by Barth is taken by Tschackert, 245, who traces the idea of the election of pagans to a weak view of sin.

19. *Commentary on True and False Religion* (1525), Z 3, 643, 1ff.

20. Ibid., 3, 692, 16ff. Luther, *Disputatio pro declaratione virtutis indulgentiarum* (1517), WA 1, 233, 10f.

21. Zwingli, Z 3, 695, 20.

and us. Nevertheless, again at one with Luther in principle, beyond that abyss and in light of the divine possibility, he not only saw but thought he could tread with a sure step the ground of our relative possibilities, the ground of ethics and history. The paradoxical confidence with which he not only demanded this step but thought it through and carried it through with all its implications is what distinguished him from Luther. At first he envisioned a carrying through of the Reformation, of the renewal of life, in the very banal and local form of opposition to the abuses in the Switzerland of his day associated with foreign mercenary service.[22] But then he had the vision of a renewal of the whole of Western cultural life in the spirit of the Pauline doctrine of justification. He not only dreamed up this possibility but thought it out clearly and set to work soberly enough to achieve it even to the point of the daring plan of a European alliance against the Hapsburgs as the leading papal power.[23] This was the *perrumpamus* that Luther took so ill.

We must do justice to Luther's objections. As criticisms of Zwingli's attitude they were right. But the attitude of Luther underlying them was also not free from criticism. We might well say to Zwingli: Where is the humility? Where is the waiting? But we can just as well say to Luther: Where is the courage? Where is the hastening?[24] There is no reason to accuse Zwingli one-sidedly if we keep in view the dialectic of the whole Reformation. It will not do simply to depict Zwingli's common sense as a lack of religious depth, his clarity of understanding as intellectualism, his urgent cry from the heart for a brave deed as moralism, his total and boldly direct relating of God to the things of this world as pantheism,[25] his more lofty and more mundane political action as typically religio-social arrogance. We must try to understand, in the first instance without evaluating, the intention and intuition behind all such things, the Reformation offensive that he had in view. Certainly he often gave a bad impression with what he did and said, but in the opposite sense this was no less true

22. Cf. the sermon to the Swiss Eidgenossen in May 1522, Z 1, 165ff.

23. Cf. G. W. Locher, *Die Zwinglische Reformation im Rahmen der europäischen Kirchengeschichte* (Göttingen and Zurich, 1979), 514ff.

24. In the two terms from 2 Pet. 3:12 Barth found the two aspects of Christian life in light of the eschaton as he saw it esp. in C. Blumhardt; cf. Barth, *Römerbrief,* 1st ed., vol. II of *Gesamtausgabe* (Zurich, 1985), 126 n. 20; and idem, *Ethics* (New York, 1981), §15.

25. Cf. Loofs, 800; Tschackert, 243; W. Dilthey, "Das natürliche System der Geisteswissenschaften im 17. Jahrhundert," 225, who speaks of Zwingli's panentheism.

of Luther's hesitation. In reality Zwingli, too, kept in mind the infinite gap between Creator and creature, the "finite not capable of the infinite,"[26] and much better indeed than his later critics and teachers.

It was precisely this awareness, however, awareness of the remoteness of God that is also his nearness, which in relative distinction from Luther would not let him hesitate but drove him sharply into action. We may stand before his incomplete life and work as before the fragments of an unfinished house, and shaking our heads ask whether it could ever possibly have been complete, yet not forgetting that beyond our human wisdom the truth still holds that in great things it is enough to have the desire.[27] And what do we really know? Perhaps if Zwingli had lived any longer he might have been like the man who wanted to build a tower without counting the cost [Luke 14:28], and his enterprise would have ended up choked and sterile and brutalized and secularized and divorced from the church because the power and worth of its origins were no longer in it. But was not that the fate of the whole Reformation, even of the Lutheran Reformation with its much more modest spirit of adventure? It might also have been, however, that the great thing that Zwingli expected from God, and that he believed he should fight for, would actually have come to pass. Zwingli's vitality, at least, was not broken even when he fell on the field of Cappel.

No matter how we assess the possibilities, however, one thing is sure: in the work of this remarkably restless and remarkably cold-blooded man from the Toggenburg, who was well adapted for it both by nature and by grace, we see an attempt to do what Luther wanted to do purely but also for profound reasons did not want to do. In other words, we see the Reformed possibility in its most distinctive form. Dilthey said of Zwingli: "No man of the Reformation age understood Christianity in a way that was more manly, healthy, or simple" (1, ch. 525).[28] This secular verdict is unjust to Luther. For in a way no less manly, healthy, and simple, Luther was at the opposite pole of the movement. We must not expound his concern for the purity of the cause as the antithesis of the qualities extolled

---

26. Z 5, 354, 6ff. The actual formula does not occur in Zwingli or Calvin, but we find it in Lutheran-Reformed controversies in the later 16th century. Cf. A. Adam, *Lehrbuch der Dogmengeschichte*, vol. II (Gütersloh, 1st ed. 1972), 396; Barth, *Die christliche Dogmatik* (1927), vol. II of *Gesamtausgabe* (Zurich, 1928), 251f.

27. Propertius, *Elegies*, II, 10, 5.

28. Dilthey, *System*, 226.

in Zwingli. There was also a restraint that was manly, healthy, and simple. Nevertheless, we must not take it amiss if a secular philosopher like Dilthey is especially warm to the second meaning of the Reformation, its ethical turn. The children of the world are often wiser than the children of light [cf. Luke 16:8]. And if Dilthey found a type of this in Zwingli, as his words surely indicate, then in this regard he was right.

§6 CALVIN

Not only historically but also materially Calvin was relatively independent of Zwingli, though he represented with him the second or Reformed turn in the Reformation. Calvin was also manly, of course, but with a different kind of manliness from what we find in either Luther or Zwingli, and I would not venture to use such terms as healthy or simple of Calvin. If we are looking for these qualities let us stay with Luther and Zwingli. And in the long run let us see to it that we are not wrong about them, too. For Calvin, who was neither healthy nor simple, perhaps did no more than bring to light a pain and problem that was the deepest secret of the other two.

We best illustrate the relation between Calvin and Zwingli that we now need to clarify by an obvious concrete example, namely, by looking at the epistles with which the two dedicated their main systematic works, the 1525 *True and False Religion* and the 1536 *Institutes,* to the same typical Renaissance prince, Francis I of France.[1] If the way of relating the new knowledge of God to the reality of the world was the great critical problem of the Reformation, the point of division, then here — where Zwingli and Calvin addressed to a worldly judge the considered result of their Christian thinking, where externally, by human judgment, the further advance of their movement depended mostly on the attitude of that judge,[2] on the man whose judgment, by reason of his position and outlook, was typical of the prevailing political and cultural opinion — here what is common to the two will be particularly plain but will also decide what it is that divides them.

A few words about the third party on the stage are called for in this connection. Francis had come to the throne in 1515. He had won the battle of Marignano, with the Swiss for the first time on the losing side,

1. Z 3, 628-37; OS I, 21, 36; BI 1ff.
2. MS *ankam,* corrected by the editor to *abhing.*

including a Glarus contingent with Zwingli as their chaplain. He had been defeated by Charles V, even though he had papal support, in the imperial election of 1519; and in 1525, when Zwingli dedicated his work to him, he had just lost a war against his more successful rival. After the manner of rulers of his day, he loved art and learning, and in this field, though in this alone, it would seem, he won an honored name in history and did real service to his country. He was himself a worldling, but he had a mother and sister who sincerely supported the Reformation.[3] He protected the biblical scholar Lefèvre d'Etaples [Faber Stapulensis], who was intellectually akin to Erasmus even in abhorrence of all religious radicalism. For a time, it seems, he was not totally opposed to the idea of a spiritual Lutheranism that would remain within the church, so that in 1535 he could invite Melanchthon and Bucer to a disputation at Paris even though burnings were then in progress there. For though he was a most unreliable supporter of the papal church, for fear of the revolutionary tendencies that he suspected in his evangelical subjects he was ready to persecute anything that went beyond the innocuous evangelism of Faber Stapulensis.

When in 1534, giving vent to his annoyance at the policies of Rome, he threatened the papal nuncio with a break from Rome after the manner of Henry VIII of England, the nuncio told him frankly that he would be the first to be duped, for a new religion among the people would later demand a change of prince (Henry, I, 99).[4] This warning was too much in line with what he himself suspected. Enraged by the publication of some very radical pamphlets aimed at the church and the clergy, at the end of January 1535 he ordered a so-called lustration in which he himself and his three children went through Paris carrying white candles while six adherents of the new teaching were burned alive on the main city squares. With this pious atrocity came even wider persecution of the Protestants. This was the period, in the mid-1530s, when Calvin's *Institutes* was written. Francis I died in 1547. The optimistic view of Beza ([CO] 21, 125)[5] that in spite of everything he was really "not alien to us" seems to me to be totally refuted by his physiognomy alone. Judge for yourselves!

---

3. His mother, Louise de Savoie (1476-1531); his sister, Marguerite de Navarre (1492-1549).

4. P. Henry, *Das Leben Johann Calvins des grossen Reformators,* vol. I (Hamburg, 1835).

5. *Ioannis Calvini Vita* (Geneva, 1575). For Beza's positive evaluation of Francis I cf. Henry, 72.

What are we to make of it that it was felt necessary to dedicate a Protestant dogmatics, unsolicited, to so questionable if important a figure. After all, Zwingli, who had been a prominent opponent of Swiss mercenary service on behalf of France, was surely just as unwelcome there as Calvin, the even more suspicious friend of the suspicious Rector Cop.[6] Yet both of them were seriously hoping, it seems, if not to convince, at least to instruct this monarch. It is a situation in which we cannot see Luther, the comparison that Henry (I, 72) makes with Luther at Worms being feeble in every respect.[7] It was the more characteristic, however, of these two reformers, both together and individually.

Let us hear Zwingli first. The style is that of a man of the world or of the courtliness of a Humanist. From the very first lines, however, the content is confident, bold, brash, and aggressive. It has a Swiss frankness that plants itself bombastically in front of the royal throne and issues its manifesto. There is something threatening about it, something openly threatening in the superior manner not merely of the religious prophet but of the political adversary who at the time is two moves ahead but is magnanimous enough to break off the game for a time and to give good advice as at a game of chess. Francis I had been put to shame at Pavia. "All is lost save honor," he is said to have cried when taken prisoner by Charles V.[8] The situation at home was also an adverse one. The people were suffering under the burden of his wars, under high taxes, under the oppression of the nobles, under the extortions of a greedy clergy. The king could no longer count for sure on the loyalty of his subjects. Will he accept good advice? What Zwingli commends to him is his own cause, the renewed gospel, as the only thing that can save him in this sorry situation. As once Hilary of Poitiers took the truth from Gaul to Germany, so Zwingli now wants to take it to France in the name of the German Reformation.[9]

Is it not evident — this is the point of his epistle — that the world

6. See below, 142ff.

7. As Luther once withstood Emperor Charles in defense of his faith, so Calvin and his companions withstood the king of France.

8. Cf. Francis's letter to his mother after the defeat (2.24.1525) in J. A. Dulaure, *Histoire physique, civile, et morale de Paris,* vol. III (Paris, 1837), 209. The usual rendering: "All is lost save honor," is not actually what we find in the letter, which reads: "All I have left is honor and my life that has been saved."

9. Z 3, 634, 29ff. Hilary dedicated his *Liber de synodis seu de fide Orientalium* to his brethren and fellow bishops in the two German provinces. In what follows Barth stays closely with Z 3, 628-37.

and its kings and peoples are sick, that they suffer from one another and all of them from the corrupt church, and that the new proclamation which the Creator of all things has now caused to go forth is the remedy, the only remedy, for this sickness? It is not without punishment that we neglect the Word of God. There is the cause of all the evil. The darkness in which people live has become most intense, but light has now drawn near, for God neither can nor will abandon the world to darkness. The day of the Lord is dawning, not the last day, Zwingli adds significantly, but the day when the Lord will radically improve present conditions.[10] We must be ready and willing, then, to let ourselves be helped by the only Helper. Amos [3:8] is quoted: "If the lion roars, who will not fear?" That is why this most Christian commentary is dedicated to the most Christian king, the bold writer dares literally to say.[11] It is not that the commentary and Christianity need the king but that the king needs the commentary and Christianity — that is the unconcealed meaning.

Recall the point of the drama. On to a world stage on which the severest of political and economic battles are being fought comes Protestant theology saying that it has the solution, not making a request, not simply craving toleration or recognition, but aware of being a power, a force, having something to offer, yet also something to demand! Let the theologians of the Sorbonne come; for what do they know of language, of philosophy, of the Bible, of things human or divine? If only the king will bring them face-to-face with the Protestant teachers, he will have no difficulty in choosing between them. Is he afraid of revolution because of what has taken place in Germany? Well, if earthly authorities oppose the heavenly Word, it is not surprising if they alienate the very best of their subjects; let them end their opposition and the very best will be on their side. Those who read this book will see for themselves what recovery (*quantum respirationis*) may be expected from the resolve on moral reform according to the word of the gospel.[12] Thus far Zwingli.

Let us compare Calvin, writing similarly to the same man ten years later. He, too, is very correct. He does not give an inch as regards either himself or his cause. He writes with dignity and clarity. But how different is the picture! For the one who now writes is one who on behalf of his faith has been driven out of his French homeland, who is now addressing

10. Z 3, 633, 16-18.
11. Z 3, 629, 9-13.
12. Ibid., 636, 31-33.

his own king from abroad, and who is pleading to the supreme judge of the country with all the skill of rhetoric on behalf of fellow believers who are still in France.[13] To this end he originally wrote his *Instruction in the Christian Religion* as a textbook, he says. He[14] wanted to show the king what those whom he was persecuting really taught and to ask him whether they really deserved such horrible punishment.[15] The charge against them — in the main that of revolution — should not be accepted without examination. It is not a matter of Calvin's own return to France, he says with pride, for he can just as well stay where he is. His concern is for the cause of all the devout and of Christ.[16] His plea is not that those who espouse this cause should merely be pardoned as poor people who are ignorant and inexperienced. Justice should be done to them. The king's task is to protect or restore the inviolability and dignity of God's glory on earth. For in his office the king is either a servant of God's glory or a robber.[17] Let not the king make a mistake because those who now appeal for justice are poor and abject little people.[18] We know that we are the refuse and offscouring of the world. Before God we may boast only of his unmerited mercy and before our fellows only of our weakness. But our doctrine is very different. It stands sublime and invincible over all the world's power and glory, for it is not ours but that of the living God and his Christ, whom the Father has installed as king. Christ rules, however, by holding the whole earth in terror, notwithstanding all the power of its iron and bronze and the splendor of its silver and gold, simply by the "rod of his mouth" (Isa. 11:4).

What the king should learn from the book that is dedicated to him is that adversaries castigate the new teaching in vain, for what they find scandalous in it is in keeping with the analogy of faith (Rom. 12:7). It is what it should be as the doctrine of faith,[19] making us so small and God so great that precisely in this way it sets us in the peace of sure expectation of salvation and eternal life. It is on account of this hope of the living God — and twice here Calvin sums up the essence of evangelical teaching in the word "hope" *(spes)* — that adherents of this teaching now have to

13. OS I, 21-36; BI 1ff.
14. MS *sie,* corrected to *er.*
15. OS I, 21; BI 1.
16. OS I, 22; BI 2.
17. OS I, 23; BI 3.
18. OS I, 23; BI 3.
19. OS I 24; BI 4.

suffer so severely.[20] Who are their foes? Who has set the persecution in motion? The clergy, whose basic concern is simply to safeguard their rule, whose belly is their god, whose religion is a kitchen religion, and of whom not one shows the slightest sign of true seriousness.[21] They see this teaching as new. The answer is that it is new only to those to whom Christ and the gospel are new, but both can appeal by right to their antiquity. They call the teaching uncertain, but trusting in it we fear neither death nor the judgment throne of God. They ask for new miracles to bear witness to it. But the old gospel needs no new miracles, and in any case the miracles they adduce count for nothing against the truth of God, for Satan, too, can work miracles. They appeal to the church fathers.[22] We freely recognize their authority, but why do our opponents simply honor their errors and mistakes without following, but instead concealing or twisting, the true things that they say. They appeal to custom, but it has never been true of the human race that the majority wants what is better.[23] Because we have been accustomed to what is bad, should we reject the one means of salvation from all the sins, pestilences, and disasters from which humanity now suffers (the single passage in which the leading theme of Zwingli's epistle may also be found in Calvin).[24] This is a mistake that has no place at least in God's kingdom, where eternal truth holds sway.[25] They confront us with the dilemma that either the church has been dead thus far or we are now in conflict with it. Our answer is that the church of Christ lives and will continue to live as long as Christ reigns at the right hand of the Father. But with this church we are not in conflict. To the existence of this church, however, we can never point with a finger and say: Here it is or there. The Lord knows his own, but the true church is not outwardly visible as such.

It is a horrible judgment that this is so,[26] but a judgment under which we must bow. Where was the true church when Elijah confronted four hundred prophets of Baal alone,[27] when Jeremiah's adversaries were the official priests, or when the lawfully elected pope of the lawful Basel

20. OS I, 24; BI 5; OS I, 25; BI 5.
21. OS I, 25-27; BI 5ff.
22. OS I, 27-29; BI 8ff.
23. OS I, 30; BI 10.
24. OS I, 30; BI 11.
25. Loc. cit.; OS I, 31; BI 13.
26. OS I, 31; BI 13.
27. OS I, 32f.; BI 14.

Council was simply deposed and a cardinal's hat was flung around like a piece of meat for a dog? Where has it been during the time when we can trace back everything that is called pope, bishop, or priest to Eugene IV, who unlawfully forced himself in as pope?

Finally there is the charge of revolution. What has Calvin to say to the king who was so worried on this score? "It is a certain characteristic of the divine Word that it never comes forth while Satan is at rest and sleeping."[28] Was not Elijah asked whether it were not he who was leading Israel into confusion?[29] Was not Christ a leader of sedition in the eyes of the Jews? Were there not those who said that Paul was leading people into sin? But are we to deny Christ because he is a stone of stumbling and offense, a fragrance of life to life for some and of death to death for others? The king may rest assured that our God is not a God of strife but of peace. What reason for suspicion have we given? When have we talked about overthrowing the state? When have we not made it plain that our only concern is to fear God and to serve him? If there are really some who on the pretext of the gospel stir up trouble — but where are they? — then the law and its penalties must come into play, but the gospel of God should not be blasphemed because of the wickedness of lawbreakers. Calvin concludes:

> Your mind is now indeed turned away and estranged from us, even inflamed, I may add, against us, but we trust that we can regain your favor, if in a quiet, composed mood you will once read this our confession, which we intend in lieu of a defense before Your Majesty. Suppose, however, the whisperings of the malevolent so fill your ears that the accused have no chance to speak for themselves, but those savage furies, while you connive at them, rage against us with imprisonings, scourgings, rackings, maimings, and burnings. Then we will be reduced to the last extremity even as sheep destined for the slaughter. Yet this will so happen that "in our patience we may possess our souls"; and may await the strong hand of the Lord, which will surely appear in due season, coming forth armed to deliver the poor from their affliction, and also to punish their despisers, who now exult with such great assurance. May the Lord, the King of kings, establish your throne in righteousness, and your dominion in equity, most illustrious king.[30]

28. OS I, 33; BI 15.
29. OS I, 34f.; BI 16.
30. OS I, 36; BI 18f.

It is immediately obvious that not merely under the pressure of the situation this address to the king is the address of someone who is on the defensive. That is the position of Calvin. That is what differentiates him from Zwingli and defines his position in the Reformation more generally. To be sure, the eternal truth of the gospel is not at all for him a passive thing, an object of meditation or speculation like the God of the Middle Ages. It is a power that breaks in and presses forward. Think of the apocalyptic passage at the beginning in which he speaks of Christ's kingly rule with the rod of his mouth.[31] As the French Calvin scholar Bossert (p. 38)[32] rightly stresses, Calvin, too, does not ask for mere toleration for his cause. He, too, presents his church, not as a new one alongside the old, but as itself the old, the one, and indeed the true church in place of that which then obtained. He, too, could offer the threat that God's kingdom presents to the world's kingdom (the last extremity),[33] and in spite of the inoffensive interpretation, excluding any human threat, that this is at once given, or perhaps because of it, this has a very sinister ring. He too, as I have pointed out already, calls the gospel the remedy for a sick world.[34]

But his restraint in saying all these things is in marked contrast to the lively and cheerful *perrumpamus* of Zwingli. Calvin does not frankly tell the king everything that is on his mind. With calm dignity, and without concealing or denying in the least what the gospel itself is and says, he can even put this in a stronger and more unsettling and pointed way than Zwingli. Think only of the paradox of the passage in which he speaks of our human nothingness and the divine mercy, apparently giving up on himself and his clients as poor little people, but then stressing all the more how sublime and invincible and powerful is their cause, their doctrine[35] — a passage that in its boomerang effect has no parallel at all in Zwingli's epistle. Calvin, however, makes the application only to Protestants themselves, whose faith has its basis of assurance in this paradoxical truth. He refrains from making the obvious application to the situation, to the king and his own need to believe, and this is in keeping with the tenor of the

31. OS I, 23; BI 4.

32. A. Bossert, *Johann Calvin*, quoted from the German translation by H. Krollick (Giessen, 1908).

33. OS I, 36; BI 18f.

34. OS I, 30; BI 11.

35. OS I, 23; BI 3.

whole address. The only exception is when he says that kingly rule that does not serve God's glory is "brigandage."[36] And even there the conclusion he draws is simply that the king is under an obligation as such to procure justice for the cause of Christ, to be the protector of its soundness and dignity *(incolumitas* and *dignitas).* He does not try to claim or win the king himself for the cause.

For all the Gallic liveliness that can flash forth at times, profound seriousness goes hand in hand in Calvin with restrained politeness. He was the aristocrat among the reformers. In comparison Zwingli's zealous urging and commending seems like a plebeian casting of pearls before swine [Matt. 7:6]. We might say that Calvin's approach is more resigned, that it does not grip so energetically. But it is also calmer and more mature, and takes into greater account what is possible. The basic Reformed view is the same, but it is more enthusiastic and utopian in Zwingli, more prudent in Calvin, more adjusted to the world and therefore more viable, a match for the vile reality of this world as a Francis I might see it, and yet at the same time showing more awareness of the distance between God's ways and ours, and not putting up for sale the solemnity of divine things. For Calvin activism meant moderate action after due consideration. He had come to terms with the fact that the world resists the gospel. He did not dream of any dramatic breakthrough or victory for his cause. His concern was to establish the most favorable possible conditions for the conflict. Francis might not understand or even perhaps read the epistle. Calvin had no illusions on that score. From the very first, as an advocate of Christianity, he was reaching beyond the unreceptive mind of the Most Christian King to a broader court, to the whole Christian world. Indeed, as he liked to put it later, he was playing a role in the theater where God and angels make up the audience.[37]

Who is to say which of the two, Zwingli or Calvin, chose the better part? All we may say is that in the transition from the one type to the other the same basic Reformed view experienced a break. It was still the same basic view. We cannot say that Calvin's restraint was the same as that of Luther. The church of Calvin, too, was the OT church militant as Luther's never was. In what Calvin says to the king, for all the moderation, we sense that fundamental lack of respect and reverence for provisional human authority that is only with difficulty concealed by its provisional

36. Ibid.
37. *On the Eternal Predestination of God* (1552), CO 8, 294.

recognition. We sense the political rationalism that recognizes human authority in the first instance only on the condition of its divine appointment, but which only tolerates bad government "as sheep being led to the slaughter,"[38] letting it be but holding out before it the threat of coming judgment. Calvin, too, knows only *one* kingdom, that of God; only *one* truth, that of God; and only *one* goal, the glory of God. He is thus at odds with all other kingdoms, truths, or goals.

But his stance in the conflict is different. On earth, though not in heaven, the offensive has broken off. A strong position has been taken up and established. The troops are being mustered. The rear is made secure. Contact with the enemy is being systematically organized. Protestant activism seems all the more vigorous, threatening, and dangerous, however, in this second restrained, concentrated, and organized form, which does not merely face the real world but is aimed at it, adapted to the historical situation. Only in this second form did Reformed Protestantism become a serious force that could no longer be confused in the last analysis with Enthusiasm. In this form it made inwardly necessary on the Roman Catholic side the Jesuit order and Council of Trent.[39] Nevertheless, we cannot ignore the fact that the first glory of spring had now passed,[40] that with fulfillment the end was plainly coming. Here is a contrast that in its inner necessity has to be explained in terms of the general situation of the Reformation movement on the one hand and its significance in principle on the other, but certainly not just in terms of difference in the situation, character, and so on of Zwingli and Calvin. Though the persecution of Protestants in France had to affect Calvin deeply, in itself this was a local phenomenon and by no means enough to account for the distinctive character of his theology as we see it in the dedicatory epistle. It was simply a storm bird heralding what was to come. What was to come was the visible power of the Reformation movement to expand and the accompanying development of reaction, the Counter-Reformation.

To understand Calvin, the *Institutes,* and the whole of his theology, it will repay us to see what had happened in the first half of the 16th

---

38. OS I, 36; BI 18f.

39. The Jesuit order was founded in 1539; Paul III sanctioned it in 1540; Trent met from 1545 to 1563.

40. Cf. the opening of H. Heine's *Tragödie* (1829), *Werke,* vol. II, ed. O. Walzel (Leipzig, 1912), 83.

century. When the *Institutes* came out in 1536, the first third of a long series of events had roughly ended, events that in different ways might all be taken as passive markers of the Reformation. In 1525 had come the Peasants' War, which meant the end of Luther's true and undisputed popularity. The years 1525-1529 brought the controversies between Luther and Zwingli. In 1531 Zwingli fell at Cappel. The compromising events at Münster took place in 1534. French Protestants came under persecution in 1535. Later, 1540 would see the bigamy of Philip of Hesse and the founding of the Jesuits. Paul III set up the Inquisition in 1542.[41] In 1543-1545 Charles V was successful abroad against France, the Turks, and the Netherlands. Trent opened in 1545. Luther died in 1546, while 1547 saw the hateful battle of Mühlberg, 1548 the Leipzig Interim, and 1549 the beginning of inner doctrinal controversies among the Lutherans.

Under the shadow of these past and coming events Calvin wrote his first version of the *Institutes*. It is no wonder that he was so different from both Luther and Zwingli. He was Zwingli, one might say, with the vision and the possibilities of the older Luther. Unlike Zwingli, Calvin had to reckon with the bitter possibility, so often weighed by Luther, that the Word of God, having run its course, would be taken away again from the earth.[42] The possibility was there in obvious forms. But unlike Luther, Calvin, in confrontation with this danger, could not take comfort merely in the cherished hope of the last day that would make all the damage good by a divine miracle. Like a soldier at a threatened and perhaps lost position, he had to resist desperately, to save what could still be saved, and perhaps even to defy and to regain what could be regained. Here, then, we have a man in bitter and bloody earnest, who like Zwingli cannot refuse bravely to make the Reformation inference that we must set up the Word of God as a force in the world, as an order of life, but who also, like Luther, can wage the war on the innermost line, avoiding all that was so plainly ambivalent and overly hasty in Zwingli, and championing with ruthless self-discipline only the one thing that was essential.

Staehelin (II, 395) quotes a saying of Ebrard to the effect that if Luther and Zwingli depict Reformation hope, Calvin depicts Reformation

41. Paul III reconstituted the Inquisition with his *Licet ab initio* of 1542.
42. WA TR 4, 151, 9ff., 34ff., no. 4123, in which Luther saw so much ingratitude, contempt, and arrogance that he feared God's Word had run its course and hoped the judgment day was near. Cf. also 3, 542, 18ff., no. 3697; 4, 509, 1ff., no. 4788; 5, 469, 31ff., no. 6064.

care.[43] I say again that Calvin is the tragic figure of the Reformation, not although, but just because, he was more successful than the others. He represents the most mature and complete and consistent expression of the Reformation, but the expression with which it brought itself to an end, taking on definitively an earthly, ethical, historical form. Evening had come, the day was far spent [Luke 24:29]. The year 1555 tells the whole story in this regard. It was the year when Calvin successfully and finally defeated all his foes and made himself master of Geneva, the year when he had finished building the city of God, the new Jerusalem, as his friends called it, the new Rome to his enemies. It was also the year when the Peace of Augsburg finally made of Luther's Reformation a recognized confession but in so doing halted its assault upon the church and society.

If we add to the historical facts the principial consideration that Reformed Protestantism, in the situation that Zwingli had put it in and that Calvin represented, was aware of the danger of being politicized and secularized, and that without surrendering the position, but rather advocating it the more vigorously, thus putting strong emphasis on the basic theme of Luther that we also often detect in the ethos of Zwingli, in this way strengthening the link of the second phase of the Reformation to the first, then in my view we have the standpoint from which we can and must understand the distinctiveness of the theology of Calvin as compared to that of Luther or Zwingli.

H. Bauke has tried to use the Romance origins of Calvin to explain his theology. He depicts him as a brilliant dialectician and systematician,[44] a second Abelard, one might say, who skillfully unites in his thinking disparate elements from the Bible, church tradition, and Luther, and who finally, not without the aid of rhetoric, can put them together in a single doctrinal structure. This suggestion undoubtedly has value in helping us to understand Calvin, just as it helps to remember that Luther was from Saxony and Zwingli from the Toggenburg. Nevertheless, the explanation leaves much to be desired if we are to gain an understanding of the whole Calvin. We may use the unfathomable depths of nationality as a principle by which to explain an author, but we must not make historical theology a subdiscipline of anthropological geography, instead resorting to the latter

---

43. E. Stähelin, *Johannes Calvins Leben und ausgewählte Schriften,* 2 vols. (Elberfeld, 1863). The quotation is from J. H. A. Ebrard, *Das Dogma vom heiligen Abendmahl und seine Geschichte,* vol. II (Frankfurt, 1846), 406.

44. Bauke, *Probleme,* 14.

only when other possibilities are exhausted, which is by no means the case with a person like Calvin, who is set in plain historical and principial context.

Karlfried Fröhlich treated Calvin along the lines of the Otto-Heiler school.[45] He took as his explanatory principle phenomenology, which conscientiously notes Calvin's use of terms like light, fire, lightning, majesty, wrath, sword, battle, and so on whenever he is speaking forcefully, and which then puts together these features drawn from the aesthetic realm to present us with a picture of Calvin's piety or his God — a picture that I would call a gruesome waxwork model from which, having surveyed it with startled interest, we can only turn aside because there can be no possibility of rational discussion with it. As for the famous "numinous" and *tremendum* that has naturally been found in Calvin too,[46] just as Bauke found that he was from Picardy, it is normal and praiseworthy to mention such things, but regrettable to have to refer back to this feature or that instead of achieving a true understanding, and it is a sign of poverty to write whole books about them.

In opposition to these very modern explanations of Calvin I would insist that we must understand him in terms of the inner necessity with which the truth that is the same yesterday and today [cf. Heb. 13:8] and that is not far from any one of us [cf. Acts 17:27], challenged and awakened this specific man at a specific time in its historical movement four hundred years ago. If we could succeed in following the course of this truth with understanding through all the human errors and human confusion, participating as though we were ourselves present, all eyes and ears for what took place then, much better than what we have done or can do now, then we would know in advance and say in advance that no other could stand at this point in history than he who was in fact Jean Calvin, born at Noyon in Picardy in 1509, and with his own specific experience of God, if we want to use that term. Uniting the context of history with that of principle, we could only suspect and not really be surprised that in that context he was the man he was, but would have to say that this is how he

---

45. K. Frölich, *Die Reichsgottesidee Calvins* (Munich, 1922); F. Heiler (1892-1967), who with R. Otto's help was appointed Professor of the History and Philosophy of Religion at Marburg. Fröhlich's book was vol. III in the series Aus der Welt christlicher Frömmigkeit, ed. Heiler.

46. Fröhlich, 9f., with a reference to Otto's *Idea of the Holy* (1923) (*Das Heilige* [Breslau, 1920]).

had to be. It seems to me that only when we are in some sense aware of this necessity, and therefore do not come up against the block of an astounding fact, are we in a position to do justice to Calvin, to be taught by him, and to learn to respect and love him in his individuality, which is the supreme goal of a monograph of this type.

Unlike many older Calvin scholars, then, I would not try to understand Calvin in terms of a single thesis in the *Institutes* such as the glory of God, predestination, providence, or meditating on the future life,[47] then using this as a master principle from which to derive all else. Nor would I begin with a contingent fact of history or psychology like the theologians to whom I have referred. Instead, I want to try to evaluate Calvin the man and the theologian in terms of his place in the historical and principial context. For this double place is the vital individual factor, that which points us to God in his work. I also note that we cannot distinguish here between the man and the theologian, and for this reason I cannot in principle approve of Wernle[48] when he separates the faith of the reformers as far as possible from their theology. What would be the reaction if we tried to separate the man Michelangelo as far as possible from his art? But again, how can we understand a person's work without understanding the person? We must not insult theology by giving the impression that in this field differentiating the person from the work is especially necessary or profitable. At the end of this section then, and before passing on to a survey of Calvin's life, let us provisionally sketch the man and the theologian as he had to be at his own specific place.

I have pointed out already that we cannot expect anything other than that we will have to do here with one who was zealous for the Lord like Elijah [cf. 1 Kings 19:10]. The Reformed turn in the Reformation included this implication from the outset. But in Calvin there is a note

---

47. Cf. Bauke, *Probleme,* ch. II, 1, pp. 21ff. On the centrality of the glory of God in Calvin cf. F. C. Baur, *Geschichte der christlichen Kirche* (Tübingen, 1863), 405f.; also Ritschl, *Gesammelte Aufsätze,* vol. II (Leipzig, 1896), 94ff.; E. F. K. Müller, *Symbolik . . .* (Erlangen and Leipzig, 1896), 445f. On predestination as Calvin's central doctrine cf. Kampschulte, *Calvin,* I, 263; A. Schweizer, *Die protestantischen Zentraldogmen . . .,* vol. I (Zurich, 1854), 17. On providence as Calvin's central doctrine cf. J. Bohatec, "Calvins Vorsehungslehre," in *Calvinstudien,* ed. Bohatec (Leipzig, 1909), 339ff.; A. Lang, *Der Evangelienkommentar Martin Bucers* (Leipzig, 1900), 365. On the centrality of meditation on the future life cf. M. Schulze, *Meditatio futurae vitae* (Leipzig, 1901).

48. Wernle, *Glaube,* Preface, iii, who notes Calvin's increasing encapsulating of his faith in a system of biblical theology, and his own desire to draw it out again.

of melancholy irritation about this zeal that we do not find in Zwingli. He has become almost wholly a man of the OT, a Jeremiah. There is nothing wooing, inviting, or winning here. It is almost all proclamation, promise, threat, either-or. His is truly a consuming zeal. Calvin is not what we usually imagine an apostle of love and peace to be. If what he represents is love and peace, then these things must be very different from what we think. What we find is a hard and prickly skin. The blossom has gone, the fruit has not yet come. An iron age has come that calls for iron believers. To have dealings with God one must be fully in earnest. God overtook Calvin like a robber — remember how at the decisive hour G. Farel kept him in Geneva by threatening him with the curse of God.[49] The strong and jealous God wanted him totally. His signet ring depicted a heart lying in an open hand. His motto was: "My heart I offer as though slain in sacrifice to God."[50] The seriousness that was alive in this man and that emanated from him was a bitter and almost unbearable seriousness. But recall how earnestly Luther described the point at which the path opens up to God as desperation, humility, fear of God.[51] In what Calvin thought and said we have the path that leads from God. Are we really surprised that he immediately and powerfully fixed on the same point? Could he really be a different person from the one he was?

Calvin's God is the Lord, and to go with God he had to be God's servant. God's will is a will for power; therefore obedience to it is a will for subjection. What is manifest in Christ, too, is the royal dominion of God. If we are God's children in Christ, we have to know what we must do. If God has glorified himself in us, and caused us to be what we are, then there is no point in asking what is the meaning of what we are. This was Calvin's response to the question of the Lutheran Reformation regarding what has to be done in time, in this world, in life, in the secular sphere. Could he have given any other answer? But his God is also the Lord in the sense that the grace with which he calls us is itself a sovereign act. In a way that we can never fathom God is majesty, freedom, supreme over every human yes and no. Those who are obedient should never forget for a moment that they are not the recipients of grace because they are

49. Marginal note "31, 26!"; cf. CO 31, 13ff.

50. Cf. Calvin's letter to Farel dated 10.24.1540 in CO 11, 100; also Henry, I, 379f.; and for a copy of the seal cf. E. Doumergue, *Jean Calvin,* vol. I (Lausanne and Neuilly, 1899), 569.

51. See above, 44, 46.

obedient, but obedient because they are the recipients of grace. They may and must obey, but they have no rights because they do so. Rights are God's alone. Those who are obedient might have been condemned to disobedience. That is the heart of Calvin's doctrine of predestination. We may debate whether his concept came to him from Duns Scotus or from Luther by way of Bucer. We can be sure, however, of his primary interest in this view of God. He experienced too many human errors and weaknesses and defeats even in those who were supposedly obedient not to have an urgent concern for the safeguarding of the purity of the origin of all obedience, the divine character of grace, against every confusion with our own actions that are always so questionable. Just because Calvin was so much an ethicist, he had to be such a strong dogmatician. His own Reformed, ethical reformation had to raise the question what we are to think of that which actually takes place in time, in the world, in life. His concept of God, which at once puts another great question mark after all human action as soon as it takes place, was Calvin's own answer. This concept shows us how sharp was the criticism under which he placed himself and his own primary thrust. Neither a religious admiration of his individual genius nor a doctrinaire approach can help us at all precisely at this central point in explanation of Calvin.

In this context I might say a provisional word about the distinctiveness of Calvin's theology. I noted earlier, and it is also an implication of what I was just saying, that I regard his concept of God, insofar as it is characterized by the doctrine of predestination, as a return to Luther for the sake of safeguarding his own ethical thrust, though in the process the Lutheran concept acquired a certain frenetic sharpness that we see only rarely in Luther himself, above all in his *Bondage of the Will*.[52] If, as so often happens, we find the distinctive feature of Calvin in his concept of God as it is characterized by the doctrine of predestination, the thesis suggests itself that his theology is simply a new edition of Luther's with a greater stress on ethics. Apparently supporting this view is the fact that Calvin almost always spoke of Luther in grateful recognition while often to some extent disparaging Zwingli.[53] But perhaps we should not attach basic significance to such personal sympathies and antipathies, which in

52. WA 18, 600-787 (1525).
53. Cf. Calvin to Bullinger, 11.25.1544 (no. 586), CO 11, 774; to Farel 2.26.1540 (no. 211), CO 11, 24; and *The Second Defence against the Calumnies of Joachim Westphal* (1556), CO 9, 51.

any case find expression, so far as I know, only in his letters. Especially in relation to Zwingli I would hazard the guess that what instinctively offended the aristocratic Calvin was simply the brash, bombastic, even rather vulgar element in him. The two shared the same starting point in contrast to Luther. What we have just said cannot alter this fact.

As I see it, the idea that Calvin's theology is deutero-Lutheran will not hold because it fails to see that the doctrine of predestination in Calvin's concept of God was only one characteristic feature, and in view of its position in the *Institutes* it was simply a second feature that is dealt with only in book III as a corrective designed to emphasize and strengthen the doctrine of justification. The first feature of Calvin's concept of God is the thought of his divine sovereignty, which we also find, of course, in Luther, but not at any rate in the primary way in which it was at once for Calvin the basis of the relation between Lord and servant, the ethical relation between God and us. It is here in the first feature that we find that which is common to the starting points of Calvin and Zwingli. It is not, so far as I can see, that Calvin took over Zwingli's approach directly, just as we cannot prove that he took over Luther's concept of predestination directly. Why should he not have arrived at both independently, since they were both so important and necessary to him in his own context? It is true that the two concepts were not first thought out by him. Luther was the first to advance the thought of justification by faith alone, and Zwingli was the first, resolutely at least, to advance that of the indirect identity of faith and obedience. Clearly in view of Calvin's relation to his predecessors, Dilthey allowed himself to call Calvin a powerful but not a creative thinker.[54] The question arises, however, whether we should not regard the way in which Calvin combined the two thoughts as itself very creative.

But however that may be, it is obvious that as regards originality Calvin stands most improbably in the middle between the pure types, Luther and Zwingli. These two had in fact exhausted the two great possibilities of the Reformation. Only the possibility of synthesis remained. Synthesis, or union in the serious sense of the term, was the original contribution of Calvin. In keeping with the situation of conflict in the later Reformation period he built a structure that was open to fellow believers on both sides. Synthesis is not possible without renunciation. That meant forgoing any further new possibilities. It meant the end of reformation. To have made this act of renunciation was Calvin's theological

54. Dilthey, "Das natürliche System," 229.

greatness. Undoubtedly connected with this is the fact that his writings and sermons do not, when we read them, make anything like the direct impression of spirit and life that those of Luther particularly do. If we look at this Frenchman for what one might call *esprit* or *pointe* we will be disappointed. His originality is for the most part not one of detail. If we do not see it blazing across the whole, we will not see it at all. Present here is something of the renunciation that characterizes his whole life's work. It is part of his tragedy, a necessity.

Calvin was a man over whose vitality a deep shadow lay. He himself also cast the same deep shadow over the vitality of others. Over his whole life and works we might inscribe the saying in John's Gospel: "He must increase, but I must decrease" [3:30]. For undoubtedly this deep shadow is the same as his knowledge of God. What did that knowledge mean for him but obedience? And what did obedience mean but subjection, order, discipline, to which the lively and colorful movement of natural life had to adjust itself? "Man is something that has to be overcome" (Nietzsche).[55] Thus Calvin as a man became an ascetic, not to gain merit like the usual ascetic, but simply for the sake of his ministry, for how can one give God the glory without strictly disciplining oneself? As a Christian, then, he became involved in politics and organization, not because he had any natural desire for such things — he would rather have become and remained a quiet scholar — but how could he be a Christian without cooperating in the building up of the community of God which to the glory of him who has called it shapes its life according to his commandments in things both small and great, both inward and outward? Hence again, as a theologian, he became a systematician, surely not by inclination, for by inclination he would rather have been a historian, but how can we think and speak about God as we should so long as caprice reigns, so long as a comprehensive survey has not found out of the fullness of the possible that which is true and valid, and given it a self-contained structure?

I need hardly point out how closely this tendency in Calvin is related to the total historical situation of Protestantism between 1525 and 1555. *This* flame was what was needed now. The older Luther could not be this flame, even less so Melanchthon. Zwingli was dead and might never have blazed up in this way. Calvin *was* the flame. But the flame necessarily consumed even as it flared up. Not without penalty does one become an

---

55. F. Nietzsche, *Thus Spake Zarathustra* (1883-84); cf. *Werke*, vol. II, ed. K. Schlechta (Munich, 6th ed. 1969), 321.

ascetic, organizer, or systematician. A man of this kind is the first to feel the pressure he brings to bear on others, and it weighs heaviest on himself. Look at portraits of Luther and Calvin together, and you will see what I mean. Are we not tempted to think that it was no accident that all his life Calvin was a sick man, and that at the end he was visited by a whole series of serious illnesses?[56] This man could not be healthy. It was as if God in all his holiness stood between him and what we call a happy life, taking from him all that is visible in order to be able to give him all that is invisible.[57]

He had much the same impact on others. The constraint and threat under which he stood worked as such on those who witnessed this life. On his deathbed he said of the people of Bern that they always feared him more than they loved him.[58] But this was true not only of the people of Bern. After his death the secretary of the Genevan council wrote of him that God had impressed upon him a character of so great a majesty (Staehelin, II, 372).[59] Among all the tributes of admiration and respect that have been heaped on Calvin I know of none more profound or powerful, but also more disquieting. Majesty as a human quality! How much else, how much that is beautiful, or worthy of love, or prized by all of us, has to be lacking or given up or sacrificed for matters to be thus and this impression to be left! But again, could we think in any other way of the last reformer, the man of the late Reformation summer?

Calvin became a moralist. I intentionally say moralist and not just ethicist. The way in which he put his thoughts into practice in Geneva leaves us in no doubt that the first of the two terms is appropriate here. Certainly Calvin preached God and grace and faith, and did so unambiguously. Before God we have no righteousness, no moral righteousness either, only unrighteousness, and then either mercy or eternal perdition. But once his glance leaves this height of knowledge to fall on us — and

56. On Calvin's health and illnesses cf. his letter to the Montpellier doctors, 2.8.1564, CO 20, 252-54.

57. Marginal note: "21, 44!" In CO 21, 21-50, we find Beza's account of Calvin's life. Barth in his copy at col. 44 underlined the saying of Calvin to Beza: "Lord, you pound me, but it is enough for me that it is your hand."

58. *Discours d'adieu aux ministres* (1564), OS II, 404, 6f., with a probable reference to Bern.

59. Stähelin gives as the source of this the council minutes, but it does not occur there in CO 21. For a slightly different version cf. E. Choisy, *L'état chrétien calviniste à Genève . . .* (Geneva, 1902), 9.

it is distinctive of the Reformed to look from the height of God directly at us — nothing remains but a *moral* outlook and accusation and demand. In Calvin, as we see from his sermons, even the proclamation of grace wears a moral garb. *This* is what we have to hear and understand and take to heart and believe. For Calvin divine service was a parade ground on which imperatives held sway in every relation. We cannot really learn to know the details of the Genevan system that is so much admired without words like "tyranny" and "Pharisaism" coming almost naturally to our lips. No one who has proper information would really have liked to live in this holy city. But that simply shows that we do not live in a time of Reformation conflict, or in a time of Reformation at all. Without the severity of "Thou shalt" there would never have been a Reformation nor will there ever be again.

It is part of being a prophet — look where we will — to be at least very close to tyranny and Pharisaism. Prophets who want to translate their visions into reality — and those who did not want this in some way would not be genuine prophets — will usually end up, unless they meet an early heroic death like Zwingli, perhaps as tyrants and Pharisees, but at least as moralists. The logically necessary end of the historical path from Luther to Zwingli and Zwingli to Calvin was Calvin's Geneva, just as the logically necessary end of the path from Moses to the prophets and the prophets to Judaism was the synagogue. Who would have the boldness to argue that this historical path of the Reformation did not have to be taken and trodden to the very end? There is no standing still in history, not even at points like Luther's Wittenberg tower experience, at which one might say to the moment: "Please linger, you are so beautiful."[60] Or was the worldly post-Lutheran Wittenberg with its carousing in the shadow of the forgiveness of sins the legitimate outcome of the Reformation? Certainly it was a shattering tragedy that the triumphant establishment of Calvin's ordinances should be the necessary and legitimate outcome of what Hutten and Albrecht Dürer had once hailed as the dawn of a new human day.[61]

---

60. Cf. Goethe's *Faust*, I, 1700.

61. Cf. Hutten's letter to W. Pirkheimer, 10.25.1528, in *Ulrich von Huttens Schriften*, vol. I, ed. E. Böcking (Leipzig, 1859), 217. No similar saying of Dürer is known, but cf. Dilthey's "Auffassung und Analyse des Menschen im 15. und 16. Jahrhundert," in *Weltanschauung und Analyse des Menschen seit Renaissance und Reformation*, vol. II of *Gesammelte Schriften* (Leipzig and Berlin, 1914), 51. For a saying of Erasmus like that of Hutten cf. J. Huizinga, *Herbst des Mittelalters . . .* (Stuttgart, 1938), 39f.; and cf. Schwenckfeld above.

But we can wish this tragic conclusion away only if we do not see that the true goal of all such historical paths lies on the far side of historical reality, so that the end of all such *historical* paths cannot be anything other than tragic, cannot have any other meaning than that of a return to the beginning, and beyond the beginning to the origin and goal that within the human and historical and temporal are always and everywhere the concealed meaning and purpose of all such paths. If we see that, then we will certainly not want to varnish over or glorify Calvin's parade ground, but we can integrate it into the peaceful work of a truly historical view that reckons with the ultimate things and can thus bear it that here and now we encounter only penultimate things. In that case we cannot avoid admitting that in spite of the not unjustified charge of tyranny and Pharisaism this end to the Reformation had its own greatness and worth as compared to other possibilities.

Calvin dealt rather harshly with those who opposed his thoughts and plans, which he equated with the cause of God. In this regard we do not find the coarseness of a Luther in his writings, but we do find a wholly distinctive sourness and bitterness that give us some idea of what it meant to be harried by him, when once recognized as an enemy, until he had finally made an end either one way or another. We cannot excuse this side of his nature by pointing out how loving and sensitive he was with his friends and with all who were favorable to him. This fact was of little help to a Servetus or a Bolsec or a Castellio. We have to say, however, that Calvin's severity was closely related to the historical situation at the end of the Reformation. Calvin was confronted by Ignatius Loyola, the Spanish Inquisition, and the Council of Trent. In his beleaguered fortress suspicion was rightly or wrongly rife. In the evil 1540s even Luther, as we know, lost for the most part his urbanity and sociability.

Calvin's severity was also linked — and this is the main point — to the great saving or destroying either-or that hung like a sword of Damocles over humanity and over every individual, and that for him resulted directly from the knowledge of God, a thought whose critical significance he felt like no other reformer, and perhaps like no one at all until we come to Kierkegaard, in whom we find the same severity. May I remind you again of the opening of the Geneva Catechism, which tells us expressly that those who do not glorify God in their lives have sunk to the level of the beasts.[62] Those who saw the value and meaning of human life in this way

62. Cf. above, 76; and OS II, 75, 10ff.; BSRK 117, 15-17.

were engaged in an existential conflict of which they were themselves truly the first and most suffering of victims, but the horrors of which they did not think they could spare others. Calvin was not giving way to passion when even in his Bible commentaries he at once spoke of dogs and swine if he saw the sanctuary of truth violated.[63] It was instead his calm and well-considered view that those who did such things did not deserve to be called human. On one occasion (Staehelin, II, 377f.) he solemnly protested that it was not out of personal hatred that he dealt with his opponents as he did.[64] Even allowing for every possibility of self-deception, why should we not just as well believe him as not believe him? But he thought — and this is connected with the unity he saw between being a child of God and a servant of God — that he might and should be angry on the basis of God's own anger. In the short sketch of his life in the preface to his commentary on the Psalms he saw himself in the situation of King David, the type of Jesus Christ, who was constantly burdened with wars against the Philistines and other foreign peoples, but who was even more harassed by the disloyal among his own people. Hardly had he achieved rest before he had to endure another conflict.[65] And almost always the battles were for that which was for him highest, for the totality. When it was a matter of the glory of God and his truth, he would rather be enraged than not, lest the dishonor staining the divine majesty should fall back on his own head. That was what he said in his fight against Castellio (381).[66] Referring again to his anger later, he said that it was as if he could do no other, as if he were caught up by a whirlwind (383).[67]

We cannot ignore the fact that in such claims, and in the reality behind them, we reach and perhaps pass over the frontier that separates the divine from the demonic. Calvin himself was aware of this frontier and would often at least to some degree restrain himself. We may draw too close to the fire of God from which the average person is too distant. When that happens, what is holy turns into what is definitely unholy. At this point the word "tragedy" suggests itself again, and we must remember

---

63. On Ps. 10:16, CO 31, 119.

64. Calvin to N. Zurkinden, 7.4.1558, no. 2908, CO 17, 235f.; and Stähelin, II, 381f.

65. CO 31, 27.

66. Calvin to Zurkinden, February 1559, no. 3023, CO 17, 466. Barth quotes from Stähelin, II, 381.

67. A 1556 letter, no. 2573, CO 16, 369, quoted from Stähelin, II, 383.

that there is no tragedy without guilt. But for all our sympathies with the unhappy victims of this elemental event, we are called to be judges of Calvin only if we, too, consciously stand in the great crisis in which he stood day and night, and if in this crisis we show more humanity than he actually did. Those who live with smaller views of a smaller cause than Calvin's really find it much easier to be less severe than he was.

As a final point I would mention the decided orientation to the next world that governs all Calvin's life and work. No reformer was more strongly shaped than he was by the antithesis of time and eternity. For him, what we may be and have as Christians was promise and no more. Those who really have the promise have the gift of the Holy Spirit; they have all that we can have here and now. And for him this having was wholly and utterly expectation and no more. The saved are those who stand in this expectation and who, expecting, are obedient servants. It is at this point that we find Calvin's distinctive christology and eucharistic teaching in which Christ, not omnipresent but enthroned at God's right hand in heaven, is present to his own by the unheard-of miracle of the Holy Spirit in faith, a sign and pledge that is visible to faith. We cannot possibly explain this teaching in terms of the secondary need to mediate between Luther and Zwingli. We find expressed in it an original concern that we find everywhere in Calvin, a concern for the distance that true fellowship between God and us involves. This concern explains why Calvin confronted the whole colorful world of phenomena with such remarkable and painfully serious restraint. Whenever he spoke about the world and humanity as they are, he at once turned with an almost audible jerk to that which is before and above all creation.

Reference has been made to his asceticism in the world, to his pessimism.[68] In him we find as little of the supposedly French joy in the concrete and real as we do of the French *esprit,* so that Bauke's idea of the decisive significance of the fact that he was French seems as little illuminating from this angle as from the other.[69] Thus far I have been able to discover, along with theology, church, and state, only one field in which with some forgetfulness of self Calvin displayed an affectionate material

68. Cf. M. Weber, *Die protestantische Ethik und der Geist des Kapitalismus,* vol. I of *Gesammelte Aufsätze zur Religionssoziologie* (Tübingen, 2nd ed. 1922), 118, where Weber argues that Calvin's asceticism differs from that of the Middle Ages by dropping the evangelical counsels and coming into the world.

interest. That, strangely enough, was everything connected with astronomy and meteorology, a field that by its nature was adapted to serve as a parable at least of his great "Lift up your hearts."[70] We have to search his works with a magnifying glass to find any traces that he could laugh. He did not play the lute like Luther and Zwingli. He once took a modest six-day vacation in the environs of Geneva. He liked to play with house keys in what is described as a rather doleful way. But these seem to have been his only pleasures.[71] He apparently saw little of the aesthetic charm of Lake Geneva over which his windows looked. He was totally devoted to his cause. He resembled very closely one who was spiritually akin to him in the Middle Ages, Bernard of Clairvaux, who once rode the whole length of Lake Geneva without being able to remember that he had seen it.[72] To this day Reformed Protestantism has not been able totally to rid itself of this dedication. It will not and should not. Yet we are surprised.

We may well ask why there was this turning *from* the world when the Reformation became Reformed and sought to turn *to* the world. We will try once again to apply our double principle of explanation. When Calvin looked back on his decisive years, he finally saw the burnings under Francis I in Paris. Throughout his life his daily thought was to care for the persecuted, for those languishing in prison or the galleys, for those anywhere in the world who for the sake of the gospel were threatened with death or were the victims of it. He was also concerned for the pressure and threat under which the cause of God itself stood. Calvin felt that he had a part in all this, that he bore responsibility. No other reformer felt the burden of responsibility so keenly. Can we be surprised, then, that he could not live lightly; that he quantitatively restricted his attention to and affection for this-worldly things; that he concentrated all his energies on the minutest point, for theology is indeed the most minute of this-worldly things; that he found in looking at eternity not only the comfort but also the courage to work and not despair[73] in evil days? Yes, that is how it is

69. Bauke, *Probleme*, 14.

70. On Gen. 1:16 (1560), CO 23, 22; also *Advertissement contre l'Astrologie qu'on appelle judicaire . . .* (1549), CO 7, 513ff.; and on meteorology, CO 38, 78, on Jer. 10:13 (1563), and CO 28, 376, on Deut. 28:12a. Barth refers here to the eucharistic *Sursum corda* to denote a main concern of Calvin; cf. his *La Forme des Prières et Chantz ecclesiastiques* of 1542, CO II, 48, 24-32; cf. *Tracts and Treatises*, II, 121f.

71. Stähelin, II, 402, and the whole section 393ff.

72. Ibid., 397f.

73. The familiar title of a Carlyle selection by K. R. Langewiesche (Düsseldorf,

when a person really turns from God to the world in order to understand the world in relation to God, and to win it for him. Basically at least there will then usually be that jettisoning and disparaging of this-worldly things. For there can be no understanding or winning of the world without an overcoming of the world, and no overcoming of the world without abstinence from the world.

The point of asceticism, of the attempt to win freedom from the world, is the attainment of the assessing and shaping and controlling of the world that this freedom alone makes possible. Already in the Middle Ages this necessary link had brought two apparent antitheses, the papacy and monasticism, into alliance. Precisely in Platonism, too, we find the strictest turning aside from the world of sense, and even a death wisdom,[74] alongside the world-affirming founding of logics and ethics. And beyond both monasticism and Platonism we find in primitive Christianity a link between eschatology and ethics by which both take on the significance that we find again in Calvin. Whether and how far there is a direct relation between Calvin and the contemporary Humanism, to which yearning for eternity and the thought of eternity were by no means alien, is a separate question. We need not assume this, for the decisive juncture at which the power of the next world becomes the power of this world[75] lies in truth along the line of Christianity's own logic. This logic reached a climax in the theology of Calvin. It need not astonish us that meditation on the future life crowns and defines this theology. With the doctrine of predestination this is the basis of Calvin's ethos that protects its authenticity and secures it against the danger of superficiality which threatens every ethos. It is not a foreign body in Calvinistic teaching. It is the true whence and whither of its way.

1902): *Arbeiten und nicht verzweifeln,* based on the last sentence of Carlyle's rectoral address at Edinburgh in 1866, in which he quoted from Goethe's *Symbolum,* using "work and despair not" for the original: "Wir heissen euch hoffen." Cf. T. Carlyle, *Critical and Miscellaneous Essays,* vol. IV (London, 1899), 481f.

74. Barth took the term "death wisdom" from F. Overbeck, *Christentum und Kultur . . .,* ed. C. A. Bernoulli (Basel, 1919), 2379; cf. his *Epistle to the Romans* (Oxford, 1933), 424ff.

75. See 73, n. 6 above.

PART II

LIFE OF CALVIN

Cf. the autobiography in the preface to the *Commentary on the Psalms,*
1556 (31, 13f.), especially the passages on his conversion, his meeting with
Farel, and his struggles; Beza, preface to Calvin's *Joshua Commentary*
(1564); Beza's *Panegyrikus,* a loyal but not very critical account that gives
factual material.[1] As a living portrait it may well be more historical than
an objective account by a nonparticipant. Nicolas Calladon (1565) am-
plifies Beza.[2] Beza wrote a Latin *Vita* in 1575.[3] For all three of these cf.
21, 21ff. New biographies: P. Henry, 3 vols. (1835-1844); and E. Staehelin, 2 vols. (1863).[4] Both are erudite, sympathetic, and anxious to set
forth the Reformed side so as to do justice to Reformed reformers who
are often overshadowed by Luther, but in my view they are more valuable
as collections of materials and too edifying to be instructive, Staehelin

1. For the preface to the commentary on Psalms, see CO 31, 13-36; for the preface
to the Joshua commentary, 22, 21-50. By *Panegyrikus* Barth is probably referring to the
editors' preface in CR: *Notice Littéraire,* CO 21, 9f., which notes the inadequacy of Beza's
panegyric and the need for a more detailed and methodical account.

2. CO 21, 51-118. Colladon was a pastor at Geneva from 1553 onward and in
1564 succeeded Calvin as a professor at the academy. He came from a French refugee
family. See M. Haag, *La France protestante,* vol. IV (Paris, 1853), 4f.

3. CO 21, 119-72.

4. P. Henry, *Das Leben Johann Calvins des grossen Reformators,* 3 vols. (Hamburg,
1835-1844); E. Stähelin, *Johannes Calvins Leben und ausgewählte Schriften,* 2 vols. (Elberfeld, 1863).

being much superior. Kampschulte, 2 vols. (1869 and 1899),[5] is nonsympathetic, stresses the objections against Calvin too much, but is a corrective to the former two and should be consulted but not made determinative. E. Doumergue, 5 vols., folio (1899-1917),[6] is probably the best of all Calvin scholars; he searches the ground thoroughly and does a good job, though inclined to try to justify Calvin through thick and thin, so that he does not finally help us to understand, being so much the pupil who reproduces the teacher. For short accounts cf. A. Bossert (1908) in Krollick's translation; A. Lang (1909); G. Bayer, a popular but well-documented and vivid presentation, in which the author tells us on p. 1 that if he were not a Lutheran he would like to be Reformed; K. Holl (1909); F. Barth, *Calvins Persönlichkeit* (1909); and Schwarz, *Calvins Lebenswerk in seinen Briefen* (1909).[7]

I have not found an account that combines the thorough knowledge of Doumergue, the sympathy of Staehelin, and the critical glance of Kampschulte, and that also so profoundly grasps the historical and principial contexts of the Reformation as to be able to treat them with detachment. But that is perhaps a combination of qualities that is beyond our human capabilities, so that we should be glad to have at least the parts in the works cited, with here and there at least a glance at the whole.[8] But now to work.

If in the course of these lectures I try to take a look at the life of our hero, it is not because this is something that for the sake of completeness we should not omit. From the two preceding sections on the Reformation and the Middle Ages and the interrelations of the three main reformers

---

5. F. W. Kampschulte, *Johannes Calvin: Seine Kirche und sein Staat in Genf,* 2 vols. (Leipzig, 1869-1899).

6. E. Doumergue, *Jean Calvin . . .,* 7 vols. (Lausanne and Neuilly, 1899-1927; vol. VI, 1926; vol. VII, 1927).

7. A. Bossert, *Calvin* (Paris, 1906); German translation by Krollick (Giessen, 1908); A. Lang, *Johannes Calvin . . .* (Leipzig, 1909) (Schriften des Vereins für Reformationsgeschichte 99); G. Bayer, *Johannes Calvin . . .* (Neukirchen, 1909); K. Holl, *Calvin,* an address in Berlin in commemoration of Calvin's birthday 400 years before, delivered on 7.10.1909; reprinted in expanded form and with notes (Tübingen, 1909); then in *Gesammelte Aufsätze zur Kirchengeschichte,* vol. III (Tübingen, 1928), 254-84; F. Barth, *Calvins Persönlichkeit . . .,* a commemorative address (Bern, 1909); *Johannes Calvins Lebenswerk in seinen Briefen,* a selection in German translation by R. Schwarz with an introduction by P. Wernle, 2 vols. (Tübingen, 1909); new ed. with introduction by O. Weber, 3 vols. (Neukirchen, 1960).

8. Cf. Goethe's *Faust,* I, vv. 1936-39.

you will have gathered that my chief concern in the whole enterprise is to see the inner and outer connections and the place of intersection on the historical and principial line on which Calvin stood. If we could see these contexts exactly, infinitely more so than we have succeeded or can ever succeed in doing, then in my view we could at once see the subject of our study and no further special examination would have to be devoted to it. In viewing the contexts we arrive at what I call our presuppositions. By this I do not simply mean preparatory materials but prolegomena in Kant's sense, and therefore ideally the whole.[9] If we still have to look at Calvin's theology as a special second theme after the presuppositions, this is more for the hardness of our hearts [cf. Matt. 19:8] than for any other reason.

We now come to the third and most inward circle of these presuppositions, Calvin's life. In its own way this life is also, or ought to be, the whole of his theology. As I said yesterday, we cannot separate the man and the theologian if we are dealing with an important person, a theologian who has to be taken seriously. Those who achieve a full grasp of his life cannot fail to see that here was a man who preached, who expounded the Bible, who engaged in polemics, and who had to shape in a particular way his doctrines of the Lord's Supper, predestination, and justification. My own father in his lectures on Calvin used to give no more than an explicit and vivid account of his life from beginning to end, and we finally saw something of Calvin's theology even though there were only incidental references to it.[10] I regard that path as more artistic and more pertinent to the theme than the one we ourselves are taking. To repeat what I said yesterday, the nature of historical understanding consists of insight into the necessity imposed by that double context. Yet I do not trust myself to be able to tread such a path consistently, and so I choose a more broken method. Equipment is needed for the first method that I do not even remotely have. Yet I would ask you to note that in the arrangement of our main material into preaching, exegesis, polemics, and system, we have a pointer at least to the biographical link and therefore to the ideal of a historical presentation. If this pointer leads you to a consideration from eternal and temporal angles at the same time, then you have perhaps gained the very best that I can give you apart from what Calvin himself gives.

9. Cf. Kant's *Prolegomena to a Future Metaphysics* (New York, 1950), 22f.

10. Fritz Barth, Barth's father, taught church history at Bern University from 1899 to his death in 1912. He does not seem to have taught a special course on Calvin but frequently lectured on Reformation history in general.

I see no reason to divide up Calvin's life in any way but the traditional one: (1) The beginnings to the arrival in Geneva, 1509-1536; (2) the first stay in Geneva, 1538-1541; (3) the Strassburg period, 1538-1541; (4) the years of conflict in Geneva, 1541-1555; (5) the victory and final years to Calvin's death, 1555-1564. If thus far we have rightly fixed the place where Calvin stood, our true theme of the story that we shall now sketch must be his distinctive *will*, how it was formed in the first period, made a first beginning in the second, was inwardly confirmed in the third, wrestled through defeat to victory in the fourth, and finally prevailed and came to full expression in the fifth. You know already that I finally view the whole of this extraordinary self-contained and complete and heroically successful life as a tragedy, as I do all else in history. I will not repeat that verdict at detailed points.

3

Early Years, 1509-1536[1]

§7 Introduction

Calvin's father, Gerhard Cauvin, of Pont d'Evêque, had risen from humble origins — his own father had worked on riverboats — to become a well-situated middle-class lawyer who acted as financial counsel to the bishop of Noyon in Picardy (the ancient Noviodunum) and also to the cathedral chapter, which was often in conflict with the bishop. From all that we know, his relation to the church as represented by his clients was a purely objective and financial one. His educational ambitions for his children were also primarily practical. He had his second son, the later reformer (born July 9,[2] 1509), first study theology, and made it possible for him to do this by securing for him when he was only 14 years of age, first a quarter share in a benefice, then a whole benefice (i.e., its income). Later, when he had fallen out with his clerical clients, he unhesitatingly transferred Calvin to the study of law as a better means to bring him to wealth and fame. It made little difference. The church was a worldly possibility like any other. Things really were different with Calvin's mother Jeanne, née Lefranc, who had brought a dowry to her husband. Though of no special intellectual gifts or maternal qualities, she seems to have been fairly devout and even bigoted, zealously hauling off her children to prayer, to church, to processions, to the revering of relics, and the like.

1. This heading is in the margin of the MS.
2. In the biographies of Calvin listed by Barth, and in more recent works, July 10 is given as the date of Calvin's birth.

It is not irrelevant to note that the atmosphere in which Calvin, unlike Luther or Zwingli, was reared was that of a middle-class and in particular a lawyer's home. The sober way, free from every illusion, in which the middle stratum of society usually views human things would later distinguish Calvin, too. We also note that the form in which he met the church in his youth was not, as especially in Luther's case, that of titanic asceticism or works righteousness, but the very opposite. In his father's profession he saw the dubious secular and economic side, and in his mother's piety a superstitious deification of the creaturely. It was natural that his opposition to this church would develop primarily on the ethical side in the broadest sense. Calvin was well aware why later he had such zeal for the glory of God. He had seen something of the dishonor that God suffered at the hands of Christians.

The very best things that Calvin owed to his parents' home derived from the prudent concern of his father to secure early on a good education for his children. The second son received this first in a kind of local private school at which he excelled for his talents and industry, then in the house of the noble family of de Montmor along with the sons of the family. The rather aristocratic side of his nature was first enhanced here. Later he had a surprising number of noble and even princely friends and correspondents. The path from the working class to the middle class and then to the upper class that his own family had trodden in three generations was in fact a natural one that could easily be traversed.

With means provided by those early ecclesiastical positions, and with a tonsure signifying at least his imaginary spiritual dignity, the boy went in 1523 to the Collège Lamarche in Paris to prepare for the university. His honored teacher there was Mathurin Cordier, a first-class innovator in the teaching of Latin, but also a fine educator at the personal and moral level. In 1550 Calvin gratefully dedicated to him his commentary on 1 Thessalonians.[3] For reasons that are not wholly clear he then moved on to the Collège Montaigu, at which not only late scholastic dialectic but also the whip and other nonpedagogic brutalities held sway. As Bossert notes, however, good students can gain profit for themselves even from poor methods, and Calvin learned the art of verbal warfare that would later be one of his main strengths (18). This was probably the time when the serious, all too serious, young man earned from his fellow students the

3. Bossert, 16, tells us the dedication was to Cordier. For the dedicatory epistle of 2.17.1550 cf. CO 13, 525f.

nickname of *accusativus* or accuser.[4] Recall what I said yesterday about Pharisaism. When Calvin left the Collège Montaigu at the end of 1527 or the beginning of 1528, another promising student enrolled, Ignatius Loyola. So closely enmeshed things often are spatially![5]

Already during these student days Calvin must have been in touch with thoughts of Reformation, or at any rate reform. When he had come to Paris in 1523, the great battle that pitted Lefèvre d'Etaples, whom we have mentioned more than once already and who was supported by all the Humanist groups and at that time by Francis I and his court, against the Sorbonne, the high seat of Scholasticism, which was supported by the Parlement, had reached a climax. The occasion was the declaration by the Sorbonne that Lefèvre was guilty of heresy in his historical thesis that the NT speaks of three different Magdalenes, whereas in the liturgy Mary Magdalene, Mary the sister of Lazarus, and the sinner who anointed the Lord's feet are supposedly one and the same person.[6] Profound differences were concealed behind this strange problem: grace or works righteousness, scripture or human decrees, faith or automatic efficacy, all stirred up to some degree by the Lutheran Reformation in Germany. Melanchthon in fact entered the Parisian debate directly with a polemical work against the Sorbonne.[7] It is quite impossible that so alert a man as the young Calvin should not have had an inner part in these controversies. It so happened that a relative, Peter Robert, known as Olivetanus (or Olevian),[8] stood alongside Lefèvre as one of the most stalwart and religiously most zealous champions of Humanistic biblicism in Paris. This man apparently drew Calvin's attention to the Bible. With what result? Who was John Calvin, and where did he stand, when, obedient to his father's wishes, he left Paris in 1527 and moved to Orléans?

It is Calvin himself who at this point in his career tosses to historians

4. Cf. Kampschulte, I, 225 n. 1. But the source is unsubstantiated Counter-Reformation polemic. Cf. E. Pfisterer, *Calvins Wirken in Genf* (Neukirchen, 1955), 111ff., on Calvin as *Accusativus.*

5. Cf. F. Schiller, *Wallensteins Tod,* act II, scene 2, 789.

6. Cf. Doumergue, I, 91-93; and Bossert, 19f.

7. Barth is obviously referring to the work of Melanchthon mentioned by Doumergue, I, 91ff., and Bossert, 20, though Melanchthon, of course, was not concerned about the debate as to the number of Magdalenes but was opposing the Sorbonne's attack on Luther.

8. Olivetanus (ca. 1506-1538) is best known for his translation of the Bible into French, for which Calvin wrote a preface. C. Olevian (1536-1587) was a Reformed theologian who had a hand in writing the Heidelberg Catechism.

a bone of fierce contention. In the little autobiography to his commentary on the Psalms (31, 22), directly after mentioning his transfer from philosophy to law, with which the account begins, he goes on to say that he was then so obstinately addicted to papal superstition that it was hard for him to draw himself up out of the deep slime, but that he (God), by a sudden conversion, brought his heart to obedience even though, considering his youth, it had already been truly hardened. As, then, he received a certain taste for true piety ("goût et cognaissance de la vraie piété"), he was set on fire to continue this study, even though he did not abandon his other studies, if now with less interest.[9] He then goes on to tell how he would much rather have had isolation and rest even though he was the leader and center of a whole group of like-minded people.

What does all this mean? When are we to date the sudden conversion? Doumergue[10] and Holl put it in 1527/28. In favor of their view — I am following Holl[11] — it is argued that in 1542 Calvin said he had come to know only the earlier works of Zwingli. Why only the earlier works? Because Zwingli was still alive, his later works had not yet come out, hence the end of the 1520s. Again, in 1538 Calvin was accused of ingratitude to the Catholic church whose education he had enjoyed for fifteen years and more. Adding eighteen to 1509 brings us to 1527. Again, the passage in the Psalms commentary refers plainly to a once-for-all break in Calvin's religious development. Again, Calvin later argued so strongly against following the example of Nicodemus, against a concealed Protestantism, that it is unthinkable that he was himself a secret believer from 1527 or so to 1533. Again, Calvin's reference to his great hardness considering his years makes sense only if he was really young at the time, that is, 17 or 18. Again, in the commentary on Seneca,[12] which was published in 1532, and in which the absence of any new religious thoughts, or any religious thoughts at all, is a main argument for the other side, we must know how to read between the lines to find traces of the sudden conversion. Finally, the fact that in 1533 Calvin was at a chapter meeting in Noyon, and gave up his benefice only in 1534, may very well be explained

9. CO 31, 21.

10. Doumergue, I, 327-55.

11. See Holl, 37-44 n. 1 (255-59 n. 1), for a discussion, with references, of Calvin's conversion. Also see n. 7 above for first and expanded editions of Holl.

12. CO 5, 1ff.: *L. Annei Senecae* . . . (Paris, 1532).

by a certain broadness of outlook and the hopes that he might still have had for the church.

The other view, advocated by Staehelin, K. Müller, Wernle, and Lang,[13] dates the conversion to early 1533. The basis of this view is that there is little evidence that real Protestant influences might have affected Calvin in any dramatic way in his early years. Again, why did not the alleged change manifest itself in the young man's life from 1528 to 1533? Why did he write his Seneca commentary of 1532 along such Humanistic lines? Why did he not emphasize the superiority of Christian ethics over philosophical ethics? Why are there only three biblical quotations in a sea of classical references? Why is he apparently only seeking a name for himself as a scholar? Must we not date the conversion to the time when he acted as a converted person, as stated in the Psalms commentary (Lang)? Among supporters of this view there is a difference inasmuch as K. Müller takes sudden conversion to be the last decisive breakthrough after a longer period of preparation, of a desire for the other things of true piety after the manner of Nicodemus, whereas Lang no less vigorously than Holl on the other side rejects any intermediate period and takes the word "sudden" literally, though unlike Holl putting the conversion no earlier than 1533.

As I survey all the material adduced on both sides, it seems to me that everything hinges on how we understand the word "sudden." Both sides, though intentionally only in the case of Müller, appear to shed light by showing that the period from 1527 to 1533 was the critical and ambivalent one in Calvin's life. He received a jolt but did not yet make a move. He was under impulsion but did not yet decide. He saw something but did not yet sufficiently understand himself to make the inferences. We cannot possibly deny that they surprisingly left no imprint on, for example, the Seneca commentary. This being so, a sudden conversion as an incomparably sudden spiritual event was just as unlikely at the beginning of the period as at the end, at the beginning because it did not really lead to anything, and at the end because then something had already happened.

---

13. Stähelin, I, 21-28; K. Müller, "Calvins Bekehrung," *Nachrichten der königlichen Gesellschaft der Wissenschaften zu Göttingen, phil.-hist. Cl.* (1905), 188-255; P. Wernle, "Noch einmal die Bekehrung Calvins," *ZKG* 27 (1906), 84-99; and in response to Holl, "Zu Calvins Bekehrung," *ZKG* 51 (1910), 556-83; A. Lang, *Die Bekehrung Johannes Calvins, Studien zur Geschichte der Theologie und Kirche,* ed. N. Bonwetsch and R. Seeberg, vol. II (Leipzig, 1897).

What does a sudden conversion mean? It seems to me that here again we see how inappropriate it is that modern theology thinks it should have to read the NT and church history with Pietistic spectacles and therefore to see conversion as a spiritual event in time. With the same premise, and the same defective insight into the relativity of time, it seems to me that the understanding of Romans 7, and also of expectation of the parousia and its history, was obstructed and made impossible from Revelation to Blumhardt.[14] Is there not something humorous about the debate of these scholars as to whether that act of God by which Calvin became Calvin took place, with or without preparation, in 1527 or 1533? Must not anyone who is not involved in the debate raise the crucial issue? What are we really talking about? The act of *God!* If an act of God, then we have here a vital existential event, as both parties and Calvin himself believe, and can there be any question of 1527 or 1533, of yesterday or today? Is it not obvious a priori that a man who was essentially a thinker, and we have every reason to say this of Calvin, if he calls an act of God sudden, will have in view a change which compared to all the changes that take place in time is absolutely unique, so that to the extent that it is seriously placed in a temporal sequence it can denote only a stretch of time, a permanent crisis, not a crosscut, something that happened with unheard-of suddenness in 1527 or 1533?

I also believe that I can prove this a posteriori, at least from the text in the Psalms commentary. If you read through the whole preface you will see that the guiding thread in Calvin's account of his life is not at all the chronological sequence, so that we are not forced to think of the sudden conversion in terms of a moment in time. The thread is the parallel between David and Calvin, and the point is that the power, the goodness, the grace, the miracle of God stands over both lives. This preface is not a

14. Barth dealt with gaps in modern theology in his Overbeck essay, "Unsettled Questions in Theology Today," in *Theology and Church* (New York, 1962), 55ff. He thought the two Blumhardts, Zündel, and Overbeck had not received in their day the respect they deserved, the result being that 19th-century theology failed to deal with the question of biblical eschatology. Barth is in agreement with the thinkers mentioned (ibid., 64): "But in any case, after the expectation of the Parousia had lost its reality, Christianity lost its youth and itself. It has become something wholly different; it has become a religion." Cf. Barth's retractions on this theme in *CD,* II/1, 633ff., and then his verdict on the way in which Blumhardt's contemporaries found his concern a strange one, *CD,* IV/3, 170f. For Barth on the Pietist misunderstanding of Rom. 7 cf. his 1st ed. of *Römerbrief* (1919), reprinted in part II of *Gesamtausgabe* (Zurich, 1985), 276ff., on "The Law and Pietism."

biography if we mean by a biography the history of an individual and the progress of the personality of that individual through time. The history of the individual is here a means by which to recount the eternal history of the acts of God that we do not see as such on the plane of historical things. Hence at the decisive point, as Holl rightly argues against Müller,[15] Calvin equates the sudden conversion with the taste for the things of true piety that is much less evident. This is how what is divine impinges on what is human. The radical sudden conversion means a relative taste for other things, the wholly other becomes a modest something.[16] The Seneca commentary fits well enough with this modest something without any artificial reading between the lines.

In fact Calvin did see something in 1527 but without achieving full clarity about himself. Friends and foes might or might not have found something new and strange in him! As others later wanted to be, and as he himself, when his ambivalence was recognized, renounced for himself and opposed in others, he might have seemed to be a Nicodemus, who out of fear came to the Lord by night.[17] He could very well visit the Noyon chapter in 1533 and enjoy his income up to 1534. All this is basically in keeping with his desire for other things that would later grow and make it all impossible, for the light of that desire dispelled unambiguous darkness and brought the first light of dawn. But the sudden conversion, God's own act, was written in *another* book, all that is said in the preface about God's comfort, help, judgment, and presence being something different from what Calvin experienced in his life in time under this promising sign. It was against his own expectations and wishes,[18] he tells us, that God drew him up out of the slime of papacy, out of his obduracy, out of his natural prejudice and perplexity. This is the point of the celebrated passage. Historians will note that at the time of his first Parisian stay — it did not have to be in 1527 — something did begin to happen in the life of Calvin, namely, conscious contact with Reformation thinking. They will also note that Calvin himself perceived in this something, this new taste for other things, incomparably more than that, namely, God's con-

---

15. See Holl, 256f.

16. See above, 16 n. 6.

17. An allusion to Calvin's controversy with those who followed the model of Nicodemus in John 3:2. Calvin coined for them the label Nicodemites.

18. Barth paraphrases here Calvin's statements in his preface to the Psalms commentary, CO 31, 21.

verting act. Seeing that, they will understand to what distinctive logic a life of this kind was subject no matter what it might finally mean at every stage. They will thus be on guard against trying to assess historically what Calvin himself calls the act of God. For historical assessment can deal only with the new taste, not the sudden conversion. The new taste is the event, the sudden conversion the recognition of it. The new taste is in time, the sudden conversion beyond all time in eternity.

After this digression we may resume our account. Calvin had left Paris as one who had been awakened and unsettled and gripped by the thinking of the German Reformation, for which he was not unprepared. At the time when he had given up theology, he was not clear whether he was not really for the first time beginning the study of theology. He was reading the Bible. He found like-minded people, unsettled just as he was, and to his own added unsettlement, against his will he became their leader. His other studies, which he still diligently pursued, secretly hampered him. So he came to Orléans. As the same man he was? No, not the same! As another man? No, not another! But thirty years later he saw that the great sword of Damocles, the great either-or, had visibly hung over his life at the time, that the great crisis in which he stood and would always stand had come, so that he felt the power of the eternal hand in which he always was and always would be, and was therefore elected and called. Yet what we see of all this in time [cf. 2 Cor. 4:18] is simply a student, a jurist, a Humanist, a Roman Catholic, a scholar of fine-tuned and nervous disposition, rather ambitious, rather cautious, in short, one human, earthly, questionable possibility among others. He moves only slowly, like the hand of a clock, yet no less inexorably than the hand of a clock. New things will take place in this life. From 1533 onward new and surprising possibilities will open up. The awakening will become conscious, the unsettlement stronger, the pressure of the hand stronger. But those who see that this life was pushed by the eternal hand will not make of this movement, of his sudden conversion, at any given time a datum in time and history. It belongs in his biography precisely because it is so much the meaning, the totality, of the biography.

Calvin was in Orléans from 1528 to 1529 and Bourges from 1529 to 1531, in both cases studying law at the university as his father wished. His feelings regarding the questions raised by Luther cannot have grown weaker during these years. When he was in Orléans in 1528 Protestants came under persecution there. The new teaching had confronted him in Paris just as it did now in this situation of antagonism. In both Orléans and Bourges there were many German students, so that interest was thus kept alive in the great events taking place in Germany. Bourges in particular was in the territory ruled over by that friend of the Reformation, Margaret of Angoulême, the sister of Francis I.[19] Calvin even seems to have preached there occasionally, not without attracting attention.[20] His works after 1533 seem to indicate that he was doing some theological study, which gradually gained in incisiveness. It is not impossible that already in 1528, when in Orléans, he paid a short visit to Bucer and Capito in Strassburg (Kampschulte, I, 231).[21] In Bourges he learned Greek from Melchio Volmar of Württemberg, to whom he dedicated his 1546 commentary on 1 Corinthians.[22] One of this man's students at the time was the young Theodore Beza, who twenty years later would be Calvin's most loyal fellow worker in Geneva. It seems that in spite of what he said later,[23] Calvin was not a little interested in his legal studies; we read at least that by way of the preface to a friend's work he took part publicly in a legal debate of the time, between Stella in Orléans and Alciati in Bourges,[24] and to the end of his days he could not suppress the old, or, shall we say, the born, jurist.

It was at this time that by overly assiduous academic labor he must have begun to undermine his health. Certain character traits like his nervous punctiliousness and his extreme personal sensitivity begin to appear in his letters. In 1531 he broke off his study of law, and with the death of his father in the same year returned to Paris, showing his desire for the things of true piety by studying Greek and Hebrew under the famous teachers Danesius, Buddaeus, and Vatable. Kampschulte is perhaps right when he says that this was the happiest time in his life (I, 237).

He had not yet come dangerously close to the theological problem. We see this from the Seneca commentary *De clementia,* which came out in 1532 (5, 1ff.).[25] Was the repetition of this warning of the Stoic sage meant as a hidden exhortation to Francis I, who was now becoming intolerable? Was he concerned about the problem of good government in

---

19. Margaret (1492-1549) later became queen of Navarre.

20. Bossert, 27; Kampschulte, I, 232.

21. Kampschulte, I, 231 n. 2.

22. Cf. Beza, *Johannis Calvini Vita,* CO 21, 30; Bossert, 28; Kampschulte, I, 229. For the dedicatory epistle of August 1, 1546, cf. CO 12, 364f.

23. Cf. n. 104 n. 3 above.

24. Kampschulte, I, 228f., CO 9, 785f.

25. See n. 9 on 136.

general and hence enticed into a discussion with Seneca? Neither interpretation is impossible, neither is probable. On the basis of the preface
and letters of the period it seems most likely that the work was undertaken
as an example of Humanistic scholarship evoked by Erasmus's edition of
Seneca, as one of those academic exercises about which we need not ask
too urgently what the purpose was. The later iron Calvin, who knew what
he was about, reveals himself in the strictness and industry that the work
displays. Materially, in spite of all his past, he was obviously capable of
following a different course. The door to a career as a Humanist scholar
was still open to him.

But that changed abruptly in 1533. The year saw a new flaring up
of the twenty-year struggle between the Sorbonne and the Humanists,
whom the king favored. The scholastic party, attacking the king's sister
Margaret, who was sympathetic to the Reformation, had gone too far.
Impertinent scholars had even taken the liberty of making fun of this noble
lady in a theatrical performance, a kind of revue such as Paris is still fond
of today,[26] and the time seemed to have come for the Humanists to launch
a counterstroke that would make them masters of the situation. By ancient
tradition the newly elected rector of the University of Paris, the young
professor of medicine, Nicholas Cop, was to take up his office with a
solemn address on All Saints Day. As was not unusual, he had the address
written for him by his intimate friend Calvin, and so the strange result
was that the jurist put on the lips of the teacher of medicine an address
that was from first to last theological, in form and tone even a sermon
(10/II, 30ff.).[27] Recently, it is true, Calvin's authorship has been contested,
especially by K. Müller.[28] In this case, too, the address is still typical of
the circle in which Calvin moved even if he was not the leader. I see no
reason why it should not have originated with Calvin himself.

We have the impression that the author has entered with some
vehemence a field that is unfamiliar to him with the intention of striking
a powerful blow. It is rather like student sermons in which the aim, as we
know, is often to say all that is to be said. Lines are drawn boldly and with
assurance in all directions from a point that has been discovered with great
enthusiasm. It is thus hard to sum up the content in a few words. One
unmistakable feature is the Pauline doctrine of justification as Luther

26. Kampschulte, I, 243.
27. OS I, 4ff.; BI 462ff.
28. See n. 13 above.

understood it, the message of the forgiveness of sins by grace alone. This teaching is extolled in the introduction, developed in a first part, and recommended for courageous promotion in a second. That a novice is saying all this is unambiguously clear from the fact that Luther's 1522 All Saints Day sermon is quoted in the Latin translation of Bucer even to the point of verbal reminiscences (as Lang discovered), along with discussion of Erasmus's supposedly reformed preface to the third edition of his New Testament, from which Calvin takes the description of the gospel as "Christian philosophy" when extolling it in the introduction.[29] That it was not impossible for him to make use of both Luther and Erasmus in the same breath never entered his head, nor did it trouble him that he could close his Erasmian exordium with a solemn invocation of the most blessed virgin, Ave Maria, and so on.[30]

Along with Luther, Erasmus, and a tiny remnant of Romanism, we find a fourth line of thinking, namely, that those who hold the Christian philosophy differ from others as humans do from animals. This philosophy enables us to keep within bounds the turbulent impulses of the spirit. God's greatest blessing is to have given us his Word.[31] Luther's trust in Christ alone is equated with seeking God's glory alone.[32] Luther's thought that God wills our *heart* is obviously but unwittingly changed by the author into the different thought that it is *God* who wills our heart, the result being an urgent appeal to renounce other things so as to be able to stand before Christ's judgment seat. The exposition of the thought of forgiveness of sins reaches a climax in a thought already known to us from the Geneva Catechism, that those who do not grasp this are as far from salvation as animals.[33] A strong challenge[34] comes at the end: Dare to bring the church peace by adhering to the Word of truth, the Word of God, and not to human dreams, and even if necessary dare to accept the charge of heresy and persecution.[35] That is obviously Calvin! But it is so mixed with what is taken from Luther and Erasmus, and the decisive Lutheran element is so dominant that it can be no more than an accompanying element, thus

29. For Luther see WA 10/III, 400-407. Cf. Lang, *Bekehrung,* ch. 4: "Die akademische Rede vom Allerheilgen-Tage 1533." For Calvin, see OS I, 4; BI 462.

30. OS I, 5; BI 463.

31. OS I, 4; BI 463.

32. OS I, 6; BI 464.

33. OS I, 7; BI 465; OS II, 75, 10ff.

34. The MS had *Anlauf* here, corrected by Barth in the typescript to *Anruf.*

35. OS I, 9; BI 467.

leaving the impression that with the main statement the author also wanted to say something else.

There is something chaotic, contingent, and tumultuous about this work. The various thoughts are integrated into one another like unhewn blocks. One suspects that the author still has a good way to go before he can make an assimilated and independent totality out of all the things that in part he repeats and in part he adds from his own knowledge. But we cannot rule out the possibility that all this is accidental, a Humanistic whim, the product of a scholar's study, when, having previously devoted his attention in the main to other things, but inwardly moved for some time by the plight of theology, this scholar is now testing himself in the theological genre. From such bold sorties many ways at that time also led back to Rome. This bold amateur theologian who hastily poured out his whole heart, who in so doing showed a certain lack of independence, who did not yet see all the connections and was not yet aware of the implications, was the Calvin of 1533. Was he converted by then? But again, what does conversion mean? I would say more cautiously that he was being increasingly awakened, that he was coming to himself, that he was discovering the theologian in himself. We can say that much if we read the address attentively. This man had probably immersed himself so deeply in theology that he would probably not be able to reverse himself or call a halt.

But what takes place here is not heroic advance. If we follow the interaction of inner pressure and outer counterpressure in this life, we will probably conclude that here the latter was much stronger and more determinative. Not for nothing, and not just to evoke flattery, did Calvin repeatedly refer later to the natural modesty of his character. He felt himself to be much more forced than forceful. He was not aware of the majesty that others saw in him. So it was now. The necessity that he foresaw in the second part of the address, namely, that we must adhere to the Word of God once it is grasped, and maintain it even at the risk of being persecuted, was indeed in tune with events. The time had come to play this part, which had been adopted for reasons we do not know how profound.

The reaction of those who heard this address left Calvin no option but to take up his own enterprise in all earnest and automatically prevented him from being afraid of where his courage was leading him. The attempt to carry through Humanistic reform in Paris was a complete failure, and among its leaders this failure upset the career of Calvin in particular. The public was not ready for the insights put on the lips of Cop, nor for the way in which they were presented, which was not calculated to instruct the public. In short, the effusion provoked only anger. The Sorbonne and the Parlement made a common complaint against Cop and his speech-writer, the university was divided and impotent, the king was unwilling to offer protection, and so the two, to avoid anything worse, had to flee. Calvin was openly forced into the position of the persecuted, the typical Huguenot situation that would characterize his whole life's work, even before he had achieved full clarity as to the meaning of this situation.

There now began for him a period of wandering. At the end of 1533 he was in his hometown of Noyon, then for a short time, protected by Margaret of Angoulême, he was back in Paris, then early in 1534 he was in Angoulême with his friend, the cathedral canon, Louie du Tillet, whose fine library he used, in whose house he studied Greek, and where he began the *Institutes,* not least to teach himself. In April 1534 he was in Nérac at the court of that princess Margaret who so distinctively combined a disposition for Renaissance and Reformation. She herself wrote comedies and pastoral pieces but also a *Mirror of the Sinful Soul,* she provided a final shelter for Faber Stapulensis, and she was always favorable to Calvin, though, like other women, she sometimes found that he went too far.[36] It was in relation to her that Calvin would later make his famous statement that if a dog barks when its owner is being attacked, why should he keep silent when God's truth is under assault.[37] For the time being, however, this Kierkegaardian absoluteness did not show itself on the surface of his nature.

In May 1534 he was again in Noyon, and having now reached the canonical age (25) he had to decide whether to continue to receive the ecclesiastical income he had been given as a boy or whether to renounce it. He chose to renounce it, but not without taking compensation, which was obviously not against his conscience. What happened next? According to a note in the chapter register at Noyon, unless there is some confusion with his brother Charles, who had broken with the church, he was arrested for causing a tumult in the church on May 26.[38] This seems to suggest that in these years he was actively propagating his convictions at times, and later all kinds of unsubstantiated reports of this activity would circu-

---

36. Stähelin, I, 34; Kampschulte, I, 243ff.

37. Calvin's letter of 4.28.1545, no. 634, CO 12, 67.

38. In the Noyon 1534 archives we read of the arrest of a Jean Cauvin for causing a disturbance, but whether this does or can refer to Calvin is disputed. Cf. Doumergue, I, 426.

late.[39] But there is little inner probability that this was so. However that may be, a short time later he was again in Paris and seems to have engaged in debate with spiritualizing Enthusiasts who had now made an appearance in France, though it is not clear whether they were of the older or newer observance. A meeting with the well-known antitrinitarian Michael Servetus failed to materialize because the latter did not show up at the appointed time. In view of Calvin's painful love of punctuality it was doubtful whether this beginning of a relationship could in any case have led anywhere.[40] Angoulême, Poitiers, and Orléans were then further stops on Calvin's travels, though there is much obscurity as to why he went to them or what he did there.

§8 *Psychopannychia*

In Orléans toward the end of 1534 Calvin seems to have finished his second major work, the *Psychopannychia*. On the advice of his friends, however, it was left unpublished and came out only later, in 1542, in a revised form. But we must discuss it here as a stage on the way of Calvin's inward development (5, 169ff.).[1] The title, usually rendered "soul sleep," means literally "night of the soul," perhaps in the sense of a night banquet. Certain Christian teachers, whom Calvin calls Anabaptists, were promoting the thesis that at the death of the body the soul sinks into a sleep resembling death, or actually dies, and that only at the resurrection of the dead will it be awakened again to life with the body. Calvin's counterthesis is that the departed souls of the elect are indeed at rest, but not asleep, not in a state of indolence, sleepiness, or intoxication — his interpretation of the opposing view — but with the rest and assurance of conscience that comes with physical death (5, 188), contemplating God and his peace, from which they are still at a distance, but of which they are sure. With no impatience or pain of deprivation they await the revelation of perfect

---

39. Kampschulte, I, 246ff.

40. On this incident cf. CO 8, 481, in Calvin's 1554 defense of the doctrine of the Trinity against the errors of Servetus, with a French translation by Beza in 1565 which adds a sentence to the effect that Calvin was willing to risk his life to win Servetus, but Servetus would not accept his offer.

1. CO 5, 169-232.

glory (5, 190f.). If not yet in possession of the kingdom of God or in beatitude, they are saved in certain hope of the blessed resurrection. They now see what we here can only believe in hope (5, 213).

What is the point of this work? How does Calvin arrive at such thoughts at this particular moment? We are rightly surprised at the arbitrary isolating of the theme. Calvin students often unadvisedly ignore the writing. Even the faithful Staehelin (I, 37)[2] regards it as so alien that he remarks that the debate that evoked it has long since died away, and that we are now all agreed on what it seeks to prove, so that he is content to take pleasure at this juncture in the sincere belief in the Bible that Calvin displays. Kampschulte (I, 248)[3] can even suggest that after his conversion Calvin had a burning desire to emerge as a theological author as well. I cannot say that I am satisfied with the great silence that reigns on the matter apart from observations of this kind. A work of Calvin written two years before the first edition of the *Institutes* demands that at least we try to understand it and fit it in in some way. Look upon what I now say as an attempt at explanation. If the explanation is not good, it is at any rate better than nothing. I will present my observations and conjectures in sequence as material for further work.

1. Biblicism.[4] If we ask what Calvin was really doing in the period of wandering from late 1533 to late 1534, the *Psychopannychia* at least supplies us with an answer. At the various places where he stayed during that year Calvin did an astonishing amount of new and intensive theological work. He was no longer just an amateur theologian. The author of this work had plainly studied the Bible in its full scope and with a thoroughness that is not even remotely apparent a year earlier in the Cop address. He knew it now almost as well as he knew antiquity when he wrote the Seneca commentary. He proved his statements already in the way that characterizes the later Calvin. His positive presentation follows well-chosen biblical passages closely, but his attack, especially on what he regards as the false interpretation of his adversaries when they quote scripture, is also very biblical, leading us both in attack and defense throughout the whole of the OT and the NT and if necessary the church fathers as well. This achievement gives unambiguous proof that now, and only now we might say, Calvin has moved ahead of others and become in

2. See 129 n. 4 above.
3. See 130 n. 5 above.
4. Heading added in the margin.

a serious sense a theological Humanist. The question arises: What impelled him in this direction?

2. Urgency of the Theme.[5] As regards this work we cannot so easily buy the idea of a chance theme as we can in the case of the work on Seneca. It is true that in the second preface written in 1536 he did not clearly succeed in making his point that the subject is more important than many think.[6] We can read through the work and still shake our heads as much as when reading the title. There is in this respect, perhaps, something youthful about the work. It smacks of the scholar's study. For he did not yet see how to present the matter of principle lying behind what so greatly stirred him in a way that would make it apparent to us, too. Yet the whole tone of the work, of which Calvin himself said that he had softened it in the new edition,[7] tells us that this time he was in grim earnest. In the first preface of 1534 he feared that he would be called a traitor to the truth if he did not speak out in this emergency.[8] He expected to be accused of violating love by taking up the fight, but he replied in advance that there is no unity except in Christ, no love in which he is not the bond. Love is preserved only when the faith is kept intact.[9] In the second preface of 1536 he anticipated the further charge that he was making much ado about nothing.[10] His answer was that the light of God was under threat of extinction by the devil's darkness. The guilt in this conflict lies with those who have caused it.[11] Both objections, probably raised among his friends, and both replies, probably given to them, offer us with remarkable clarity a profile of Calvin the relentless polemicist of his later years. It might well be that when Calvin brought these guns to bear he was not putting on a purely academic performance, even if it is not clear at a first glance what his purpose really was.

3. Historical Context.[12] From a historical perspective we may obviously say this about the *Psychopannychia*. In Paris in the summer of 1534, and perhaps in other places, Calvin had run up against the people called Anabaptists. Like Luther and Zwingli he had first to deal with the question

---

5. Heading added in the margin.
6. CO 5, 175 and 176.
7. Ibid., 173 and 174.
8. Ibid., 169 and 170.
9. Ibid., 171f.
10. Ibid., 175 and 176.
11. Ibid.
12. Heading added in the margin.

whether the opposition of this group to the church was not the same as his own, whether it might not be possible or even necessary to go along with circles of this kind. As pointed out already, he even held out a hand to Servetus. But the answer that he gave to the question, and that he wished to be loud and public, was a round, flat No. The preface tells us that he was not just afraid of the unjust infamy of being an innovator, but he also did not wish to accept every novelty as the winds of change directed. No matter how true a teaching might be, he was not ready to lend an ear to it apart from the Word of God. He displayed a real aversion to those who, having digested a few chapters of *loci communes,* proclaim mysteries from the Pythian tripod and thus cause schisms, scandals, and heresies.[13] He feared — note this well — the threat of Jesus that the kingdom of God can be taken away and given to others. His cry was that we must always hang on God's Word.[14] We must present ourselves to the Lord as the students he would have, poor, wholly emptied of our own wisdom, eager to learn, but not knowing and not wanting to know anything but what he teaches us, fleeing above all everything exotic as though it were poison.[15] We see that Calvin's confrontation with what we might call the Baptist possibility was swift and sure. Almost as soon as he met it, he knew uncannily well and quickly what his reaction must be: Not that! For that is wantonness.[16] It is exotic, arbitrary, aberrant. The complete antithesis to it is the Word of God, which stands above even the truth that is known so well and that is so full of vitality.

4. Antithesis to Wantonness.[17] What is the thrust of Calvin's opposition to Anabaptism? Formally it is this. As is usual with him, his encounter and acquaintance with the Anabaptists had made clear to him that in no case can we understand what in 1533 he called Christian philosophy as a tumultuous, random, capricious thing like this, no matter what fine and profound justification might be offered for it. The aversion came surprisingly promptly in Calvin. It was for him in truth something primary, his

13. CO 5, 173 and 174. Melanchthon's *Loci communes* came out in a 1st ed. in 1522 and a 2nd in 1535. Calvin read the 1st ed. in one of the many impressions that differed textually. He probably had the 2nd ed. before finishing the 1536 *Institutes;* cf. A. Lang, "Die Quellen der Institutio von 1536," *EvTh* 3 (1936), 106f.

14. CO 5, 175 and 176.

15. Ibid.

16. Ibid., 173 and 174, though the reference is to Calvin himself avoiding wantonness.

17. Heading added in the MS margin.

first serious step in the world of theology. Of a moment when everything still hung in the balance, when the Anabaptist message seemed to him to be a serious possibility like that he proclaimed as the gospel in the Cop address, of such a moment, at least, we know nothing. When, plunged willy-nilly from Humanism into theology, he considered what he had to do, at once he was constrained to take pen in hand to refute this thesis. It would never be able to make any appeal to him. He could point out that he had never had anything in common with it.

If the Cop address shows us on what path he was setting out, we now see him striding ahead rapidly on that way. What counts now is not the Lutheran, the Erasmian, nor the sparse Catholic element in that address, but the fourth element that is genuinely Calvin's own, what he says about the Word and obedience, the element, it seems, that is lying in wait, that has only to be awakened, and it will result in a distinctive life and control everything. The Anabaptists were the ones who brought this element to life precisely by misunderstanding faith and obedience and thus embodying the danger that led Calvin to feel dissatisfaction with Luther and Erasmus and instead to forge his own sword out of what they had given him. Calvin's store of thoughts in the *Psychopannychia* appears to be much thinner and more one-sided than in the expansive Cop address. In no case wantonness — that is the bass note underlying the whole melody, though there is, of course, much else in the melody — instead God! And if because truly God, then God in his Word, God as the authority over all human conceits, obedience not caprice! By grasping this thought Calvin became a biblicist. He took hold of the Bible as the supreme critical principle and used this principle to distinguish the freedom of God's children from the freedom of fools. Laying so much store by the fact that knowledge of God is a motivating force, he had to stake everything on ensuring that it had inner force, that is, clarity and certainty. He found the means to do this in the Bible. This is the general formal significance of the *Psychopannychia*.

5. Opposition to Quietism.[18] But the work also has a special material significance. It seems to me to be clear that its theme is by no means an accidental one. With sureness of instinct Calvin seized on a point that was distinctive for both him and his opponents, and at this one point he not only had in mind and attacked all that his opponents were teaching; he also set his own view over against theirs and instructively characterized

18. Heading added in the MS margin.

150

this view within the Reformation as a whole. What is meant by this abstract-sounding doctrine of soul sleep?[19] And what is meant by Calvin's opposing view of the rest of the righteous in Abraham's bosom? It seems to me that we should not simply overlook the eschatological-metaphysical form of the controversy but also not simply shake our heads over it. I propose first to translate the concepts from the metaphysical into psychological terms. It is then clear that soul sleep or the soul's night festival is nothing other than what we know from mysticism as Quietism.

As distinct from Luther, Calvin is dealing in the main with mystical Enthusiasts. The doctrine of soul sleep is simply a metaphysical version of the attitude to life that by passivity, renunciation of all things, abandonment of all thinking, willing, and doing, finally thinks that by the mystical death of the soul in God it can attain to the supreme summit of human striving. Commendation of this approach can now come in formulations that confusingly resemble the Reformation insight into the way through death to life as Luther proclaimed it.[20] We have also seen that Luther himself in his younger days could hardly differentiate it from his own insight, but hailed it as an ally. In Calvin the distinction between faith and mysticism is the beginning, the starting point. It is so because for him faith must be free at once for life, for ethos, for the glorifying of God in thinking, willing, and doing. Nothing is more intolerable for him than an intermediate religious state where the issue is not obedience. For him faith means putting one's hand to the plow and not looking back [Luke 9:62].

What is his answer, then, to the mystical thesis? He, too, apparently unfolds a wholly metaphysical-mythological picture, that of the rest of souls in tranquility and assurance of conscience and certain hope of the blessed resurrection.[21] But it seems evident to me that in fact he is here describing a specific approach to life that he wants to set over against the mystical approach. It is no accident that more than once he finds it hard

19. Soul sleep was taught in the 16th century by groups and individuals whom it is hard or impossible to identify. It is not certain whether Anabaptists advocated it as Zwingli (Z 6/I, 188) and Bullinger assumed. Bullinger opposed the doctrine in a letter to Paul Beck in the summer of 1526 (*Werke* III, vol. II [Zurich, 1991], 127ff.). But he was not yet attributing it to the Anabaptists. He did this only in his 1530 work against them (Zurich, 1531). Possibly the Zurich reformers were echoing Wittenberg verdicts on the theme; see n. 26 below.

20. Cf. Luther's *Romans Lectures* of 1515/16, WA 56, 375, 21f.; LW 25, 365; and his 1519-21 *Psalms,* WA 5, 167, 40-168, 4.

21. CO 5, 188, 213.

to give cogent reasons for distinguishing the state of deceased believers from that of those still living. The righteous in Abraham's bosom who are awaiting the last things are Calvin's devout, whether in this life or after it. The alert conscience, wakefully waiting on God, still imperfect yet with a sure and clear sense of the peace and glory of God, the peace of the living (5, 190),[22] this is what Calvin wants to proclaim in the work in opposition to that which in mystical waiting, silence, and absorption seemed to him to be simply indolence, sleepiness, and intoxication. The soul does indeed bear within it the image of God, but his image equips it with the knowledge of God (5, 180).[23]

We have to ask, then, whether there is any such thing as a sleeping knowledge of God. That this possibility is mooted, that pious Anabaptists let themselves call the sleeping soul the essence of Christianity and the climax of piety, is what arouses Calvin's aversion as though a slug were touching him. For him this was the summit of what is wanton and exotic and poisonous, almost as though he foresaw the invasion of silent worship of God from India that we witness today.[24] No *psychopannychia*, no soul night festival, is his battle cry. To say nothing against this is to betray the truth. In opposition to it he finds himself forced to resort to God's Word and to do biblical theology.

Why specifically in opposition to this? I would say: Because he is scared to death that this possibility, the soul sleep of the devout, might replace knowledge and obedience, and because in the Bible he found nothing about soul sleep but very much about knowledge and obedience. This aversion had to follow his understanding of Luther's thinking as thunder does lightning. Luther's gospel could not be construed as a pointer to a comfortable indolence that shames God afresh and even worse. There can be no eternity of idleness and inaction. Otherwise the kingdom of God will be taken from you [Matt. 21:43].[25]

In this saying we catch the Reformation concern of Calvin that never

22. Ibid., 190.

23. Ibid., 180.

24. Barth is alluding to a concept promoted by R. Otto in his essay "Schweigender Dienst," *CW* 24 (1920), 561-65. The form of this worship is described (col. 562) as kneeling in silence until the prayer bell has sounded three times. Inner speech replaces the outer Word, with prayer as dedication to him who is present. Inner silence of the soul corresponds to the outer silence, a quiet sinking into the eternal ground, the lofty wonder of union. Cf. also Barth's *Vorträge und kleinere Arbeiten 1922-1925*, ed. H. Finze, part III of *Gesamtausgabe* (Zurich, 1990), 31, 81, and 172, along with Barth's criticism in *CD* III/4, 111f., esp. 112.

left him his whole life long. He is the man who, appropriating the knowledge of the God of judgment and mercy, at once feels the need to express and confirm this knowledge as wakeful expectation, as will and action; who at once fears the very worst, the loss of this knowledge, if there is a pause, a religious siesta, between death and resurrection, that is, between justification and sanctification, between faith and life. The peace of the conscience that is comforted by forgiveness is the peace of the living and not for a single second anything else.

In this strange work then, if my interpretation is correct, we have decisively important evidence of Calvin's starting point and his whole position in the Reformation. And if, as I now hear from Hirsch, Luther, who also knew the doctrine of a soul sleep, agreed with it, or at least did not expressly disagree,[26] then we have, if not proof, at least a further indication that this interpretation is right. Although Luther was not a Quietist, as I constantly repeat, it is here that the first and second roads of the Reformation part company.

6. Time and Eternity.[27] We still have to ask why Calvin had to clothe his opposition to Quietism in the garb of what seems to be so totally a metaphysical-eschatological issue. Of primary importance in this regard is that Calvin himself chose the field of battle. According to his own testimony he does not seem to have had any attack from the other side, any opposing Anabaptist work advocating the doctrine of soul sleep. He expressly says in the preface that he had heard of the matter only through murmurings and suppressed mutterings, that he had heard of relevant *schedulae* but never seen them (and none from that time is known), and that he knew the teaching only from what friends told him they had learned from the spoken addresses of Anabaptist teachers.[28]

Support for this statement may be found in an undated letter from Capito of Strassburg to Calvin (10/II, 45f.) in which he said that he had read the manuscript, was somewhat put off by how unreadable it was, and advised against publication, particularly as we cannot fight such errors unless we first

---

25. See n. 14 above.

26. E. Hirsch (1888-1972) was a Göttingen colleague, professor of church history. See WA B 2, to N. Amsdorf, 1.13.1521 (no. 449). Later Luther often made positive statements about the doctrine, e.g., WA 10/I, 117ff.; 10/III, 191; 11, 70; 12, 456; 15, 475; 17/I, 169; 17/II, 235; but he did not seem to think that soul sleep involved a long night for the soul, or its complete decay until the judgment day, as Calvin understood it.

27. Later marginal heading in the MS.

28. CO 5, 169f.

really know them. In his view the matter lies outside the analogy of faith and dealing with it can only create strife and be a temptation for many uncertain people. Calvin should devote his literary zeal to a more plausible argument. Capito is plainly of the view that Calvin replies to in his preface of 1536, namely, that the enterprise is contrary to love and in any case superfluous. He does not see the need to say precisely *that* at any time.

The situation, as so often in the life of Calvin, is that like the alert dog, if we may use his own comparison, he senses an enemy at a time and place where no one else is aware of any need to see danger, and to the alienation of all others, he lunges in this unexpected direction to give warning of the enemy that only he himself has noticed until at last all are awake to the threat. The initiative in the fight against soul sleep is all on his side, and it must be something in himself that impels him to fight *this* fight against what is only a murmuring and muttering. He is obviously not of the view of many that in the last things all may hold their own arbitrarily chosen views without peril or penalty. It is not for him an indifferent matter whether souls sleep or are awake after this life, whether they are at rest inactively or in tense expectation of fulfillment. Everything depends precisely on this question.

We finally come back here to the point we touched on in our general account of Calvin's theological character, to the essentially eschatological orientation of his Christianity, to the sharp and never to be ignored antithesis and connection between time and eternity on which all his thinking rests. Already here I would draw your attention to two works of Martin Schulze, of which at least the first is for me the most important and the most valuable of all the works on Calvin that I know. The two works are *Meditatio futurae vitae . . .* (Leipzig, 1901), and *Calvins Jenseitschristentum in seinem Verhältnis zu den religiösen Schriften des Erasmus* (Görlitz, 1902). Here Schulze works out instructively and convincingly this side of Calvin in a way that is one-sided but that contributes essentially to our understanding of him. In a much more pregnant and emphatic way for Calvin than for Luther, the real life is the future eternal life. We might put it this way: For him the thought of death and the hereafter was much more directly linked than it was for Luther to the concept of salvation that Luther's doctrine of faith and justification had clarified for him.

We first ask with astonishment how that can be so when his theology is marked specifically by a turning to this world, by a stress on obedience and the glorifying of God in the present life. In reality the two things go together. The thought of eternity is taken strictly. Eternity is seen as the negation of all time and the position that underlies time, hence not as a second and different thing in a moment of time, but as the primary-finite thing of every moment of time, its meaning, its transcendental content. This concept cannot devalue time or empty it out. Or rather, it does this completely, but only in order to fill it to the full. It makes time serious and important as the place of training where nothing, nothing at all is eternal, but everything, everything is judged and determined by its relation to the eternal, full of meaning, full of tasks.

I cannot agree with Schulze when he thinks that by way of Erasmus he can claim Calvin as a Platonist,[29] though there can be no doubt that Calvin knew Plato fairly well and valued him above all other philosophers, and though it can also be taken as proved that the one who directly led him to an understanding of the world of Platonic thinking was in fact Erasmus. The truth seems to be rather that for the new version of Luther's insight that was hovering before him in the Cop address, namely, an ethicizing version, Calvin found the right lever in the formulas in which Erasmus understood Platonic philosophy.

But much more important than this thesis of formal dependence is, I think, that of the material identity of Calvin's meditation on the future life and Plato's *meletan apothnēskein*.[30] Facing Luther's doctrine of grace on the one side and the need to relate this vertical in all its unheard-of character to the horizontal of human life and striving, that is, truly to set the latter in the light of grace, Calvin forged ahead to the point where a theological view of life and a philosophical view have always met and always must. He saw in the thought of death the standard by which all things living are measured. He became the strict essential thinker who sought what is truly positive and existent, not in greater proximity to, but precisely beyond the negation of, all that is apparently and provisionally positive and existent, but for which this infinitely distant thing, just because it is the true thing, becomes what is most close and immediate and serious and important, the most urgent concern and the most compelling motive in everything present.

Calvin is an eschatologist as an ethicist and an ethicist as an eschatologist. The meaning of the next world is this world, and the power of this world is the next world.[31] Looking to eternity seriously and taking

29. Schulze, however, also sees a direct derivation of Calvin's thought from Plato (*Calvins Jenseitschristentum*, 1f. n. 1).

30. *Phaedon* 67e; see also above, 64.

time seriously are for him one and the same thing, two sides of the same coin. Just because he sees here connections that escaped the excellent Capito and so many others, the state and life of souls after this life — as the subtitle of *Psychopannychia* runs[32] — cannot be for him a matter of indifference. Those who speak about what follows this life are speaking, whether they realize it or not, about what is true and primary. Those who are in error here are in error about God, and those who know here know in God. It is precisely the departed soul, the soul after this life, the soul that we think of only eschatologically, that has to be thought of as motivated and feeling and strong and knowing; otherwise it is not the immortal soul, the bearer of God's image, and all that we say about the fellowship between God and us is not true because it is not authentic or solidly based (5, 182 and 184).[33] If life after death is a night festival, a *pannychia,* then so is all life. But if life after death is an alert and lively waiting for God, then we know what we must think about all life.

7. Evaluation.[34] We have said already that in 1534 Calvin did not know how to work out the actual significance of the theme. Among all the Enthusiasts' topics he seized on this one without even well-meaning people like Capito knowing why. His own counterthesis does not sound credible because the need for it is not clear. It seems to be a product of the study, remote from life, which sets one eschatological notion alongside another. Only in the *Institutes* does the relation that gave Calvin so lively an interest in the subject become clear, so clear that he can now return to the specific problem only in passing.[35] But as an exercise preliminary to the *Institutes* the treatise is an important part of Calvin's work, and if we are to understand the genesis of his approach we must go past it much less hastily than Calvin students have thus far done.

31. Cf. Troeltsch, *Soziallehren,* 979; cf. n. 20 above.
32. On this heading, which follows the two prefaces in the older editions between 1542 and 1565, cf. the editors' note, CO 5, 177.
33. CO 5, 182.
34. Marginal heading in MS.
35. Cf. the 1559 *Institutes* III, 9 and 25; in passing, 25, 6.

§9 1536 *Institutes*

Introduction

Meantime the events in Paris from the end of 1534 to early 1535, of which we have spoken already, had been taking place. Radical Protestant circles made a new push for Reformation and now failed more tragically than in 1533. The placards against the mass came out that called it blasphemy and seduction and described priests as false prophets, deceivers, wolves, idolaters, liars, and murderers of souls, more abhorrent than the devil.[1] Posters of this type were attached even to the doors of the royal palace. As a result, Francis I was annoyed, decided firmly to oppose the Protestant cause, and initiated the gruesome persecution of 1535 to which Calvin refers in the dedicatory epistle of the *Institutes*.[2] In a statement meant especially for the ears of related German Protestants he can say with some credibility that the problem lies with Anabaptists, madmen, agitators, and people about whom it is best not to speak.

For the moment the situation was a hopeless one in France. Tactically Calvin no doubt knew well why he had attacked the Radical wing of the movement in the *Psychopannychia*. But it was too late. At the end of the year, to evade persecution, Calvin went by way of Metz over the border to Strassburg en route to Basel. He spent 14 or 15 months in great seclusion in Strassburg, where he lodged with Katharina Klein, a fine woman, in the suburb of St. Alban, which would later boast of his having stayed there.[3] In a way that would prove important later, he made acquaintance in Strassburg with Simon Grynaeus, rector of Basel, Heinrich Bullinger, Zwingli's successor in Zurich, and Pierre Viret, later reformer in the Vaud. For the rest he was wholly claimed by work on his now maturing magnum opus, the *Institutes of the Christian Religion,* or rather on the first version known to us,[4]

---

1. For an extract from the text of the placards cf. P. Henry, *Das Leben Johann Calvins,* vol. I (Hamburg, 1855), 52f., based on the edition *Livre der martyrs.* On the incident cf. Stähelin, I, 34f.; an original example was found in the Bern city library in 1935, cf. H. Bloesch, *Un original des placards d'Antoine Marcourt de 1534* (Musée Neuchâtelois, 1943), no. 4. In English see BI 437ff.

2. OS I, 21; BI 1ff.

3. According to Peter Ramus, who in 1568/69 lived in the same house as Calvin had done in 1535. Cf. P. Wernle, *Calvin und Basel bis zum Tode des Myconius 1535-52* (Basel, 1909), 3.

4. OS I, 37-283; BI 21ff.

for work on it in one new version after another, in which it remained the same but was always totally fresh, would continue without a break until 1559, five years before his death. It was primarily this book that made Calvin one of the main factors in the history of older — and not just older — Protestant theology.

A glance at this first version is essential if we are to understand Calvin's life itself. "Institutes" has the sense of "instruction" (not "foundation," as M. Bossert suggests).[5] In keeping with this is what Calvin says at the beginning of the dedicatory epistle regarding the first aim of work. In answer to a need, especially in France, he wants to expound certain main teachings that will help those who have a religious interest on the way to true piety.[6] We have to remember that the man who felt called to this vast task, with no external motivation, for we do not hear of anyone asking him to do it, was then 27 years of age. The urge to present and unfold his insights, to intervene in history as an instructor, and to direct the religious movement must have been a deep and original one within himself. He believed, and in this again he was akin to Plato, that virtue may be taught.[7] If there is no obduracy, and if the witness of the Holy Spirit speaks the last and decisive Word, it is possible not merely to proclaim the truth of Christianity, but to expound it in a way that enlightens and convinces. At the beginning of the history of the Reformed church that would be so influential historically stood a schoolmaster with his textbook. That is from the very first its strength and its weakness. Those who would be Reformed should not in any event be ashamed of this beginning and this distinctive feature.

A second aim of the book, as Calvin himself tells us, was to defend the Protestant cause to those outside: before the court of the French king and before the French public.[8] We have already discussed the dedicatory epistle prefacing the work and do not intend to come back to it here.[9] Calvin did not think he had failed to achieve this second goal because the book made no discernible impression on Francis, for later changes and expansions still in large part move in this apologetic direction. He used

5. Cf. Bossert for this rendering of *institutio*.

6. OS I, 21; BI 1.

7. Plato discusses but does not decide whether virtue can be learned (taught?) in *Menon* 99e and *Protagoras* 319b.

8. See above, 108f.

9. See above, 108-12.

the work especially to give a necessary authoritative defense and answer to old and new objections and misunderstandings on the part of ill-disposed opponents or fatal friends of the Protestant cause, and to give an authentic interpretation of the Protestant gospel to those who were at a distance from it. He originally planned it as a redoubt with two main fronts but gradually built it up into a fortress with guns trained in every direction. Reformed Protestantism was militant from the first.

We cannot be experts in Reformed theology unless we are aware of Calvin's sense of responsibility, the keenness of his gaze on every hand, his need constantly to sharpen up and delimit his own insights and statements, his feeling that he was always on the watch. If we call this thrust in Calvin apologetic, however, we should note that it is not an apologetics that seeks to justify Christianity before courts outside itself, for example, philosophy or science. The standard by which Calvin's theology measures itself in justification lies instead within itself. It is its own generating principle, holy scripture, which, of course, is related so closely to reason, and therefore to true philosophy and science, that no need for external vindication can exist. The power of Calvin's apologetics, so far as it has any, consists of the fact that basically it is simply a conversation with itself. Its initial premise is that there are not two truths but only one, and hence from the very first it feels no temptation to barter. It proceeds with the silent summons: Those who have ears to hear, let them hear! [Mark 4:9].

Calvin himself did not state his third motive, but we need to take note of it because it is the presupposition of the other two, the educational and the apologetic. I refer to the intrinsic need to systematize. Calvin has always been called the born systematician, the great systematician of the older Protestantism and perhaps of all Protestantism.[10] A systematician is not just one who wants order and purity of thinking and has some skill in arranging and structuring thoughts. It may be that these qualities are not so essential in a true systematician as is thought. In truth we see little of them in the first edition of the *Institutes*. They usually develop in time when something very different is present first. This first and very different thing, however, is a profound need for synthesis and an ardent desire for it.

Synthesis is something original and creative. It precedes all detailed

---

10. Cf. Tschackert, 394, who calls Calvin "the greatest dogmatician of the Reformation"; and Loofs, *Leitfaden* (4th ed. 1906), 882, who calls the *Institutes* the "masterpiece of Reformation theology."

discussion. It is not itself discussion but the subject in every discussion. It is an ability and desire to see antitheses together, no matter whether we are thinking of spirit and nature, the inward and outward, eternity and time, faith and ethos, revelation and history, intuitive and discursive thinking, or whatever. All of us by nature incline to synthesis. Yet there are differences in disposition. Some have a religious bent like Luther. Others have a one-sidedly intellectual or moral or political or aesthetic bent like the great majority in the Middle Ages and today. In both these types the need and the ability to see things together is weakly developed. They can neither debate nor come to terms with one another in any true or meaningful way. They do not understand one another. They can only confront one another as strangers.

But a third group consists of those who are strongly inclined to synthesis. They have a powerful urge to present a total view, to set forth the whole. All that they do presses on toward this whole. They do not perhaps have any specific or outstanding endowment on any one side. For this reason they are the great warriors and at the same time the great peacemakers of history. They are the born teachers and fighters and debaters and soliloquizers. But before that, they are the born systematicians. Whether they actually erect what we call a system is of secondary importance. They are systematicians long before they do so, and would still be even if they never did. Those who succeed in erecting a real academic system with all the chicanery that this entails are perhaps not born systematicians but systematicians at a later stage, like carters who find work where kings build.[11] We recognize born systematicians by the fact that they are not wholly successful. Calvin was a systematician in this sense.

Already on a previous occasion I have called the *Institutes* a primeval forest.[12] It is certainly not a real academic system. In its way, however, it is the brilliant work of a synthesizer, of a man for whom synthesis was really the primary and original thing. Remember that the beginnings of work on the *Institutes* go back to the stay in Angoulême, that is, to early 1534. Already, just a few months after the Cop address, his first improvised Protestant statement, the author felt himself compelled to offer something

11. Cf. Schiller's poem *Kant und seine Ausleger,* which includes a line on carters having work when kings build.

12. Cf. 41 above, and Barth to Thurneysen on 6.8.1921, in which he calls Calvin a waterfall, a primeval forest, something demonic, direct from the Himalayas, absolutely Chinese, marvelous, mythological.

total and comprehensive, not just bits and pieces of Christianity, but instruction and training in it;[13] and if our understanding of the *Psycho-pannychia* is correct, that work, too, was not simply a bit of specialized dogmatic research but a contribution to fundamental principles. Calvin did not merely synthesize something already there, a mix of his own thoughts with those of Luther, Erasmus, Bucer, and Zwingli. He was first a systematician, and *then* he saw what was right for him in all these thoughts, *then* he found them, now here, now there, in the writings of contemporaries. He can always see both sides of the antitheses that crop up, for even before he knows the two sides their connection and unity are there for him. He can contend against the one side in the name of the other because both are reconciled in him. He can bring the two sides together because both are really at odds in him. He can think as Luther does against Zwingli, as Zwingli does against Luther, as Erasmus does against both of them, and as Bucer does against Erasmus. He *can* do all this, but he also *must*. He always understands the one through the other.

It is Calvin the systematician who on his own initiative becomes the educator and apologist. For thus understanding naturally produces a need to teach and a need to defend the whole as such, and both are needs that the one-sided on either side cannot know. In 1536 he had certainly not become a systematician in the sense of a system-builder, nor did he really do so in 1559. As a systematic structure the 1536 edition is just as unsatisfactory as Melanchthon's *Loci* in 1521 or Zwingli's *Commentary on True and False Religion* in 1525. It surpasses both, however, in the synthetic power that distinguishes the born systematician.

The order of the first *Institutes* is that of Luther's Catechism; law, creed, Lord's Prayer, sacraments, but with two powerful appendices, an attack on the five added medieval sacraments in ch. 5 and an exposition of Christian liberty in ch. 6, where unexpectedly under this title the main issue discussed is the form of life in the church and society. This is not the place to follow Calvin in detail, but we must try to work out briefly the dominant themes in the outward chaos of individual thoughts, and therefore the systematic element in Calvin in the true sense.

13. Borrowing from Kierkegaard, Barth used the title "Training in Christianity" for his last two parish confirmation classes in 1920/21 and 1921/22, *Konfirmandenunterricht 1909-1921,* ed. J. Fangmeier, part I of *Gesamtausgabe* (Zurich, 1987), 263, 405.

Knowledge of God and Man

We must begin with the famous opening sentence, which remained the same in every edition: Nearly all wisdom *(doctrina)* consists of two parts: the knowledge of God and of ourselves.[14] We may say fairly definitely that the impulse to adopt this formulation came from Zwingli, in whose *Commentary on True and False Religion* we read in the second small section that since it is God whom religion strives after and we are those who strive after God in religion, we cannot speak aright about religion unless first of all we know God and ourselves.[15] The difference, as we see, is twofold. First, to differentiate between the knowledge of God and ourselves, Zwingli uses *agnoscere Deum* but *cognoscere hominem,* there being nothing similar in Calvin. Second, it emerges from the "first of all" *(ante omnia),* and also from the whole structure of Zwingli's work, that the two sections 3 and 4 of the work (on God and man) are obviously viewed as a kind of prolegomena, whereas the inclination of Calvin, as we see especially clearly in the later structure, is actually to view the whole *(summa)* of doctrine from this double angle. The use of the formula is thus much more significant for the one who adopts it than for the one who coins it. We can and even must say that Calvin discusses this twofold theme throughout, that he is always speaking about God and us. Here is the synthesis in which more or less clearly all the theses and antitheses of his theology unfold in their dialectic of opposition and relationship, and to which, when rightly understood, they all seek to point.

If we now look at what Calvin has to say about God on the one side and man on the other on the first pages of his 1536 *Institutes,* one thing that strikes us is that so far as possible he sets God at once in the light of a full and sufficient knowledge of *man,* and that he at once speaks of man in such a way that we note that this is the man who is seen and known by *God.* In neither case is there any trace of a restraint that might indicate that we have here only a first and provisional stage of knowledge, for example, a natural theology and anthropology. Basically, can more be said about God on some higher stage than what we at once read here, namely, that he is infinite wisdom, righteousness, goodness, mercy, truth, meaning, and life, and that there is none beside him? All such things come from him, and all things in heaven and earth are created for his glory. He is the

14. OS I, 37; BI 20.
15. Z 3, 640.

judge who is over us all and who puts the fateful question whether we really serve his glory. But he is also the merciful God who takes up the cause of the needy when they flee to him and appeal to his faithfulness, ready to forgive, to help, and to save those who put their whole trust in him (I, 27).[16]

And can one basically say more of us than is said there, that we are created in God's image and likeness for full fellowship with him? But this image is obscured and forgotten as a result of the fall. We are far from God and alienated from him. All that is left as our innermost being is ignorance, wickedness, weakness, death, and judgment; even our holiness that shines brightest is an abomination (I, 28).[17] What we are of ourselves, intellect or will, soul or flesh, is concupiscence (I, 113).[18] From head to foot no good may be found in us (I, 45). If there is anything good, we owe it to God's grace (I, 45).[19] Yet the unmet obligation remains to serve God's honor and glory (I, 28).[20]

It is plain that in both cases the knowledge rests on an unstated presupposition, a "cognition" that contains the other two "cognitions" in itself and unfolds them. We *do* know God and God *does* know us: that is the unstated, primary, synthetic knowledge of God and ourselves with which Calvin begins and in the light of which he has to say all the rest. This original cognition is full, sufficient, and beyond emulation. Everything else that has to be said is simply a development, expansion, and elucidation of this original knowledge. It is simply an expression and naming of it. It is not something new and additional, a further step. Calvin knows no steplike difference between natural and supernatural revelation, no way from the one to the other. If he later makes a distinction, the latter is properly no more than an explanation of the former, its actualizing, one might say, and the Bible, for example, is the pair of spectacles by which to read the Word of God in nature and history, as he will later say expressly.[21]

This comparison should not mislead us into thinking that in the final edition Calvin was setting the knowledge of God the Creator and the knowledge of God the Redeemer over against one another in books I

---

16. OS I, 37; BI 20.
17. OS I, 38; BI 20.
18. OS I, 131; BI 132.
19. OS I, 57; BI 42.
20. OS I, 38; BI 21.
21. *Inst.* I, 6, 1; OS III, 60, 25ff.

and II. Without the biblical revelation that defines God the Redeemer Calvin sees no real knowledge of God the Creator, and conversely knowledge of God the Redeemer is simply a sharper and clearer seeing of the revelation of God the Creator. Materially the two forms of knowledge are exactly the same. We differentiate them only at once to grasp more truly their essential unity.

Hence I think it is wrong to say that Calvin did not gain his insight into God and us from Christ or that he simply forced Christian elements into a general metaphysical, philosophical view.[22] We need to note above all else that for Calvin there is no basic distinction between the elements of knowledge, but that Christ is from the first the key with which he unlocks the whole. Christ is that unspoken original presupposition in terms of which we see God a priori as the ground and goal, the one who judges us and shows us mercy, and in terms of which we see ourselves a priori, when measured against God, as sinners, and are thus pointed to grace. Looking from Christ at God, we have knowledge of God, or, as it is put later, knowledge of God the Creator. Looking from Christ at us, we have knowledge of ourselves, out of which arises later knowledge of God the Redeemer. It is the same light, however, that shines on both sides. The Christian element in Calvin is not a special higher possibility of knowledge, but the first and only possibility by means of which we may establish and say what is essential about God and us. Calvin does not try to do honor to Christ by putting him on one side, by putting him, as it were, on a higher lampstand, and then putting out all the other lights so as to let this light shine triumphantly; he sees all the other lights from the very first in the light of this one light.[23] We have seen already that this does no harm to the radicalism of his thinking about God and us — quite the contrary. It is true that in the process the borders between philosophy and theology become fluid, but that is perhaps not the least advantage of his theology.

We note the same trend and synthesis when we look at his thinking on law and gospel, that is, on the biblical revelation. Strictly, says Calvin, God's law is written in our hearts. It is the same thing as conscience (I, 29).[24] But because of our arrogance, which prevents us from finding it in ourselves, God

---

22. Cf. R. Seeberg, *Lehrbuch der Dogmengeschichte,* vol. IV/2 (Erlangen and Leipzig, 3rd and 4th ed.), 571.

23. Cf. the later Barth on the relation between Christ the one light and the lights and truths of the creaturely world and the cosmos, *CD,* IV/3, §69.2.

24. OS I, 39; BI 22.

had to give it to us in written form as well. Here again, then, the primary thing that Calvin never lost sight of is the unity. The same relation repeats itself on a higher stage when the law is written in its double form as the threatening unmasking of our sin and misery and the comforting promise of our deliverance from both. In fact Calvin cannot recognize at all any real distinction in principle between law and gospel. Christ is not a second Moses,[25] he says with Luther. But as distinct from Luther he does not mean by this that Christ was something totally different from Moses, for Moses already preached Christ. Increasingly in later editions[26] Calvin sees law and gospel together. The whole of the OT is full of promise, full of Christ, so that the NT is in the OT. Conversely the NT does not set aside but confirms and purifies the law that the Pharisees had perverted.[27] Both apostles and prophets preached the same unchangeable will of God both to judge and to save. Few thoughts were so much on Calvin's heart in his own time as that of the primary unity of the biblical revelation both with itself, and then further back, and less evident, with what God has said and still says to us in nature, history, and conscience.

In Calvin the thought of revelation is freed from all historical caprice and contingency. The one God meets us majestically, if more or less in concealed form, all along the line.[28] We can none of us make the excuse that we do not know the law or are not under its authority. Again, we none of us should regard ourselves as lost for not knowing the promise that always accompanies the law. There is no escaping divine judgment, but also no total distance away from divine mercy for those who can and will hear God's voice. Christ once more stands between the contradictions or rather above them, as the principle of knowledge, showing us both the full terror of judgment and the full depth of grace, yet not accepting the fact that these two both are and always will be two things. Calvin has been charged with Judaism because he would not let go of the essential relation of the OT and the NT but like the early church upheld their unity.[29] He has also been charged with rationalism[30] because for him God's revelation

25. OS I, 54; BI 39.

26. *Inst.* II, 9f.; OS III, 398ff.

27. For this thought cf. already in 1536 OS I, 54; BI 39.

28. Cf. esp. *Inst.* I, 5, and II, 12-17; OS III, 173ff.; 254ff.

29. Seeberg, 566, thinks Calvin's legalism inclines him to erase the boundaries between the OT and the NT.

30. Bauke, *Probleme,* 13ff., thinks the first feature of Calvin's theology is dialectical rationalism.

is simply his bringing to fulfillment our most profound and compelling human disposition. In spite of Marcion and Harnack,[31] we may regard the first fault as an advantage, and in view of the hints that Calvin gives us we should perhaps think more cautiously about the relation between reason and revelation in him. At any rate, no special gains accrue from cutting the threads between the OT and the NT.

If we now turn to what Calvin thinks about Christ when speaking about him expressly, we see at once that we have here the seat and origin of these and all the other tensions and antitheses that characterize his theology. The first thing he has to say in 1536 is that Christ, one with the Father, assumed our flesh and thus concluded the covenant with us, drawing us very close to God, from whom our sins had greatly estranged us (I, 30).[32] He has been made righteousness, sanctification, and redemption for us [1 Cor. 1:30]. This means for Calvin two things that are always distinct yet never separate. Christ died for us and thus freed us from the curse and judgment that lay upon us. In our flesh, and therefore in our name, he went up to heaven and is there at the right hand of the Father, interceding for us, our only hope, by participation in whom we are already in heaven even though on earth. That is the Godward, not the manward, side of Christ. He places himself in front of us, covering and justifying and liberating us, because in our flesh he is so wholly other than we are, the Son of Man who is the Son of God, and in whom, even though we are so far from God, we can put our trust.

Nevertheless, we cannot follow through this side of the matter to the very end without at once coming upon the other side. If Christ represents us in this way, then we are no longer afar off. In him we, too, are in heaven, chosen before the foundation of the world according to the same good pleasure of God that has made him ours, redeemed, accepted, reconciled, put under his protection, planted in him, in him already entering in hope the kingdom of God. There takes place here the wonderful participation that we who by our own works could never be justified or capable of justification are now what he is, a new creation, and we

---

31. The 1st edition of Harnack's classic study of Marcion had just come out in 1921 (Leipzig); cf. *Marcion* (Durham, North Carolina), pp. 134ff., where Harnack argues that the early church was right to retain the OT but the OT became a fate overhanging the Reformation in the 16th century and in the 19th keeping it in the canon weakened the Protestant church and religion. Barth's evaluation of Marcion was much influenced by this work.

32. OS I, 40; BI 22.

cannot be anything else when we deny ourselves and take up the cross, giving active expression to our heavenly calling by the good works that *God* gives (I, 49-52).[33] We have here, we might say, the opposite manward and not Godward side of Christ. But always Christ is in reality both the one who justified us *without* us and the one who dwells and works and initiates *within* us as the giver of the new life in us. The two can never be separated, yet the union is also true only insofar as each is on its own side the whole. Always in Christ we are those who are afar off, sinners, poor, ungodly, referred only to grace. Yet in Christ we are always close, God's children, hoping and already attaining, inseparably related to God. This is a secret and hidden philosophy that we may not know by syllogisms but that God makes known by opening the eyes of some, so that in his light they may see light (I, 82).[34] Always in fact Christ is the covenant and the one who concludes the covenant between God and us, the enacting of the inconceivable and impossible thing that when enacted is also the most simple and most natural.

The place where God's revelation comes to us is holy scripture. We all know that with special strictness Calvin stresses scripture's objective validity and authority. Already in the 1536 *Institutes* it is plain that he handles the Bible like a legal book whose wording must always have the final decision. Calvin forged the dogma of inspiration. Yet we cannot be content merely to say that. He never spoke about the inspiration of the Bible without also advancing the principle of its opposing highly subjective character. I refer to the inner testimony of the Holy Spirit,[35] the voice of truth that makes itself heard not merely in the Bible but also in the believing reader or hearer. Hence the process by which the content of the Bible becomes certain and authoritative is not merely an enforcing of the dictate of the letter and the subjection of the human understanding to it, but, if we take Calvin in the living sense that he had in view, it is also a conversation of the truth with itself. As the Holy Spirit is in the letter and also in the hearts of believers, the truth only seems at first to be twofold. In reality it is one, and inevitably it will find and know itself again on both sides. Precisely here, to do justice to Calvin, we must see that in his thinking he moves from but also toward a single point that is above the antitheses of objective and subjective or outward and inward, and that he

33. OS I, 60ff.; BI 46ff.
34. OS I, 96; BI 42.
35. *Inst.* I, 7, 4; OS III, 65ff.

167

can now very specifically speak of the one, now of the other, only because primarily he always has their unity, the totality, in view.

The same may be said about the thinking of Calvin on the appropriation of revelation, on faith. More strongly than the other reformers Calvin stresses the purely other-sided basis and content of faith. Faith does not come from us, not even as the recognition of our need. Even when we believe, and precisely when we believe, we have nothing good in us; our treasure is in Christ in heaven. It is the nature of faith to pierce the ears, close the eyes, wait upon the promise, and turn aside from all thoughts of human worth or merit.[36] For, he hammers home tirelessly, the object and goal of faith is the Word of God as such, and for us, then, it is the divine promise that we cannot see or touch. By nature faith is a mystery and always will be. It is something that we have in hope. We cannot possibly have it without self-renunciation, without ever new humility. The only guarantee of its truth and reality is the truthfulness of God, which no experience can attain to, which comes to us only in God's Word, and which can be accepted by us only in the trust in God's Word that the Holy Spirit creates in us. Faith is acceptance of God's truthfulness, namely, that he cannot deceive us. But this is always the truth of *God,* the invisible thing, the mystery, the promise, that which we accept in Christ, and precisely in Christ, when we believe. At its core faith is always by nature hope. All this, however, does not mean for Calvin any uncertainty, hesitation, or doubt. The very character of faith as hope is its character as certainty. For where is there certainty except beyond ourselves in God? Where can we rest except in what we cannot see or touch? Where is the Archimedian point for our life on earth except in heaven? Just because we have here *only* promise, *only* hope, we have certainty, assurance, undoubted possession. Hope, not having, is true having vis-à-vis God. All having must again and again be understood as hope. Those who would boast, let them boast in the Lord [1 Cor. 1:31]. But those who can boast in the Lord can and should boast.

With each detailed statement in Calvin's theology we should note how, when it is pressed, we reach a kind of joint where a new and apparently opposing statement comes to light that makes the meaning and content of the first one really clear if we can resolve upon following the dialectical movement in which all the statements engage. The point of this movement is always the same, namely, to think together the divine and

36. OS I, 60; BI 46.

the human or the vertical and horizontal side, to relate the insight of Luther to the problem of the Middle Ages and the modern period, or to put the latter in the light of the former, to see God from our side and ourselves from his. Good care is taken, then, that this theology will have to remain humble. There can be no question here of building a proud medieval structure. There has to be constant reference back to a first and original thing that cannot be put in any one statement but that simply stands creatively and critically behind all statements. In other words, all statements can only point to an inexpressible center, and to do so they must turn into apparently opposing statements. We might well say that the systematic element in Calvin consists of the applied insight that with words we can engage only in good polemics, and that with words, and the Word, we must be zealously polemical indeed when necessary, but that we cannot make a system of words, for only the theme of all words, God himself, can really be the system, the synthesis.[37] When theology remembers this unattainable synthesis and sets itself under its constraint in all its words, that is in itself a great thing.[38]

I would like to give a few more examples in order to make this feature in Calvin's theology clear. As a good Lutheran, when he hears the term "good works," Calvin never wearies of declaring that with all our efforts[39] and exertions we are worthy only of death and confusion. He was afraid that faith would collapse the moment it ceased to be totally the faith of promise, faith in God's mercy. We do not simply have the forgiveness of sins; we have constant need of it. Even the good things we do in faith on the ways of God cannot make us pleasing to God in ourselves. Only the imputed righteousness of Christ can stand in the eyes of God (I, 47, 49).[40] God's people can build only on this righteousness (I, 113).[41] Even those who have gone a long way on God's paths are still far from the goal. They have the desire and the will and they try, but in them is no perfection. If they look at the law, they see that every work they attempt or plan is under a curse. For what is imperfect is not even partially good or acceptable, but bad and accursed. This is what we are assured with unyielding severity (I, 197).[42] Hence we need

37. Cf. Goethe's *Faust,* I, vv. 1997f.

38. Barth had here a graph in the margin that he no doubt put on the board.

39. The MS erroneously had "temptations" here; cf. OS I, 59; BI 45, which Barth was paraphrasing.

40. OS I, 58ff.; BI 44f.

41. OS I, 131; BI 132.

42. OS I, 225; BI 243.

forgiveness for our stains and impurities, always needing to be covered by Christ's purity and perfection so as not to come into judgment until the hour, the hour of death, when the goodness of God, perfecting us, giving the new Adam, Christ, the victory over the old Adam, takes us into his blessed peace, and when we await the day of our Lord, the day of resurrection, on which, in our new and incorruptible bodies, we will enter into the glory of his kingdom (I, 49).[43]

Yet all this does not alter in the slightest for Calvin the seriousness of the task that is posed for our lives by the divine law. How can the Holy Spirit not be given as Leader and Ruler into the hearts of those to whom Christ's righteousness is imputed before God? But that is a seizing of our flesh. It means that our will can will no other than in every respect the glory of God. On the basis of the election of grace a life must be built up in which we demonstrate what we are: vessels of mercy [cf. Rom. 9:23] chosen for glory and therefore for cleansing. Those who are God's are changed and have become a new creation [cf. 2 Cor. 5:17]. They are on the way, moving from the kingdom of sin to the kingdom of righteousness. Holiness of life is the way, not the way that leads but the way on which the elect are led by their God to the glory of his heavenly kingdom. It is the training that we have to undergo, a school for recruits *(tirocinium)*,[44] when we are justified by grace alone before God. Between the cursing that Calvin pronounces on all our works as such and the school for recruits in which we must receive training in good works for the glory of God there is apparently an unbridgeable gulf. There is indeed. We do not misunderstand Calvin, however, but perhaps suspect something of the fear and trembling [cf. Phil. 2:12] with which this man would see Christians standing before God, if we remember that it is again the line that is broken in God that he wanted to describe, and could obviously describe in no other way.

More keenly than the other reformers Calvin felt and emphasized the provisional and questionable nature of our temporal life. How often do we read in this man of only twenty-seven years of age expressions like "so long as we live in the flesh" or "so long as we are confined in this prison of the body"[45] we are sinners and stand under judgment and have to bear the burden of this earthly life, so that we must be ready to journey

43. OS I, 61, 47f.
44. OS I, 67; BI 55; cf. n. 47 below.
45. OS I, 59; BI 45; cf. 133, 138.

on here below. Strangely seldom does he sound a triumphant note as Luther so often does. With earnest agreement he repeats the familiar thoughts of Luther that cause him at this point to use words in which we unmistakably recognize a restrained rejoicing. But it is always restrained. It is as though he is lifting up his hand to show us that the situation is really too serious for us to let ourselves go even for a moment. We never trust God enough except in mistrust of ourselves. Our courage in him is never so high that it does not have to be broken in us. We never find enough comfort in him unless we are without comfort in ourselves. We can never really boast of ourselves in him unless we renounce all self-boasting (I, 48).[46]

Or listen to his description of the lives of Christians who, looking to the divine promise in faith, have ventured to tread his way. Scripture, he says, has left us nothing of which to be proud before God. Its whole aim is to suppress our arrogance, to humble us, to make us small, to keep us within bounds. But it comes to the aid of our weakness, which would crumble at once were it not sustained and comforted by expectation. How hard it is to give up and abnegate not merely what is ours but our very selves is something that we must all consider individually, but that is the school for recruits in which Christ trains his disciples, that is, all the pious. He then disciplines us all our lives with the discipline of the cross so that we do not lose our hearts to the desire for temporal goods or to trust in them. In short, he treats us almost as though, wherever we look so far as the eyes can see, we see meeting us only despair. So that we do not go down under such heavy pressure the Lord comes to us and reminds us (so that we may lift up our heads and learn to look further ahead) that we may find in him the felicity that those in the world do not see (I, 54f.).[47] Or listen to what he says about faith in another context. To believe with our whole heart, he tells us, is not to cling perfectly to Christ but simply to lay hold of him sincerely, not to be fully satisfied in him but to hunger and thirst and sigh after him with burning desire (I, 104).[48]

Naturally all these notes may be caught in Luther, too. The difference is that they have become the basic note in Calvin. He correspondingly draws the lines more strongly on another side. Above the problems and assaults of the present life there shines always the thought of the day of

46. OS I, 60; BI 46.
47. OS I, 67; BI 55.
48. OS I, 120; BI 120.

the consummation of the kingdom with the revelation of divine judgment when God alone will be the sun and all in all, when his own people will be gathered in glory, and when the kingdom of Satan will be shattered and overthrown (I, 94);[49] or, in less eschatological terms, in an exposition of the fourth commandment (I, 37), the eternal sabbath which is already dawning wherever we rest from all works that are not done by us as the fruit of the Spirit, and will dawn with eternal rest the moment the divine "then" comes that confronts our human "then."[50] To be fair to Calvin we must look at both the harsh and stringent appraisal of time and the bright prospect of eternity in which we often almost think we hear the notes of a Tersteegen. When we do this we see from a new angle what the sure secularity of Calvinism is all about. It is the diagonal[51] between a sober view of temporal things that is free from all illusions and a looking ahead to the reality of the Absolute at an unheard-of upward angle. There are portraits of Calvin in which we can nearly grasp this conjunction of reasonable sternness with almost radical enthusiasm.

Sacraments

Always from the same standpoint we must take a preliminary look at Calvin's doctrine of the sacraments. We are in the mid-1530s and the issue is one that divided and still divides adherents of the Reformation movement. On which side would the young Calvin come down? What was the debate really all about? The historical facts are well known and so are the historical explanations. I can only say that the usual comments on the matter do not satisfy me.[52] An issue on which Luther would sooner see the whole Reformation confounded than yield had to be in some way more important and central than we view it today with the help of the usual slogans. But what was the important point of the sacramental controversy? Why did this issue stand at the heart of all the controversies?

I will first try to explain Luther's insistence on an almost material

49. OS I, 109; BI 108.

50. OS I, 47; BI 31f.

51. Cf. Bohatec, *Calvinstudien,* 353, for the term "theology of the diagonal"; also Bauke, 16f.

52. This sentence in the margin replaces an original (erased): "I admit that I am in some difficulty here because I do not rightly understand (inwardly) what the controversy was really about."

presence of the divine in the sacred actions in terms of his general tendency to make of the divine an independent material entity. Thus in him faith and the Word of God and the kingdom of God always have a remarkably isolated position from which at best we have then to find connections and bridges. His experience, the great Reformation experience, is before him as a something in time and place like the Wittenberg tower. We must let the Word stand.[53] It may be that Luther had in mind here something that no one since has really considered, something for which, for us latecomers, the antennae are in some way not available. For him everything depends on the Word enduring in its purity and distinctiveness. "*This is* my body" [Mark 14:22 par.]. The thought of sacramental objectivity had value for him as an expression of that other objectivity which in the mere Word seemed to be too little safeguarded against human caprice and unbelief.

Zwingli, as we saw earlier,[54] did not have this interest in the objectivity and purity of the divine element, or had it in a different way. For him all the stress fell on application, on practice. He could see in Luther's view only a relic of the medieval idea, which it was not. For him the divine element, the Spirit, the object of faith, was wholly and utterly a relation, a movement, *theos* being derived by him from *theein* (I, 165).[55] It is flesh and not spirit that is thing, body, a matter of sense, and the flesh is of no avail [John 6:63]. Hence: *significat.* Zwingli's sacramental teaching has its own fervor and force; let us make no mistake about that, and let us be careful not too speak too hastily about profundity and less profundity. An interest in relation is in truth a profound interest, too. Here, then, were the great opposing views with which Calvin had to deal in 1536.

In that year negotiations for union were in train between Wittenberg, Strassburg, and Zurich that reached a provisional and not very promising conclusion in the so-called Wittenberg Concord.[56] We might expect in advance that in relation to this controversy Calvin would display the greater perseverance and desire, for concerns of both Luther and Zwingli were present in him. With Luther he laid all the stress on the objectivity of the divine element, and with Zwingli he staked everything on the real

---

53. An allusion to the last verse of Luther's *Ein feste Burg* of 1529 (based on Ps. 46).

54. See above, 96.

55. Cf. Zwingli's *True and False Religion,* Schuler and Schultess III (Zurich, 1832), 165.

56. For the text of the Concordat, which Melanchthon composed, cf. CR III, 75; and Tschackert, 261f.

relation to humanity and the world. Hence both the sacramentalism of the former and the spiritualizing of the latter were alien to him, or, rather, he saw the element of truth behind the two as one and the same, so that he had to go his own way between the two contending brothers.

I must also say at this point that Calvin did not opt for a mediating path either here or elsewhere. He was not a man of no fixed opinions like Bucer busily rushing back and forth between Wittenberg and Zurich.[57] He really did go his own way, already in 1536 when he had France chiefly in view, but also later as well. The implacable anger of Luther and the Lutherans was soon enough directed at him as well, and by 1560 Calvin's name was in as much ill repute in North Germany as was Zwingli's.[58] If Calvin's theology did in fact prove to be ecclesiastically mediating, this was only to the extent that in some areas of Germany it made the Reformed version of the Reformation possible, giving it a more acceptable form than Zwingli's theology had done.

But let us now get to the point. Calvin calls a sacrament an appendix of the promise by which God seals the promise and makes it more credible to us. He stresses that the promise itself does not need this seal. God's truthfulness is sure enough in itself. It is our "imbecility" that needs it. The sacrament thus bears testimony to the grace of God by means of an outward symbol that confirms our faith (I, 102).[59] The water of baptism is not itself our cleansing and salvation, but simply the instrument of these, mediating to us the knowledge and assurance of this gift of God that takes place through the Word (I, 110).[60] What happens is not the forgiveness of sins but a strengthening of faith in forgiveness (I, 115).[61] Similarly the Lord's Supper is not the bread of life or Christ himself, but it reminds us that Christ is the bread of life (I, 120).[62] In it the Lord seeks to nourish the soul rather than the stomach. We are not to seek Christ in the body, as though we could grasp him with our bodily senses, but in such a way that the soul knows and grasps his presence (I, 121).[63] Here is the basis

---

57. Cf. Tschackert, 263, on Bucer's attempted mediation.

58. Barth obviously refers to the controversy between Calvin and Westphal of Hamburg; cf. OS II, 263ff.; CO 9, 51ff. and 141ff. The controversy hardened the rejection of Calvinism in North Germany and Lutheran northern Europe.

59. OS I, 118; BI 118.

60. OS I, 127; BI 128.

61. OS I, 133; BI 134.

62. OS I, 138; BI 141.

63. OS I, 139f.; BI 142.

of the belief that in the flesh Christ is in heaven in our place.[64] Those who would say that his body is not there but here with us really mean the spirit. Hence Calvin argues that he is truly and effectively exhibited, not naturally *(naturaliter)*.[65] We are given, not the substance or the true and natural body of Christ, but the benefits that he has mediated to us in his body (I, 123).[66] The point of the sacred action is (1) to remind us of the goodness of God in Christ and to summon us to recognize it, (2) to enable us to perform an act of confession, and (3) to bring us to a fresh awareness of our fellowship with the brethren and to lead us to love of them in *Christ* and of Christ in *them* (I, 126).[67]

I do not really understand how Wernle can arrive at the thesis that in this question, and in his approach to the sacraments, Calvin may be seen as a Lutheran when he really sought to stay clear of the far too strong material element in Luther's thinking.[68] Instead we are tempted to take the line actually taken by many of his contemporaries and claim him as a rather cautious Zwinglian. Yet that again would not be correct, of course. We must take note once more of the hinge that suddenly sheds a different light on the picture. Calvin did not go along with the liberal antisacramentalism of Zwingli that under the sign of spirit and faith left no place for the objectivity of the divine element. Under the form of thinking that was Zwinglian, or close to that of Zwingli, he did in fact speak no less strongly than Luther about the objectivity of the divine element in the means of grace, but developed the thought without the massive materialism of Luther. When Calvin referred to the appendix of the promise, the exercising of faith, the act of confession, or the act of fellowship, he did not add any "merely" to these concepts or weaken the presence of the divine element. As we saw yesterday, promise for him was the supreme and proper form in which God now draws near to us. Faith in the promise, eschatological faith in things that we do not see, was for him full and profound saving faith. This faith precisely, and this faith alone, which is set on Christ

---

64. OS I, 140; BI 142.
65. OS I, 142; BI 145.
66. OS I, 142f.; BI 145.
67. OS I, 145f.; BI 148f.
68. P. Wernle, *Der evangelische Glaube nach den Hauptschriften der Reformation*, vol. III, *Calvin* (Tübingen, 1919), 92, argues that Calvin undoubtedly saw himself on the side of Luther, not the Swiss, but just because he felt so strongly Lutheran he thought he should fight the more vigorously against a superstitious confusion of the external sign with the thing signified.

enthroned in heaven, and which is awakened by the Holy Spirit whom Christ has sent from there and given us from above, is an assured and certain faith that fully suffices.

Spiritualizing for Calvin does not mean any volatilizing, any subjectivizing. It is supreme objectivizing. Unlike Zwingli, on no account did he want, of course, a Spirit that freely roams and rules. As he brought Spirit and letter into a dialectical relation, so he did Spirit and sign. He always had two sides strongly in view, the eternal and majestic God in his unsearchable loftiness and freedom, and we in all our imbecility and arrogance who cannot do without external words and signs. For this reason Calvin expressly defends the sacrament in a way that is plainly directed not least of all against Zurich, against the arguments that faith does not need it, that it restricts the Holy Spirit, and that it infringes on the honor of God by bringing in such a creaturely element.[69] His basic response is always to recall how needy and provisional is that which we call faith — a consideration that was by no means unnecessary face-to-face with the overconfident folk at Zurich — yet also to recall[70] the way in which God himself wills to meet us by such means, and finally to recall how obvious it is that we should not trust in the sacraments but in God alone, the ministry of the sacraments being to help us to do this (I, 104f.).[71]

Along these lines, then, baptism is important and meaningful; it is good to have assurance that it is God himself who speaks to us through the sign.[72] We certainly need a lifelong testimony that we are not only growing into the death and life of Christ but that we are one with Christ in God's sight and share his blessings (I, 114).[73] In the same way the Lord's Supper documents the promise and bears witness to it. Where the promise is, faith has something on which to base itself and with which to comfort and strengthen itself (I, 118).[74] We are offered that here and not elsewhere; it is as though Christ himself were present before us and could be seen and touched by us.[75] Note that Calvin puts this in the conjunctive. For

---

69. The editor at OS I, 120 n. 30, thinks that the second and third objections discussed by Calvin go back to Schwenckfeld.

70. By an oversight the MS has here an *auf* for *an*.

71. OS I, 120; BI 120f.

72. OS I, 132; BI 134.

73. OS I, 132; BI 133.

74. OS I, 137; BI 139.

75. OS I, 137; BI 140.

him the corresponding indicative is of a higher order that does not belong in this context. Yet he leaves us in no doubt that it has its place. We are to move by analogy from bodily things to spiritual things. We must listen to the words: We are told to take, and that means that it is ours; we are told to eat, and that means that the other thing that we cannot see or take or eat becomes one substance with us.[76] The whole force of the sacrament, says Calvin, lies in the Word: "given for you," "shed for you." Those who take in the language of the sign truly take the thing signified. In later editions of the *Institutes* Calvin used formulas that came even closer to Luther and the Lutherans. He could do so with calm confidence. The ground on which he moved, not Lutheran or Zwinglian but his own, was solid and broad enough to allow of free movement without peril. His failure to win over the Lutherans shows outwardly that he had made no concessions. The more the pity for all of us that this farsighted and superior intelligence did not succeed in calling the confused minds on both sides to order!

Church

By way of orientation let us look finally at the doctrine of the church as Calvin presented it in 1536. The breadth of his whole conception, the almost titanic nature of his theological enterprise, is nowhere perhaps so clear as at this point. At issue is the antithesis that is usually depicted under such headings as visible and invisible church or church of faith and church of holiness. I myself would like to put it more one-sidedly and yet also more ambivalently as the divine church and the human church. Who are those who belong to Christ? What is the nature of their membership? How do we distinguish these people from others? Here obviously we have a very important field of battle for decision regarding the Reformed and Reformation interest in the relation between the vertical and the horizontal, the above and the below, eternity and time, Lutheran and medieval or modern thinking. Can we succeed in simultaneously saying the two things as one, that the church is God's work and yet that as such it is also a human reality? Can we trace membership of Christ wholly to free grace and yet precisely for the sake of the truth of God's grace see another angle and make a distinction from nonmembership? Can we attribute God's judg-

76. OS I, 137; BI 141.

ment on individuals wholly and solely to him and yet, just because this judgment counts as the most valid of all life's realities, establish the point that it means a strict and pitiless distinction?

From the outset we must say that even Calvin could not succeed in really establishing and upholding both aspects, at least as one and the same. As everywhere, so here, too, he had to be content to put the two alongside one another and to show how they are interrelated and affect one another. And as everywhere, especially in his sacramental teaching in which it is plain enough where his heart is, so here he is closer to Zwingli than to Luther, staking everything on God's *relation* to us and therefore on the visible holy human church, though also with Luther as distinct from Zwingli, we must immediately add, staking everything also on the *what*, on the content of the relation, and therefore also, even if rather against the grain, on the invisible church of God that we can only believe. But if Calvin's undertaking did not and could not succeed — the person who has found the right word in this predicament has not yet been born — his intention is plain and instructive enough.

It is interesting to see how the Calvin of 1536, in dealing with the article regarding the holy catholic church, the communion of saints, was never more Lutheran than precisely at this point, a sure sign that here especially he thought of going further in the opposite direction. For he here defined the church as the sum total of the elect *(numerus universus)*, whether angels or humans, and if humans, dead or alive, and if alive, living in various lands and scattered among many peoples. There is *one* church, *one* communion, *one* people of God, of which Christ our Lord is the prince and leader, the head of the body. In him they (all) are elected by the kindness of God before the foundation of the world so as to be gathered into the kingdom of God (I, 72).[77] From the foundation of the world there has been no time when the Lord did not have his church on earth, nor will there ever be such a time. For out of the corrupt mass he always sanctifies to himself some vessels to his glory, so that there should not be any generation that does not have experience of his mercy (I, 74).[78] For Calvin, then, the concept of the church rests on that of election, or predestination, which in the 1536 *Institutes* is worked out here and only here. Note in this regard two points.

1. When we see that this is how predestination comes into Calvin's

---

77. OS I, 86; BI 78.
78. OS I, 87; BI 80.

theology, we certainly cannot say that it is the starting point or center of that theology. Such an idea rests on an optical illusion deriving from the fact that later Calvin would stress so vividly this theologoumenon whose content is so arresting, and that he would defend it against all attacks, even the slightest. In so doing he was defending his commitment to the Lutheran doctrine of justification by faith more vigorously than Luther himself thought necessary, for Luther did not go so far in the sponsoring of a visible church of the sanctified and obedient. For the same reason the doctrine of predestination had already been much stronger in Zwingli than in Luther, but Calvin, the synthesizer, knew far better what he was doing. Modern Reformed theology, which for sentimental reasons thinks it may or must throw the concept of predestination overboard, has burdened and punished itself, as we see in Switzerland and America, precisely with what Calvin wanted to avoid by means of his sharp insertion of the concept. It has burdened and punished itself with great moral leveling, with a highly industrious and astonishingly visible churchiness that knows little, however, of the fear and trembling at the grace of God [Phil. 2:12] that is the basis and meaning of the real nature and life of the church. Things will not get better until those who are thus occupied see in some way that the ancient master of Reformed theology had good reasons for introducing this counterweight precisely at this point.

2. But we have also to take note of what the counterweight means precisely at this point: a strict election of grace as the constitutive principle of the church! Where, then, is all the rest, the assurance, the continuity, that at least today we regard as essential for the development of a so-called flourishing congregational life? Is it not clear that we are constantly facing the beginning again, or nothing again? Who of us have the courage today to base our congregational work on proclamation of the God who truly elects and rejects according to his good pleasure, and whom we can never anticipate? Would not this be like laying a foundation at which we solemnly put a big load of dynamite on the foundation stone instead of engaging in the harmless ceremonies that are customary? Calvin had this courage, as we see not only in his dogmatics but also in his sermons, in which again and again he ruthlessly begins at the beginning.[79] In this regard we can only note with astonishment that he achieved a success in

---

79. A common phrase in Barth; cf. *Christliche Dogmatik,* part II of *Gesamtausgabe* (Zurich, 1982), 390f. n. 14; and *Römerbrief,* 1st ed., reprinted in part II of *Gesamtausgabe* (Zurich, 1985), 163, 171, 382.

upbuilding that none of us today can emulate, and that obviously it was precisely with this rediscovery that he had the courage and the good conscience to take much more energetic steps in building up a true visible, holy community than we moderns do who shrink back from what he discovered.

For him — and again we must face the paradoxical connection — it was precisely the apparently uncertain thing that lies beyond us, predestination, the unconditional freedom of God's dealings with us, that gave him the possibility of taking firm steps in this world, and good reason to do so. Of the elect who make up the church he said that their salvation rests on such secure and solid planks that it would not collapse or fall even if the whole cosmic machine *(tota orbis machina)* were to break in pieces. For it is linked to God's election and could change or fall only with this eternal wisdom. The elect may thus tremble and be tossed hither and thither and even fall, but they cannot perish, for the Lord holds them with his hand (I, 73).[80] I think we can see expressly how the other side already comes to light in these eschatological statements, namely, the church, but not the church as a mere ideal or conceptual entity, not an invisible church in the watered-down modern sense of the term. No, cost what it will, here is something that will take shape visibly on earth during the reign of the emperor Charles V, not in spite of, but precisely because of, the fact that it has its roots where other plants do not, that is, in heaven.

But let us tarry for a while on this side. We naturally ask who these elect are who make up the church. Calvin replies that we can only believe the church as we regard ourselves as also called and elect, leaving the position of onlookers and questioners and standing by the answer that is given us in Christ, by the goodwill of God toward us.[81] The one thing we must not do, he cries out with Luther, is ignore Christ as we put the question. Any secondary guarantee of our election that ignores the origin, the revelation, would instead provoke God's wrath against us, and as we plunge into the abyss of his majesty we could only be crushed by his glory.[82] This terrible threat shows us how seriously Calvin took the danger of finding a basis for the church and its membership in this world. At the end of this road he can see only the plight, indeed, the despair of those who want to have dealings with God but not seriously. Calvin knows

80. OS I, 87; BI 80.
81. Ibid.
82. OS I, 88; BI 81.

something of the fact that it is a fearful thing to fall into the hands of the living God [cf. Heb. 10:31]. By humility, objectivity, and worship we learn not to ask whether we are elect.

Clearly the prompt yes with which Calvin can answer believers as to their church membership simply underlines the thesis that the church is the church of God that rests on the revelation of his goodwill. As regards others the answer is not so simple, for in the strict sense we can all believe only for ourselves. We obviously cannot deny to even our nearest neighbors the venture of trust or the seriousness of obedience, nor can we ascribe them to them. But for the same reason we must refrain from any final decision either way. It is God's prerogative to know those who are his [2 Tim. 2:19]. Even the lost can still convert, and even those who seem to stand the most firmly can still fall.[83] When he referred to binding and loosing for the kingdom of heaven [Matt. 16:19], Christ was not putting in our hands a judicial means of determining plainly who the bound and the loosed are.[84] The final truth is, then, that the church is God's and his alone. The last sentence of the whole section on the church tells us that the church is not a carnal thing that we may know by the senses or locate in a set place or restrict to that place (I, 77).[85]

Calvin spoke in a more succinct and one-sided and Lutheran way than Luther himself about the church as the church of faith — of faith, that is, of God alone. In 1536 he came close to the spiritualizing concept of a church that we may see only in terms of God. We must be surprised at the manner in which he found his way back from this point. But he *did* find his way back. The extreme manner in which he spoke about predestination seems to me to be a proof that from the first his intuition was twofold, that from the first the concept of a visible church, a very visible church, was his goal, that it was not suggested to him, as Wernle thinks, only by wrestling with the practical problems of church life after 1536.[86] We can be so radical on the one side only if we are no less radical on the other, and with even greater need, I would say, in Calvin's case.

How about that other side in Calvin? As regards others, he says, we

83. Ibid.

84. OS I, 89; BI 82.

85. OS I, 91; BI 83.

86. Wernle, *Calvin,* 56, argues that a few years of church work after the 1st edition were enough to shift Calvin's thinking from the invisible ideal church to the visible church, so that in the next edition he was no longer hovering between heaven and earth but had both feet firmly on the ground.

cannot know the elect with any certainty of faith. But we do have some signs or indications by which we may at least have some probability. You all know what are the "notes" of the church according to the Augsburg Confession: "The church is the congregation of saints in which the gospel is rightly taught and the sacraments are rightly administered."[87] Here is an attractive solution. The sanctity of the church has an objective basis in its institution. The saints are not saints; they are the sanctified by participation in that institution. Visibility, then, means such participation, or, more strictly, the disclosing and communicating of the primary accounts of it, that is, the right proclamation of the gospel and administration of the sacraments. We seem to have here a happy solution to the problem how the invisible can be visible without losing its objectivity and becoming something contingent, human, and limited, and we can well understand why modern Lutherans (Stange!)[88] do not seek any closer definition but constantly retreat into this sure and tested stronghold. When Calvin came to speak about the visible church, why could he not be content with this classical Augsburg formulation to which he subscribed[89] and of which he undoubtedly approved?

This is not the only point at which the difference between Lutheran and Reformed theology is not one of deviation but of agreement and yet with something extra, a further dialectical refraction, on the Reformed side. We shall perhaps see that as regards the Lord's Supper, too, where the extra is apparently on the Lutheran side, the situation is no different. Here in the concept of the church it is plain. No, Calvin could not be content with Augsburg's definition of the "notes" of the church. We may really doubt whether the definition, even though its obvious purpose is to secure the objectivity of the concept of the church, actually does this in face of every velleity[90] and constriction. The history of the Lutheran church at any rate seems to me to give us good reason for such doubt. What is meant by right teaching and right administration? Obviously only the founder of the church can decide, and he only directly. Luther (in a 1521 sermon; Tschackert, 104) said that we humans can consecrate bishops and

---

87. Augsburg Confession, article VII, has "pure docetur" according to BSLK 59f., but in J. T. Müller, *Die symbolischen Bücher der evangelisch-lutherischen Kirche* (Gütersloh, 3rd ed. 1913), 40, which he used, Barth found "recte"; and cf. Schaff, 12.

88. Carl Stange (1870-1959) was a Göttingen colleague of Barth, professor of systematic theology.

89. 1541 at Regensburg; see 398 n. 18.

90. *Willkürlichkeiten.*

make parsons, but only the Holy Spirit can make good preachers, and if he does not, then all is lost.[91] Again (in his 1518 Psalms commentary, EOL XIV, 66) he said that the church, God's holy city, is where Christ most purely teaches Christ.[92] That is the authentic interpretation of "rightly." It has to be so, for would not any other more obvious and more readily comprehensible interpretation at once interfere with the aim of the whole formula, namely, to secure the purity and objectivity of the concept of the church? But if there is no other interpretation of the decisive "rightly," then clearly it says no other than what Calvin is saying in his "number of the elect," that is, that the Lord knows who are his [2 Tim. 2:19].

At the end of his discussion Calvin thus adopted the Augsburg concept, but with some not inessential changes or, better, sharpenings. He says that where the Word of God (not just the gospel) is sincerely (not just an objective "rightly") preached (not just taught) and heard (again not just taught), and where the sacraments are administered according to Christ's institution (not just an indefinite "rightly"), where we see all this we cannot doubt that the church of God is also there[93] — note the caution as compared to the assurance of Augsburg: "The church is . . ." Nor does Calvin ever speak here of notes, let alone of notes of that which it is his final concern to seek. He speaks thus only to give final comfort face-to-face with the fact that there can be no ultimate certainty as to individual membership or nonmembership of the church. In this matter he does in fact seek notes or indications, things to which we can cling. But he does not do this in the impersonal matter of the true church, which we cannot know in practice. The changes that he proposes in the Augsburg definition obviously point in this direction, though he does not himself specify them. The Word of God that embraces both law and gospel (not just the gospel) as it is sincerely preached and heard and the sacraments as they are administered according to Christ's institution — *they* constitute the true church. But here is only Calvin's final comfort where all else fails. As proper notes or signs he does not adduce the qualities or activities of the church as such but only those of the people who as the elect of God have a share in it.

What did Calvin fear most? The spiritualizing imprecision that leaves

91. WA 9, 603, 6-8.
92. Cf. WA 5, 60f. on Ps. 2:7.
93. OS I, 91; BI 85.

it open whether the "rightly" is expounded authentically in Luther's sense? Certainly he did not want to stop at the number of the elect that such an interpretation would finally give but saw clearly that if there must be notes something more is needed. Or did he fear institutionalizing more, the objectivity of the pastorate to which the other interpretation would inevitably lead? We have no data on which to judge. The most we can say is that he had simply no antenna for the specifically Lutheran concept of the ministry. Positively, at any rate, he wanted a truly visible church against the background of the invisible church, a human church that might dare with fear and trembling to equate itself with the invisible church, but without being condemned thereby to passivity in this world; in short, a congregation of saints in which there would be no need to take the term saints so strongly that of the subjects of this holiness, the living persons concerned, no more would in truth be left than a kind of church roof arching in friendly fashion over them. When he inquired into the elect, the members of the church, Calvin was seeking the living persons to whom they relate. We should not really regard his aim too hastily as a kind of relapse from the Reformation and denounce it as a new monasticism or Humanistic velleity.[94] The relation of the knowledge of God to the living persons, and thus to the culture, or lack of it, in which they live, is also, as I said last time in regard to Zwingli, a serious and a profound concern. What would the knowledge of God be, and what would come of it, if there were no such relation? Can there be such a thing as a knowledge of God in itself? We must see the valid reasons for the concern that drove Calvin beyond Luther and Augsburg, just as we must understand the concern of the latter when they did not go beyond that definition. Only when we have grasped Calvin's concern have we any right to shake our heads because he could find no way of meeting the concern.

Calvin's notes of the church are as follows. We must have regard to a person's (1) confession of faith, (2) example of life, and (3) partaking of the sacraments. If in these three things the person confesses the same God and Christ as we do, then we should accept that person as one of the elect and a member of the church, but if not, then for the time being we should not.[95] In Calvin's view church membership, or election, will necessarily show itself in certain subjective signs, and he himself specifies the above

94. Cf. A. Ritschl, *Geschichte des Pietismus*, vol. I (Bonn, 1880), 76; Troeltsch, *Soziallehren*, 627; Loofs, *Leitfaden*, 893; also in n. 156 below.
95. OS I, 89; BI 82.

three, especially the first two. But this means that notwithstanding his almost spiritualizing or at any rate extremely Lutheran concept of the church, he has to demand church discipline, the right of the congregation to excommunicate. This is essential (a) lest anything unworthy be imputed to Christians to the dishonoring of God, as though his holy church were a conspiracy of lawbreakers and openly ungodly people, (b) in order that the bad example of such people should not corrupt others by their accepted presence, and (c) in order that by being put to shame such people should repent and make public confession.[96]

To his well-known demands Calvin did, of course, attach some provisos that put the matter in a different light from that in which it is usually seen. We are not to be simply offended by the moral imperfection of others, at least so long as they have not totally fallen victim to it. We are not to regard temporary exclusion from the church as though those thus punished had fallen from God's hand, from the number of the elect, and were lost — unless, as he adds, those concerned are openly condemned by God's Word, opposing the truth, suppressing the gospel, extinguishing God's name, and resisting the Holy Spirit.[97] By the nature of the case this limitation of the limitation, that is, the possibility of directly recognizing those directly marked by God and treating them as such, had to be more influential in practice than it should have been according to the theory. In his later life Calvin met a surprising number of people whom he would recognize to be wicked in this sense. But this was, perhaps, inevitably his destiny in view of his distinctive witness. At any rate, we must not overlook the fact that he wanted to exercise the church discipline that he envisioned with great caution and restraint. We cannot limit God's ability or make rules for his mercy. God can change the worst of people into the best. He can bring in the alienated. He can put those who are outside inside. He can thus shatter all human thinking. We must mutually think the best of each other, and if we cannot we must commend ourselves to God's hand and at least hope for something better from one another. In this way we shall maintain peace and love and refrain from foolish prying into the mystery of God's judgments. Even though Paul may hand over someone to Satan in 1 Cor. 5 [v. 5], that is only a condemnation in time for the sake of salvation in eternity.[98]

96. OS I, 89f.; BI 83.
97. OS I, 90; BI 83.
98. OS I, 91; BI 84.

In a word, we are not to condemn others. Their persons are in God's hands. For our part we can only evaluate their deeds by the standard of the law of God that is the rule of the good and the bad.[99] Our purpose with the excommunicated, then, is simply to motivate them to bring forth better fruits and hence to return to the society and unity of the church.[100] There follows a passage that perhaps unfortunately but at least significantly Calvin omitted from later editions. In it he stated that we were not to treat only the excommunicated in this way but also Turks and Saracens and other enemies of true religion. We must totally reject the ways in which thus far many have tried to convert them to faith by withholding from them water and fire and other common necessities of life, by refusing to discharge to them the duties of humanity, and by persecuting them with iron and the sword (I, 77).[101]

From all this we see that Calvin was well aware of the ambiguity and danger of his movement in the direction of a visible church. But we must also note that on the basis of the subjective notes that he boldly advanced these were only restrictions on the demand he made for church discipline. What he really wanted deep in his heart was a church that can honor God in the world, a church that has the advantages of a sect without the disadvantages, a church that knows what it wants and does not want, a church that knows its people, a church militant that could be compared to the Jesuit order in external power if not perhaps in inward organization because after all it is not an order or society but in spite of everything a church. Here was the step, then, that Calvin took beyond the Augsburg Confession. In later editions of the *Institutes* he worked out this side of his teaching with increasing force and more and more pushed the other side, the Lutheran side, into the background, though he never abandoned it altogether. Precisely at this point we see in a distinctive way the synthetic approach in his theology. He knew what he was doing when he dared to be a resolute and blunt churchman. He also knew what he was doing when he dared to be a resolute and blunt predestinarian. Even today we should take note of his pointing finger in this regard: Not the one side without the other. Both sides are valid.

99. OS I, 90; BI 83.
100. OS I, 91; BI 84ff.
101. OS I, 91; BI 85.

False Sacraments

We have now familiarized ourselves with the main content of the first four chapters on law, faith, preaching, and sacraments. We have still to take a look at the last chapters on false sacraments and Christian liberty, which, as we have said, expand the schema offered in Luther's Catechism. But since these two chapters together make up no less than half the main work, we must be on guard against claiming Calvin here as a kind of translator of Luther into French. Calvin did not really find Luther's Catechism exhaustive, and, as we have seen, he would often go his own way even when following it. The two chapters do not, of course, make easy reading. In them we get some impression of the ambivalence of the fact that Calvin completed Luther's work. What we see and hear now is reformation that has truly and finally come down from heaven to earth. We now have a detailed answer to the momentous question facing all religious movements: "Men and brethren, what shall we *do?*" [Acts 2:37]. How could this question fail to call forth a detailed answer in the Reformation, too? The threatening foes and uncertain friends of the cause force the leader to say precisely how all things would now be. It was a thankless task to give this answer. Luther played his part in shouldering the burden. But Calvin carried more of it. For in his case the insight into its inevitability was not the bitter end but the beginning that already stared the twenty-seven-year-old in the face as he realized that there was no option.

I do not know whether it is apt to do as Wernle often does and speak about Calvin being inspired.[102] Those who from the outset had to undertake that thankless task had to have much more than inspiration or whatever else we might call it. Much more apt, I would think, is a description like harnessed enthusiasm, which Wernle also coined for Calvin in one place.[103] Seen on the highest level, this attitude is perhaps one of the greatest and most heroic one can find among us. But at a first glance, it might easily seem to make a person dry and dull and all too human. Calvin could never achieve popularity either in his own lifetime or later. He could not become a theme of myth like Luther. It is more understandable that unlike the latter, he walked rather than flew. The 1909 anniversary in Geneva was thus a celebration for pastors and professors,

---

102. Cf. Wernle, *Calvin,* 20, who sees here a personal relation to Christ rather than theology.

103. P. Wernle, *Einführung in das theologische Studium* (Tübingen, 2nd ed. 1911), 225, views a repressed, restrained enthusiasm as integral to Calvin.

not for the people.[104] There was too much resignation in Calvin's whole attitude for things to be different. Indeed, resignation was with him from the beginning. For proof enough we have the fact that when he went over to Protestantism he became a theologian, and indeed a dogmatician and ethicist. To become a theologian in the way Calvin did is perhaps the most sober and secular and unromantic thing, the most free from illusions, that anyone can do. Instruction, apologetics, synthesis — these three terms are the distinguishing motifs of his theology. All three denote a descent into the arena. It is easy in contrast to extol the purer figure of Luther or the bolder line taken by Zwingli. A person has to be very open to undertake that descent. For that reason Calvin is at least no less a figure, no mere successor. It is in this connection, it seems to me, that we should read the two last chapters of the first *Institutes,* out of which later the enormous book IV on the external means of salvation would develop.[105]

In the first of these chapters we see Calvin with sword in hand hewing away with all his skill at the chief enemy of the gospel, Roman sacramentalism — a veritable slaughter of the innocents as he casts a severe and hostile glance on all the beautiful little plans of ingenious institutions and practices that had flourished under the warm medieval sun, as always happens in religious history, first plucking them up, then digging out the roots and energetically throwing them on the rubbish heap — not perhaps an edifying but a very human spectacle! Those who know in any sense what was at issue can hardly raise any serious objection. On this matter of the sacraments we have a plain either-or. Either friends and foes alike knew what was at stake, or they gained adherents without knowing what they wanted, willing to make a peace with opponents that would be the beginning of the end. A true leader could not be crisp enough in giving the order here to halt and advance. If the need for this is no longer really clear today, if, not without reason, there seems to us to be something nonessential and superfluous in what now passes for the fight against Rome,[106] this is more relevant as a judgment on our own age than on that of the Reformation.

---

104. Barth's library contained an illustrated account of the July 1909 anniversary in Geneva, *Les Jubilés de Genève en 1909.* Cf. W. Niesel, *Calvin-Bibliographie 1901-1959* (Munich, 1961), 32ff., for the related literature.

105. The full title speaks of the external means and supports by which God invites us into the fellowship of Christ and keeps us in it.

106. Barth plainly alludes here to the partly political Protestant distrust of ultramontanist Roman Catholicism; cf. K. Scholder, *Die Kirchen und das Dritte Reich,* vol. I (Frankfurt, 1977), 35f.

That precisely this chapter is so fundamentally and ruthlessly negative undoubtedly made it a liberating and reconciling chapter for hundreds and thousands at that time who were not clear about the matter. Behind the no with which Calvin challenged his adversaries his own Reformation position could be seen all the more clearly, the "Glory to God alone" which was the essential message of Luther *and* Zwingli *and* Calvin in opposition to the well-graded medieval pathway of grace and salvation. In France and Germany there was certainly special gratitude to Calvin precisely for this chapter because of the perspicacity and care with which he worked out the simplicity, directness, and credibility of the relation to God, if also the unheard-of paradox of it, in contrast to all the ingenious and even profound and certainly sentimental things that in the last resort could only conceal the simplicity, and also because of the energy with which, to use his own expression, he had partly stripped the lion's hide off the asses,[107] showing up that which was human for what it really was. This chapter unquestionably did much to clarify the situation regarding the opposition. In this context I must refrain from going into details and be content to share with you some of my own inquiries.

The first section is on confirmation.[108] The reference is to the Roman practice, the ostensible equipping of those regenerated in baptism with the Holy Spirit for the battle of life. But where, asks Calvin, did God ever promise any second equipment of this kind alongside baptism? A servant's first duty is to obey. Where is the word of command to which those who call themselves ministers of the sacrament may appeal here?[109] Who has taught them to seek salvation in the oil that plays so decisive a role both here and in the whole Roman Catholic sacramental system? Is not baptism itself an adequate equipment for the battle of life? Is it not a devilish doctrine that so devalues the promise that God has given in baptism?[110] The wisdom of God, celestial truth, all Christian doctrine, really institutes and anoints a Christian (I, 145).[111] A sacrament is not from earth but from heaven, not of us but of God alone (I, 146).[112] Away, then, with confirmation! If we are perhaps to retain what the practice was originally,

107. OS I, 223; BI 170ff.
108. OS I, 163ff.; BI 170.
109. OS I, 163; BI 172ff.
110. OS I, 165; BI 172f.
111. OS I, 166; BI 174.
112. OS I, 168; BI 176.

we might put catechetical instruction in its place, teaching children the main points of religion in a short formula, and thus doing something that can only be useful in view of the general ignorance.[113] I might note in passing that with a few slight alterations what Calvin says about confirmation might still be said against the great abuse that from the days of Pietism and Rationalism has gained a footing even in Protestant churches. Apart from oil and bishops, there is really nothing missing of the things against which Calvin inveighs here. For the rest his friend Bucer seems to bear some guilt for the development of this Protestant confirmation.[114]

The second section is on penitence (penance).[115] Like few passages in the whole work it breathes a Lutheran spirit. The enemy here is the idea that penitence can be a single act which as such effects forgiveness of sins. Plato comes in at this point with his thesis that the life of the philosopher is a meditation on death. Even more truly one might say that the life of a Christian is a constant striving and training in the mortification of the flesh until it is fully destroyed (I, 150).[116] We thus learn not to dwell upon our own contributions and penitential tears but to direct both eyes to the mercy of God and to give him the glory in true humility (I, 152)[117] — the surest way to avoid the despair and the lightheartedness between which we vacillate when we make penitence a sacramental act. Penance has to go. We have sinned against God alone, God alone can help us. To him alone we can and must confess our sins.[118] The power of binding and loosing is either the power of God's Word in the preaching of the gospel, which God acknowledges and in which we hear God himself speaking with his Word of judgment and grace, or it is the authority that the church has been given to discipline its members, and that has nothing whatever to do with the remission of sins.[119] Ideas about special priestly powers, a treasury of good works that the church can draw on, works of satisfaction that must follow absolution, mortal and venial sins, and pur-

113. OS I, 169; BI 176.

114. For Bucer and the church orders influenced by him confirmation still had sacramental significance; cf. *Martini Buceri Opera omnia,* ed. F. Wendel et al., series 1: *Deutsche Schriften,* vol. VII (Gütersloh and Paris, 1964), 313: Laying on of hands and prayer as an act of blessing.

115. OS I, 169ff.; BI 177ff.

116. OS I, 172; BI 181.

117. OS I, 175; BI 183.

118. OS I, 179; BI 188.

119. OS I, 186; BI 196f.

gatory (a "deadly invention of Satan") are all human and misleading fabrications.[120] Penitence as an act is not a sacrament. It does not have the sign and promise that alone make a sacrament. The true sacrament of penitence is baptism, which offers sufficient comfort to the penitent.[121]

We then move on at once to extreme unction, ordination, and marriage.[122] An important point here, stressed in the case of ordination, is that in place of the hierarchical omnipotence that had thus far instituted and deposed ministers Calvin envisions at least some powerful cooperation on the part of the congregation itself,[123] something, as we well know, that even the Protestant church has not yet fully achieved. Dearest to Calvin was the appointment of pastors by the civil authorities on the advice of tested older ministers.[124] He had no objection to the laying on of hands at institution, but it ought not to have any religious, that is, sacramental, character.[125] The enemy again was cultic materialism — the relating of oil and spirit (I, 190), inept gestures (I, 189) — in presumptuous imitation of the appointment of the apostles by Christ.[126] With savage scorn Calvin calls this an ingenious fabrication, trying to show historically how the priesthood developed out of Christendom, Judaism, and paganism patched together to make one religion (I, 190).[127] He does not regard the anointing of the sick in the Epistle of James [5:13] as a basis for extreme unction, nor the story of the Samaritans in Acts 8 [v. 16] as a basis for confirmation, for even though the latter were baptized, and had yet to receive the Holy Spirit, the apostolic age had gifts and needs that are no longer present,[128] a thesis that the churchman accepted with remarkable rashness. His conclusion is the triumphant statement that in part he has torn off the lion's hide from the asses.[129]

In reading all this we do not really know whether to laugh or to cry, to go along with the powerful attacks or to hold somewhat aloof from them. Calvin does a successful and convincing job for us in the chapter

120. OS I, 187, 190ff., 200; BI 200ff.
121. OS I, 201; BI 216.
122. OS I, 202ff.; BI 216ff.; OS I, 205ff.; BI 219ff.; OS I, 220ff.; BI 236ff.
123. OS I, 214; BI 229.
124. Ibid.
125. OS I, 218; BI 233f.
126. OS I, 217; BI 233; OS I, 216; BI 232.
127. OS I, 217; BI 233.
128. OS I, 203; BI 217f.; OS I, 164; BI 171.
129. See n. 106 above.

only to the degree at least that he makes his own strong position clear through all the negations and proposals for amendment. As regards the negations I believe that we may in good conscience vacillate between the thesis that once we are caught in the wasps' nest of Romanism we have to attack vigorously and uninhibitedly[130] and the thesis that we certainly cannot do real justice to the Roman Catholic problem along these lines. On our lips Calvin's polemic would undoubtedly not sound good. Both theses are true. It seems that one of the evils, either slackness in principle or injustice in principle, can hardly be avoided. May we decide carefully which of the two we choose!

Historically the following points are to be noted regarding this controversial chapter. (1) The direct impression it leaves is that here is a man who can handle Roman Catholicism well, really well. He shows no sign of devotion to the world of its piety, or love for it. At every point he looks pitilessly only at the ancient and evil foe. Again and again he calmly puts the stereotyped question: Where is the sign for this supposed sacrament? or: If you have a sign, where is the divine promise that makes the sign a sacrament? He does not say farewell to the opposing position that he fights as one might to a dear friend who has, perhaps, become unfaithful — Luther's attitude to the Roman Catholic church. He does so as a judge who dismisses a convicted and condemned malefactor. This mood cannot have been of recent origin. A sudden conversion in 1533 thus seems to be ruled out completely. His abandonment of medieval Catholicism must have taken place much, much earlier. His stubbornness in clinging to error, to which he refers in the Psalms commentary, cannot have gone that far, or it must not be regarded as a serious adherence to Romanism. Who knows, the seeds of his break with the church might have been sown already in his parents' home in Noyon.

(2) Nowhere except in the Seneca commentary of 1532 does Calvin speak so plainly as a Humanist as in this chapter. Naturally that does not detract from its value, but we have to take note of it for the sake of understanding. Nor does it mean that in the chief point at least Calvin does not launch his polemic wholly from the center. Especially in the great chapter on penitence, which is typical of the whole, a grim seriousness holds sway, a constant recourse to the final and profoundest arguments. But the subject meant that the battle front here was in many ways similar

---

130. Cf. M. Claudius, *Asmus omnia sua secum portans oder Sämmtliche Werke des Wandsbekker Bothen* (1775; new ed. Munich, 1968), 551.

to that[131] of contemporary *illuminati*. Hence we can well imagine that some portions were read favorably by those who rejected the Reformation gospel but approved of the fight against Rome and joined in it. In contrast, serious and thoughtful Roman Catholics would hardly be reached at all by the work. The method of proof is biblicist, more so than in other parts of the book. But formal biblicism was originally a Humanist achievement. The simple way in which the question: What is written? rather than other questions is used against tradition may sound orthodox in our ears but there is something of the Enlightenment and liberalism about it. In large part it goes with the eternal conflict between Romanticism and rationalism, and it is only that which hides from us a little the significance of the fact that in this case, unlike a century ago, rationalism is the younger and fresher and more vital of the two contestants. The crisp fighting style and the irony and mockery which often enough break through all the seriousness point in the same direction. Finally, the polemical arguments themselves, at least in some passages, hardly differ from those of a decided rational skepticism vis-à-vis the Roman world of miracle. At this point we plainly see an intersection of the two lines of the movement of the time. This was unavoidable in Calvin. It was he who was really, and would increasingly become, the chief fighter against Roman Catholicism, never clearly distinguishing for himself the difference of motifs in the conflict. This was both the strength of his polemic and its weakness. Calvin would not have been Calvin if there had not been this side to him, too.

In the chapter on false sacraments we see Calvin with sword in hand. Unique to him there is the energy with which, more like Zwingli in this respect than Luther, he burns his boats behind him and says farewell to everything medieval, to all that goes along with consecrated oil. Note that without the antagonism expressed in the chapter one might perhaps be a good Lutheran but one cannot be a good Reformed. Reformed Protestantism has two problems: the glory we must give the Lord God (thus far it is only a sharpened Lutheranism), and the demonstrating of this reverence by a corresponding attitude in secular life in the world (a concern not so strongly on the heart of Luther). There was no place for an independent third thing between the two, both sacramental and cultic. The cultus, even in the form of the sacrament, can only be instruction on the invisible relation to God and its visible implications, not an objectifi-

---

131. The MS incorrectly had *denen* here.

cation or reification of what is divine. It is not an end in itself but only a means. It is not basically a tarrying but a hastening. There is no relation between oil and spirit.[132] In this spirit the Heidelberg Catechism could later call the papal mass "an accursed idolatry,"[133] displaying a fierceness that was never known in Lutheranism because this knew nothing of that hastening from the sacred to the profane, but in its own way, if perhaps in a spiritualized manner, it cultivated a tarrying in the sphere between the two. This spirit impresses on Reformed Christianity a certain nonreligious, sober, and in some sense critical and openly or secretly aggressive character from which it cannot and should not break loose so long as it understands itself. Precisely this chapter on false sacraments is thus a primary Reformed note. We can calmly contemplate and accept its humanity and human questionability but in no case should we suppress or overlook it if we are to understand what is at issue.

Christian Liberty

In the sixth and last chapter Calvin took tools in hand with the aim of showing in outline how he thinks about the Christian attitude in secular life in terms of reverence for God. He suggests three themes: (1) Christian liberty; then more narrowly (2) ecclesiastical power, and (3) political government.[134] In the three titles we find expressed both the borrowing from Luther and the difference. When at the end Calvin seeks to speak expressly as an ethicist in the more precise sense, we do not have an added second or new thing, nor the law as a second thing alongside the gospel. His concern is simply for a right use of the freedom that is opened up for us by the gospel. The statements that speak about life in terms of faith and the world in terms of God are not synthetic but analytical. No new factor emerges. The aim is to understand the one old factor aright and to put it into action aright. The Enthusiasts, who are here the enemy, misunderstood and misused Christian liberty. A violent, chaotic, and capri-

132. See n. 123 above.
133. Heidelberg Catechism qu. 80.
134. Chapter 6 has the three headings in its title, but Barth puts the break between the first two sections at a different point from the editor of OS I. See n. 139. On ecclesiastical power see OS I, 234ff.; BI 252ff.; on political government, OS I, 258ff.; BI 284ff.

cious relation to the historically evolved world and its forms of life was for them the consequence of the new knowledge of God. A situation threatened that we today know only too well, namely, that those who came down from the newly discovered mount of transfiguration [Mark 9:9 par.] into the depths of everyday life, as they had to do, would wander around in an intoxicating mist of Enthusiasm, all of them as seemed best to them [cf. Judg. 17:6] adopting a basically negative attitude to everything that might have any claim to represent valid order in daily life.

Calvin, like Luther and Zwingli, did not think that this had to be, that this was real Christian liberty, nor did he take this view merely as an apologist for Protestantism to Francis I, who feared revolution. He could do so because nothing was more alien to his approach from the outset than that cloudy freedom. For a synthesizer, who tried to see antitheses together, what could Christian liberty mean in practice but discipline and order, just as in practice the number of the elect was identical to the militant church of the saints, the voice of the holy God was one with that of the written Word, and the divine gift and fulfillment was one with the promise that is all we can have? The remote, the divine, the wholly other was in fact so remote, so divine, so wholly other for him that he could not fail to do justice to what is near and human and ordinary. In contrast to all intermingling of heaven and earth, he had now for the first time to show the near and the human and the ordinary in their own true light, in their unavoidability but also in their crisis. *So* radical and sudden was his conversion that the usual confusion in conversions between overcoming the world and greater or lesser withdrawal from it or fighting of it, between Christian freedom and some other freedom, could never find any place in him. *So* radical was it that he did not have to give up his Humanist and juristic leanings and interests; we find no trace of this in Calvin. Instead, he could at once find a place for them in the resoluteness of a Christian who was not ready to put his light under a bushel in the human and properly ordered world.

Two things are true and call for notice. Calvin was wholly Lutheran when he did not put his ethics under the rubric of good works, fulfillment of the law, or the new obedience, but under that of Christian liberty. In view of this fact we can hardly say that he did not rightly understand or adequately value the intention of Lutheran ethics, which is best summed up under the phrase "Christian liberty." Christian life is life in the liberty of the children of God [Rom. 8:21]. All that might seem to have to be added to faith as life, good works, obedience, keeping the commandments, or however else we might put it, has substance and truth only in the atmosphere of this freedom. Hence nothing has to be added to faith. Faith has simply to come into action. This is what Calvin expounded so powerfully here.

But then we must note the second truth. Calvin is not at all Lutheran when he associates or, more precisely, interrelates Christian freedom and ecclesiastical and political order. Could we really imagine Luther's famous *Freedom of the Christian* having a second and third part on these themes? As Calvin tried to grasp Christian freedom both specifically and positively, his eye fixed on church and state as the two great forms of life on and in which we must practice and demonstrate it. Decisiveness unrestricted by any asceticism is the distinctive feature of Calvin's ethical approach to the relation here. Or, in other words, we might find the distinctive feature in the fact that the concept of love, which plays so big a part in Lutheran ethics, has for Calvin no role at all, or only a subsidiary role, in this whole context. If love is precisely the great step out of world renunciation and false freedom toward the neighbor, the world, and orderly action in the world, one might argue that it was something that Calvin took for granted. But one might also argue that when Calvin the lawyer and Humanist at once fixed his eye on church and state in making the step, he had good reason to handle the concept of love with caution and restraint. The latter interpretation is probably closer to the truth. Realism is the strong side of all Reformed ethics, love perhaps the weak side. No one can have a strong side without some penalty.

But let us now turn to the details. In a first section of the chapter Calvin deals with Christian liberty as such, that is, in its negative significance. As he sees it, the gospel means liberation for us in three ways. (1) While not challenging our obligation to make our lives a meditation on piety, it does challenge the idea that by such efforts we can achieve the righteousness that counts in the judgment of God. So, then, without weakening the seriousness of the divine commands, it turns our gaze away from ourselves to Christ, that is, to the mercy of God.[135] (2) Without hiding the fact that what is perfect is demanded of us, and that the imperfect obedience that even the best of us renders is reprehensible disobedience, it tells us that God in his fatherly leniency accepts even our imperfect practice, that in Christ we are not household servants but children, and that in spite of, no, because of our basic insight into the

135. OS I, 224; BI 242.

judgment under which we stand, we may meet and obey the divine summons with great and joyous alacrity.[136] (3) It frees us from an anxious conscience in our use of God's earthly gifts, though not concealing from us the truth that conscience, and regard for the consciences of others, obviously limits our freedom, and yet in such a way that we might have to give offense to Pharisees, and that there is no place for a vacillation of conscience, for its being torn in different directions.[137]

If we look at the three negative descriptions of freedom together, it is evident that nothing, absolutely nothing but faith is made the basis of ethics here, a relentless looking past oneself to God, a good will that stands totally under judgment and finds its possibility precisely therein, a certainty, finally, that has its footing and its natural limit in that eternal foundation. Christian liberty is in every part a spiritual thing (I, 199).[138] The truly free person is the one who is captive to God. For this very reason there can be no confusion between the freedom that is grounded in God and the freedom that we assert in relation to others. This is where the themes of the second and third sections come in, that is, distinguishing and relating the spiritual government of the church and the political government of the state.

The second section deals with ecclesiastical power (I, 205, 208).[139] Calvin's purpose is indubitably to show that in contrast to fanatics who misuse Christian freedom, discipline and order are unavoidable and good even in the church of the gospel. What is remarkable, however, is the way that he takes to reach this goal. He arrives at it only at the end and deals with it only briefly. He devotes the main part of the section to showing that there is no ecclesiastical power that fixes our relation to God or binds our consciences. Freedom itself, true freedom, must overcome false freedom. It must do so by showing that it is itself at the same time captivity to God. And so again he gives centrality to what can be described only in negations. The authority and dignity of prophets, priests, apostles, or the successors of apostles is not their own, not a human authority and dignity, but the authority and dignity of the ministry they fulfill, or rather of the Word that this ministry serves (I, 205f.).[140] But there is only one Word

---

136. OS I, 225; BI 243; OS I, 225f.; BI 245.
137. OS I, 226ff.; BI 246ff.
138. OS I, 234; BI 254.
139. OS I, 234ff.; BI 252ff.
140. OS I, 234; BI 254.

of God. From this source all those have drunk to whom God gave the honor of knowing him: Adam, Noah, Abraham, Isaac, and Jacob, and all like them. The time of the NT, however, the time of Jesus Christ, is called the last time because it brought the conclusion of revelation, the revelation of the unity, exclusiveness, and definitiveness of the Word of God (I, 207).[141] What kind of other human authorities come into consideration now that the Word has become flesh, the age of many and varied prophecies and revelations has been brought to a close, the one Word to which all revelations point has been spoken? Every human mouth must stay closed now that he has spoken in whom the heavenly Father willed to hide all the treasures of wisdom and knowledge. . . . The one Christ must speak and all others be silent — the one must be heard and all others ignored and even despised.[142]

On this basis, however, there is an authority that is given to the church and indeed to all its pastors: the power confidently to venture all for the Word of God as whose ministers and administrators they are instituted; to make all worldly power, glory, and greatness bow to its majesty and obey it; to rule all, from the highest to the lowest, by the Word; to build the household of Christ; to destroy the kingdom of Satan; to feed the sheep; to slay the wolves; to admonish and instruct the obedient, to correct and upbraid and oppose the rebellious and arrogant; to loose and to bind them; and finally to deal with them with thunder and lightning; but to do all these things with the Word of God, whose spiritual power is as different from that of bishops as Christ is from Belial (I, 280f.).[143] This saying stamps the character of Calvin and Calvinism as few others do. By both outer and inner necessity imperialism and militarism are here made a likeness — a likeness, be it understood — of the kingdom of God.

But let us hear more. When people do not bow before the Word of God but before something human, then ecclesiastical authority is a deception and illusion, contrary to Christian freedom and indeed to God himself. Nowhere does God recognize anything as his except where his Word is heard and very carefully *(religiose)* obeyed (I, 211).[144] Nothing injures God so much as to be venerated in a new form of religion that is

---

141. OS I, 235; BI 256.
142. OS I, 236f.; BI 257.
143. OS I, 237; BI 258.
144. OS I, 240; BI 262.

of human invention (I, 212).[145] Hence there can be no appeal to the authority and tradition of the church. What is the church? The Holy Spirit makes Christians, makes the church. This is always true considering the imbecility to which even the most gifted are always subject.[146] But the Spirit's presence is guaranteed only by humble attentiveness to the Word. The church is certainly that church that must be heard.[147] But it is the company of those who are united in Christ and it dare speak only out of God's Word. This company is to be heard, and no other church.[148] The truth does not always flourish in the bosom of pastors, and the wholeness of the church does not depend on their state (I, 216).[149] A pastorate that is not based on obedience to God is a matter of caprice *(licentia)*.[150] Against it may be brought all that Jeremiah and his like had to say against the priests and prophets. But that is how it is with the pope and bishops and councils. The royal rule of Christ puts an end to all human dominion.[151]

But what about the order that Calvin did not wish to give up but sought to maintain and establish against the fanatics?[152] He himself admits that at a first glance it is not easy to distinguish this order from the clericalism he was opposing (I, 225).[153] It can be justified only if we see its totally human and temporal and earthly character and divest it of any religious character. For the sake of peace and concord and seemliness and humanity, he says, every human society is of necessity a *politia*. Without order and decorum and observances and "bonds of humanity" the church could not survive in view of the great number of different people in it.[154] These things are not necessary to salvation. They do not bind or loose consciences. They do not serve God. We cannot even claim their detailed necessity or validity.[155] But they are useful if they are not pressed too hard and if the instruction of good pastors protects them as far as possible against misunderstandings. Among the bonds of humanity Calvin lists not

145. OS I, 241; BI 262.
146. OS I, 242ff.; BI 264ff.
147. OS I, 244; BI 267.
148. Ibid.
149. OS I, 245; BI 268.
150. OS I, 245; BI 269.
151. OS I, 245ff.; BI 268ff.
152. OS I, 253ff.; BI 277ff.
153. OS I, 255; BI 280f.
154. OS I, 255; BI 281.
155. OS I, 256ff.; BI 281f.

only such things as Paul mentions in 1 Corinthians 11 and 14, for example, women keeping silent in the church [14:34] or liturgical order and all that it entails, but also church discipline, which is so important for him. But there must be no clinging to such things at all costs, not even to things that came in long ago by good human right or even by divine command. Thus King Hezekiah had to destroy the brazen serpent [2 Kings 18:4] with the same necessity with which Moses once set it up [Num. 21:8]. God's Word stands over every yes or no in such matters.

This was Calvin's last word on ecclesiastical authority in 1536. When we recall how much, as we noted earlier, he was concerned to establish discipline and order in the church, and when we also recall that the struggle with the people of Geneva, which at least outwardly became the main theme of his life and which, all unawares, he would enter upon this same year, revolved around this very point, we can never be surprised enough at the restraint that he exercised in this section. You will certainly be astonished that apart from the remark about the value of church order for decorum and humanity he has nothing positive to say in justification of it. The point of his argument is simply to make plain that it is compatible with Christian freedom, and under what restrictive conditions. For him everything depends on basing ethics on freedom. If freedom is ensured, ensured even against self-misunderstanding, that is, the freedom of the divine Word that itself provides for order in human affairs, then Calvin believes that the order he desires so ardently is secure. In this context he sees no reason to do more than indicate the way in which Christian freedom can and indeed must be used to set up in the human sphere a church law at least as rigorous as that of Rome, and the form that this use should take.

For him everything depends on the grounding of the *possibility* (not the *reality*) of what he thought, of course, to be unconditionally necessary as the human side of the church. We thus coarsen and falsify Calvin's thinking if we say that his concept of the church is a revival of that of medieval Catholicism.[156] The two look alike but they are not the same.[157] Appearances deceive. In any case Calvin's church was not at all the same. It rested no less invisibly and spiritually and exclusively on God's Word

---

156. Seeberg, 631, sees here a movement back to medieval thinking and away from the Reformation overcoming of this. He put this view even more sharply in the 1st ed., II, 405.

157. Terence *Adelphi* V, 3, 37.

than Luther's. Indeed, it was perhaps even more invisible since Calvin experienced and conceived of faith more paradoxically than Luther, of Christ's eucharistic presence more miraculously, and of the merciful character of justification more keenly. Just because he drew the line on the one side to the very end here, it was natural and necessary for him to continue it on the other side, and to do so with full awareness, with a good conscience, and with no hampering consideration that we have here only the other, human, earthly side of the matter, the visible church with its strict order, the step from heaven to earth. We must not view Calvin's church of holiness as a catholicizing confusion of divine and human commands, at least not as far as Calvin himself was concerned, no matter what misunderstandings might have arisen later among his successors. Calvin himself clearly saw the possibility of such a confusion. Under the pressure of the order and holiness that he found in God, he realized that order and holiness are incommensurable. They cannot be imitated on this side in the human sphere that is not to be confused with the other world, in the little city of Geneva that even at the pinnacle of his success he never truly regarded or described as a Jerusalem. With a certain resigned wisdom and grim humor, if we might put it thus, he spoke only of honoring God by bonds of humanity[158] so far as this is possible seeing that we live on earth. Calvin did not fall victim to the illusion that gripped the whole of the Middle Ages and that has gained force again in the modern age, the illusion that there is a continuous path that leads step by step from an earthly city of God to the kingdom of heaven. For him the divine was always divine and the human always human.

But precisely this sense of distance that finds such surprisingly strong expression in this section of the first *Institutes* makes the human symbolical and plastic for him and full of promise. For this reason it is an object of serious work for him as it can never be when heaven and earth are confused. What was the origin of this insight? We might again pose this question here. Did he derive it from the NT, from Plato, from Luther, or from Erasmus? Did he derive it from all of them? My own view is that we do not derive such an insight from any source. If we have it, we have it. But in any case we must not confuse the insight that he so wonderfully expresses in these deliberations on church authority, both against it and for it, with any of the medieval or modern banalities.

The only remaining section of Calvin's ethics is on political govern-

158. See n. 154 above.

ment.[159] I want to go into this rather more thoroughly both because of its relevance and even more so because we really find the theological uniqueness of Calvin with special clarity again in this area. Let us look first at the frame of mind with which Calvin undertook to tackle, in a teaching manual, what was then a dangerous issue, that of the relation between Christianity and politics. It is important that we should be clear about this in order that we may rightly evaluate the surprising content of this final section of the work. Let us keep the following points in view.

1. As a lawyer Calvin had expert knowledge of the field. Here if anywhere we might expect this to become apparent in the knowledge displayed and the concerns addressed. Yet when we read through the section we are disappointed in this regard — whether pleasantly so or not is a separate matter — at least to the degree that he refrains from introducing anything that is not strictly relevant in this area of his special expertise, or from expressing any thoughts that would not be immediately understood even by those who have no legal training. The reason for this cannot be that he had forgotten his legal knowledge, for he gave ample demonstration of it later in Geneva, and he showed that he knew how to make good use of it in given cases.

2. There can be no doubt that Calvin wrote this last section of his book with a specific material interest. He was not a monk emerging from the cloister and realizing that there was secular as well as spiritual government, so that for good or ill he had to try to wrestle with this alien fact. Calvin was a man of the world who had certainly investigated the questions of public life — whether anarchism is right or wrong, what is the best form of the state, whether revolution and tyrannicide are permissible — before he ever took up the question of the content of the NT. We must remember with what profound skill and liking he participated all his life in high politics, even the highest. In fact, if not in form, he was the statesman as well as the pastor not only of his Genevan but also of his international congregation. In a symposium that has just come out entitled *Masters of Politics* (Stuttgart and Berlin: Deutsche Verlagsanstalt, 1922) Calvin is the only theologian represented, and in a brilliant depiction of him H. von Schubert ventures to compare him to Napoleon.[160] Today we

159. OS I, 258ff.; BI 284ff.

160. H. von Schubert, "Calvin," in *Meister der Politik . . .*, ed. E. Marcks and K. A. von Müller, vol. II (Stuttgart and Berlin, 2nd ed. 1927), 67ff. On pp. 94ff. Schubert argues that Rousseau, too, saw the importance of religion in Geneva, as did Napoleon, who for

might well imagine Calvin as a most industrious reader of newspapers and writer for them, and modern politicians of all parties and countries would probably learn something from him. But if we expect to find anything of this great ability and interest in the section, we will again be disappointed. His thoughts about government and law and society as he expresses them here are perhaps clearer and more acute and consistent than those of other theologians who then dealt with such matters, but they do not show more of the statesman. He had to put a deliberate curb on his interest as well as his knowledge.

3. We may not doubt that to this field as well as that of the church he brought specific insights and goals as well as knowledge and concerns. Behind his exposition of the different possibilities and requirements of public life stands not only an exact knowledge of the subject, and not only abstract attentiveness to what was going on in this theater such as we might have when, as is best for us, we are not committed to any party dogma but for this very reason are forced into the frustrating role of onlookers. As would soon come to light in Geneva, Calvin had specific ideas of what he wanted, very specific ideas, for example, of the best form of government (he was an aristocratic republican),[161] of civil and criminal law, of the European situation and its demands, and even of economic relations and possibilities. In such matters he was anything but an unworldly idealist; he was supremely practical. To mention only one thing, for a good part of his life he flung himself body and soul, and expended much of his energies, in a fight against the policies of Bern, and in this fight he knew how to achieve what he wanted and needed!

But in the *Institutes* we find no sign, almost no sign at all, of his wanting anything, not even in the later editions that came out in the heat of all the conflicts. He can discuss the most prickly of political issues without playing politics (even by hints) on a single line, without making a plea for or against one thing or another. The more closely we look, the more clearly we see that there are in fact no specific decisions in individual matters, that questions are left open, that even if we regret it, we are not set on a particular course of Calvinist politics. If an uncommitted person were given the section to read without knowing who its author was, such

---

a moment thought of favoring Protestantism, regretted that it had lost its chance in France in the 16th century, and might well have reached out his hand to Calvin had he lived at that time.

161. See 225f. below.

a person would find it hard to identify the man who not unjustly has been called a father, if not *the* father, of the political and economic ideal of Western European liberal democracy,[162] but would be more likely, perhaps, to see here a North German legitimist who is perspicacious enough to look beyond his legitimism. How self-controlled this author must have been, or, better, how controlled by some other interest, to be able, when giving instruction in the Christian religion, not to say what he, John Calvin, was really aiming at with all the fervor of his heart and the brilliance of his mind!

4. Finally, we have to remember how much the predisposition and thrust of Calvin's whole theology lead us to expect that he would have to give a plain, down-to-earth statement here. Did he not attempt a synthesis of divine and human knowledge? Did he not aim to supplement the Lutheran systole with the Reformed diastole?[163] Did he not insist firmly on justification by faith and yet as an ethicist keep both feet solidly on the ground and thus seek to apply the Reformation insight (as a crisis) to the horizontal problem of the Middle Ages and our own time? Why, then, is there no program of a theocratic state or Christian Socialism? Why are there not at least precise and unambiguous indications of Calvin's view of the way in which Christians should approach the problem of society? Why does he not at any rate pacify us with an attempt to derive from the gospel a way of fashioning life and the world that is in keeping with the gospel, and thus lead us to the goal to which with some impatience we want to be led when someone undertakes to give us instruction in the Christian religion? Is it not the agelong weakness of theology and theologians that the moment we expect them finally to redeem the promise they have long since given and say to us: "Do this and do not do that for such and such reasons," they leave us in the lurch again on fresh dialectical pretexts? At least on the basis of some writings on Calvin and Calvinism, do we not look for better things from him?

Yes, we do have here a weakness of theology, at any rate of Protestant theology, if we want to call it a weakness. I myself would, of course, say that it is the venture of Reformation and Protestant theology, which distinguishes it from medieval and modern theologies, that it neither can

---

162. Cf. M. Weber, *Spirit of Capitalism* (London, 1940), 43ff., vol. I of *Gesammelte Aufsätze zur Religionssoziologie* (Tübingen, 2nd ed. 1922), 17ff.

163. Barth crossed out a further sentence in the MS: "You know, of course, these medical terms for the two functions of the mechanism of the heart."

nor will do anything but leave us in this predicament, or, rather, make it fully plain to us that the final word: "Do this and do not do that," must, of course, be spoken (the "must" is specifically Reformed), but that it can be spoken only by God himself as his own Word; and if Reformed theology, when addressing ethics, wanted things to be different, this would mean apostasy from the Reformation! Those who look for a program, or even simply a system of directions, in instruction in the Christian religion must turn to Thomas and not to Calvin. (I already pointed out to you on an earlier occasion that we modern Protestants of all trends can probably fare better with Thomas than Calvin.)[164] Longing for the smooth and well-lighted paths of medieval and Roman Catholicism is a very understandable emotion, and it is too much alive in us Protestant theologians for us to take offense at others when they accuse us of leaving them in the lurch at the most relevant point in our expositions. But it is not we who do it. It is the Reformation that leaves us in the lurch the moment we think: This is it! Or, rather, it leaves us to God. It shows us clearly that all else that has been said can only be an experience that helps us discard all other possibilities of salvation and leads us to the point where we must hand over ourselves — our conscience, insight, and will — to God.

We should not expect anything else from Calvin, not even in his ethics, otherwise he would not be Calvin, but Thomas, or Bernard of Clairvaux, to both of whom he was in fact related in some ways, though we should not fail to see that he was so under a changed sign, that is, with the Reformation knowledge of God, with the theology of the cross that is also the point of his ethics. Everything becomes totally different in him. It cannot be, then, that in his synthesis he again wants either peacefully or stormily to point to a way from earth to heaven, or even to a heaven on earth, as though the parallel lines were again meeting in the finite sphere. No, God is still God, and we are still human. Calvin felt this antithesis, or at least expressed and emphasized it, much more sharply than Luther, and he thus worked out much more sharply than Luther the thesis that God is our God, the God of real people living in the real world, that there can be no fleeing from his presence to another world, that there is no world that even as it is, is not God's world, that precisely in *this* world we stand under the *command* of God. Yet under the command of *God*. The burden that is laid upon us by the fact that God is the Lord who issues the commands cannot be lifted from us by anyone, not even by a

164. See above, 40f.

good Christian lawyer, no matter how great his political interest may be or how well he knows what he wants. If anyone were to take the burden from us, even an angel from heaven, and if we were gratefully to exalt that one into heaven as the being that had finally, finally brought us clarity and given us directives — that one would be the most dangerous and abominable deceiver.

Calvin was not a deceiver of that kind. He was not Dostoyevsky's Grand Inquisitor.[165] Often he might almost seem to have been so. I myself have sometimes thought that he was more dangerous than all the popes and generals of the Jesuit order put together because, under the Reformation banner, he was doing the work of the worst kind of Counter-Reformation. But precisely the surprising thing in this last section of the *Institutes* shows us, if nothing else has yet done so, that he was *not* a deceiver, he who knew better than any others the temptation of the Grand Inquisitor and indeed the justifiable concern that he had. This is why he does not set up any Christian state or Christian Socialism or Christian civil or criminal code, even though he is obviously not lacking in ideas and plans in that field, and even though, once the time comes for him not to instruct but simply to live, he will regard the most far-reaching experiments in that direction as not merely legitimate but divinely commanded, and will for this reason conduct them with incomparable historical success.

Yesterday we saw how he would make no exceptions in his criticism of all ecclesiastical power that does not have the force of the Word of God itself even though he really knew what he wanted in this regard and also sought and achieved what he wanted (church discipline). The decisive point is, however, that he set the specific and well-considered and to him truly important content of his willing and striving and achieving fundamentally on a very different human level, where also, of course, God has to be heard and obeyed, but where human imbecility rules as well, where face-to-face with the eternal majesty of God there can be no human eternities, where, as we saw yesterday, the brazen serpent that Moses set up may be destroyed again by order of the same God. Human willing and striving, even when obedient to God, and especially then, has to have specific content. We cannot obey God without willing and seeking something, this or that. But what we human individuals will and strive after, even though it be ever so important and significant, even though it be a

165. See F. M. Dostoyevsky, *Brothers Karamazov*, II, 5.

whole city of God, always stands as such under the shadow of the relativity of all things human. It neither can nor should become a theme in instruction in the Christian religion if it is not to have the force of a new enslaving of conscience. This instruction, if it is to remain pure and true, can provide only a basis for the *possibility* of what can and must happen on the human side in obedience to God, at the creature's infinite distance from the Creator yet also with a view of the Creator. It cannot provide a basis for the *reality*. For this reality is always human, temporal, this-worldly. If God in his paternal leniency will accept it as well-pleasing to him, that is his affair.[166] But we neither can nor should count on making it, as though this were for us to decide. Not making this distinction is a feature of Roman Catholic theology. I say yet again that not unrightly we have the feeling we would be better off not having to make it. But Calvin did make it. Hence his great silence precisely where we are most curious. Calvin's synthesis is the synthesis between God in his majesty and us in our imbecility, between the holy God and sinners. No other! Since we are Protestant theologians, we must try in some way to accept this.

Let us now analyze briefly the content of this last section.[167] We recall that in the second section on church law, which gives us no law, he used the title "Christian Liberty." This in itself tells us the whole story. Calvin certainly wants those whom he is instructing to plant both feet firmly on the ground. He certainly wants to answer the question: What shall we do? But he can give his answer only in the framework of Christian freedom. Remember that "freedom" is the catchword under which Dostoyevsky distinguishes Christ from the Grand Inquisitor.[168] Only one thing is at issue even when demands are put: that we should be forced into a situation in which we are thrown back upon God and therefore free, that we should be freed from illusions that might still hold us and that are remote from freedom.

Hence Calvin's aim in this section is not, as it might seem, the positive one of founding and establishing the ideal state. As before, when he discusses the church, his aim is to show what is God's will in the orders

166. See n. 136 above.

167. OS I, 258ff.; BI 284ff.

168. The reference is to a passage in Dostoyevsky's novel in which the Grand Inquisitor tells Christ that all will be happy under them, neither rebelling nor exterminating one another as they would under Christ's freedom. He would convince them that they would be free only by renouncing their own freedom in the church's favor and becoming subject to it.

that exist, with the emphasis not on the existing orders, as in a conservative worldview, but on the divine will! There can be no Christian freedom without submission to the divine will. The rights of government and law and the duty of citizens to obey arise only out of Christian freedom. For in government and law we encounter the order of God that Christians particularly should not seek to avoid.

The enemy whom Calvin combats here is the view of the Radicals that salvation involves total world reform,[169] the setting aside of imperfect government and law. For Calvin this view is so bad that he refrains from expressing his own concern for better government and better laws. We must avoid this "Judaic illusion" that would make Christ's kingdom part of this world (I, 228).[170] We must not fuse into this world that which does not belong to it but must follow its own logic *(ratio)*. As different as soul and body are Christ's spiritual reign and civil order.[171] Spiritual liberty is truly compatible with political subjection.[172] Our human status and the national laws under which we live are not the thing that counts, for Christ's kingdom does not consist of such things (I, 229).[173] So says the father of modern democracy, the man to whom it was not really a matter of indifference whether he continued to live under the laws of old Geneva! But that concern yields to the other concern, that in our desire for better human laws we should never forget or neglect that law of God that is always and everywhere present.

Does this distinction make the civil order an object of indifference and contempt? Not at all! That order is a different thing from the reign of Christ but it does not stand in contradiction with it. The celestial kingdom begins already with the reign of Christ in us, and in this mortal and perishable life we thus have a prospect of immortal and imperishable blessedness. The point of civil order, however, is to integrate our life, so long as we live among others, into human society, to frame our ways of life according to justice, to make us mutually responsible for one another, to nourish and to cherish peace and tranquility.[174] All that will be super-fluous when the kingdom of God that is now hidden in us brings the

169. OS I, 258; BI 284f.
170. OS I, 259; BI 285.
171. OS I, 258f.; BI 285.
172. OS I, 259; BI 285.
173. Ibid.
174. Ibid.

present life to an end. But while it is the Lord's will that we should wander as pilgrims in expectation of our true homeland, our pilgrimage demands instruments of that kind, and to strip us of them is to strip us of our humanity (I, 229).[175]

Note the double meaning of the term "humanity" *(humanitas)* here. It first denotes our earthly pilgrimage far from our true homeland, and hence something no less imperfect than necessary. But this imperfect and necessary thing is the Lord's will under which we stand here and now. We must not try to evade it even though we see how superfluous such supports for our pilgrimage will be when it is over, when there is no more here and now, when the kingdom of God brings our present life to an end. How lacking in insight it is to try to evade this relative divine will that is valid here and now! As though it were not simply barbarity *(immanis barbaries)*[176] to give free rein to evil because of some dream of a perfection that is already possible.

Calvin then goes on to list what civil order entails: first, simply seeing to it that life is possible; then seeing to it that there is no idolatry, no blasphemy against the truth of God, no other offense against public religion; that public peace not be disrupted; that the property of all be protected; that regulated dealings between people be possible; that Christian worship be ordered; and again, and obviously unambivalently, that humanity obtain among us.[177] Calvin excuses himself for makng the care of religion a political matter when it is in truth outside the sphere of human competence. He would rather not do this, but his concern is simply to protect true religion against public calumny and slander.[178] Here we are obviously on the level of relative considerations, and Calvin himself points this out. We do not owe our lives to the authorities but to God. God does not need the state to protect himself and his truth. Private property and free trade are not of supreme importance. Humanity is not the key to the door of heaven.

We naturally do not need Calvin to tell us all this. But does it then follow that these postulates, including a loyal protection of the church by the state, do not have a relative justification? The seriousness of the human situation forces Calvin to say that they do, and its humorous side permits

175. OS I, 259; BI 286.
176. OS I, 260; BI 286.
177. Ibid.
178. OS I, 260; BI 287.

him to do so. We must not confuse Calvin's justification of the state with political conservatism, for although the general need for the state rests on a command of God, this command is valid only for a time, and, as we shall see, the details are based only on time and place, not on divine institution.

In Calvin's doctrine of the state and society we find three trains of thought.

1. Authorities.[179] Calvin starts out from the fact that the Bible does not merely recognize civil authorities but eulogizes them. He even thinks John 10:34: "I have said, 'You are gods,'" has to be related to the civil authorities. He takes it that this and similar passages give those who hold political office a divine mandate and therefore the divine authority to play the part of God in every relation (I, 230), seeing to it that to some degree they act as his representatives.[180] What kings and their advisers and other officials decide and carry out is thus God's work. The divine providence and sacred ordinance are a sufficient reason why human affairs are regulated in this and not some other way. Civil authority is thus the most sacred and honorable of things of this kind in all our mortal life.[181] After what I said last time I need hardly give a detailed explanation of these statements that should sound strange to us. We today no longer know what eternity is, and we thus find statements of this kind strange. But those who are as clear as Calvin was that the life we live here and now has the character of parable and pilgrimage can safely venture to make the statements. And we can rest assured that they will not fail to put them in proper light by means of other statements.

What does this dignity that is ascribed to public officials actually involve? Above all things a duty, a responsibility. Having to rule, those who are God's vicars or legates must remember that in their own persons they have to offer to others a picture, as it were, of the divine providence, protection, goodness, benevolence, and righteousness. If they fail to do this, they sin not only against their fellows but against God, whose justice they besmirch.[182] In their dignity they do have, of course, the comfort that as God's servants they do what God does, so that those who reject them always reject God.[183] The office of kings certainly differs from that

179. OS I, 260ff.; BI 287ff.
180. Ibid.
181. OS I, 261; BI 287f.
182. OS I, 262; BI 288.
183. OS I, 262; BI 289.

of apostles, but both rest on divine appointment,[184] even the dangerous office of the monarch. Monarchy or republic? That is a matter of circumstance, conditions, and usefulness. Both forms may be right in the right place. Calvin warns against disputation on such issues.[185] In the light of God's will it is for us to be obedient where the one or the other exists (I, 231-33).[186] The task of government?[187] Calvin issues a reminder that he is not speaking *to* the powers that be, but *about* them. He is thus content with the affirmation that, as is necessary on earth, they must reward the good and punish the bad; this is the judgment or justice to which Jer. 22:3 refers. There is thus no disguising here that we are in the field of opportunistic or relative considerations, that the fact that God is in heaven and we on earth [Eccl. 5:1] applies also to the "gods" on royal thrones and in royal council chambers. For Calvin the divine justification of civil authorities lies precisely in the relativity and humanity of their task as he soberly sets it forth. In his view we may not and should not fail to see the finger of God in this very relativity.

Three short excursuses follow that show us what problems fanatical circles in France had caused at this particular time. First, government means the shedding of the blood of wrongdoers. Should it? Yes, says Calvin without hesitation. He well knows the prophecy of the holy mountain where no one will hurt or destroy (Isa. 11 [v. 9]). But the death penalty is simply the unavoidable answer to the fact that in this world the commandment "Thou shalt not kill" [Deut. 5:17] is constantly broken. It is a divine judgment on this transgression.[188] The devout, of course, must not hurt or destroy. But it is not hurting or destroying if the unjust suffering of the devout is punished by divine command. It is not human arrogance to exact this penalty. Since the judgment of God is concealed in it, failure to do so would be human arrogance. From this standpoint, Moses and David, both lenient and peaceable by nature, as Calvin thinks he can state, sanctified their hands by the use of force, and would have stained them had they not used it. They executed the vengeance that is the Lord's but that the Lord commits to them for its execution.[189] Natu-

184. OS I, 263; BI 289f.
185. OS I, 263; BI 290.
186. OS I, 263; BI 291.
187. OS I, 263ff.; BI 292ff.
188. OS I, 264; BI 292.
189. OS I, 265; BI 293.

rally kings and judges have to remember that clemency is their supreme ornament, but they must remember, too, that there is a superstitious softness that face-to-face with the horrors against which they have to protect us is in fact the most dreadful inhumanity.[190] Note well that what Calvin is arguing for here against the fanatics is obviously not the right of society to defend itself against those who disrupt it but the thought of the divine judgment, which in this world must first take the form of that self-protection of society. Calvin also realized that this is not the *ius talionis* of eternal law, but as temporal law it is the fearful reflection or likeness of that law, and for that reason it must be upheld.

The second special problem is that governments wage war. Should they do so? Calvin again answers yes. But a conditional and limited yes! They must not resort to the sword under the impulse of passion. It must happen only as a last resort. All other steps must be taken before a decision is made for arms.[191] But finally we have a full and unqualified yes. Wernle comments that Calvin was not aware of the problem that the Radicals discerned.[192] He did at least know, however, the horrors of the reality of war and he had a strong impression of its ungodly nature, as we learn from many passages in which he speaks of it. Is it by chance that he does not mention the name of God here but is content simply to say that the same right which makes governments the protectors of their subjects, guardians of the laws, and a terror to malefactors is also the right to wage war when necessary, but also the right to anticipate what waging war involves, to have standing armies, and to enter into defensive alliance?[193] Naturally he might have mentioned the name of God in this connection as well, not merely because on his view of God and the world God's action is also concealed in some way even in our ungodly human action as its ultimate determinative basis, but also because our human action that evokes such horror — and this is the point here — is sanctified when it is performed in obedience to God's command. The function of government in both peace and war, however, stands under God's command. We must see to it that justice is done to this command and how it is done, but we should also be on guard against overlooking the fact that in observing the command ultimate and humanly speaking unheard-of possi-

190. OS I, 265f.; BI 294.
191. OS I, 266; BI 294.
192. Wernle, *Calvin*, 147.
193. OS I, 266f.; BI 294f.

bilities are present. To overlook this would be to overlook the seriousness of the human situation, the seriousness of the fact that while the kingdom of Christ is the beginning and the goal, it cannot be or become an element of this world. All the required restraint regarding the ultimate unheard-of possibilities of drawing and using the sword will not and should not prevent us from constantly realizing how serious the situation is.

This was what Calvin wanted to defend against the pacifists of his day. The step from there to what we neutrals in recent years called a theology of war[194] is a very small one, or no step at all. But we must not fail to see the distinction. To defend the right to wage war with the help of divine right is one thing, to illustrate divine right with the right to wage war is another. The latter was what Calvin was doing. Again recalling his own example of Hezekiah destroying the brazen serpent [2 Kings 18:4], we will not ourselves use this overworked example. But that should not prevent us from seeing that for the sake of divine rather than human order Calvin exalted something that is most imperfect and yet most necessary into a duty and a right.

The third excursus is on the raising of taxes, not just for truly necessary because generally useful state expenditures but, as Calvin remarkably and expressly emphasizes, to achieve domestic splendor, to carry out duties of representation, and to make possible the pomp and magnificence that are indivisibly associated with government of any kind.[195] To play the parts they had undertaken, David, Hezekiah, Josiah, Jehoshaphat, other pious kings, also Joseph and Daniel, used public funds to achieve this splendor "without offending piety," as Calvin strangely assures us, untroubled by the doubts that might assail us in this connection.[196] But then, of course, comes the sharp warning that the state treasury belongs to the people. It is the "lifeblood of the people" that is in the hands of the government, and it would be the worst possible inhumanity to squander it.[197] Unjustifiable tax burdens are tyrannical robbery. That is now the passionate cry, not perhaps without some allusion to the government of Francis I, which, as we recall, had made itself hated on this very score. Princes must see to it that what they venture in this field they venture with a good conscience. Wicked recklessness here can easily become contempt for God.[198]

---

194. Cf. Barth's letters to M. Rade (8.31.1914) in the Barth-Rade *Briefwechsel*, ed. C. Schöbel (Gütersloh, 1981), 95ff.; also to W. Herrmann (11.4.1914) in ibid., 113ff.
195. OS I, 267; BI 295.
196. Loc. cit.
197. Loc. cit.
198. Loc. cit.

Why, we might ask, was the right of governments at this point so important to Calvin? Wernle conjectures that it is the practical Calvin who is speaking here.[199] I do not know. That explanation seems simplistic to me. The directions are not really very practical; we might equally well call them visionary. Perhaps in the representative splendor of those in high and responsible places, which private citizens, the public, could not and should not hope to achieve,[200] he saw something divinely significant, a reflection of the majestic divine right that he did not wish to be assailed on obvious rational grounds. Perhaps he was motivated by complaints of fanatics unknown to us, complaints only too comprehensible in view of the lifestyle of Francis, but that Calvin now used, whether they might be justified or not, to clarify once more not the right of princes but Christian liberty.

2. Laws. We now come to a discussion that will help to shed light on all that is puzzling and paradoxical in the first train of thought regarding government. It is not as if Calvin wanted simply to absolutize the given reality of princes and others who happened to be in charge, or of their whims. We find the nerves, or indeed the soul, of the state, he says, in law. Without law there is no government, though the converse, of course, is also true. The law is silent government, the government living law.[201] Calvin's concept of the state thus loses that element of the contingent and capricious that seems to cling to it and to the state functions that he has discussed. For Calvin, being blessed by God, if we might put it thus, is identical with the strictest subjection to laws. This being so, the wind is knocked out of pure "legitimism." For even if, as we saw, Calvin issues unconditional warnings against all revolution, with this question of the legality of a regime the axe is laid to the root of the tree and blind obedience on the part of subjects is made impossible. It is this close link between government and law that distinguishes Calvin's concept of the state from Luther's.

But what is this law that gives legitimacy to government and with it constitutes the state? In what precedes we have seen that it is a divine command that makes the king a king and that permits and even commands him to draw and use the sword and adopt a kingly style. We have seen

---

199. Wernle, *Calvin*, 148, states that for the practical Calvin it was obvious that a king should live as such and show himself to be a king to the people.

200. OS I, 267; BI 296.

201. Loc. cit.

that it is not for his own sake but for that of the command of God that we cannot deny him these rights. But whence comes this divine command, we might ask, and what is its content? Calvin replies that it is no other than the moral law, which itself is the basic content, valid for all ages, of the revelation to Moses, but which again, as is added by way of explanation, is simply a witness to, and co-knowledge of, that natural law which God has engraven on every human soul.[202] Its content, however, is the eternal and unalterable will of God that we all worship him and love one another.[203] Understood and written thus, it is the magna carta or basic law of human society in all its forms. As the ceremonial parts of the Mosaic law were subject to the moral law, and in contrast to it[204] had only transitory significance, and as the detailed legal provisions of the Mosaic law applied only to Israel, so in laws that are valid today we must distinguish between law in the broader sense *(constitutiones)* and the sustaining and motivating basis of all laws, namely, that revealed moral law which is simply an explication of the natural law that is innate in everyone and that Calvin sums up in a very sober and practical word, equity.[205] It is typical and noteworthy enough that Calvin can here associate the worship of God and neighborly love, and force them, one might almost say, into the Procrustean bed of equity. What resignation, one might say, what a withdrawal from absolute requirement! Naturally Calvin realized that the demand for love of God and neighbor went far beyond the demand for equity. We see this from the fact that he quietly drops the word "love" and uses the more restrained term. The frenetic need to assure us that paying taxes, governing, and waging war are works of love that we find in Luther,[206] Calvin wanted to avoid.

The puzzle remains, however, that in him the basic command of God remains here in this strikingly shrunken form. It obviously does so because here only the absolute requirement had to come on the scene, because Calvin had no intention of sketching a plan for the ideal state. But what is the issue? He has to show that the state which has in fact evolved historically does not rest on chance or caprice, that it does not

202. OS I, 269; BI 298.
203. OS I, 268; BI 297.
204. The MS had *jenen* here.
205. OS I, 269; BI 297.
206. WA 19, 625, where Luther argues that in spite of appearances what soldiers do is in fact a work of love.

rest on any uncontrollable institution, on any intrinsically sacred origin, or on any arbitrarily invented human orders or statutes, but that it finally rests on the one law of all laws known to us all. That this law is not pure or absolute in a historical, human, earthly entity like the state, or in this or that person or institution, Calvin takes for granted, not because, as Wernle says once more, he is so practical,[207] but because he has too great a sense of distance to have any such expectation.

But even if in the foreground that which is unclean and imperfect, in this case pagan-sounding equity, is all that remains of the law of all laws, this does not alter the fact that worship of God and love stand in the background,[208] and that the unclean foreground has at least a share in the dignity and significance of this background. Equity is the form in which the divine command appears in human laws. It is the meaning inherent in all initially meaningless laws, thus forbidding us to free ourselves from existing laws. The question of equity is the question that we can fairly put to state representatives and institutions when, as the fanatics fail to see, there would be no point at all in putting the question of the absolute demand in such cases. The relative is only relative. But it is not for this reason a matter of indifference. Let us see that in the different legal enactments of every age and country one meaning, one requirement, lies hidden. Let us see God even in the imperfect reflection of the human. Let us fear God by honoring the king whom the law of equity legitimates (cf. 1 Pet. 2:17)! This is what Calvin wants to impress upon us. The divine mandate of government is not an irrational sacred cow but a necessity that we can well understand to be rational.

3. People and Government. May we and should we accept the state in practice? This is the last question. The Enthusiasts say no, Calvin yes. But here if anywhere we see that Calvin's real concern is not the state. He does not begin with the state but by way of it, and above it he begins first with God. Though from what we have heard thus far it might seem so, it is really no surprise that in the long run Calvinism was never and nowhere reactionary or merely conservative. In the long run it always had a reforming, unsettling, and even revolutionary effect on state life, and it did so just because it suppressed and stifled all the usual and most obvious

---

207. Wernle, *Calvin,* 150, states that Calvin, being very practical, took it for granted that in the main he could speak only of equity. In everything relating to life he stayed close to the realm of the possible.

208. OS I, 268; BI 297.

reasons for revolution and left only the great contrast that what is simply is, that it is the order of pilgrimage, the humanity that is necessary in all its imperfection, and that over against it, truly over against it, is the celestial country.[209] This contrast justifies humanity but also unavoidably brings to light its questionability. The great contrast that gives its due to what is cannot but have a most unsettling effect even on what is. When seen in this light, even though justified in this light, the state must be on the watch for what will become of it when its reality is in all too great contradiction with its claim.

Calvin begins with the question whether one may go to law.[210] This was a well-known problem for Radicals. Calvin's reply is that legitimate complaint and defense at law have a place. Without bitterness, and trusting in the courts, we should seek what is just and good.[211] We should not wish harm to opponents, nor seek revenge, nor insist unconditionally on our own rights. We should look for the friend in the foe. We should handle the dispute in a superior way as though it were already settled. No strife, anger, or hatred, yet still litigation! For if not, says Calvin, pursuing even the most righteous cause is ungodliness. Even Wernle dare not say that Calvin is speaking here as a practical lawyer. A lawyer could hardly speak about litigation in a more unpractical way. How does he mean it? Here again there is method in the madness. To use Calvin's own phrase, he is depicting a kind of miracle.[212] That is the point of litigation. It is far too easy to cry out that in reality the miracle will not take place. Naturally it does not, or very seldom does. But what does that prove? The thing itself is still good and pure.[213] The point of it, the meaning, is the heavenly justification of the meaninglessness.

Those who simply reject the seeking of justice before human judges must realize that they are rejecting the divine order, and that if they keep hammering away at this order they will never be aware of it anywhere. We are certainly commanded to suffer injustice rather than commit it [Matt. 5:39]. We must be ready to find nothing good in this life but bearing the cross, seeking to overcome evil with good [Rom. 12:21], not repaying eye for eye or tooth for tooth. But we can unite all such things and even fulfill

209. See n. 169.
210. Barth has *prozedieren,* which equals *prozessieren.*
211. OS I, 271; BI 299.
212. OS I, 271; BI 300.
213. Loc. cit.

them by earnestly seeking justice, whether on our own behalf or as the public interest demands.[214] Christians will suppress the love of battle that plays a part in every trial. They will keep alive in their hearts the love that bears all things even when they are in court. But for that very reason they can go to court. Is Calvin defending litigation or is he defending the great and secret possibility of a common striving for justice and truth that lies concealed in this unpleasant garb? I think that to put this question is to answer it. It is obvious, however, that on this view litigation must be something very different from what first appears, that it necessarily effects a revolution of its own. And we need to ask ourselves: Which is really more revolutionary, the refusal of the Anabaptists or Calvin's rejection of it, his apparent connivance and cooperation with the world?

After that odd example Calvin takes up the main theme of the final train of thought which also concludes the whole work. The duty of subjects to rulers is that of respecting and obeying the divine mandate entrusted to the latter.[215] We should not view government as a necessary evil. We should warmly and sincerely cherish it. We should meet its demands with a ready mind.[216] Temperately renouncing self-will, we should realize that the authorities and not private citizens are the true subjects in public life.[217] It is for them to act and take the initiative. Citizens do so only to the extent that the constitution provides. If it does not, they must be content to play a part in achieving what they regard as needed for improvement.

The problem of bad government, of the tyrant, arises here. What if the ruler is not what he should be, the father of the fatherland, the shepherd of his people? Does the obligation of obedience and respect fall to the ground because nothing may in fact be seen of the divine image that he ought to reflect?[218] Calvin begins with the natural and obvious right to revolt. In all ages a hatred of tyrants has been innate in our hearts no less than a love of good rulers. But this sentiment or resentment must not be the deciding factor. Divine right is still present in the right of government even when those who rule are not worthy of it. But the divine right is then disclosed more plainly in its true character. It is the right of the divine Judge and Avenger that is revealed in the injustice of a bad ruler against

214. OS I, 272; BI 301.
215. OS I, 273; BI 303.
216. Loc. cit.
217. OS I, 274; BI 304.
218. OS I, 275; BI 304f.

his people. A wicked ruler is the wrath of God on earth. Hence that ruler, too, shares in the divine majesty. Even the most terrible man who holds office, unworthy of any honor at all, is still as such the holder of that wonderful divine power which the Lord of justice and judgment has committed to his servants, and he must be honored by his subjects accordingly.[219] Along such lines we must view even the most unjust of rulers from the standpoint of his divine appointment.[220]

What Calvin has in mind he illustrates by the so-called right of kings in 1 Samuel 8, which without exaggerating depicts the power of the king over his subjects in terrifyingly harsh colors. Are all these acts of violence the right of kings? No, by right, by law, kings should not act in this way. But it is their right in relation to the people, and though it is personally wrong for them, subjects must not contest it, for they are kings.[221] As Jeremiah says, God, the Creator of all things, has delivered the peoples into the hand of Nebuchadnezzar his servant, and woe to all those who resist his hand. But serve the king of Babylon and you will live. Thus it is sedition against even the worst of rulers to think we should treat them as they deserve.[222] Instead, seek the best for Babylon to which the Lord has taken you (Jer. 29 [v. 7]). Again, even though David was himself chosen to be king, he did not harm Saul. Why? Because Saul was the Lord's anointed.[223] We should not have regard to individuals but to their role, which that "inviolable majesty" encircles.[224] We cannot want to repay authorities tit for tat anymore than in the case of husbands and wives or children and parents. In marriage the law of love obtains even though the other[225] be a fragile vessel. The command to honor parents holds sway even though they do not do their duty. Similarly, the command to obey governments obtains even though the regime be bad.[226] Calvin is willing to go thus far, not so as to overvalue or glorify the state (I can only repeat that that is not his point), but out of concern to clarify by this actual problem what Christian liberty is, the divine right under which we are set in Christ.

219. OS I, 275; BI 305.
220. OS I, 276; BI 306.
221. OS I, 276; BI 307.
222. OS I, 277; BI 307.
223. OS I, 277; BI 308.
224. Ibid.
225. I.e., the spouse.
226. OS I, 278; BI 309.

I do not know whether my understanding of this section has convinced you so far. I freely admit that it is not the most obvious or the clearest, especially when we read the section alone. Here, as in Romans 13, which deals with the same problem, what seems to be the most faithful historical interpretation is that we have an acceptance, justification, exalting, and extolling of the state, and how we are to explain that, well, it simply is so by God's command unless one can find some external pragmatic explanation or other.[227] As an example of the latter I will take Wernle's explanation because it is the most recent and the most illuminating that I know. Wernle concludes that Calvin was (a) a French royalist, (b) a follower of Paul tied to the wording of Romans 13, and (c) a practical man.[228] I can only say that if I had to be content with this type of explanation, then at this decisive point, but basically in relation to Calvin as a whole, I would be confronted by a blank hole of which I could have absolutely no understanding at all. Wernle speaks of the glorifying of state power as such, but what would be the point of that here at the end and climax of Calvin's instruction in Christianity? With what inner right does such a thesis come into connection with what Calvin thinks and desires? What in the world does the fact that Calvin was a French royalist, a literal expositor of Romans 13, or a practical man, have to do with the title "Christian Liberty" under which Calvin has contingently set these contingent matters? A man who had so little idea of what he wanted, or was so little aware of what he was doing, would not in my book be a living man but a wax figure, like the author of Romans 13 if, as almost all expositors say, he followed up what he had to say about divine wrath and righteousness, human misery and redemption, election and self-offering, with an immediate and disconnected but enthusiastic eulogizing of the state, and then just afterward, as though nothing had happened, proclaimed the end of all things, the imminent day of Jesus Christ. If such contradictions are to have the last word just because a superficial literal

227. Cf. Barth's *Römerbrief,* 2nd ed. (Munich, 1922), 424ff., on 13:1f., where Barth argues that only apparently do we have here a positive basis for total subjection, since the decisive word "God" does not have here alone in the epistle the significance of what is metaphysically unequivocal and given. What use is faithfulness to the wording if it is purchased at the expense of unfaithfulness to the Word?

228. Wernle, *Calvin,* 158f., states that no one glorified the power of government more than Calvin. In spite of everything Calvin spoke as a French royalist, yet also as a disciple of Paul, and it is hard, he says, to see how a Christian who is so closely tied to what Paul says can take any other position on this issue.

reading that is out of context seems to support them, then Paul and Calvin were poverty-stricken opportunists and amateur theologians and their historical influence is a riddle whose solution we cannot even sense, since there is no solution, either with God or with us.

Pardon this polemical digression. I entered into it only because I suspect that in the last hours there might still have been some distrust among you, that you might perhaps have suspected that I have been reading into Calvin something that is not there. I *have* been reading something in, namely, the presupposition that Calvin could not be teaching such resounding nonsense in contradiction with himself. But I think I have shown that even the literal wording does not force such a conclusion on us. I have not opposed but accepted the fact that Calvin does emphatically affirm the state. But I am asking: In what sense? And I reply: In a parabolic sense, not directly, but indirectly, not as it stands but in its relation, as a temporal image of the eternal righteousness of God, to what is thus its meaning and origin.

Relation means relativity. The Radicals wanted to bypass the relativity and plunge directly into the origin, the absoluteness of God. That is for the most part the tendency of the medievals and us moderns as well. The Radicals thought they could base this tendency on the newly discovered insight of the Reformation that God is really God, that absoluteness is absoluteness, that eternity is eternity. They showed thereby that in thus understanding this insight they were misunderstanding it. For if God is God and eternity eternity, then the only thing for us is the relativity, the relation, of all things human and finite and temporal to their origin. We must avoid leaping into that abyss, whether in the form of serious objective knowledge of the significance precisely of the relative, in the form of reverent and obedient pilgrimage with all that that entails, or in the form of meditation on the future life that is necessarily one and the same thing as taking the present life with basic seriousness. The state as the most primitive and the most developed form of life in society and not just a future ideal state (even if there were ever to be such), the present state no matter how it is constituted, is what reminds us impressively that as we live in the body we stand under the divine justice and judgment; in other words, that God's command is now valid for us as we live in the body, that there can and should be obedience here and now, that we do not have to wait for Christian freedom because it is itself the great waiting for God. This is what Calvin wanted to defend in this crowning chapter of his book against what I have called the brilliant misunderstanding of the Radicals. And in my view Calvin and the other reformers, in rejecting the Radicals' hostility to the state, were even more brilliant so long as we do not make of their opposition a banal friendliness with the state.

You are naturally right to ask me how it is that this whole line of interpretation is not more obvious, that Calvin himself does not seem to have worked it out in this way. I can offer in reply only the general observation that Wernle, too, expressly emphasizes (p. 164), namely, that the uniformity of the *Institutes* is not immediately apparent, that we have to read the work from a certain distance in order to perceive the unity that is still there.[229] Calvin speaks of each subject, in this case the state, in such a way that it seems almost to stand alone, and we have to look closely to be able to see that in fact the totality is always there behind what he says, shining forth from hundreds of points. Reformation theology, like NT theology, does not meet our systematic needs as we might desire. It counts on readers having intuition, the ability to divine things and to put them together, gifts that are not as plentiful in every age as they were then. It poses riddles. As Wernle again says regarding this section, it speaks in hard paradoxes.[230] It flings out one Cyclopean block after another and counts upon us having eyes to see how they all fit together. If we do not, then the worse for us. We will see only blocks being flung around and falling and lying there, and we will excuse our failure by saying that the Reformation was a wonderful event even though, when we look at it, we do not understand it. If, then, you ask whether the teaching of Calvin really hangs together, I can only ask you to read the *Institutes* for yourself with the question whether you do so presupposing that this section has to be part of the whole and has to have a meaning that a better interpretation can wrest from the literal wording.

Yet I have not yet fully analyzed the third train of thought in the section, the discussion of the right relation between people and government. Listen, then, to the conclusion of this final section of the *Institutes*. Is it really the case that the affirmation that even bad rulers are God's envoys and representatives for the sake of the role that is given them and

---

229. Wernle, *Calvin*, 164, does not think it easy to find any guiding thought in the 1st edition of the *Institutes*. A first glance suggests that Calvin deals with each theme separately and leaves it to his readers to tie them together. Calvin certainly handles each question with a specific interest and feels no compulsion to systematize. We have to look at the work at some distance to achieve awareness of its inner unity.

230. Wernle, *Calvin*, 155.

that sanctifies them in their total lack of sanctity — that this is really the last word on the problem of tyrants? In ordinary life we would say that people usually deny the most vehemently that which is the most obvious implication of their own thinking. You remember perhaps my review of the last passage in the dedicatory epistle to Francis I, in which we read unequivocally that when all appeals and explanations to the king have failed to halt the fury of the persecution of believers, we will then be led as sheep to the slaughter and reduced to extremes, but in such a way that we possess our souls in patience and wait for the strong hand of the Lord, which will undoubtedly be stretched forth armed in its own good time both to rescue the sufferers from their distress and to execute vengeance on the despisers.[231] What does that mean? Is it just a pious flourish, or does Calvin know something else about the relation of a tyrant to his victims apart from their having to honor him in all circumstances since he is God's representative? And if the latter is true, if Calvin, seriously if not threateningly raising a warning finger against his king, is showing that he really does know something different, can we really expect that the conclusion of the book, unlike that of the epistle, will insist on the duty of unconditional respect and obedience? That would have to be so, of course, if Calvin were really the royalist and statist that he seems to be according to the wording at least of many passages. But if Calvin had really aimed to glorify the power of government as such, if he had been a French royalist and a disciple of Paul tied to Romans 13, then how could he have thwarted his own purpose at the end by pointing out the possibility of an appeal to the supreme court, from the representative to him who is not just a representative, and how could he have shown in no less than three ways, and more plainly than when he spoke about the right of kings, that there is a limit to the power of tyrants?[232] Certainly the Calvin of a Wernle, for example, could not have done this.

But he does it. And that is how the *Institutes* ends. What are we to do when we suffer under a bloodthirsty, avaricious, spendthrift, idle, and ungodly ruler? Answer: We are to remember our sins that have merited this punishment and consider that it is not for us to ward off such evils.[233] Note here that the loyalty that Calvin so urgently recommends is again apparent. It is not the tyrant who plagues us but God who punishes us. And if we were

231. OS I, 36; BI 19.
232. Cf. Schiller's *Wilhelm Tell* II, 1, v. 1275: "No, the power of tyrants has a limit."
233. OS I, 278; BI 309.

to set out to remove the tyrant it would not help us. Our only help comes when God ceases to chastise us through the tyrant. Our one resort is to call upon God. There is really no such thing as the power of government on earth. What we describe as such sinks into oblivion when the one who has appointed rulers his servants comes on the scene in opposition to them. He is God and he will stand in the assembly of gods and judge them in the midst. All kings and judges of the earth who have not kissed his anointed will fall down before him and will be cast down (Ps. [82:1;] 2 [vv. 10-12]), all kings and judges who have passed unjust laws in order to wrong the poor in judgment and to do violence to the cause of the lowly, in order to rob widows and to seize the goods of orphans (Isa. 10 [vv. 1f.]).[234] It will then be clear that these rulers and judges are only servants.

God also has other servants. This is the first bar to tyranny. From among them, if need be, God raises up avengers and gives them a commission to punish wicked rulers and to liberate people from their misery. To this end he can even use the fury of those who have in mind and before them something very different from the will of God.[235] There is a legitimate divine vocation to oppose kings without violating their divine appointment because a greater power is now restraining the lesser, as when a king can and may proceed against his ministers.[236] We have examples in Moses and the judges when they avenged and liberated their people. There is also, however, an unwitting doing of God's will here when those concerned may perhaps themselves have only evil in mind.

It is still true, however, that no matter how we are to evaluate the human actions, the Lord uses them to do his own work of breaking the scepters of bloodthirsty kings and toppling regimes that have become impossible.[237] Thus the Assyrians executed judgment on Egypt, the Egyptians on Tyre, the Medes and Persians on Babylon, the Babylonians on Judah and Israel. Wernle sees it as a sophism that Calvin thinks a legitimate divine vocation to resist government is possible, and he conjectures that out of sheer biblicism, since all the examples of the overthrow of tyrants are taken from the Bible, Calvin is in self-contradiction in advocating a right of resistance.[238] If we think the power of government as such is the

---

234. Ibid.
235. Ibid.
236. OS I, 279; BI 309f.
237. OS I, 279; BI 310.
238. Wernle, *Calvin*, 156f.

theme here, then we must, of course, accept this kind of exposition. But we ought not to think that. Calvin's thinking is clear and not at all sophistical, and it has nothing whatever to do with biblicism, once we see that his real theme is the rule of God, which may today wear the mask of tyranny and tomorrow the mask of revolution, but is always the same.

All the democratic impulses that we find in Calvin are for him the next bar against tyranny. Private citizens have simply to obey and to suffer. The law of subjection is strictly valid for them in all circumstances. Nevertheless, there are people's magistrates who are specially appointed to curb the whims of rulers. By way of example Calvin refers to the demarchs of Athens, the ephors of Sparta, and the three estates of France. They, too, are divinely instituted to protect the people's freedom, and they will be guilty of serious unfaithfulness if they do not fulfill their office.[239] It is here, if we will, that we can call Calvin, the herald of a divine blessing of the strictest observance, a father of modern democracy. In his day he himself could not see how broad was the breach that he made in the wall of the conservative principle with this thesis. But how could the modest beginnings of democracy that he knew and earnestly acknowledged fail to lead at last even to a social democracy whose representatives are not by a long way to be excluded from divine appointments? No party, right or left, can claim direct support from Calvin. In truth we have to say that in him the breach was no more important than the wall. It is only for the sake of him who appoints that he speaks at all of those who are appointed, whether they be kings or ephors.

A third and the strongest bar to tyranny is for Calvin the freedom of conscience in relation to God that even kings may not violate. How perverted it would be to please men by injuring him for whose sake we obey them. The Lord is the king of kings who, when he speaks, alone must be heard before all others and above all others. We are subject to those set above us, but not at this point.[240] In this regard, however, we in no way fail to render rulers the respect that is their due. We simply place them on the step where they belong face-to-face with the supreme power of God. How dangerous this is, is clear. The king's anger at such conduct can be the messenger of death. Nevertheless, we must obey God and not humans. We have been dearly bought in Christ. Hence we have to do two things. On the one hand we must not be enslaved by common human

239. OS I, 279; BI 310.
240. OS I, 279; BI 310f.

lusts — this is obviously aimed at the revolutionaries. On the other we must not become servants of "impiety" out of fear of suffering for the sake of obedience to the will of God — this is obviously aimed at legitimists who have forgotten that there is a supreme court over the one immediately below it.[241] Calvin belongs neither to the one group nor to the other.

Naturally the conclusion of the *Institutes* is not establishing the right to revolt. But neither, as we have seen, is it establishing the right of kings. Either way, it is establishing the divine right measured by which all human and relative rights both stand and fall. Yes, the right of kings may also fall and that of revolt against it may also stand. Calvin unquestionably sees that there is a divine vocation, a legitimate vocation, to offer resistance in the three different forms of direct divine revelation, democracy, and the freedom of conscience, and he clothes this vocation with the same dignity as that of rulers. But the applause that here breaks out perhaps from the left, and that makes Calvin a forerunner of Rousseau and human rights, is just as lacking in understanding and insight as that of the right that would make him the defender of dark Romantic forces. There neither can nor should be any complete right on the human side in such matters.

I am not speaking theoretically when I speak of applause from the left and the right. In Switzerland at least it has been our experience that Ragaz and Wernle[242] thought they could appeal with equal enthusiasm to Calvin, the one for revolution, the other for reaction. The last word of the *Institutes* is neither the one nor the other but Christ, Christian liberty, and the celestial country, in the light of which training — serious, relevant, zealous training, yet no more — is the proper term for what we ourselves ought to be doing.

§10 Basel to Geneva

After this great digression, which was forced upon us by the completion and publication of the first *Institutes* in 1536, we take up again the thread of our historical account. It was once thought that there was a French

241. OS I, 279f.; BI 311.
242. Cf. M. Mattmüller, *Leonhard Ragaz und der religiöse Sozialismus: Eine Biographie*, vol. II (Zurich, 1968), 80, 430f., 452f. Barth clearly has Wernle, *Calvin*, 158f., in mind.

edition of the *Institutes* before the Latin, but this has been shown to be a misunderstanding.[1] At any rate, Calvin finished the Latin, which he had perhaps brought with him in part in manuscript from France, when he was in Basel in 1535, and it was printed and published by Thomas Platter of Basel early in 1536. At the same period Calvin wrote a second preface to his *Psychopannychia*[2] and perhaps completed a revision of the work, though this was not published. We recall the letter from W. Capito that warned him not to publish it and to clothe his zeal in a more plausible line of argument, an admonition that in every way rested on ignorance of the situation, for even Capito could not deny that the *Instruction in the Christian Religion* constituted the more plausible line of argument he requested.[3] But Calvin's simultaneous work on that earlier publication shows that in his view the step from the *Psychopannychia* to the *Institutes* was not a step from nonessentials to essentials, that he saw a link between the former thesis and the thrust of this main work, and that he thought he had to keep up this link even if, following the advice of friends and for other reasons, he at first refrained from publishing the revision. I would ask you, now that we have gained some acquaintance with the *Institutes*, that you look again at what was said about the *Psychopannychia*, and that you realize that we do not have there a mere chance throw but the key to the way Christianity is presented in the *Institutes*. It would be a rewarding and important task to work out and to set forth in detail the inner unity of the two works.

At a stroke with the *Institutes* Calvin achieved renown not only in France, where he was known already, but throughout the Protestant and anti-Protestant world. The impression he made on contemporaries was not that of someone who was here repeating what they might just as well read in Luther, Bucer, or Zwingli, but of a new and independent fighter who had now entered the field, and in all whose Protestant views they could rejoice without identifying him with anyone else. He left the impression of the welcome intervention of a fresh and untapped force and gift in a situation that was becoming more and more complicated for the

---

1. Cf. E. Doumergue, *Jean Calvin*, vol. I (Lausanne, 1899), 589, 592. Doumergue concludes (192) that materially and morally it is impossible that the 1536 Latin edition of the *Institutes* should not have been the first. So, too, E. Stähelin, "Calvin," *RE*, III (1st ed.), 658.

2. CO 5, 173ff.; cf. above, 148ff.

3. CO 10/II, 45f.; cf. above, 153f.

Protestant cause at the time. This impression has to be for us a confirmation that we do well, when explaining Calvin, not to give prominence to the question of his dependence on predecessors but to seek signs of uniqueness at every point, as we have tried to do. This course commends itself even and precisely when we say, as we certainly can, that Calvin's *Institutes* met what had become a general need in the third decade of the Reformation: the need for a work that with vigor and openness, but without surrendering anything, would deal with the relation of the Humanist question of time to the Lutheran question of eternity; the need for a comprehensive compendium that, without shrinking from the final implications, would sum up the Reformation paradoxes and at the same time make clear that these are paradoxes of real life; the need for a treatment of the antithesis between the Reformation and the Middle Ages that would be more sharply and ruthlessly defined than Melanchthon's *Loci* or the Augsburg Confession, but less personally and contingently than Zwingli's first great systematic effort along these lines, his *Commentary on True and False Religion;* the need for a deep and serious presentation that would satisfy all kinds of strangers in theology to whom Luther's Catechisms might seem to be too childish or too deeply German or too edifying to accept.

To meet this need, to be able to speak strongly and with full eternal certainty of the glory of God, and yet at the same time, and for this very reason, to be eminently practical and contemporary, a special gift was required that neither Luther, Melanchthon, Zwingli, nor Bucer had, and that gift was Calvin's. How far it was seen to be unique at the time is another matter. The entrance of a uniqueness that is new and strong is almost always *felt* first and only *then* understood. Yet Calvin's uniqueness was understood as it became clearer what he was and what he wanted. This is proved by the fact that the first impression that his *Institutes* was important became an abiding and growing impact that as it were stamped the face of the Reformation in this second period more strongly than did the influence of the older Luther.

The people of Basel were unaware of the important event that took place in the St. Alban suburb in 1535-36. It was not their fault. Always, even to the days of Friedrich Nietzsche, Basel has made too much rather than too little of celebrated strangers. The fault lay with Calvin himself, who lived there under the name of Martianus Lucianus, so that when the *Institutes* came out under his real name, at first no one knew that it was he who had written the "catechism of a certain Frenchman to the king of

228

France" (Wernle, *Calvin und Basel,* 6),[4] his associates at the time being only very few, and most of them aliens. Calvin seems to have done biblical study or had conversations with the rector Simon Grynaeus.[5] We see this from the dedication of his commentary on Romans, which he wrote and published in Strassburg in 1539, and which carries a reference to this period.[6] Probably even before the *Institutes* was published, and certainly before it became known and famous, Calvin had left Basel. As he noted in his commentary on the Psalms (31, 23/24), his aim was not to put himself forward or acquire renown, and he quickly left,[7] almost like a fugitive abandoning his place of work once the work was done.

In March 1536, using the name Charles d'Espeville and accompanied by his friend Louis du Tillet,[8] he went by some unknown route to Italy. According to Beza (21, 125) he went there because of a great desire to see Italy, and if that is correct he was one of many famous northerners gripped with an almost incomprehensible homesickness for the south. There is a 1535 picture of Calvin painted by Leonhard Limousin[9] — whether it really depicts him is open to question — in which he appears as a young and distinguished man, pale, of eager glance, with full beard, and in a scholar's robe. The expression conveys seriousness but also give signs of fatigue and overwork, of a certain shyness and reserve, and yet also of something childlike and thoughtful, with a suggestion that impulses of a romantic nature might not have been absent at this period.

The practical aim of the journey was a visit to, and perhaps a longer stay at, one of the secret half-Humanist and half-reforming centers of the movement of the time, the court of the duchess Renata of Ferrara,[10] daughter of Louis XII of France, the predecessor of Francis I. The Ferrara

---

4. P. Wernle, *Calvin und Basel* . . . (Tübingen, 1909).

5. Simon Grynaeus (1493-1541) was professor of Greek language and NT in Basel, 1529-1534.

6. For the dedication, dated 10.18.1539, cf. CO 10/II, 402ff. (no. 191). In the margin Barth noted that he did have the preface to Olivetan's translation of the Bible of 1535 (9, 791ff.), which he must have been told might shed further light on this period in Calvin's life. Calvin's two prefaces show him at work on the problems of interpreting scripture prior to the publication of the *Institutes* in 1536.

7. CO 31, 23. In the French (24/26): "de me monstrer et acquerir bruit."

8. Louis du Tillet later went back to Roman Catholicism and doubted Calvin's vocation. Cf. A. Ganoczy, *Le jeune Calvin* . . . (Wiesbaden, 1966), 335ff.: "Le problème de la vocation."

9. Cf. Doumergue, I, 13ff.; and Bossert, 54.

10. Renata of Ferrara (1510-1575), wife of Duke Ercole II of Este.

court, in the Lower Po Valley, is the scene of Goethe's *Tasso.* You will perhaps recall the inspired words of Leonore San Vitale describing it (I, 1).[11] Goethe's Leonore was Renata's daughter. But in Renata's day everything was not so happy and harmonious as there depicted. A tragedy lay between mother and daughter, described by the latter in Goethe's play in III, 2.[12] Renata had great knowledge and cleverness but these did not protect her from what was called "foreign error." The tragedy was closely linked to Calvin, for the foreign error that threatened and finally split apart the princely family was none other than Calvinism. If, as in Goethe's *Tasso,* classical princely hospitality was extended to poets like Ariosto and later Tasso, it could be dangerous to entertain foreigners of Calvin's stamp as Renata did.[13] This Renata was like her friend Margaret of Angoulême, one of those tragic women whose gifts and position as such enable them instinctively to sense what is authentic and right with a perception that[14] we seek in vain in their more or less clever husbands and brothers, but unable or too little able to follow up on what they know with the energy and consistency that the men usually show when they reach the same stage. Renata was not beautiful but she was intellectual, had studied Greek, Latin, mathematics, and astronomy from her youth, and although regarding herself as a good Catholic, had a basic dislike for the papacy, so that, continuing the honorable tradition of Ferrara in offering hospitality, her court became a center for all the enlightened, all those who had been driven into opposition, all malcontents, all Protestants after the manner of Stapulensis, especially those of French origin. Her husband, Ercole II of Este, a son of the infamous Lucrezia Borgia, was a well-educated but dissolute Renaissance ruler — he even seems to have written some fairly good Latin verse (Bossert, 56) — but for political reasons, as an ally of Charles V, he did not trust what his wife was doing, and the situation seems to have become especially critical that spring.

I have gone into all this in some detail because the situation was a typical one for the younger Calvin: a mixture of the Renaissance, a high aristocracy that would ultimately act for political reasons, and Protestant sentiments. Into this, under an assumed name of course, and invited

11. Lines 70ff.

12. Lines 1792ff.

13. For the reference to *Tasso,* III, 2, cf. T. Schneider, *Calvin und wir* (Wiesbaden, 1909), 6f.

14. The MS had *bei,* altered by the editor to *nach.*

because he was French, came the brilliant scholar and the malcontent, not as an agitator but as one who scattered the seed in judicious conversations with the duchess, so that he did not bring peace but a sword [cf. Matt. 10:34]. A Humanist physician from Germany, named Sinapius,[15] was also in Ferrara at the same time. He was friend of Bucer and Grynaeus. But Calvin did not take him into his confidence, just as he had not told the people of Basel who he really was. We are not entirely clear why the author of the *Institutes* engaged in this concealment, which was much in vogue in that day, but we should take note of it if we are to understand what it meant when we see the same man very publicly at the helm a few years later.

One thing is clear: his own inclination and constraint were not to occupy the position of a reformer. He wanted to be a Christian scholar working through his books and through private conversations with people like Renata of Este who, he believed, might come to think as he did. There is something academic, almost esoteric, about what he did for the Protestant cause from the Cop address [to the 1536 *Institutes*]. Even if, as we saw, with some final reservations, he did proclaim the need for active participation in church and state, saying what ministers of the Word, rulers, and citizens should do, for his own part he kept such participation to a minimum, feeling little compulsion to act, practicing his understanding of life in time as a pilgrimage[16] literally and directly by wandering from place to place as an anonymous pilgrim scholar with no abiding city [cf. Heb. 13:14], whispering rather than blowing trumpets, desiring nothing less than achieving prominence or renown.[17] What he was able to do, he did provisionally by writing his book and the epistle to the French king. He obviously had no further plan in view and therefore no reason to expose himself unnecessarily to danger.

During the weeks Calvin was in Ferrara the latent crisis between the Estes flared up. In March 1536 inquiry came from Rome whether there were Lutherans in Ferrara. This was a provocative question. On April 14, Good Friday, one of the Frenchmen present in the church refused to offer adoration to the cross. The duke had him arrested and tortured, and like-minded friends of the duchess scattered. Calvin must have been one of those who fled Ferrara at the end of April. His stay, then, can have been

15. Johann Sinapius (d. 1561); cf. Bossert, 159; and Doumergue, II, 63f.
16. See above, 208f. and 216f. n. 208.
17. See above, 229 n. 7.

only for a few weeks.[18] Beza tells us that Calvin said he had arrived in Italy only to leave it again (21, 125). For the duchess this was the time of the beginning of the tragedy sketched by Goethe. Rich in all kinds of episodes, it came to a head in 1554, when her children were taken from her and she herself was condemned to imprisonment for life. Two weeks later, however, she declared herself ready to go to mass again. She was restored to her princely dignities, but on her husband's deathbed had to swear to have no more dealing with heretics. She had been in correspondence with Calvin all this time, and he pronounced the oath to have been forced upon her and therefore invalid.

She left Ferrara in 1560, since her son (Goethe's Alfonso) was just as much in the hands of the Counter-Reformation as his father. Confessing herself a Protestant, she went to France, where her castle Montargis became a place of refuge for the persecuted during the Huguenot wars. She evenly bravely withstood a siege there. She outlived Calvin, who counseled her until his death. She died unbowed in 1575, three years after the St. Bartholomew's Day Massacre, and as Goethe's Leonore put it, she did not give her children the final consolation of "dying reconciled to God." Her life, her whole physiognomy, is a remarkably characteristic reflection of the life work of her mentor, both in its greatness and in its questionability.[19] This was what might happen when people became Calvinists in the 16th century. They might well be secular to start with, then show human vacillation as they went on, and finally be heroic after the manner of antiquity. The mother deserved poetic depiction no less than the daughter. But Goethe had his reasons for seeing his own problem in Tasso and not in Calvin. That is how it will always be when artists come face-to-face with this distinctive story. The drama of Renata will no doubt remain unwritten, and surely it is better so.

From there[20] at the end of April Calvin directed his steps to France, where persecution of Protestants had to some extent eased (Edict of Concy, 1535). The story that he fell into the hands of the Inquisition but fortunately escaped rests on a late fiction, as does the report that his journey through Piedmont was a kind of evangelistic tour. It is hard to decide, too, whether he left there by means of the 2786-m. Col de Fenêtre to reach the Rhone Valley. In Aosta there is today a cross with an inscription

18. Cf. Doumergue, II, 52.
19. Doumergue calls Calvin Renata's "directeur de conscience"; cf. II, 67ff.
20. Doumergue, II, 85ff.

(1541) to record his flight, obviously a monument to the victory of the Counter-Reformation, and there is a tradition that links the cross to the repulse of a Protestant minority in which Calvin played an active part on his return journey by way of Aosta, and with whom, when the Romanist party triumphed, he took flight to the Rhone Valley and from there to France, using the difficult detour of the Col de Fenêtre because the Great St. Bernard was blocked. The truth behind this tradition is that Protestantism advanced into the Aosta Valley in 1535/36, not without some support from Bern, which was then entering into the period of its entanglement with Savoy, and that the estates of the province passed a resolution to live and die in the Catholic faith and in loyalty to the ruling house.[21]

It is more than doubtful, however, whether Calvin had anything to do with all this, for the estates met on February 25, 1536, when Calvin had hardly left Basel. And what about the date 1541 on the cross? Calvin's whole attitude in these years up to his arrival in Geneva makes it most unlikely that he should have been an agitator for the Protestant cause in this corner of Upper Italy. Furthermore, the goal of his journey was not west Switzerland but Basel, so that from there he might move on to France. This being so, going by way of Aosta would have been a strange detour. Finally, a Swiss theologian, E. Bähler,[22] regards the whole story as most improbable from an Alpinist standpoint, for the Col de Fenêtre would still be impassable in May. In my view this whole Aosta episode belongs to the sphere of legend, though we may regret the fact that it robs the life of Calvin of a dramatic feature. In those years Italian fugitives were by no means rare in those valleys, and recollection of the events of spring of 1536 might well have come to be linked later with the name of the most famous and the most hated of the fugitives. It is at least historical that in Italy, and in Savoy in particular, people later made the sign of the cross when the Genevan reformer was in view.

We thus find Calvin in Basel, and then at the beginning of June in Paris to settle his parents' affairs. He then wanted to go to Strassburg, but a German-French war blocked the direct path through Alsace-Lorraine, so that he had to go further south, and at the end of July or the beginning of August he reached Geneva. His plan was simply to spend a night there,

---

21. Ibid., 86.

22. E. Bähler, "J. Calvin in Aosta und sein Alpenübergang," *Jahrbuch des Schweizer Alpenclub* 39 (1903/4), 189ff.

but it would become his permanent residence. The most decisive hour of his life had come, the moment we might well call a sudden conversion in the usual sense as distinct from all earlier moments of decision. It is certainly odd that that great but long forgotten war should have had a part in it. That Calvin had to make the detour became its decisive contribution to world history.

Writings: De fugiendis impiorum illicitis sacris *and* De sacerdotio papali abiiciendo

Before we turn to the next stage in Calvin's life, his first stay in Geneva, we must look at two little works that came from his pen at this critical time, written during the Italian journey according to Beza. The two pamphlets were both printed and published together in Basel in 1537.[23] They seem to me to be important for an understanding of what went before and what came after. Our general impression of the Calvin of the first period is that of a theoretically perspicacious person but one who was definitely more inclined by nature to contemplation. What has been recounted of his varied reforming activity in France and Italy seems to rest more on an understandable projection back of the later Calvin to the earlier period. There is nowhere any solid evidence for it. Suddenly, after 1536, we find Calvin, having discovered fields of action, at work as an agitator and fighter. When he himself tells us that this was not what he wanted,[24] we must surely believe him. It is also in keeping with the external image that he had fashioned up to that time. Nevertheless, the change naturally did not take place unprepared. We have already seen something of the agitator and fighter in the *Institutes,* though within the whole theological system and in the material context it is less prominent there. We have also seen earlier in discussing the Cop address and *Psychopannychia* that at root Calvin did not want to do the work of a mere scholar but to speak to his contemporaries. If we had more of his earlier letters, we would surely know more of the urge to act, to go to work, that was already awake in him even if it was still severely restrained.

Why was it restrained? Why the incognito in Basel and Ferrara that

23. For the full titles cf. OS I, 287ff. For the short titles used by Barth cf. CO 5, 239ff., 279ff.
24. Cf. below, 243ff.

raised a question for us yesterday? Why was it, as we shall hear next time, that Farel had to take extreme measures to break through the restraint? Should we try to explain the matter psychologically as an inferiority complex that secretly dogged this strong man, perhaps attributable to his strict father, and that remained with him until Farel in that famous scene counteracted it and roused him to an awareness of his own powers? Or is it that until he came to Geneva he did not find the object of action that was needed to provide adequate opposition? His relation to this city was remarkable. It was so different from him and for that very reason suited him so well. In 1538 he left it with a feeling of deliverance but in 1541 he would return to it for good, drawn by invisible cords. Or are we to say it was simply the cause, God's cause, to which he had devoted himself, that proved to be the motor but was also the great rock in his path?

In discussing the *Institutes* we have seen how he himself constantly checked and thwarted himself and his inclinations even as he developed them. Especially worth pondering in this regard is that he did not entitle his sixth chapter "De civitate Dei," but contrary to all we might have expected "De libertate christiana." We must also add that even afterward Calvin was never unfaithful to the restraint. If his synthesis was tilted overmuch to one side in the first *Institutes,* he would also allow for a powerful tilt on the other side. Especially in his personal life, to his honor, he took the step from waiting to action most impressively, making clear that the Christian's pilgrimage does not find fulfillment in the contemplation of the sage but in the practice of an active life. Nevertheless, the uplifted finger that he obviously saw raised against himself in Basel and Ferrara almost prevented him from ever becoming Calvin, and it would be raised over him throughout his life — the doctrine of predestination that so firmly reminds us of what we cannot do is the most powerful sign of this but not the only one — and without this restriction again Calvin would not have been Calvin. One thing, however is certain. Even before 1536 that other element, the urge to act, the urge to play a part, was burning in him, and it was surely a more burning and consuming urge just because of the even stronger restraint. We might perhaps compare it to a river flowing underground. Farel's adjuration might well have awakened something of this sort but could hardly have created it.

In this respect the two works written just before the accidental arrival in Geneva are an important signpost. We might perhaps say that if the Cop address shows how the new knowledge of God that Luther and Erasmus mediated had broken tumultuously on the young Humanist, if the *Psychopannychia* shows how Calvin then began to think out Reformation ideas for himself, and if the *Institutes* shows him provisionally relating these insights at each point to issues of the day, these two products of the Italian journey indicate the place where Calvin, personally obeying his own genius and the demand of the hour, thought of bringing his powers to bear, thus initiating the process that would have his most striking successes and impact as a result.

But what will he actually do when he takes the stage? We can almost see what he will do in advance as we read these works. He will give Protestantism a keener edge by making it clear to Protestants that in venturing with God they have ventured on something dangerous that makes a claim and demands consistency and decision; that the new knowledge must show and confirm itself in significant actions, actions that issue a loud no on the one side and a loud yes on the other. Calvin will strip away from Protestants the illusion that the forgivenss of sins and Christian freedom are soft pillows on which they can rest and thus comfortably forget the great medieval unrest, achieving in this way a medieval rest instead of unrest as Catholics who no longer believe in their Catholicism but with their better knowledge have the consolation of a good conscience. No, he will shake them and tell them that the new unrest is greater than the old, and that come what may, there can be no peace with medieval Catholicism. Calvin will become the father of a militant Protestantism that will again produce heroes and martyrs as Christendom had not done for some time. By making Protestants aware that they are in a conflict, of course, he will also make the rift in the church incurable and irreconcilable. Again, as we have said, he will bring the Reformation finally into history as a force alongside other forces, as a For and Against with specific contours even by human standards. He will thus summon into life something great, something very great, but in the process also destroy for good many flowery dreams that might have been dreamed with a good conscience fifteen years earlier, and either way he will meet the demand of the hour.

The two 1536 pamphlets have the same motto, 1 Kings 18:21: "How long will you halt between two opinions? If the Lord be God, then follow him; if Baal, then follow him."[25] The first work also has 1 Pet. 2:9 as a motto: "But you are a chosen generation, a royal priesthood, a peculiar people, that you should show forth the praises of him who has called you

---

25. OS I, 287.

out of darkness into his marvelous light."[26] And the second work also has the text Rev. 3:2, 15f.: "I know your works, for you have a name that you live, and are dead. Be watchful, and strengthen the things that remain, that are ready to die, for I have not found your works perfect before God. . . . I know your works, that you are neither cold nor hot; I would that you were cold or hot. So then because you are lukewarm, and neither cold nor hot, I will spew you out of my mouth."[27] One might say that the whole of Calvin's program is present in these three quotations from the Bible. The two works have the form of open letters, and although no recipients are mentioned they were addressed to two definite French contemporaries whose names were quickly guessed by the public.

The first work (5, 239ff.)[28] on shunning ungodly rites was for Calvin's Paris friend Nicolas Duchemin.[29] The question is whether Protestant Christians as a minority among Roman Catholics should conceal their convictions by cultic participation. Many at the time had subtle arguments in favor of this course, and not all were cowards who did it. Calvin would often have to take up his pen later to oppose these so-called Nicodemuses. In 1545 they were still asking Melanchthon, Bucer, and Peter Martyr as well as Calvin for theological opinions on the matter, and that of Melanchthon was not wholly unfavorable to them.[30] Their justification was as follows. We can take part externally in the practices of those who believe differently with full inner freedom and clarity. The mass is simply the Lord's Supper.[31] We must do what the times demand. Is now the time to worry about such trifles? Is it not more important to educate people first in true piety, love, kindness, and patience, and only when the time is ripe to undertake external change?[32] How can we educate them if we separate ourselves externally from them?[33] Is it not perverse to deny the Christianity of one who goes to mass when one who does not do so perhaps shows much less of the Christian life?[34] Is it a good thing to give incurable offense to many earnest and devout people, who are not so far

---

26. Ibid., 328.
27. Ibid., 362.
28. Ibid., 287ff.
29. A layman, a former Paris school friend.
30. For the responses, also from the Zurich pastors, cf. CO 6, 621ff.
31. OS I, 310.
32. Ibid., 316f.
33. Ibid., 290.
34. Ibid., 317.

off, by ostentatiously not taking part in the cultus, when we might avoid giving offense by Christian moderation?[35] Do we not by such nonparticipation incur the charge of atheism?[36] Is not the intransigent attitude of Calvin and the like a bitter and morose one?[37] Is it not all too easy for those who stand outside to philosophize quietly in the shade about the conflict and to condemn those who have a much harder time than they?[38] This side could even produce their own good proofs from scripture, for example, the permission that Elisha gave to Naaman to worship with his king in the house of Rimmon in 2 Kings 5:18, or the striking account of Paul bringing an offering for purification in Jerusalem in Acts 21:26.[39]

Calvin's reply has the effect of a torrent. He must have been invited formally to answer along the lines he did, but it needed only the slight opening of the sluices and he burst out. He had the advantage that those who deal in basics always have over opportunists, even pious opportunists. But he also had the disadvantage that always arises in meeting a specific challenge. His opponents at least seemed to have the NT on their side, Calvin only the OT, apart from Naaman, in whose case, as in Paul's, he could hardly find an adequate answer. In both these cases the other side was exegetically right. In general, however, Calvin had incomparably the stronger position, as we see at once. What does he really have to reply to? His position is strongest when he simply appeals directly to God. Those who are ready to be trained by God, and who learn to check their own desires, cannot even raise such a question, he says at the outset.[40] All attempts to suit both others and God rest on such desires, which those who are serious with God will suppress and forget. If we deviate a nail's breadth from obedience to God, even if only, as in such considerations, by making distinctions between outward and inward obedience, between important and nonimportant commands, then we are in the typical human situation, and the last state is worse than the first. Christian freedom cannot consist of such deviation from God. It is a weakness, too, to abandon the post at which God has set us. True piety involves true confession.[41] For those who truly love God, can there be any other law

35. Ibid., 324.
36. Ibid., 325.
37. Ibid., 304, 316.
38. Ibid., 328.
39. Ibid., 321, 323.
40. Ibid., 290.
41. Ibid., 294.

than that of manifesting his sacred majesty in every possible way? Our only goal must be to let this majesty be seen on every possible occasion, and in an unbroken sequence of moments genuinely to do in this regard what we have ventured to do.[42] It is not for us to share the honor we owe to God between him and idols.[43]

The mass in particular is a blatant encroachment upon the all-sufficient atonement Christ made with God.[44] Its liturgy is an abjuration of Christ that cannot be compared to the Lord's Supper.[45] It makes God a finite object, and, as Calvin sees it, the priest's facing the altar with his back to the people is part of this process.[46] Does the fact that all is done in the name of God and Christ make it any different from paganism?[47] Is not participation in it to be rejected since Romanists are looking for this and see in it a sign of assent?[48] Is not the differentiating of outer and inner worship intolerable when the latter is a judgment on the former?[49] Since God is now seeking to purge his church, can there be any more rational course than to correct radically and at a single stroke all the things that have simply come from the devil's school?[50] Better be suspected of atheism than of idolatry, thinks Calvin in conclusion, and he is not afraid to call upon his friend to consider that what he is saying is not just human advice but an oracle from the sacred mouth of the eternal God that has for him the force of a command in this matter.[51] So sure of his cause is Calvin!

For the rest, we cannot say that he was inattentive to the practical problems that scattered Protestants faced. Thus he says that it is not necessary and should not even be right for everyone to emerge as a proclaimer of evangelical truth. We must all follow our own vocations.[52] Distinctions may also be made. Fasts and celibacy are matters of Christian freedom. We may break fasts and marry, but do not have to do this.[53]

---

42. Ibid., 295.
43. Ibid., 304.
44. Cf. ibid., 306f., 310.
45. Ibid., 307, 311.
46. Ibid., 308f.
47. Ibid., 312f.
48. Ibid., 315.
49. Cf. ibid., 309f.
50. Ibid., 303.
51. Ibid., 325.
52. Ibid., 294.
53. Ibid., 303.

Yielding is thus possible in such areas. This situation is different, however, with images, unction, indulgences, holy water, and especially the mass.[54] To give way on such matters is to betray God and to give real offense even if by only a semblance of participation. To give even the appearance of approving of the Roman Catholic cultus is reprehensible participation. This is what must not happen in any circumstances, and raising one's hat to an image is included.[55] Yet one may quietly and modestly attend a Roman Catholic church.[56] Paul very skeptically inspected the altars at Athens to see what was going on [Acts 17:23].[57]

Calvin concludes with some positive hints and directions. Protestants must conduct themselves in such a way that they are not seen to be despisers of God. In the eyes of others their whole life must have a clearly religious cast.[58] Others must see so much good in them that they have to recognize them as servants of God! To avoid the difficulties created for them by servants who might betray them, they must insist that the whole household join with them in the knowledge of God so that it constitutes a little church. They will then not regret having been obedient.[59] There is an urgent warning against mixed marriages, for these entangle people in a labyrinth, and there is no basis for the usual consolation that the person of different beliefs will be won over.[60]

All in all, this is not a secondary matter but involves the very heart of religion.[61] Calvin does not ask anything specific of his friend — simply that he not deny Christ. He should not cling so much to this life. He should see that it is worse to be cast off by Christ than to be regarded by others as an ungodly apostate and traitor. As regards the accusation that he himself was philosophizing about the conflict in the shade, Calvin believes that God will arm him with his Spirit when he finally leads him into the thick of the battle. He did not think out what he had written in the shade. It had been tested in the sufferings of the martyrs. These did not suffer in order that we might comfortably surrender the truth for which they died but in order to teach us how, trusting in God, we might

---

54. Cf. ibid., 303ff.
55. Ibid., 304, 325.
56. Ibid., 314f.
57. Ibid., 315f.
58. Ibid., 325.
59. Ibid., 325f.
60. Ibid., 327.
61. Ibid.

become invincible face-to-face with the whole battle array of death, hell, the world, and Satan.[62]

The second open letter was to one of the best-known advocates of the Protestant party in France, Gérard Roussel, who under the protection of Margaret of Valois had become bishop of Oléron.[63] Calvin's letter to him on the sacerdotal ministry of the papacy is a sharp criticism of this step. "Amid the stream of congratulations I come to you morosely accusing, complaining of the very things on which others are congratulating you."[64] The glory is only in appearance.[65] Calvin then gives a graphic depiction of what the ministry really entails: not outward pomp but divine appointment, heavy responsibility, nervous tension, no slackness, watching.[66] In contrast, a Roman Catholic bishop's chair means wealth, indifference, evil influence, the contradiction of its own claims.[67] A beleaguered city in which the plague breaks out![68] It might just as well be a robbers' cave.[69] His friend should either do something bold or resign. Otherwise he is neither a true man nor a Christian.[70]

In this way Calvin summons to decision. The hour when he himself had to go on to do something decisive had struck.[71]

---

62. Ibid., 328.

63. Gérard Roussel (ca. 1500-1550), bishop of Oléron from 1536.

64. The reference is to the episcopal office; cf. OS I, 331f.

65. Ibid., 329.

66. Ibid., 331ff.

67. Ibid., 335ff.

68. Ibid., 340.

69. Ibid., 342.

70. Ibid., 362.

71. Obviously Barth had not been able fully to prepare his lecture here, so that he simply gives the contents of the second work under headings.

4

First Genevan Stay

As regards the circumstances in which Calvin came to settle in Geneva on his way back from Paris to Basel, he himself tells us in the preface to his Psalms commentary (31, 26) that he had resolved to live a retired life, but finally Master Guillaume Farel kept him in Geneva, not so much by counsel or admonition as by a terrible curse, as if God from on high had laid his hand on him to hold him fast. For the direct route to Strassburg where he wanted to go was blocked by war, so he decided to go by way of Geneva, but not to spend more than a single night there. Just before, the papacy had been chased out of the city by that excellent man whom he had mentioned and by Pierre Viret, but things had not yet been put right and there were bad and dangerous splits and parties in the city. Now it happened that a man who later shamefully apostatized and went back to the papists recognized Calvin and made him known to the others. [This was none other than Calvin's friend and travel companion du Tillet, who had left him on returning from Italy and settled in Geneva; Kampschulte, I, 280. His relapse took place at the end of 1537 or early in 1538.][1] The result was that Farel in his burning zeal for the cause of the gospel made every effort to keep Calvin in Geneva. When the latter told him that he planned some private studies for which he wanted to remain free, and when Farel saw that he could gain nothing by entreaty, he called upon God to curse the leisure and tranquility for study that Calvin sought if he turned his back on such great need and denied his help. This saying

---

1. Barth's brackets.

terrified and shook Calvin to such an extent that he abandoned his intended journey. Yet with a sense of his shyness and timidity he did not want to pledge himself to take up any specific office.[2] According to Beza'a *Life of Calvin,* Farel, a man of heroic spirit, told Calvin that if he hid behind his studies he predicted in the name of almighty God that God would curse him for not joining with them in this work and seeking self rather than Christ (21, 125).[3]

In this way Calvin was torn away from the contemplative life of the theological Humanist, of the Protestant sage, of the radical but not practically engaged observer, speaker, and writer, and plunged into the fulfillment of his own deepest urge, into the active life of the Genevan reformer. I must ask you, as you survey what we have said about Calvin thus far, to keep in mind that *that* was the beginning. A portrait of Calvin without the great restraint that expressed itself plainly enough in the decisive scene we have just described; a portrait of Calvin as simply the theocrat who is zealous and races and runs and speaks and writes and organizes and deposes and burns and burns up for the glory of God without considering whether this can ever be a human affair; a portrait in which it is forgotten that this man of organization and system was not really concerned about organization or system, that this captain was not really concerned about the battle or the positions under attack, that this new and energetic worker on the medieval problem was not really concerned about the city of God on earth, that behind all his actions there lie at root such nonactivist thoughts as meditation on the future life, alien righteousness, predestination, and Christian liberty, that is, the reality on behalf of which we can strictly do nothing; a portrait of this kind, whether favorable or hostile in intention, can only be not just distorted but false.

If we want to understand Calvin aright under the sign of action — and he does indeed come under this sign, and under it, from the standpoint of church history and world history, and under it he became what he was — then we have to realize that for him this action was, to a very different degree than for Luther, basically demanded and necessitated by his understanding of Christianity, even though it was for him also a descent to the

---

2. The key words are as follows: "et avoye deliberé de continuer de mesme iusqu'à ce que finalement maistre Guillaume Farel me reteint à Geneve, non pas tant par conseil et exhortation, que par une adjuration espouvantable, comme si Dieu eust d'enhaut estendu sa main sur moy pour m'arrester."

3. Beza, *Ioannis Calvini Vita,* CO 21, 125.

basement. We have to realize that all the great and also the little things that he did along this line, all the important and often the questionable things, were done in this basement, and that they cannot be understood properly without the great proviso of eternity, grace, and freedom that Calvin himself always kept more or less clearly in view. Calvin could work alongside Farel, but Calvin was no Farel, who had been born in that basement as a vassal of the good Lord. Nor was it just the aristocratic element in Calvin's character that constantly prevented him from saying and doing the far too obvious things that his friend Farel confidently thought he could venture to say and do. Farelism, that is, pastoral daring and rashness to the glory of God and the improvement of conditions, is not really Calvinism, and it can hardly have escaped Farel himself that in pressing this man at any price to join him in his work he was summoning someone who was something very different from a better edition of himself.

It is the more typical of Calvin that in the ultimate weapon that Farel, like many zealous pastors, used so freely, he still thought he could see the hand of God that he could not escape. What he really heard was the voice of his own innermost genius. But no, we do best to take him at his word and see here the hand of God that terrified and shook him afresh in the security that he had achieved with his knowledge of Luther's gospel; that diverted him afresh, as he thought, from the path that he had marked out for himself; that tore him away from the sober, clear, satisfying, superior position of one who sees the true relation of God to the things of this world and who for this very reason takes care to become involved in these things only so far as is absolutely necessary; that plunged him into the ambivalent, dangerous, compromising position of one who on the basis of the knowledge of God cannot take leave of that knowledge and discipline, but at the risk of being defiled becomes involved in the problems of the world of things. By this movement he placed himself under judgment but also under promise. The situations in which he became entangled would often not be without their tragic aspect, but also — and this is perhaps harder to bear — not without their comic aspect.

Yet behind all these situations there would be a more than usual and more than historical necessity. His actions would be ambivalent on this lower ground, as everything human that is done there is ambivalent. God's wrath and God's judgment would blaze forth almost indistinguishably from these deeds, arousing both love and hate, both admiration and horror, a savor of life to life and of death to death [2 Cor. 2:16]. But in the last analysis who may presume to judge, seeing these acts rest on knowledge and are acts of obedience? A consideration has its place here that we learned to know in discussing Calvin's ethics (at the beginning of ch. 6 of the *Institutes*) and that Calvin urged against the Lutherans at the Worms Colloquy of 1540, namely, that there is a fatherly indulgence in the law, too, in virtue of which God accepts even our defiled works, not on account of their worthiness, but on account of his kindness, if only, as God's children in the NT sense, we have regard to the promise that is ours, not as those who act but as those who trust in his fatherly benevolence (21, 269).[4]

The urge to dare to go to work in faith was the hand of God which in that hour Calvin saw embodied in the pious impertinence of the good Farel. Here once again Calvin was humbled and broken and converted, and this time more penetratingly and with more momentous results, perhaps, than in his earlier conversion from the papacy to Lutheranism. In truth, this was not just a step out of the study into practical life as Farel was demanding. Hidden behind this in itself insignificant switch was the step from the humility *(Demut)* of faith to the courage *(Mut)* of faith. And what can be more humbling than to have to prove humility, which is thought to be already present and practiced, by courage? The very essence of the Reformed or Calvinist branch of the Reformation lies in that demand. It is no wonder that this second change lived on in Calvin's memory much more vitally and vividly than the first, as we see from the preface to the Psalms commentary. For it was by this second change that he became what he was. Naturally he did not do so for the first time in that hour with Farel, for we see the controlling influence of the change already in the first *Institutes* and even in the *Psychopannychia*. But the hour with Farel became for him as it were the symbol of the change, for it was then that it moved out of the realm of thought and became event.

It then became unequivocally clear that God demands of us a double brokenness, the first by way of the insight that God alone is great and that we can do nothing for him and for our own justification, the second by way of the insight that we must obey this great God in faith either by what we do not do or by what we do, but at all events that we must obey him if we really believe. Disobedience is equivalent to unbelief. This means that even everything we might do in contrast to the dangerous and am-

---

4. Cf. the *Acta conventus Wormaciensis* of W. Musculus (11.10.1540), reprinted in CO 21, 269. See also above, p. 197 n. 136.

bivalent active life, for example, studying, is also human and not justified in itself. The contemplative life of study offers no salvation. It is a possibility, an opportunity, and indeed, after this hour Calvin would truly study for the first time, but it is no more than that, and if the humility that will not be courageous seeks to hide behind it, it is even less than that, an impossibility, an occasion of perishing for all our humility. "You are seeking self and not Christ, and the Lord will curse you."[5] How true that is! So, then, this path is at least under threat, and the other path, that of an active life, is at least open even though it lies under the shadow of the same threat.

We thus have a concrete and definite relation to the world by which the relation to God must in some way demonstrate itself. As we saw, we miss this in the ethics of the *Institutes,* which pointed out the possibility but not the actuality and necessity of this or that definite action, the first and last word of that ethics being Christian liberty. It had to be so. A theological ethics that would take any different attitude would be Roman Catholic and not Reformed. Only the reality of God, which is concealed in the reality of life, can fill this vacuum. On the one hand was this reality in all its full and succulent uniqueness and pregnancy, on the other was the earthly, banal, and limited Geneva on Lake Geneva, where things had not yet been put in order,[6] where very much that was conceivable but also very difficult had yet to be done. *Here,* then, was the place to obey, *here* something had to be done, *here* fatherly indulgence had to be invoked over all the human work.[7] Where else but in this earthly, banal, and limited here and now? Farel was needed to point to this here and now, to issue a call that would ring in such a way that it was like a blow, that Calvin, for whom it was nothing new, received it as though it were something very new, the very thing that was new for him. Why could not Calvin resist it? Why had he to see in Farel's demand the symbol of his second conversion? Why could he not refuse to see in *this* here and now his own here and now? There was many another Geneva and many another Farel.

At this point, of course, no further survey or discussion of what happened can help us. We confront the problem of the unique, the contingent, the divinely willed as such, and can only say that this is how it was. It is enough to see that it took place because this problem, the

5. See n. 3 above.
6. See 204ff. above.
7. See n. 4 above.

problem of ethics, was like a rock on Calvin's path that he could not remove, and nothing would be more distinctive of Calvin's life and work than that there was this rock on his path. Nevertheless — and I go back now to the beginning of what I was saying — we have to keep in mind that what we have here was an event, a change, showing that the man of Geneva whose puzzling portrait we are trying to unroll was a broken man, a doubly broken man, not a Farel, not a vassal of God, if we may use that phrase again, though it was through Farel that he was converted, and his life would now be linked to this Farel. If we fail to see the break, we cannot understand the portrait. Our evaluation of it will be wrong. We cannot hear the promise and the warning that lie in it.

§11 The Situation in Geneva

I must sketch for you in a few strokes the situation that Calvin found in Geneva. In this context I do not have time for a full account. For this I would refer you to Kampschulte, vol. I.[8] Geneva was first a stronghold of the Allobrogi, then a Roman provincial city, then a residence of the kings of Burgundy, then an episcopal city. When Calvin came to it, there were some fifteen thousand residents. It had three governing powers: the bishop; the count or his regent, who lived on an island in the Rhone and had jurisdiction; and finally the free and self-governing citizenry, which had always had a strong sense of its rights. Severe tensions had come into the relations between these forces from the time that the ducal house of Savoy had become overlords of the count in the 13th century and then seized control of the bishopric in the 15th, this time with the help of the papacy, which in this instance betrayed the freedom of the church and for this reason enjoyed little respect among the citizens. The Savoy bishops also discredited themselves among their flock by a worldly, to some extent dissolute, and at any rate unspiritual lifestyle. Early in the 16th century Geneva swarmed with clergy who did nothing for the city. There were seven parishes, five monasteries, three hundred ministers, seven hundred monks and nuns, twenty fraternities, and nine hospitals. The bad moral reputation of the clergy was typical of the day. But at first the decisive factor was political opposition to the house of Savoy represented by the

8. Kampschulte, I, 3ff. Barth follows this account except where otherwise noted.

church. In spite of everything the church as such still had many warm supporters in the city, as became plain when the conflicts shifted from the political to the religious arena.

In 1519 the citizens tried to secure their position by a so-called agreement on city rights with Swiss Freiburg. This attempt was defeated and the leaders were executed or imprisoned, but the upshot was that when the Savoyards exploited their victory too unwisely the bishop had to leave the city in 1526. Propaganda against the church was already present. In 1528 the Reformation triumphed in Bern, and when in 1530 the bishop declared the Genevans to be rebels and the Savoyards actually threatened the city, troops from Bern and then Freiburg came to Geneva. This development paved the way for the first Protestant sermon in St. Pierre cathedral. It was delivered in German by a preacher from Bern, the Zwinglian Megander.[9] A treaty with Savoy gave Geneva security against arbitrary acts, if not its freedom. A council decree ruled somewhat ambiguously that in religion they wanted to live as their ancestors had done but that the gospel should be preached without human additions.[10] This was a provisional decision that others would necessarily follow.

What happened, however, was a confused chaos of strokes and counterstrokes from which the only thing to emerge clearly is that the Reformation in this Reformation city was very little a matter of principle. In the summer of 1532 Clement VII wanted an indulgence preached in Geneva. A certain Jean Goulaz put up posters against this, arguing that forgiveness of sins is by grace and faith alone. The result was a violent clash between him and one of the cathedral clergy named Werly. In these weeks Guillaume Farel (b. 1489 at Gap in the Dauphiné) came for the first time to Geneva. This man had been a zealous Romanist, but through Faber Stapulensis in Paris he had changed into an even more zealous Protestant agitator and fighter. He was no scholar or speculative thinker but a matchless man of action, a little man, with a bristly red beard, fiery eyes, a big mouth, a shrill voice, sunburnt as a result of his many wanderings, bony, broad-shouldered, always prepared to speak at a moment's notice to the people.[11] His life was a veritable *Odyssey* or *Iliad*, for wherever he went sharp and not merely intellectual conflicts arose. More than once he himself was almost beaten to death by enraged masses in French

9. Kaspar Megander (1459-1545).
10. Kampschulte, I, 109.
11. Henry, I, 167.

Switzerland, where he chiefly worked. For the scenes in Geneva at the bishop's palace and in the streets when he came with his notorious reputation, you must read Kampschulte.[12] At first, to avoid the worst, even this bold man had to yield. A further effort was made by Antoine Froment,[13] who said first that he was a language teacher, then held secret Protestant gatherings, then dared to preach publicly on the Place Molard, but finally had to flee.

In 1533 Pierre Viret[14] of Vaud came for the first time to Geneva. As a result opposing steps were taken by the two parties to secure their positions. A council decree to the effect that each should act according to conscience, but that traditional customs should not be derided, and yet that preachers should also stick with scripture, failed to bring either clarity or peace. Werly, always ready to draw the sword for Roman Catholicism, would finally have to pay for the cause with his life. The one who killed him was executed. From a distance the bishop impotently tried to prohibit unauthorized preaching and Bible reading. An attempt by Roman Catholics to swing things in their favor by calling in the scholarly Dominican preacher Guido Furbity[15] ended badly for their cause when the foreigner described his opponents as "German heretics," which at once evoked a protest from Bern.

Meantime Froment and Farel were again on the scene, and in a public assembly they could defy Furbity, who knew Thomas but not the Bible. Early in 1534, amid a great throng, Viret administered the first Protestant baptism. On March 1, 1534, the Franciscan house was stormed and Farel preached in the church there. Freiburg appealed in vain to the earlier agreement. The bishop called in vain for economic sanctions and even a night attack on the city. An attempt to poison Farel, Froment, and Viret failed. In a second disputation the Frenchman Peter Caroli,[16] of whom we will hear more later, tried to put things back on an intellectual level. On August 8 Ami Perrin[17] led the decisive attack on the images in St. Pierre, with some shameful acts (feeding the host to dogs), but also with the unmasking of some shameful deceptions (gadgets to make the

12. Kampschulte, I, 118f.
13. Antoine Froment (1508-1581), Froment in Kampschulte.
14. Pierre Viret (1511-1571).
15. On Guido or Guy Furbity cf. Kampschulte, I, 136ff.
16. Peter Caroli (ca. 1480-after 1545).
17. Ami Perrin (d. 1561), captain general of Geneva.

images of saints sing or angels appear, and a skull of Peter made of stone). The monks and clergy had to admit they were ignorant. On August 12 the mass was ended, and on August 27 the bishop and pope were banished in favor of the sole authority of holy scripture.

By the events of 1535, at the time when Calvin was writing the preface to his *Institutes* in Basel, Geneva had ceased to be a papal city. But what had it become instead? In keen anticipation the people of Geneva chose a motto made up of the Vulgate of Job 17:12: *Post tenebras lux,* and the no less bold: *Deus noster pugnat pro nobis* (based on Deut. 3:22).[18] We should not probe too deeply into what either the spiritual and secular leaders or the image-storming youth from the alleys meant by *lux* and *Deus.* There were places where the visible, historical circumstances under which the so-called Reformation took place were more worthy and significant than in Geneva, and there were other places where they were even less worthy and significant. The great wave of change from the medieval ideal, the wave of the disturbance and disruption of all that had been customary in the West by a factor that in the first instance, since it had no home on earth, we can intelligibly describe only in more or less violent negations, but that, understood, misunderstood, or not understood, was simply there and at work, this wave had now reached these waters, too. That here as elsewhere the waters that were thus ruffled from the surface to the depths were human, all too human, should neither be obscured by a mythical depiction by Protestants nor all too triumphantly exposed by the kind of anti-Protestant account that we find in Kampschulte.[19]

Naturally everything that takes place in history, absolutely everything, has a human face, and the more closely we look, a not very edifying face. Educated people like ourselves are much too easily tempted to forget that this is true of all the processes of history and to regard what happened in the studies of Humanists and theologians during the Reformation years as something pure and detached and free. We are tempted to do this because its result, Reformation thought, has given us such fine and bold and illuminating ideas, and it seems as if we are falling from heaven when we become aware that in Wittenberg and Zurich and Geneva there were markets and alleys and council chambers where the Reformation was desperately tainted with sweat and blood and tears and money and alcohol and public papers and all the rest. To safeguard ourselves against the

18. See Doumergue, II, 139f.
19. For Barth's evaluation of Kampschulte cf. Bw.Th. I, 360.

disenchantment that might arise when we realize that the human beast had a hand in the Reformation as well as the human spirit, against the temptation to close our eyes to the way things really were, we have to be very clear that even the apparently pure religious experience and thinking that we find on the intellectual peaks of humanity in the medieval West were also human and earthly and beset with ambiguities, and that the composition of the *Institutes* and the breaking of images, vastly different though they seem to be, all come under one common denominator, so that at every point we have to differentiate between what was disturbed, and what caused the disturbance, the Spirit of the Lord from above.

The Reformation loses nothing of its importance if we allow no place for even the remnants of hagiography that we find in the biographies of Calvin by Henry and Staehelin.[20] On the contrary, it is only then that we are protected against the danger of falling victim to anti-Reformation polemics such as we find in such a subtle and outstanding form in Kampschulte's account. We may then quietly accept the thesis that the Reformation in Geneva was essentially political and economic in motivation; the suggestion that the people of Geneva did not really know what had happened to them when they suddenly became Protestant, nor what part had been played by foreign policies such as that of Bern; the question marks that we have to put against such figures as Farel and especially the Molard preacher Froment; and in my view perhaps something that is a fact even if Kampschulte offers only a little solid support for it,[21] namely, that from a human standpoint those who came out best in this Reformation were the nuns of the St. Clara convent, who with a steadfastness that was worthy of a better cause, even under severe attack, refused to let themselves be reformed by Farel and his worldly associates.

But why should we not also agree that along with others the religious motive played just as big a part in the movement; that the sermons of Farel and the biblical teaching of Froment, no matter how much we might have against their type of evangelizing, could not possibly have been mere clamor, babbling, and appeal to the lowest instincts as Kampschulte depicts them; that we can just as well put a positive as a negative sign in front of the whole movement even with all its far too human components? If we are not afraid to see how questionable are all things human, then we are

20. For Henry and Stähelin, see n. 4 on p. 129. For Barth's view of Stähelin's work cf. his letter to E. Thurneysen dated 12.14.1919.
21. Kampschulte, I, 169ff.

in a position to see, too, that all things human after their manner and on their level have at least the possibility of justification.

Let us leave, then, the question how far Geneva in August 1535 had not only ceased to be Roman Catholic but had also begun to be Protestant, how far the new motto, so genuinely Genevan and oratorical, corresponded to reality. Let us leave this ambiguous question unanswered. It was to this situation that Calvin was referring when on his arrival in Geneva he said that things had not yet been put in order.[22] But as yet Calvin had not come to Geneva. The ecclesiastical revolution of August 1535, itself strongly political, served for its part to sharpen the political situation, for it now ruled out any peaceful settlement with the bishop and therefore with the Savoyards who stood behind him. The bishop could now be content with nothing less than the complete subjection of the city, and the city could feel secure only if totally independent of the bishop. Savoy at once took up the fight with renewed energy, and the people of Geneva, strengthened now by a religious as well as a political shibboleth, resisted with fresh power. The duke overran the surrounding area with his troops, and not without heroism Geneva sacrificed the suburbs, leaving some six thousand people without protection, but making the city itself the more defensible. For the first time Farel and his colleagues now began to make a comparison between fighting Israel and God's new people in Geneva to whom God would not deny similar victory.[23] A regular siege began. Expectantly the people of Geneva began to look to the east, to powerful Bern, as whose envoys Farel, Froment, and Viret, the messengers of the new faith, had come to them. If a stalwart Christian city, Bern, had given the gospel to Geneva, wrote a chronicler in Bern at the time,[24] it could not now refuse to undertake the defense of those who were oppressed for the gospel's sake.

But now there plainly began the game that Bern would play with Geneva during this whole period, and that would cause Calvin so much trouble later. At first it was a double game. To the general surprise Bern for long enough held coldly aloof from Geneva. Remarks like "The shirt is worn much closer than the coat"[25] were common currency. But to the other cantons and to the government of ducal Savoy it posed as an advocate

22. See above, n. 2.
23. Kampschulte, I, 185, based on A. Froment, *Actes et gestes*, 179f.
24. Kampschulte, I, 186.
25. Ibid., 189.

of the interests of Geneva. When its ally Constance demanded that it should abandon Geneva in the interests of peace, it suddenly insisted on the city rights that it had to observe. But at first no actual steps were taken to relieve Geneva. The bear would not scratch until the city was in the last desperate straits, said the same chronicler[26] in an excellent understanding of his government's intentions. What was the point of this game? Very simply, the leading idea behind the policy of Bern had always been the openly imperialistic one of restoring the kingdom of Burgundy under Bern's leadership, and Geneva would be a pillar of this larger territory. For this reason Bern supported the struggle for independence from Savoy, sharpened the conflict by cleverly introducing a religious rift through the brave Farel and his companions, and then, when happily no settlement was possible, despicably leaving Geneva in the lurch so as to show plainly how useful and necessary an alliance with its neighbor was. The people of Geneva were well aware that they could have their independence at this price, but they were freedom loving and clever enough not to fall into this trap. Hence they decided first to wait and help themselves as best they could.

And help came in a way that fortunately the little powers of this world not infrequently experience. A fourth actor came on the scene. Francis I of France had plans on Upper Italy and therefore against Savoy, whose duke was related by marriage to Charles V and hence his natural enemy. Francis, then, had an interest in securing Geneva. It thus came about that the French negotiated for an alliance with Geneva and a protectorate over it, though Francis did not intend this to include the religious liberty that he was suppressing in his own country. Some inadequate attempts were also made to end the siege. Geneva handled dealings with this dubious patron cleverly, thanking him politely for his friendly intentions but making no concessions in fact. For the time being the game was already won, not by clever Bern or clever Francis I, but by the people of Geneva with whom they were playing it. For now, said the chronicler, prudent Bern summed up things correctly and resolved to help Geneva before the king led the dance.[27]

The intervention of a rival from the west worked wonders. Neither the unfavorable attitude of the other cantons nor a warning letter from

26. Ibid., 188, quoting Valerius Anshelm, *Berner Chronik,* unprinted continuation, 1534.

27. Kampschulte, I, 195, quoting Anselm for the years 1535-36.

the emperor could now stop the bear marching. Geneva had accepted the gospel, rooted out the papacy, and thus greatly increased the anger of enemies of the divine Word. Bern would cover itself with eternal shame if it did not help the beleaguered city. So said a manifesto of the government to the citizens of Bern.[28] On January 16, 1536,[29] war was declared on Savoy, and shortly thereafter six thousand men under the tested captain Hans Franz Nägeli marched through the Vaud up to Geneva. This was a swift and completely victorious march. It gave Geneva a breathing space. Roman Catholic Freiburg, Valais, and France then joined in so as not to leave all the spoils to Bern. Soon afterward the castle of Chillon was taken and the freeholder Bonnivard of Geneva, who had been imprisoned there for six years, was released from his chains.[30] This man would later be an enthusiastic writer of the history of the period and would also come under Calvin's church discipline, for good reasons. The surrounding territories of Savoy were laid waste, and the Genevans themselves took an active part in this in revenge for the sufferings they had endured so long. God's OT people were again recalled, for, as we well know, this people had punished neighboring idolatrous peoples with rapine and subjugation.[31]

Less along biblical lines was the demand that Bern made upon Geneva that it should recognize the rights of the bishop and the regent in the city. But again, even though a Bernese military presence backed the demand, Geneva managed to evade it. Without doing anything much, Geneva was again in the fortunate position of a skilled checkers player. Bern realized that if it tried to use force, Geneva would be pushed irrevocably into the arms of France. Hence, when the demand was rejected, Bern had to be content with a treaty that upheld the sovereignty of Geneva — the contested rights of the bishop and regent were transferred to the magistrates — but that also bound the city not to enter into alliance or agreement with other states without the consent of Bern, and always, in peace or in war, to keep its gates open to the Bernese, its fellow citizens.[32] What Geneva could not prevent was that Bern, having conquered the Vaud, lay almost directly at its gates, a proximity that in the event would not always prove pleasant. Understandably there would also now be in

28. Ibid.
29. Ibid.
30. Ibid., 197.
31. Ibid., 198, based on Froment, 222ff.
32. Kampschulte, I, 201f.

Geneva, in addition to the Roman Catholic Savoy party, which had been eliminated for practical purposes, a party that was more oriented to Bern and Switzerland and a party that was more oriented to France, each of which with some degree of truth could claim to represent the genuine interests of Geneva's freedom. For the time being, however, Israel had peace [cf. Judg. 3:11, 30, etc.], and it could now put into practice its newly achieved political and religious freedom, which in recollection quickly became one and the same thing.

Council records (21, 197ff.) show us how the Reformation went ahead under Farel in the spring and summer of 1536. On March 10 and 24 Farel came before the council and in a great speech strongly exhorted them[33] to give the Word of God to the surrounding city areas, bringing them to obedience and setting aside licentiousness and swearing. In this process, remarkably, an important role was played by the setting up of church bells to summon the people more effectively to worship. Above all it seemed necessary to take measures to prevent some of the Genevans from secretly attending mass in the unreformed rural areas on Sundays. On March 31 the magistrate of Vandeuvres made the naive request that his people might be allowed to hear mass on Sundays as they had always done and after it they would willingly listen to a gospel sermon. In view of this kind of failure to understand the situation it was resolved to summon all community leaders and pastors to a conference in the city.[34] This took place on April 3, 1536. To an earnest remonstration one of the community leaders made the reply: "Sirs, we are ready to live according to the gospel, but let us live as has been our custom. Our forefathers were good people and we want to follow them. But if we see our neighbors changing their manner of life, we will do the same."[35] One of the pastors present was accused of having a book by means of which he led the people astray. It seems as if he had a collection of sermons, often found, as we know, in pastors' studies, and the good man could usually find in this something to offer his people on Sundays. Farel treated him roughly: he must stick to the gospel and not to his book of sermons. Another pastor made the sensible proposal that they should be given a month to read the gospel first and then give their answer. It was then resolved that within a month they should state whether the evangelical doctrine taught in the

---

33. CO 21, 197.
34. Ibid.
35. Ibid., 198.

city was the "sacred doctrine of truth" or whether they had doubts about this. In the meantime, however, they should stop ministering in the old style and the community heads should see to it that the people came to sermons (obviously in the city). They agreed to do this.[36]

A similar conference with other pastors took place on April 5. The pastors were told that the aim was now to live as God requires. They confessed that they did not have enough learning to understand how that might be, and they were counseled to come to sermons and to stop reading the mass for the time being.[37] On April 28 it was resolved that at weddings brides should have their heads covered as Paul enjoined. On May 10 rules for clergy stipends were made. On May 12 it was resolved that some pastors who had read the forbidden mass should be forcibly brought to sermons and publicly made to confess their misdeed. On May 19 Farel and his colleagues made an urgent plea for good lives according to God's will and for concord among the people. In particular the school system was to be reconstructed to prevent young people from wasting their time. A general assembly should also be called with a view to finding out whether people were all ready to live "according to the reformation of the faith as it was now preached."[38] On the same day the Council of Two Hundred declared that it was not ready to tolerate there being people in the city who were cold in their faith in God.

The popular assembly took place on Sunday, May 21. Bells and trumpets called the people together. When the solemn question was put, the people gave unanimous consent by show of hands and promised and swore before God that with his help they would with one accord try to live "in this sacred evangelical law (!) and Word of God as it has been announced" to them, renouncing all masses and other papal ceremonies and abuses, images and idols, and everything associated with them, and living in unity, obedience, and righteousness.[39] It was also resolved to found a school that would be free for poor children and compulsory for all, the renowned Antoine Saunier[40] being appointed teacher at an adequate salary.

On July 13 a pastor came forward with the admission that against

36. Ibid.
37. Ibid., 199.
38. Ibid., 200f.
39. Ibid., 201f.
40. Ibid., 202. Saunier was French. His dates are not known.

his promise he had been saying mass frequently, and he was promptly locked up. On July 21 an arrest warrant was issued against another pastor on the same charge. On July 24 Jean Balard, a respected man and tested freedom fighter, was summoned and appeared on the charge that he refused to go to sermons. Asked why, he replied that he believed in God, who taught him by the Spirit, but not in the preachers. No one could force him against his conscience to go to sermons. When told to obey within three days he replied that he would live according to the gospel of God, but he needed no interpretation by private persons, only that of the Holy Spirit through holy, catholic mother church in which he believed. His conscience would not let him go to sermons, and he would not go against it. He had his teaching from a higher source *(par plus haut)* than the preachers.[41] This opposition could have been linked to the influence of Radicals appealing to the Spirit. The man was imprisoned on August 15, for several days taken by force to sermons, and when he persisted in his protest he was banished from the city after ten days of grace. On September 15 Farel was awarded a keg of white paradise wine *(unum dolium vini albi de paradys).*[42]

§12 CALVIN'S WORK

Meantime, at the end of July or the beginning of August, Calvin had come to Geneva. He agreed to stay on two conditions, first, that he should be allowed a few weeks of time (which he used to visit Basel); and second, that initially he should not have any specific office in the church. It is evident that a block still remained, that he did not want to be committed to any particular task.[1] By the beginning of September we find him starting some Bible studies or biblical lectures in the St. Pierre cathedral (not sermons!). He was also at work on a translation of the *Institutes* into French and called himself professor of holy scripture.[2] Obviously for the time

---

41. Ibid., 203.

42. Ibid., 205.

1. Kampschulte, I, 281f.; cf. Calvin's letter to his friend F. Daniel, 10.13.1536, in CO 10/II, 62-64 (no. 34).

2. Calvin uses this description of himself on the title page of the two 1537 *Epistolae,* OS I, 287.

being he wanted to occupy a kind of middle position between purely academic work and church work. He never became totally a pastor but always remained on the boundary, as it were, standing and working on church soil but always looking beyond it to associated possibilities as a public adviser and an independent thinker, scholar, and writer. Furthermore, in the biblical lectures, which he would not give up even when he was appointed pastor some months later,[3] we can see the beginnings of the Geneva academy, which would later[4] grow almost of itself out of Calvin's lectures.

What line did this early educational activity in Geneva take? We hardly know anything about it except that he began by expounding the epistles of Paul.[5] Zwingli opened his preaching ministry in Zurich under similar but more peaceful conditions with an exposition of Matthew's Gospel.[6] The different texts chosen are typical of both. Remember that Calvin found himself in a totally chaotic situation in Geneva. On his deathbed, saying farewell to his colleagues, he said of this that when he first came to this church there was, as it were, nothing there. Sermons were delivered, but that was all. Idols were sought out and burned, but there was no reformation. Everything was tumultuous (9, 891f.).[7] Into this situation he brought Paul and his Romans, which would be the theme of his first commentary three years later.[8]

It is hard to imagine how things really went. One thing is certain, that even decades later,[9] when he had for a long time been in the thick of it, Calvin had not by a long way developed the same direct form of eloquence that still grips us in Luther's sermons. To the end of his days he had to be content to expound, though at once going on to show the relevance and universal validity of his texts, always focusing on the main point, hence not without the fervor that is unavoidable when there is this concentration on the drift and content to the exclusion of all secondary matters; yet always very sober, bent over the Book, not claiming to bring

---

3. Stähelin, I, 122.

4. In the MS Barth first put the "later" before "Geneva academy," but then altered it to its present position.

5. Bossert, 66; Kampschulte, I, 283.

6. 1.1.1519; cf. H. Bullinger, *Reformationsgeschichte*, ed. J. J. Hottinger and H. G. Vögeli, vol. I (Frauenfeld, 1840), 12. The sermons have not been preserved.

7. *Discours d'adieux aux ministres*, OS II, 401.

8. CO 49, 1-292.

9. The MS had by mistake an unnecessary "when he" here.

or to represent anything but what stands in it[10] in all its weight and with all its implications.

At the first, when he emerged from his study to speak to the public, this was how it had to be, though we do not have any of his lectures from this period. Nevertheless, a remarkable thing happened. These biblical lectures, which to our way of thinking might seem to be doctrinaire, made an impression and were well attended, as though a mysterious underground and paradoxical relation had come into being between the mixture of error and force[11] that was then called the Genevan reformation, and the thinking of Romans that came from such a different world. Already on September 5 Farel was before the council stating how necessary the lectures were that "this Gallus" was giving in St. Pierre and asking them to see to it that they were continued and supported. It was resolved to do this.[12] But nothing much actually came of it, for in February 1537 the council itself had to report that Calvin had received almost nothing by way of remuneration and it was resolved to pay him six taler.[13]

What he surely did receive in quick time was the respect and admiration of the other pastors, though he played a secondary role in relation to Farel, and was content to serve as the latter's chief of staff. By May 1537 Farel was no longer going before the council without being accompanied by this colleague who was twenty years younger. Farel and Calvin constantly appear together now in council records, and when the crisis broke, as though by an oversight on the part of the scribe, we suddenly find Calvin and Farel.[14] The real relation between the two had probably for a long time been in this reverse order. And when, three years after they left Geneva, the situation became untenable, the Genevans knew where they had to turn, and Calvin, no, M. Calvin *ministre,*[15] had now become the only one to address the council in the church's name. That the reversal could take place without the slightest friction or dissension between the two not only arouses sympathetic regard from a human standpoint but is also an indirect proof of the strict objectivity to which the two subjected

---

10. For this formula in Barth cf. the preface to his *Romans* (Oxford, 1933) in the second and later editions, 2ff.

11. Cf. Goethe's *Zahme Xenien* IX.

12. CO 21, 204.

13. Ibid., 208.

14. Ibid., 224 (4.19f.1538).

15. Ibid., 282.

themselves. Farel understood the strange art of not just letting himself be led but also letting himself be taught by the other even in things in which he had already formed his own different convictions apart from Calvin, for example, in eucharistic teaching, in which he was originally a fully pledged Zwinglian.[16]

And to this stormy and unpredictable man, who at 69, for example, would marry a young girl over the protests of all his friends,[17] Calvin would be no less loyal. The friendship that linked two such different characters all their lives, and that on Calvin's side showed no signs of reserve or being forced, proves too that in spite of everything we might note concerning it, Farel's reformation in Geneva also took place on a different plane from that which is historically visible. Calvin could speak on his deathbed about Froment, the moral preacher, though not without a twitching in the corner of his mouth.[18] But he loved and honored Viret and Farel as well as respecting them, though going his own way and not theirs, and though it was only as his students that they became unambiguously what they were.

In October (1-8) 1536 the Bern government had arranged a disputation at Lausanne.[19] In the conquered territory of Vaud Roman Catholicism still had strong support. Viret was preaching in one of the Lausanne churches, but mass was still being said in the cathedral. Clearly the victorious state had to take steps to cut the religious ties that still linked the area to the previous government. With Viret, Peter Caroli (a Sorbonne doctor and Protestant refugee), Farel, Calvin, and two other Geneva pastors would represent the Protestant cause. On the Roman Catholic side, which was much more resolutely and perspicaciously advocated than at Geneva, a physician, Blancherose, was outstanding. But here, too, most of the priests were characterized by a total lack of counsel or knowledge. The

---

16. In treating Farel as a Zwinglian Barth follows such older authorities as J. H. Merle d'Aubigné, *Histoire de la réformation . . .*, 5 vols. (Paris, 1838ff.; ET New York, 1849ff.); and C. Schmidt, *Wilhelm Farel und Peter Viret. . .* (Elberfeld, 1860). More recent research shows that this view does not allow for nuances and has little basis in Farel's works; cf. E. Jacobs, *Die Sakramentslehre Wilhelm Farels* (Zurich, 1978), 354, who concludes that we must abandon the idea of a Farel who first followed Zwingli and then Calvin as too simple, Farel being in fact closer in his eucharistic teaching to the Strassburg reformers.

17. CO 17, 335f. (Calvin to Farel, no. 2958) and 17, 351ff. (to Neuenburg colleagues worked up about the matter, no. 2966); cf. Schmidt, *Farel*, 35.

18. *Discours d'adieux aux ministres*, OS II, 401, 36ff.

19. Schmidt, *Farel*, 19ff.

Protestant theses (9, 701f.; Müller, *Symb. Bücher,* 110)[20] laid strong emphasis, as was usual in Zwinglian circles, on the saving work of God and the spiritual nature of salvation. Christ was sacrificed for us once and for all, hence the only church is the fellowship of the reconciled and believing, Christ is present only by the Holy Spirit, the sacraments are symbols and signs of hidden things, the only priesthood is that of administering the Word and sacraments, confession of sins is made only to God and only God can forgive sins, and the only possibility of serving God is the spiritual one of love for God and neighbor.

Calvin did not speak at this disputation until the fifth day.[21] Perhaps this was because he had been sick in bed at Geneva for ten days just before it,[22] the first of many sicknesses. Or perhaps he felt a need to become acquainted first with the new situation and to let Farel and Viret take the lead. Or it may be that he had an instinctive aversion for the Bernese background of the whole affair. Or perhaps he could not be wholly satisfied with the theses because they did not contain much that was dear to his own heart: the majesty and glory of God, the authority of holy scripture, an eschatological outlook, the paradoxical presence of Christ in the sacrament, the sanctification of individuals in the community as an inescapable task. But finally on the fifth day he saw cause to make his own incisive contribution, though it would not be much more than the verdict of an expert (9, 877).[23] In discussion of the Lord's Supper Blancherose had said that the Protestants were contradicting the fathers. Farel could not answer this charge.[24] Calvin with his knowledge of the history of dogma felt that he should now join in the proceedings.

He did not forget to begin by saying that we really have enough in the Law and the Prophets and do not need to use either the living or the dead as our authorities. For this is not just a matter of temporal policy for the present life but a question of the spiritual rule of God for eternal life in which we have to recognize God as the only king and lawgiver.[25] (It is worth noting that a link between biblicism and eschatology comes to light here. It is because we have to do with eternal things that the Bible is

---

20. *Les articles de Lausanne,* CO 9, 701f.

21. CO 9, 877. Calvin stated that he had kept silence thus far and had meant to do so to the end seeing the replies of Farel and Viret were so adequate.

22. CO 10/II, 62.

23. CO 9, 877-86.

24. Cf. Schmidt, *Farel,* 21.

25. CO 9, 878.

normative rather than the fathers, in whom this orientation is not sufficiently strong.) Nevertheless, if there was to be an appeal to the fathers, Calvin thought he could show that they favor the Protestant view more than they do the Roman Catholic. His contribution was primarily a brilliant display of his erudition. From memory he could adduce a passage from Tertullian, another from Pseudo-Chrysostom, and six from Augustine, and give the sources.[26] Furthermore, he could give an outline of his christology and eucharistic teaching[27] with a precision that shows clearly that he lived and moved regularly in that whole world of thought of which he had given only one demonstration in the *Institutes*. A Franciscan monk named Todi then rose up in a kind of ecstasy and declared that he had now seen the truth, that he knew what the gospel was teaching, that in order not to sin against the Holy Spirit he must confess this, that he was asking the people to forgive him for so long leading them astray, and that he was leaving his order.[28] This was the high point of the whole disputation.

Calvin spoke again twice when the other side appealed to the authority of Pope Gregory VII, using not wholly impartial sources, again extemporaneously, to show what kind of man Gregory was.[29] When the Bernese mayor Jacob of Wattenwil, who was present for the occasion, declared the disputation over on October 8 and held out the prospect of a decision by the government, it was evident to everyone that the goal had been reached and reformation would take place in Vaud. Caroli was appointed the first pastor in Lausanne and Viret the second.[30] We shall hear more about both.

On October 16 Calvin went with Caroli to a synod at Bern dealing with the so-called Wittenberg Concord. Thanks to the unwearying efforts of Bucer and Capito this document had been drawn up as an instrument of peace between Lutherans and Zwinglians. Luther on the one side and the Swiss on the other were not enthusiastic about it. Calvin did not take part in the proceedings. As is still the custom to this day, the discussions of church and state bodies in Bern were held in dialect, and it is quite possible that the French guests were simply unable to follow the course of

26. Ibid., 879-81.
27. Ibid., 882-84.
28. Doumergue, II, 216.
29. CO 9, 884-86.
30. Schmidt, *Farel,* 22.

the lively debate. It is hard to see what other reason there could be for Calvin maintaining silence when such an important matter was under discussion.

§13 Reformation Program[1]

In the ensuing winter months of November and December the lectures and sermons met with growing success, and Calvin also drew up the chief documents for the first attempt to reorganize the church. These documents included a church order that he submitted to the council in a memorandum, a catechism that would be the basis of religious education for young people, and a confession of faith[2] to which adult citizens would solemnly subscribe in order to seal their resolve to accept the Reformation. Since the whole Geneva experiment, of which these documents were the start, is so important if we are to achieve a proper portrait of Calvin and his theology, we cannot refuse to look more closely at these pieces in their original form.

Church Order

On November 10 Farel came before the council to present some articles of church government. It was resolved to accept these as they were, to remove all images, and to establish an order for preaching according to detailed resolutions that would be passed at the next session. This at least is how I have to understand the rather obscure wording of the minutes of that session.[3] It certainly seems to me that these articles cannot have been the same as those presented by Farel and the other pastors on January 16, 1537, the articles on the organization of the church and worship at Geneva, in which nothing is said either about removing images or a preaching order. Probably the November articles were a first draft, but we know nothing about this apart from the points mentioned, and Calvin probably had little or no hand in them. It is indeed psychologically more likely that

1. In the MS the heading was added in the margin.
2. OS I, 369ff., 378ff., 418ff.
3. CO 21, 206.

Calvin, having just come back from Lausanne and Bern, and having previously been at work hardly a single month in Geneva, would not have rushed in at once with his incisive ideas on the organization of the church. He obviously had to tackle this subject, and he did so at the beginning of 1537 in a memorandum to the council (10/I, 5ff.).[4] He himself almost certainly did not draw this up, but equally certainly its contents in the critical portions are his work. We must briefly analyze it.

A first introduction rather clumsily summarizes the four main points that concern the pastors who present it.[5] A second introduction admits that the confusion of the first period of reformation did not make for the quick reducing of everything to good order but claims that it has now pleased the Lord to establish his rule rather better here, and therefore the time has come to consider what church polity should be adopted as we are directed by his Word and have the assistance of his Spirit.[6] If the council sees that the following proposals are in keeping with God's Word, then it should do its duty and put them into force as orders. For the Lord has indeed given the council the insight that the church's ordinances (an actual use of this term already!) must always rest so far as possible on his Word, which is the sure rule of all government and administration, especially in the church.[7] Who was behind these statements we can hardly fail to see. They are memorable and historically weighty statements when we remember all that would follow this first link in the chain. From this time on we not only have Calvin but we have *Calvin in Geneva, Calvinism.* The first part of the memorandum, more than three-quarters of the whole, deals with the Lord's Supper.[8] Then we have the singing of the Psalms, the catechism, and the order of marriage, but in comparison these are mere trifles. Calvin's church order is a eucharistic order.

The exposition begins with the clear-cut thesis that it would be desirable to administer the Lord's Supper at least (!) every Sunday. Jesus did not institute it to be remembered only two or three times a year but as a constant exercising of our faith and love in which the congregation should engage every time it meets. The abomination of the mass has led to decline from the original use.[9] It will be seen that Calvin had no thought

---

4. OS I, 369ff.
5. Ibid., 369.
6. Ibid., 370.
7. Ibid.
8. Ibid., 370ff.
9. Ibid., 370.

of sharing in a spiritualizing aversion from the sacrament. For him it was a constituent part of worship. He did not want to lag behind Roman Catholicism in this regard but to move ahead of it — an almost intolerable idea for us but one into which we must try to find our way somehow if we are to understand Calvin. In him as in the other reformers, even Zwingli, I have the impression that they had at their command at this point categories that we have lost but that in some manner that eludes us were linked to what was most central in their knowledge of God, the communion of Christians with Christ. They still knew what a sacrament is. Perhaps we will one day come to know this again. Calvin himself had to give up this ideal of an administration every Sunday. Because of the existing "weakness of the people" there was a danger that too frequent administration would bring disparagement on the mystery. For this reason it would be better to opt for a monthly administration, switching from one church to the other, though obviously with the whole city and not just one parish in mind.[10] We are probably not mistaken if we see in this more limited proposal, which the council later would not find satisfactory,[11] the result of a compromise among the pastors themselves. Calvin wanted to go further, others less far, so they agreed upon this middle course.

The question of frequent administration, however, was not Calvin's main concern. The "principal order" that ought to be introduced was as follows. The institution of the Lord's Supper had as its aim the uniting of the members of Christ to their Head and their uniting among themselves as one body and spirit. But this union must not be stained and besmirched by the participation of those whose evil lives declare that they do not belong to Jesus. This would be the dishonoring of God against which Paul made such serious threats in 1 Cor. 11 [vv. 17-34].[12] Those who have the power, then, must set up a polity that stipulates that only those may participate who are as it were approved members of Jesus Christ. This meant excommunication according to Calvin's understanding of Matt. 18 [vv. 15-18]. The obdurate and those who lead an unchristian life in spite of admonition must be cut off from the body of the church as members that have rotted.[13] For — and here we have three reasons familiar to us

---

10. Ibid., 371.
11. CO 21, 206. The council fixed on four times a year.
12. OS I, 372.
13. Ibid., 372.

from the *Institutes* — (1) Jesus Christ must not be exposed to the suspicion that his church is a conspiracy of perverse and frivolous people; (2) those concerned should be brought to self-knowledge and repentance by the shame of this punishment; and (3) the rest should not be unsettled by their bad example but terrified by the example of their punishment.[14] Papal excommunication is a caricature of this, for the right to punish is there taken from the congregation and handed over to pseudo-bishops.[15] It must be given back to the congregation. To put it into effect the congregation must select a number of men of excellent life and character, proven convictions, and incorruptibility.

What this involves, though the word is not used here but only in later versions of the order, is the consistory. Chosen from all the parishes, the men mentioned will keep an eye on how people live, and if they find a serious fault ("notable vice") in anyone, they will report it to a pastor, whose task it will then be to admonish the one concerned in brotherly fashion.[16] If that does no good, the fault and obduracy will be reported to the congregation. If that again does not help, the congregation will be told that although it has done its duty, it has failed. If the offender continues in hardness of heart, the time for excommunication has come, for exclusion from the "company of Christians," for handing over for a time to the power of the devil until signs are given of remorse and repentance. In token of this exclusion the person concerned will be refused Holy Communion and intimate dealings with other believers, but will still be allowed to hear sermons in order to get teaching and in an attempt again and again to see whether it will please the Lord to move the heart and to bring the person back to the right path.[17] Apart from this punishment the church will initiate no other proceedings, we are then told expressly, but if any thus excommunicated think they can laugh at this punishment, then the authorities will know ways of not leaving unpunished such deriding and mocking of God and his gospel.[18] This theory, we see, does not regard it right for the church to inflict bodily punishment *(ecclesia non sitit sanguinem).*[19] It is not unlike the Roman Catholic view

14. Ibid., 372; cf. 89f.; BI 83.
15. OS I, 373.
16. Ibid.
17. Ibid., 373f.
18. Ibid., 374.
19. On the history of this legal maxim cf. A. Erler, "Ecclesia non sitit sanguinem," *Handwörterbuch zur deutschen Rechtsgeschichte,* vol. I (Berlin, 1972), 795ff.

that heretics should be handed over to the secular arm. The difference is that jurisdiction now extends only over the moral and not the religious life of the people, an uneasy advance on Roman Catholicism, but at any rate not its opposite.

Naturally Calvin did also regard religious attitudes as a matter for church discipline. Those totally "opposed to us in religion" were even less to be tolerated in the eucharistic fellowship than evil livers.[20] For them the remedy was as follows. All the residents of the city were to make a confession so as to show who were in agreement with the gospel and who would rather belong to the kingdom of the pope than to the kingdom of Jesus Christ.[21] And it would be an act of Christian magistrates if council members would individually subscribe to the confession in the council so as to make it plain that their doctrine really is that by which all believers link themselves to the church. By their example they will show the rest what they must do.[22] A more unusual demand has seldom been made so formally of any government. The one who dared to put the demand can hardly have been a loyalist. Having made the confession, some of the council members should then go to individual citizens with a pastor to receive their assent to the confession. But this should be done only this one time when it is not known as yet what the attitude of people is to the teaching that is the true beginning of a church.[23] The thinking is obviously that a tradition will now be started to which there may be legitimate appeal should doctrinal differences arise later. In this way Calvin focused church membership, church government, and the church confession on the Lord's Supper. The purity and dignity of the supper is the standard by which to decide who are approved members of Jesus Christ, members of the church.[24] To maintain the purity and dignity of the supper a church board is needed, the consistory, but so too is the church confession if the whole structure is to rest on an authority and continuity that are more than personal and that may be invoked at any time.

It is a fact that in remarkable and instructive tension with the spiritual and even otherworldly character of Calvin's Christianity his community in its original conception is so expressly a eucharistic community, and also,

---

20. OS I, 374.
21. Ibid.
22. Ibid., 374f.
23. Ibid., 375.
24. See above, n. 13.

as we have seen, that the state, by means of the confession made by the supreme authority and the sum of its citizens, should confess its identity with this community, and should thus show itself to be a Christian state, a legitimate power that God has instituted not only in his wrath but also in his grace. The parallels to what we find in Roman Catholicism are obvious. I hinted at some of them yesterday. But it should be pointed out again and again that in contrast to this strongly developed element of visibility in Calvin's concept of the church the thought of predestination offers very sharply an element of invisibility, so that there can be no real equation with the concept of medieval Catholicism.

Let us recall again at this point that in Calvin ecclesiastical power comes under the heading of Christian liberty and has a place only there. The church is not for Calvin a saving institution, seriously though he takes it. It is the visible fellowship of believers. But in its proper place and with every necessary caveat we have to take it seriously as such. In the Lord's Supper there is no corporeal presence of God, no direct miracle, but in it we have the presence of the promise of God, the sign and image of the miracle, and where people find themselves in the fellowship of those who expect this, who look beyond the visible, *there* is the community of Christ on earth, and again it is to be taken seriously as such. Finally, even the church discipline is not a way to God that is necessary for salvation. God's judgment remains sovereign over both those who are inside and those who are shut out. It is an instrument of humanity,[25] a measure by which the community may keep its witness pure. And who permits us, Calvin thinks, not to use this visible measure, knowing its relativity? What we really have here is the force and breadth of Calvin's genius that are almost beyond our comprehension — a clear vision of the this-worldly element on the one side and the otherworldly element on the other, but with an equal appeal to both as complementary to one another. In considering the church order for Geneva with its uncomfortable concreteness, we must thus pay more attention than formerly to the transcendent, eschatological, and theocentric motifs in his theology, not being content merely to shake our heads at all that we heard yesterday.

The second matter on which the pastors of Geneva gave their advice to the council concerned the introduction of psalm singing after the manner of the early church so as to protect common prayer against coldness and to lift up the hearts of the people to God. At this point, too,

25. OS I, 256; BI 281f.

the papacy had robbed the church by making of loud praise to God's glory a thoughtless mumbling. The Psalms should first be taught to children, then adults should be taught to sing them, so that they might become a common inheritance of the church.[26]

The third article dealt with Christian education.[27] Faith and confession go together, especially for young people. In the existing situation in particular something had to be done to make possible for them an intelligent confession of the faith of the church to which they belonged. There was to be seen in them an astonishing "rudeness and ignorance" such as were not tolerable in the church of God.[28] Needed, then, was a brief and easy summary of the Christian faith by which children might be examined at certain times of the year by the pastors until they showed themselves to be adequately instructed. It was really the parents' duty to see to it that children learned this summary of the faith, and they should be admonished to attend to this by the council. As we see, we have here a primitive form of religious education. There is no talk at all of confirmation or the like. A church whose pastors knew what they wanted did not really have to take these things tragically, only seriously. Being so concerned about content and so sure of the power of Christian truth, they did not need to worry about quantity or educational refinement. Today when religious pedagogics is in full bloom and church circles show a general concern for the quantity of religious education,[29] you must answer for yourselves the question where there is a similar concern for content or a similar confidence in the power of Christian truth.

Finally, the fourth article has to do with the order of Christian marriage, especially as regards impediments, in regard to which scriptural injunctions were to be brought back in place of the complex papal rules.[30]

The memorandum closes with a challenge to the council to test what has been said by the Word of God. If the Word is in agreement with it, then it is not the pastors who have said it, and no difficulty should prevent the council from doing its duty and setting affairs in order. If we follow the commands of God, we must also have good hope that God in his goodness will bring our undertaking to a successful conclusion. God has

---

26. OS I, 375.

27. Ibid., 375f.

28. Ibid., 376.

29. Earlier Barth had been much involved in this issue. For a list of relevant writings cf. the Swiss edition, p. 364 n. 31.

30. OS I, 376.

already given the council the grace to seek his glory.[31] Before we look at the basic significance and historical outcome of the memorandum, we have still to turn our attention to the two other elements in Calvin's reforming of the church.

Catechism[32]

We are now dealing with the original form of the famous Latin and French Catechism of the Genevan Church of 1545, which became a norm and model for all Reformed catechisms until a year before Calvin's death it was put in the shade by the work of the theologians Ursinus and Olevianus, the much more practical and usable Heidelberg Catechism of 1563 (6, 1ff.; Müller, *Bekenntnisschriften*, 117ff.).[33] The Catechism or Instruction in the Christian Religion of 1538 was the direct forerunner of the 1545 work.[34] It claims to be a translation of an earlier French original[35] and was drawn up to defend the author and his colleagues publicly against the charge of Arianism that Caroli had brought against them in Lausanne. The earlier French original was for a long time thought to be lost, but suddenly it was rediscovered in 1877 in a collection in the Bibliothèque Nationale in Paris, published, and then included in CR (22, 33ff.; Latin 5, 323ff.).[36] This French original has the title *Instruction and Confession of Faith Used in the Church of Geneva,* and it is surely that brief and easy summary that the memorandum of the pastors, as we say, requested of the council. The time of its appearance is not easy to fix since it is not dated, nor is it mentioned in the records of the council, but according to the testimony of Beza's biography[37] and a letter of Calvin to Grynaeus in

---

31. Ibid., 377.

32. Ibid., 378ff.

33. BSRK 117ff.; Schaff, 307ff.

34. In a marginal note Barth refers to Calvin's quoting of the catechism in answer to Farel, but the reference should be to Caroli. In a letter of the Genevan pastors to Bern dated February 1537 (CO 10/II, 82-84), Viret is defended against Caroli's charge of Arian error. Two quotations are given from the Latin version of the catechism that agree word for word with the text in CO 5, 337f.

35. For the full title see CO 5, 323f.

36. Cf. CO 22, 9; OS I, 378ff.; Latin, CO 5, 323ff.

37. Beza, *Vita Calvini*, CO 21, 126. For the letter to Grynaeus see CO 10/II, 106-9 (no. 64), with reference to Viret and Arianism on 107.

May 1537 it must have come out at the end of 1537 or early in 1538, that is, at much the same time as the memorandum was presented.

As regards authorship, internal and external evidence leaves us in no doubt that the work was Calvin's and only Calvin's. Apart from arrangement, the original differs from the better-known 1545 Catechism in that it does not consist of questions and answers. Like Luther's Large Catechism, but more crisply, it consists of a sequence of sixty succinct presentations. Three characteristic texts from 1 Peter serve as a motto: "As newborn babes, desire pure spiritual milk" (2:2); "Be always ready to give an answer to everyone who asks you a reason for the hope that is in you" (3:15); "If anyone speaks, let him do it as speaking God's Word" (4:11). The Ten Commandments, Apostles' Creed, Lord's Prayer, sacraments, preaching ministry, and government are the topics. Seven articles on the knowledge of God and self form the introduction. Nine articles on the Commandments and the Creed deal with the significance of the law for salvation, predestination, faith, justification, repentance, and good works. Between the Creed and Lord's Prayer three articles deal with hope and prayer.

As we see, we have on the whole a repetition of the *Institutes,* and there are even some verbal echoes at times. All the same, I would recommend you to read the work and can hardly pass it by altogether here. Its relation to the *Institutes* resembles that of Kant's *Prolegomena*[38] to the *Critique of Pure Reason.* It is an authentic summary of the larger work and in it many sayings and thoughts that do not receive emphasis there take on for the first time their true color and force. At the same time there are in it no new approaches or expositions that carry us further. I will thus simply pick out certain things from this catechism. For the purpose of these lectures we cannot impress upon ourselves too strongly the distinctive expressions and concepts of Calvin's theology.[39]

Article 1[40] tells us that in view of the fragility and brevity of life it has to be a meditation on immortality. But we can find eternal and immortal life only in God; hence we have to seek God.

Article 2[41] deals with the difference between true and false religion.

---

38. The *Critique* came out in 1781, the *Prolegomena* in 1783.

39. Barth put the themes of the articles, or groups of articles, in the margin, underlined in red pencil.

40. OS I, 378. Theme: "God and Immortality."

41. Ibid., 379. Theme: "True Religion."

People constantly come up with the idea of a deity they have to fear. But true piety is not fear. Fear of the deity may well go hand in hand with an irregular life and with great security. Fear is not yet recognition of the infinite majesty of God. Fear fashions its own god according to the dreams and illusions of the heart. We have here a criticism of religion that we might well feel reminds us of Feuerbach. True piety shows itself in the genuine zeal that never tries to conceive of God as our own presumption dictates but seeks the knowledge of the true God in God himself, conceives of him only as he himself reveals himself and declares himself, namely, as Father and Lord, reaches out after his righteousness, and has more fear of offending him than of death itself.

Article 3[42] has to do with the knowledge of God. True and solid piety is faith conjoined with fear and trembling. We cannot comprehend God's majesty as such. We are simply shattered by its brightness. We must cling, then, to his works, which represent what we cannot see.[43] We see in the universe of things the immortality of our God as their common beginning and origin, his power, wisdom, goodness, righteousness, and mercy.[44] Note that here God's immortality is put before all his other attributes and is linked to the thought of creation — another instance of Calvin's basic eschatological, or, if one will, Platonic, orientation. Properly, he thinks, the universe of things ought to teach us about God, were we not blinded to the witness of this second created light as well. This being so, we need the divine Word, which tells us what we cannot see for ourselves, that every good thing comes from God and must redound to his praise. We have to come to ourselves, to the revelation of God as the living, wise, and almighty God, to the proofs of his righteousness, clemency, and goodness toward us, if we are to understand the language of heaven and earth.[45]

What can article 4[46] say about us, however, but that we have damaged our divine likeness by revolt against the Lord, against God. It is only stripped of all glory of our own that we can now know God. Everything about us is profane and abominable to God.[47]

---

42. Ibid., 379f. Theme: "Knowledge of God."
43. Ibid.
44. Ibid., 380.
45. Ibid.
46. Ibid., 381. Theme: "Self-Knowledge."
47. Ibid.

As article 5[48] puts it, nothing we undertake is the true freedom it ought to be; all is corrupt and spoiled.

Article 6[49] tells us that we are born thus and are constantly ensnared in what then happens along these lines. If this insight plunges us into terror and despair, it is essential that with no righteousness of our own, no trust in what we can do, no possibility ("expectation") of life at all, we learn to cast ourselves down before the Lord, acknowledging our poverty and shame.[50]

For — we read in article 7[51] — this very self-knowledge creates for us the possibility of true knowledge of God. Or rather, with it God himself has opened for us a first door to his kingdom by destroying the two evil pests of security against his retribution and false self-confidence. We now begin to lift up to heaven eyes that were previously focused on earth. We no longer rest in ourselves but sigh for the Lord.[52]

To bring this about is the purpose of the law of God, of which Calvin speaks in articles 8-20.[53] You must read the exposition of the commandments for yourselves.

If there are any people, we read in article 21,[54] who really exhibit God's law in their lives, they have to have the perfection that God expects. If our wills were in line with God's, the law would be enough for salvation. But that is not so. The more clearly the law reveals to us the righteousness of God, the more clearly it also reveals our own corruption.[55]

Hence, article 22 tells us,[56] God himself intervenes for us and comforts us with the confidence in his power and mercy that he gives us in Christ, his Son. In the law he seemed to be only the righteous Judge; in Christ we see him in his grace and clemency.[57] We note that here Calvin keeps in the background two thoughts that elsewhere he stresses strongly: the promise concealed in the law and the unity of the OT and the NT. He follows instead the familiar Lutheran schema of an unequivocal an-

---

48. Ibid. Theme: "Free Will."
49. Ibid., 381f. Theme: "Sin and Death."
50. Ibid., 382, n. 50.
51. Ibid., 382. Theme: "Alteration."
52. Ibid.
53. Ibid., 383ff. Theme: "The Law."
54. Ibid., 389.
55. Ibid.
56. Ibid., 389f. Theme: "The Gospel."
57. Ibid., 390.

tithesis of law and gospel. It cannot be denied that the Lutheran view of the relation is simpler and more vivid and dramatic. That Abraham saw the day of Christ and rejoiced [John 8:56] is something that is hard to explain even to adults and indeed theologians, let alone children. I do not know whether it was for this reason, to avoid upsetting the psychological simplicity of the familiar treatment, that he kept silence at this point. In fact we must not always say all that we know or might say. In the later versions of the *Institutes* he took up the matter all the more extensively, and the fact that in question 19 the Heidelberg Catechism followed Calvin and ventured to state the position so plainly[58] seems to me to be one of its most decisive theological services.

In another respect Calvin makes things easier for children than the Heidelberg, at least in this form of his catechism. I am referring to the doctrine of predestination, which even here, in contrast to the first edition of the *Institutes,* he expounds for the first time under its own heading. The condition for acquiring that comforting trust in God is faith, says article 23.[59] There is thus a distinction among people. Some receive the seed of the divine Word, others do not.

According to article 24[60] this distinction goes back to God's election, which applies to some, whereas others are rejected by the same divine decree before the foundation of the world, so that the clearest and most perspicuous preaching of the truth can be for them only a savor of death to death [2 Cor. 2:16]. Why did God decree thus? We must leave knowledge of the reason for his choice to God alone. Again, our crude minds cannot comprehend the divine clarity. Those who seek to penetrate the divine majesty will be overpowered by the glory and struck down.[61]

We should not say that it is an evasion when Calvin has recourse to mystery in this fashion. What he speaks of is not *a* mystery, but *the* mystery, the mystery of the freedom, the deity of God, of him who is and is not, of the ground of all grounds, of the light that is present for no eye, of him who goes and comes, who is eternal. This being so, faith is our only option, he is saying. Faith does not mean that everything is self-evident. It means being wrested out of the darkness of unbelief. God alone is the "why" of faith, God the Lord, God in his majesty. How can or may we make of

58. Schaff, 313.
59. OS I, 390. Theme: "Predestination."
60. Ibid.
61. Ibid., 390f.

that "this being so" an explanation, a reason? If there were a reason for faith, it would not be faith. Faith is faith only when it has no basis other than the freedom, the decree, of God. Calvin is a thousand times right when he begins his description of faith with God and God alone.[62] Whether he is equally right to assign faith and unbelief to two different human groups is another question. I for my part do not think so. It would be more consistent, I think, to speak loudly and forcefully about God's electing and rejecting but to maintain a strong and significant silence about the elect and the rejected. But it would take us too far afield to go into that here. Two things Calvin believes we should cling to face-to-face with this mystery of the election of grace. First, God is always right, for even if he wished to destroy the whole human race, who could deny him the right to do so? If he saves some, it is of his sheer loving-kindness, to which no one can lay claim. Second, we need not plunge into the abyss of eternity to know how we ourselves stand; we have only to hold fast to the witness that is given us in Christ and that grants assurance of salvation to all who accept it.

True faith, says article 25,[63] halts at the mercy of God that is promised us in the gospel. Promise and faith are correlative concepts for Calvin. Take away the promise, he says, and you take away the basis of faith.[64] A faith that is anything other than faith in the promise (in the things that we do not see but can only hope for according to Heb. 11:1) would again not be faith. Christ, however, is the confirmation of all promises, the quintessence of promise, we might say in line with Calvin. In him we see all the treasures of the divine mercy. In him they are offered to us. Hence he is the "perpetual object" of faith,[65] the lasting and definitive focus of all eyes that wait for the consummation.

This being so, article 26 continues,[66] it is obvious that faith transcends all the powers of our human nature. We are blind to the divine mysteries. We have no organ by which to perceive them. How can we be certain about the will of God for us? We who are human! Is it not a fact that the truth of God has no stability in us even when it is a matter of observing visible and perceptible things? How, then, can it be firm and

---

62. Ibid., 391.
63. Ibid., 391f. Theme: "Faith."
64. Ibid.
65. Ibid., 392.
66. Ibid., 392f.

certain when God promises us things that no eye sees and no mind understands? No, when and where faith is present, it is so only as a distinctive and precious gift of God. It is a clarity of the Holy Spirit illumining our minds and confirming our hearts so that we are firmly convinced that the truth of God is so certain for us that it is totally impossible that what his holy Word promises should not be fulfilled.[67]

Article 27 deals with justification.[68] If Christ is really the sum of all the promises, the perpetual object of faith, we can know that what we receive though faith has to be in Christ alone.[69] Stripped of our own righteousness, we are clothed with his.[70] We do not receive anything of this righteousness within ourselves. It is imputed to us as promise, imputed just as if it were our own.[71] Christ represents those who in him believe in the promise of God, and that means the forgiveness of sins, not an alteration in us, but the unheard-of and incomprehensible thing of an alteration in God's attitude to us. This alteration is the point of the sending of Jesus Christ.

For Calvin, however, there is not just a justification by faith but definitely (article 28) a sanctification by faith as well.[72] They are deceiving themselves who think they can boast of their faith in Christ without this second aspect.[73] There is for Calvin no contradiction between what he had just said and this further point, for in his view justification and sanctification lie from the outset on two different levels, yet they intersect — and this is the important thing — on the line which is Christ from an upward point of view and faith from a downward. Christ represents us before God; that is in faith the ground of justification. But Christ also gives us his Spirit; again in faith, that is the ground of our sanctification.[74] To put this in mechanical terms, a hinge has to open here. As the one thing is done for us in heaven, we on earth are put in a position to do the other. The second thing is still totally different from the first, but it has to take place in consequence of it. This other thing, the other that has to take place on earth, is the observing ("l'observation"), though

67. Ibid., 392.
68. Ibid., 393. Theme: "Justification."
69. Ibid.
70. Ibid.
71. Ibid.
72. Ibid., 393f. Theme: "Sanctification."
73. Ibid., 394.
74. Ibid., 393f.

not, of course, the fulfilling of the law. The law, once the cause of self-condemnation, now becomes the light on our path [cf. Ps. 119:105]. It is not as though we are now doing works in our own strength. We do them in spiritual strength as works by which we are made ready for the righteousness of the kingdom of God.[75]

Hence — article 29[76] — there is no faith in Christ without penitence, without regeneration. Participation in the righteousness with which Christ clothes us when representing us before God is a grace that we must not profane, for it means consecration of life.[77] In this conversion regeneration takes place through mortification and vivification. As a result, penitence is a task that is always essential.[78]

We thus move on in article 30[79] to the meaning of good works. Especially clear in this article is the way in which Calvin constantly views our human situation dialectically, from a twofold standpoint. There is no doubt, he begins, that good works which proceed from a clear conscience, that is, a penitent conscience, are pleasing to God. But why and to what extent? Because God recognizes his own righteousness in them. The only righteousness of our works before God is that which consists of this correspondence to the divine righteousness.[80] Only in faith in Christ is this correspondence really true and are we justified in what we do.

We might use the following comparison to make Calvin's meaning clear.[81] Imagine two mirrors parallel to one another. The one represents God's righteousness, the other our good works. A wall separates them, somewhat inadequately representing — every simile conceals! — the total impossibility of congruence between the perfect and the imperfect. We cannot possibly attain to the righteousness of God and our works cannot be pleasing to him. But imagine that at the end of the dividing wall a third mirror is pointed in the opposite direction, that is, turned to the first two divided mirrors. This third mirror is Christ. Then it is clear to us how far there can in fact be correspondence between God's righteousness and our good works; how Christ can stand in our place before God and

---

75. Ibid., 394.
76. Ibid., 394f. Theme: "Penitence."
77. Ibid., 394.
78. Ibid., 395.
79. Ibid., 395f. Theme: "Good Works."
80. Ibid., 395.
81. The MS margin has an illustration.

in God's place before us; how in Christ we can participate in God and God can recognize himself in us; how we can find our righteousness in God and God can find his own righteousness again in us.

What Calvin calls correspondence here signifies a relation, one that is, of course, broken and indirect, that is real only in *Christ,* but that is in fact *real* in Christ. Apart from Christ God could not find a single meritorious work in his people. If there are to be justified works of ours, the justification must lie outside us.[82] It is outside us in Christ, and now God finds in our intrinsically imperfect and polluted works nothing but a "total purity" ("une entière pureté"), calling them righteous and rewarding them with eternal life.[83] Take Christ away, the living relation, the correspondence between heaven and earth, and everything is as it was before, for only in Christ can this inconceivable thing, this paradox, be the truth.

I will pass over articles 31-40, which expound the Creed.[84] Article 41 on hope[85] is important as a significant transition from belief in the resurrection of the body and the life everlasting (in the last article on the Creed) to prayer. For Calvin the relation of hope to faith is that hope is the truly alive and active and motivated thing in faith, its pressing on from promise to fulfillment. It is true that if Calvin keeps Christ at a distance from us as the content of promise, along with the mercy of God and everlasting life, he does not do this as if there were a kind of static relation between here and there, a real this world and the next. Faith in itself, of course, is simply acceptance of the promise, but how can that take place without at once more than that taking place? Those who receive this assurance are now waiting for what God promises to take place. Faith takes it that God is truthful, hope waits for the manifestation of his truth. Faith accepts God as our Father, hope waits for him to show himself as such. Faith regards everlasting life as already given, hope waits for it to reveal itself to us.[86] The total Calvin speaks in this "hope waits" *(espérance attend).*

Articles 42f.[87] describe prayer as the great movement beyond ourselves to God to find in him what we lack. Above all, then, it is a renouncing of our own dignity and glory. In it we do not exalt ourselves

82. OS I, 395.
83. Ibid., 396.
84. Ibid., 396ff.
85. Ibid., 403. Theme: "Hope."
86. Ibid.
87. Ibid., 403ff. Theme: "Prayer."

before God but bewail our plight before him.[88] We thus do what is acceptable to him, and of itself prayer now becomes what it ought to be: petition and thanksgiving.

In expounding the Lord's Prayer in articles 44-51,[89] Calvin seeks to show how the honoring of God that is the theme of the first three petitions is for our own good, so that in praying for our own good in the last three petitions we constantly redirect our thoughts from this to the honoring of God, since we can seek our own good only to God's glory.[90]

Article 52 bears the heading "Perseverance in Prayer"[91] and is perhaps one of the most personal passages in Calvin. We must not try to tie God to specific circumstances nor to impose any law or conditions upon him.[92] The first step in prayer is to subject our will to God's so that, restrained, as it were, with a bridle, it seeks only to adjust and conform itself to that will.[93] If we have composed our hearts to such obedience and are allowing the divine providence to rule over us completely, then we learn in prayer to trust, to wait upon the Lord, and to accept delay in the fulfillment of what we desire until the time his will decides, certain that he is always present with us even when this is not apparent, and that one day he will show that he is not deaf to our cry, no matter how often it seems not to be heard.[94] And even if after long waiting our senses do not see that our prayer has been of any use, our faith affirms what the senses cannot see, namely, that we have been granted all that is needful for us, that we have plenty in our poverty and comfort in our affliction. Hence, when all else leaves us in the lurch, God does not leave us, for he cannot let the expectation and patience of his people be in vain. God himself will be an adequate substitute for all else, so surely does he contain in himself all the good that he will fully reveal in the world to come.[95] This was the way in which Calvin prayed.

Articles 53-56[96] deal with the sacraments. The sacrament is a witness to the grace of God, to his goodwill toward us, an outward sign of

---

88. Ibid., 403f.
89. Ibid., 405ff.
90. Ibid., 405f.
91. Ibid., 410f.
92. Ibid., 410.
93. Ibid.
94. Ibid.
95. Ibid., 410f.
96. Ibid., 411ff. Theme: "Sacraments."

proclamation that the imbecility of our faith requires.[97] Faith must be exercised before God and others,[98] both inwardly and outwardly, we might perhaps say, as an act of knowledge and as an act of confession, for, even though it is God's work, it is still our faith, imperfect like all things human. God trains it by putting his high and heavenly mysteries in the form of carnal things as befits the ignorance of our flesh in all that is high and heavenly.[99] It is not as though the things we are offered in the sacrament bore what is high and heavenly in themselves by nature. They do it only inasmuch as the Word of the Lord gives them this significance.[100] The promise that God's Word gives us comes first. The sign follows. It confirms and seals the promise. It sheds light on it by putting it in the realm of what we can comprehend with the senses.[101] And as we ourselves do something at the same time, we exercise our faith outwardly before others as well, and it becomes confession and praise of God.[102]

For Calvin the high and heavenly mystery is the same in both baptism and the Lord's Supper. There cannot possibly be different graces. The one always depends on the other or calls to it. Nevertheless, he possibly sees in baptism more of the sign of our fellowship with Christ, of our investing with the good things that God has hidden in Christ, of our sanctification, and in the supper more of the sign of justification, of Christ's representing us before God. All the same, baptism is also the promise of divine mercy and the supper the promise of Christ's presence. Precisely in Calvin's doctrine of the sacraments we can see how justification and sanctification, without merging or mingling (as in Osiander or in J. T. Beck in the 19th century),[103] do belong together and are alive and dynamic as the two divine standpoints from which we must see our life and whose relation can find no analogy in any natural or continuous process.

In baptism and the supper we are to avoid certain errors. Water is

97. Ibid., 411.
98. Ibid.
99. Ibid.
100. Ibid.
101. Ibid.
102. Ibid.
103. Barth knew Andreas Osiander (1498-1552) esp. through the work of his Göttingen colleague E. Hirsch, *Die Theologie des Andreas Osiander* (Göttingen, 1919), esp. 172ff. For Barth's later evaluation of J. T. Beck (1804-1878), cf. his *Protestant Theology in the Nineteenth Century* (London, 1972), pp. 616ff., where he finds him closer to Osiander than to Calvin, if not indeed to Trent.

not the cause or even the instrument of cleansing and regeneration, and there is no spatial presence of Christ's body and blood in the supper. The baptismal water imparts to us knowledge of those gifts, and the eucharistic elements give us instruction on Christ's presence with all his riches.[104] For Calvin, however, this knowledge and instruction are the most vital and direct and supreme things that God can now do for us here and now. For the knowledge and instruction come about through the Spirit.[105] Is there anything stronger or more direct and divine than the Spirit for us who are human and not God? Would not anything more in fact be less? I would warn you here against viewing Calvin's sacramental teaching as more limited than the Lutheran, as subtraction from the latter. For Calvin there was no belittling or conjuring away of the mystery. His concern was to put the mystery in the right place where it is unambiguously not just any mystery but *the* mystery of the relation between God and us, the mystery of the *Spirit*. Calvin excludes all spatial and material and natural ideas in order that that alone may remain which truly unites God and us, namely, the Spirit. If Christ has gone up to heaven and left this dwelling on the earth in which we still find ourselves to be pilgrims, even so no distance can take away his ability to quicken his own people by what is his.[106] The reference is to the Spirit, to *the* Spirit, to the supreme Spirit, to the Spirit of God.

If we are assured of this fellowship between God and us by the miracle of the Spirit, then we can hazard the further thought that was so much a concern of Luther and that we found already in the *Institutes*. As the Spirit speaks in the sign to our spirits, Christ is present to us, and truly no less so than if we could see him with our eyes and touch him with our hands, indeed, with such power and efficacy that he not only gives the hope of eternal life to our spirits but makes us certain of the immortality of our flesh.[107]

The very insight into the strictly and properly spiritual nature of God's relation to us, the recollection of the distance between heaven and earth, makes possible for Calvin, then, the insight that corporeality is the end (the *end*) of the ways of God.[108] Without the first insight the second

---

104. OS I, 412, 413.

105. Ibid., 412.

106. Ibid., 412f.

107. Ibid., 413.

108. Barth picked up this phrase from F. C. Oetinger, *Biblisches und Emblematisches Wörterbuch* . . . (1776), 407.

would be naturalistic dreaming, just as the first without the second would be spiritualizing sophistry. Together the two insights form the genuine paradox of faith. The place from which we see the spatial and material and natural in its relation to God has to be transcendent, but from this place we do see it in that relation. Thus for Calvin everything is again said in his sacramental teaching, and here perhaps most strongly. "Hope waits," he might perhaps say here too, and for that reason he stops inflexibly at the sign, but at the sign that signifies.

The final articles 57-60[109] present the doctrine of church and state in much the same words as used in the *Institutes.* Recall the militant description of the ministry of the Word of God.[110] Calvin adopted it more or less word-for-word in the Catechism,[111] though with a stronger emphasis. God's Word is what gives preachers their authority.[112] If, then, they turn back to the dreams and inventions of their own heads, they are *eo ipso* no true pastors but are to be chased off as dangerous wolves. For Christ bids us listen only to those who tell us what they have taken from his Word.[113] Of all human traditions we are to say that in no case do they bind the conscience, and in no case are they to be equated with service of God.[114] If they do bind us, if they seek to be necessary to God's glory, if they want to be spiritual laws, then they not only destroy Christian liberty but obscure true religion and violate the majesty of God, who alone wills to rule in our consciences by the Word.[115]

Calvin then moves on at once to an exposition of church discipline with the express caveat that we do not find in the memorandum but is there in the *Institutes,* namely, that it is a matter of regulating the church, not of a true restraint of evil, and also with the three reasons for it that we know already.[116] The teaching on government[117] finally repeats the demand for unconditional obedience, the one condition being that, since the demand is made in the name of God, the will of God is itself a limit.

109. OS I, 413ff. Theme: "Church and State."
110. Ibid., 237; BI 277ff.
111. OS I, 414.
112. Ibid.
113. Ibid., 414f.
114. Ibid., 415.
115. Ibid.
116. Ibid., 415f. On restraint of evil, 415; cf. 90f.; for the 1536 *Institutes,* BI 83. See above, 185ff.
117. OS I, 416f.

Here, too, Calvin's last word is that we must obey God [Acts 5:29] rather than human authorities.

This, then, is how Calvin wanted the young people of Geneva to be taught. We are astonished. But let us ask carefully what it is that astonishes us. It certainly should not be the pedagogical inexperience and hardness of Calvin that he would offer children this kind of fare. To be sure, it is difficult dogmatic food. But do not assume too quickly that the children would not understand it. It *was* understood. The whole history of Geneva for the next centuries proves that. The Genevans quickly learned to listen to Calvin on predestination and Christ's eucharistic presence, and to speak about it themselves, just as the manual workers and barbers of Byzantium and Alexandria could speak about *homoousios* and *homoiousios*.[118] Such things were for them not just pettifogging issues or matters for doctors of theology, but living questions. If they no longer are that for us, so much the worse for us! In itself Christian dogmatics, when it really speaks, is just as alive and intelligible as anything else in the world. It really speaks when necessity, spirit, and life stand behind it, when it is a hard-won answer to serious questions. Then it is an urgent matter of the day. Then it is as relevant as anything else in virtue of its special connection with the most burning of all questions. Then children, too, can understand it. But if it is no longer that, then it becomes obscure, difficult, and absurd. Then all our efforts to explain it or to give it emotional force are no help. Then sincere young people laugh at our psychological wiles, no matter how well meaning they may be. If we are in this latter position, then we need to ask ourselves how it has come about that something that did speak once will no longer speak to us. We certainly should not suppress the historical truth that it did speak once.

Confession

You will recall that in our account of the memorandum presented to the Genevan council a confession of faith was put forward as a requirement for the Lord's Supper, a confession to which the council and all citizens were solemnly to subscribe. In the preface to the Latin version of the catechism in 1538 (5, 319),[119] Calvin himself tells us what considerations

118. Cf. Gregory of Nyssa, MPG 46, 557.
119. OS I, 426-34.

moved the pastors to ask for this prerequisite. Whatever others might think of it, he said, the pastors could not limit their work so narrowly as to be content with preaching as a completed task. They had to attend more closely to those whose blood might be required of them should they perish because of the pastors' sloth. As this concern became sharper, it became a particularly burning and painful one when they had to administer the Lord's Supper. For although they viewed the faith of many as more than doubtful, all the people without exception streamed to the supper. They thus took to themselves the wrath of God rather than sharing in the sacrament of life. Should it not be concluded that even the pastors were profaning the sacrament if they could administer it with so little joy? The pastors, then, could have a good conscience only if they demanded that those who wished to be counted as Christ's people and to be admitted to the holy and spiritual meal would pledge themselves to the name of Christ by a solemn confession.[120] It was obviously the text of this confession that was presented to the council on November 10, 1536, along with articles on church government that have not survived.[121] We may also assume that reference was somehow made to the confession in the articles. As we shall see, the confession was then printed separately in April 1537 and distributed to all the houses. In 1538 Calvin then translated it into Latin along with the catechism and thus made it known to a wider public. The longer title tells us that all citizens, residents, and subjects were to swear to uphold and keep it (9, 693; 22, 85; Müller, *Bekenntisschriften,* 111; Latin, 5, 355).[122]

The question of authorship is not at all simple. The 1538 Latin translation undoubtedly came from Calvin's pen, and in whole and in detail the confession is based on Calvin's Catechism. But between the beginning and the end with Calvin another was probably the true author. For the sake of brevity this author left out an exposition of the Ten Commandments, Apostles' Creed, and the Lord's Prayer, as we did last time. He put a section on the authority of holy scripture at the beginning. He greatly shortened the expositions of the catechism. In many places he simplified them theologically by eliminating the dialectical element. He omitted the section on predestination and the second half of that on government, where God, we are told, must be obeyed first. In compensa-

120. Ibid., 428f.
121. CO 21, 206.
122. OS I, 418ff.; cf. CO 9, 693ff.; 22, 85ff. (French); and 5, 355f. (Latin).

tion he enriched the earlier work by enlarging the section on discipline with a sonorous list of vices and many sections with powerful attacks on the papacy, as in the section on the Lord's Supper, where the mass is called, almost in the words later used by the Heidelberg Catechism, an abomination and damnable idolatry, churches dependent on the papacy are called synagogues of Satan, and so on.[123] So far as possible, everything is made practical and illuminating and easy to handle. As we would see it, this confession is unquestionably more usable than the catechism itself as a means of instruction. What it offers as the first Calvinistic confessional statement is throughout Calvin's theology. There is hardly a non-Calvinistic word in it. But a thin veil of Reformed churchiness is thrown over Calvin's concepts, as would be attempted so often later with success or failure, most classically in the Heidelberg Catechism. On linguistic grounds (prolegomena to 22)[124] it may be cogently argued that the author was Farel, not Calvin.

The confession shows plainly what a strong impact Calvin's theology had made only a few months after his arrival, even on those who were so much older than its author. It is also astonishing, however, how quickly Farel learned — and how easily and swiftly this may be done with the theology of Calvin or anyone else — to remain more or less faithful to the wording and yet to make of this theology something different, something, we might say, that is more customary and that may be put more easily to use. Supposing that Calvin had died of the illness that afflicted him in the fall of 1536. The work of reformation that had been begun with the *Institutes* would have been in the hands of Farel and the other pastors once again, and they would have continued it along the lines of the confession. Farel was an open and honest man, not wanting at all in zeal. But things would have been much different than under Calvin, as they were thirty or forty years later when Calvin was no longer there: Calvin with his very theological and, for all its turning to the world, very unpractical abstractness; Calvin with his puzzling zeal for an extreme doctrine of predestination; Calvin with his incomparably paradoxical concept of Christ and the Lord's Supper; Calvin with his insistence that obedience must first be paid to God [Acts 5:29]. Much that was ambivalent and demonic would then

---

123. For the vices see CO 9, 698; 22, 93; OS I, 424f. On the mass see CO 9, 697; 22, 92; OS I, 423; cf. Heidelberg Catechism, qu. 80; Schaff, 335f. On the synagogues of Satan see CO 9, 698; 22, 93; OS I, 424.

124. CO 22, 9/10.

certainly not have happened: the disaster of 1538;[125] the rough power struggle of the 1540s; the fall of Bolsec; the burning of Servetus; the momentous development of the second, Reformed form of the Reformation in such a way that it made a place for itself and could no longer be set aside as simply a sect, a special instance of spiritualizing Enthusiasm — in short, much of that which has made Calvin such an unsympathetic figure in the eyes of the educated world.

The making of a compromise in which Reformed Protestantism would have a good and strict but not so unbearable or aggressive a form, a mild type of Reformed Protestantism linked to a necessary devotion to the shades of Zwingli, but accepting, with some discontent, of course, its destiny as a singular form of Lutheranism, which alone deserved serious consideration — all this would have been just as possible in Geneva as in Zurich, Basel, or Bern. For all their excellent qualities, and for all their respect for the Genevan reformation, how carefully and self-consciously did Bullinger, Myconius, and Haller hold aloof from it as long as they lived, with the open or secret question always on their lips: Why are you really like that? Could you not be rather simpler, rather more palatable, rather more like ourselves? How much more Farel for all his rough edges and corners, how much more the worthy Beza, would have been their man, even the man for Geneva, which would not have had to suffer all those things under them. How then a Calvin jubilee might have been celebrated in 1559 similar to the celebrations of 1909,[126] at a safe distance from the guns, with infinite joy under the shadow of the great name, but joy at what? At being so very different from Calvin himself!

As we have said, had Calvin been dead, things would very easily have returned to normal, to what was possible and supportable. Some of the difficult nails of Calvin would, of course, have been too forcefully hammered in by now for people to escape them that easily. They could not forget all that quickly the great threat under which they had lived for the last decades or the great promise which they sensed behind it. For honor's sake belief in predestination and verbal inspiration and church discipline would have had to be maintained for a time, and would in fact have been maintained with honest conviction. Yet soon enough it would have had to be admitted that these things were not meant in the same way as in Calvin, and honesty would have demanded the abandoning of all the

125. The expulsion of Farel, Calvin, and Courault from Geneva.
126. See n. 104 above.

extreme positions. The great disruption[127] would have been over. Unfortunately, perhaps the Spirit would have been lost as well. Church history could go on as usual. The thinly veiled Calvinistic confession of Farel shows that all this might easily have come to pass already in 1536.

Calvin did not repudiate Farel's work. He accepted it as though it were his own. He could do this easily. The veil was thin, so thin that it did not take much to stand by what was written. Calvin had always reckoned with the fact that there would be others alongside him who would say and do things differently. In this matter he would naturally let his old friend take the lead, at least outwardly. There was no danger in so doing, for this was a confession that was to be subscribed to only once. The Reformed church had never had confessional documents in the solemn sense familiar to Lutherans. Farel's confession was good enough for the purpose. This, in my view, is how we must understand Calvin's relation to this part of the Reformation program in Geneva. The voice was Jacob's voice, but in this instance he could be content that the hands were the hands of Esau [cf. Gen. 27:22].

But let us pause for a moment to consider what it really meant that Farel and Calvin dared to come before the council and people of Geneva with this demand for a Protestant confession. This point in their Reformation program was just as strange and repulsive as the other two, the church order and the catechism. We learn of the objections that were made to the demand from Calvin himself in his preface to the Latin edition of the catechism in 1538.[128] The objections were by no means flimsy. For example, it was asked, not merely in Geneva but by Protestants abroad, whether such a confession had any legitimate place alongside the confession that everyone made by the fact of being baptized.[129] This was an objection that Calvin himself could well understand. It is basically the same objection that many rightly make today against what is called confirmation. On Calvin's own view no human work is to be interposed as necessary for salvation between the heavenly grace that is known and confessed in baptism and a life in time that is obedient to that grace. On his view, too, baptism stood in need of no confirmation. A second objection went to the very heart of the demand. All citizens were to pledge

---

127. Cf. the heading of Barth's exposition of Rom. 12–15 in his 2nd ed. of *Römerbrief* (Munich, 1922), ET *Romans*, 424ff.

128. See n. 119 above.

129. OS I, 429.

themselves by an oath to keep the divine law that no one can keep, and they were thus inevitably being led into perjury.[130] In this regard appeal could be made to Calvin himself as a witness, for he had spoken plainly enough about our human inability to keep God's law.

In striking fashion Calvin's answer to these objections is simply one long reference to the OT. What were Moses, the kings Josiah and Asa, and later Ezra and Nehemiah doing when they had the people of Israel swear to try to keep God's law?[131] Did they forget the sacrament of circumcision in which the covenant of God was sealed without confession? Did they really lead Israel into perjury? Is it really a matter here of demanding that we seek after the righteousness of the law and not of confessing the righteousness of Christ with which we are to be clothed as we renounce all human righteousness? Is not the impossibility of keeping God's law an essential part of this confession?[132] A recklessly bold riposte, one has to say. There is thus a renewing of the covenant with God (Calvin uses this expression), but with the admission that we do not have to renew anything, but will be renewed in Christ! A confession, then, that everything we confess amounts to nothing! Yes, that is Calvin's paradoxical meaning.

For a just evaluation of this development and of the whole historical process, we have to keep in mind that Calvin was operating on two levels, an upper and a lower. The decisive process was on the upper level, and there he was in full agreement with his critics. There we are indeed poor and wretched and blind and naked face-to-face with the gracious God. There the glory of God shines over all that takes place in the transitory world. But then — and this again is distinctive of Calvin — something is also taking place on the lower level, and it ought to do so, certainly in full awareness of the relativity of what may happen there, and therefore something that is from the very first imperfect and halting and irresolute, yet precisely in awareness of the relativity, something that still takes place with the energy and solemnity of the history of God's kingdom in the OT. In this action, realizing that we are only human, we must still show, too, that we are God's.[133] In it God, impossible though this might sound, has to be glorified by us.

130. Ibid.

131. Ibid., 429f.

132. Ibid., 430.

133. Perhaps echoing the motto of Christoph Blumhardt in his third period (1896-1900); cf. C. Blumhardt, *Eine Auswahl . . .*, ed. R. Lejeune, vol. III: *Ihr Menschen seid Gottes! Predigten und Andachten aus den Jahren 1896-1900* (Zurich and Leipzig, 1928).

Just because Calvin constantly had meditation on the future life in view — and we must stress this again — he had a strongly developed feeling for significant action on earth, for what could be at times unavoidably dramatic Christian testimonies of the fellowship of Christians with Christ. This is why the Lord's Supper was so important for him, or church discipline with its solemn act of excommunicating the unworthy. This is why later in situations of conflict he would press matters not unwillingly to an almost incomparably impressive intensity, for example, in his last sermon in St. Pierre's in 1538 in defiance of the prohibition of the council, or on occasion by openly refusing to give communion to someone who was acting shamelessly, or by solemnly entering the council chamber at the head of all the pastors.[134] He also made his dying into a solemn act in several scenes.[135] We may compare him in this regard with Luther and his death. This will show us how Calvin's death had about it something of a very impressive and by no means unplanned event.[136] We find the same thing on many occasions, and above all we have to note in such matters the urge to make things vivid and dramatic, and to see the profound link between this urge and all that Calvin was and willed. When *we* become solemn, there is usually something very suspect about it because we do not really know why we are solemn. Solemnity in itself, solemnity on the lower level without the overarching light of eternal occurrence that is reflected in our action, is naturally all wrong. But it might well be that with the need to think of eternal things we can again have the freedom here below to be solemn.

First, however, we can hardly be warned too much against merely imitating Calvin in this regard. It is in this connection that we are to understand the demand he made upon Geneva for confession. He perceived the objections that might be brought against the demand, but he also saw the need for something striking and momentous at this stage in the Genevan reformation, something in which all should have a part so that expression might be given to, and everybody impressed with, the element of seriousness, decision, and irrevocability in the situation produced by the Reformation, a great sign or symbol in which everybody

---

134. On the sermon see below, 359f. On refusing to give communion see Kampschulte, II, 203ff., esp. 209-11; also I, 460f. On entering the council chamber, see ibid., II, 213.

135. Cf. OS II, 398-404.

136. Cf. Stähelin, II, 460ff.

could see clearly what the situation was and be united with others in relation to it. As clearly as a stroke of lightning, the history of the kingdom of God had to be seen as something that had not happened but was in process of happening, and the excitable people of Geneva, always disposed to high spirits and revolt, had to become again the people of the OT covenant, while he himself, Calvin, would be their Moses, Josiah, Ezra, and Nehemiah. All this had to come about like a lightning flash, an impossible event, not meant ever to be a church institution, not meant — not at all — for imitation, at root a wholly eschatological event. Nevertheless, as such, conceivable as a once and for all, a special, a most special, event, it was somehow necessary.

In the preface to the catechism, directly after his explanation of the demand, Calvin added an almost supplicatory request to other Protestants abroad who had blamed him to some extent on the matter — and this passage is one of the most gripping that I have learned to know thus far in Calvin — to bear in mind that we are all soldiers engaged in one war against the one foe, under the one leader, and in the one camp. Unity is thus demanded above all that is individual or that divides.[137] If we want to show obedience to Christ our captain, it is imperative that we bind ourselves together as one pious society and keep peace among ourselves. What? Should not the enemy, the devil, constrain us to act in concert?[138] He alone can rejoice in our conflicts. If only we were to consider that there is a danger of fighting against Christ himself should we oppose actions in which even one scintilla of piety may be seen. Ought we not to note and honor the insignia and ornaments of our God no matter in whom they encounter us?[139] Ought we to have such distrust of one another as to be always so ready to take in a bad sense all that our brethren and fellows undertake? With charity and goodwill should we not instead think the best of one another and act on one another's behalf?[140] Especially when it is a matter of ceremonies, in which we have freedom and do not have to agree? What will be asked of us at the last judgment but whether we have made good use of this freedom? Those will stand in that day who have done most for edification. May, then, our whole care and attention and diligence and concern be directed to edification, in which we can be

137. OS I, 430.
138. Ibid., 431.
139. Ibid.
140. Ibid., 431f.

successful only insofar as we go forward in earnest fear of God, sincere piety, and undissembled holiness of life.[141]

It was finally in this light and context that Calvin himself saw the Genevan confession. He can defend himself, but he can also lay down his weapons. He strongly supported the need for the act, but if the objection to it was sound, he simply replied that it was no more than a ceremony, a possible means of edification. Think of it as you will, but no conflict about it in any circumstances. As I understand it, Calvin thought the act necessary in the sphere of freedom. Freedom stands above the need, and Christ the captain above freedom. I believe that this renunciation of any justification does in fact justify the extraordinary act. Those who know what Calvin knew here of the peace of God that passes all understanding [Phil. 4:7] may permit themselves extraordinary acts of this kind. I at least would not be bold enough to stop them with criticisms.

That is how it is in some sense with the whole of the Genevan program of reformation as we have come to know it. What are we to say concerning it? We can put ourselves back in the situation of the time and thus say correctly that in the way they were undertaken the measures initiated by Farel and Calvin, the church order, catechism, and confession, met the historical needs of the hour. When the position of the gospel in this remarkable corner of Europe was under attack on every hand, what would have become of Geneva if these extraordinary men had not purposed and ventured to do these things? And perhaps we may also ask what would have become of the Reformation in general if these very well-equipped men had not come along and founded this school? The very things that scare us off from the Genevan program in fact fit only too well into the general situation of the day on the lower, secular level, just as a purely sociological study of the things that were then attempted will find real pleasure in them. It was a classical, an only too classical construct that then began to emerge in Calvin's work of reform. From the opposite angle we may also with some truth remark that Calvinism did in fact fit into this world much *too* well, that the construct was *too* classically human. Then we can point to all the things in the acts, as acts on the lower level, that were imperfect and suspect and even openly perverted: the dangerous proximity and relationship of these acts to what the enemy, Roman Catholicism, was doing in this situation; the serious temptation to revive the Middle Ages in a new and even more ambiguous and dangerous form; the

141. Ibid., 432.

acute infiltration of a political, legal, or at any rate OT element into the Reformation gospel.

We can say all these things. Nevertheless, we cannot fail to see that when we have justified and criticized, beyond all that may be said both for and against, there is finally something else to be said on Calvin's behalf, even if it be only indirectly. I refer simply to the fact that here was a man who in the Spirit dared to take a step, a dangerous step, an earthly step, yet a step that he had to take. It may be that nothing more can finally be said in his defense. But as a sign he had a promise that many more easily justified human steps do not have because they are not ventured as this step was. It is the secret of life in general to know what Calvin knew, to look beyond to what is incorruptible, and then to live and act in the world of the corruptible precisely with this higher reference.

§14 RECEPTION

I now have to tell you how the Reformation program of Farel and Calvin was received by Geneva. It will always be a fact worth pondering how it was possible that in those days a complex of abstract theories and unheard-of demands like the Reformation, opposed as it was to a centuries-old religious, cultural, and political tradition, could become not only an intellectual and religious force but also a public force that often in a few months could change visibly and palpably the whole nature and structure of national societies and most incisively redirect their total destinies. In this regard we have to remember what an inconspicuous role all churches and forms of Christianity have thus far played in the upheavals of our own day, how they have just accompanied the actions of governments and peoples and been the rearguard of world movements, at times sanctifying and transfiguring them, at times uselessly protesting against them, but never seizing the leadership or even giving a notable watchword, let alone giving the impression that in this worst catastrophe to overtake Europe since the barbarian invasions they championed a special, respectable, serious cause of their own, a cause to which political and social needs could adapt themselves and not just vice versa.

I am saying that we must keep all this in mind if we are to be clear about the elemental force and dynamic of the events of the Reformation that proved that in little things and great Christianity is at least one factor that has helped very strongly to shape the life of society, a factor that is transcendent at any rate to the degree that no one could fail to see how it calls all this-worldly factors into question and undermines their stability. What book of religion or theology today, for all the interest it arouses in specific circles, does not remain strangely aloof from the spheres in which most people seek their duty and their joy and the destinies of classes and nations are fought over and decided? For who listens seriously today to what theologians and philosophers say, at any rate so long as they speak as such?

We have to repeat, however, that Reformation writings dealt with everyday issues no matter how abstract their contents might be, and what they proposed, transcendent though it was, and just because it was, impinged upon what was taking place in the council chambers and marketplaces. The visible emergence of a transcendent factor all along the line at that time might have been very broken and imperfect. The otherworldly did not become the this-worldly. That is self-evident. But much more significant is the point that the transcendent factor did indeed become visible, or, better, noticeable, with such incomparable intensity that it was hardly possible not to notice it. Let us now try to see in some way how far this was true of Calvin's initial proposals in Geneva.

1. We know little or nothing of the reception that Calvin's Catechism first met with in Geneva, except that there was no obvious opposition. That the council, which had to make the decision, was fully convinced of the soundness of Calvin's theology, or was even in a position to be clear about the ramifications of all the details, we cannot, of course, take for granted, nor that in spite of personal impressions of the man and his proposals there was any enthusiasm for making the venture of his theology. Once they dared to take this step they learned soon enough to understand that theology, partly valuing it highly, partly realizing with horror that they did not really want what Calvin wanted. Thus for some it would be the cornerstone, for others the stone of stumbling [cf. 1 Pet. 2:6-8], but for all a benchmark. The Christian thinking of Geneva, whether for or against, would from then on really be along the lines of this catechism. Positively or negatively the stamp of Calvin would be upon the face of Genevan Christianity, and long after Calvin's death, right up to the days of Rationalism, there would be no serious rival. The best token of this truth is the realization of Calvin's indispensability after he had been chased out in 1538. It is of the nature of the case, however, that we know little or nothing of what took place in the early period.

2. Things are different as regards both council and people when we come to the proposal for subscription to the confession. It was not a matter now of a general willingness to adopt a specific type of Christian instruction but of a once-for-all, immediate, and solemn acceptance. As we saw last time, both in Geneva and outside this was not something that could be taken for granted but an extraordinary demand. We see this from the hesitation with which the council undertook the task of implementation. The confession was presented on November 10, 1536.[1] But only in April 1537 were any real steps taken concerning it. The first resolution was to the effect that residents in each district should be visited by pastors and syndics to put before them the confession they were being asked to affirm, but then the simpler plan was proposed that it should be printed and copies sent to every house.[2] Even then, however, it was only on July 29, on repeated representations from the pastors, that the Council of Two Hundred resolved that the administering of the oath should be in the hands of the leaders in the various wards. They had to make sure that the residents were willing, if necessary deal with those opposed, report the obstinate for judgment, and finally at the head of their wards assemble all the people, young and old, men and women, in St. Pierre's cathedral, where the city secretary would read the oath from the pulpit, and then have the people swear by raising their right hands, thus pledging themselves to a new city constitution.

It will be seen that the city authorities themselves thought in terms of complete parallelism between the religious order and the political. The initial question put to the citizens was the general question "how they wanted to live." The supreme and decisive answer was that "they wanted to live according to the commandments of God" along the lines of the official confession.[3] But on this basis they were also pledging themselves to uphold the liberty, rights, and laws of the city and republic of Geneva. When we consider how dialectical was the argument that Calvin put forward for the inner possibility of the whole act of confessing, that is, that it was naturally not a matter of keeping, or fully observing, the divine commands, but of faith in Christ, which meant a recognition of the impossibility of observing the commands and trust in being clothed with the heavenly righteousness of Christ, the very argument that he expressly

---

1. Cf. CO 21, 206.
2. Ibid., 210.
3. Ibid., 213.

put forward in Geneva itself — and when we realize that the Genevan council ventured to build the political allegiance of the citizens and residents on this foundation, we can see clearly for the first time how fantastic, or how eschatological as I put it last time, the whole process was. There was here none of the brutal accommodation to the level of the OT that Calvinism is often accused of; instead, the OT, in this case the oaths taken by Israel under Moses, Josiah, Asa, Ezra, and Nehemiah, are boldly given an NT sense and the commandments of God are sharply understood as the kerygma of forensic justification. That is historically the most remarkable, paradoxical, and significant feature in the whole process.

How the people concerned, Farel and Calvin, the city authorities, and the residents, actually thought of the matter is hard to imagine. Even when we take into account the possibilities of no understanding at all or of misunderstanding, the reaction must have been much more lively and spirited than it would be with most of us in our age of straight-line, nondialectical thinking. Calvin himself in the preface to the 1538 Catechism could speak of a certain alacrity *(élan)* with which the government arranged the taking of the oath and the citizens responded.[4] On the whole that seems to be true, though resistance to the demand was more active and significant than Calvin saw or wanted to see. The council itself was not so fully convinced of the need for the oath or its value, and opposition arose among many of the people that, though suppressed, linked up quietly with all kinds of other charges against the pastors and finally found expression afresh in the great outbursts of 1538. Real unanimity in such a venture would have been much too good to be true. In figures of that type we cannot usually state what took place in history.

On September 19, well after the oath had been administered, a complaint was lodged in the council that not all had taken it, that some had managed to evade it. It was resolved to call such people to account, and if they still refused, to tell them that those who were unwilling to take the oath should go and live somewhere else.[5] But on October 30 Calvin had to come before the council to complain again that some had now sworn but others had not, and it had to be resolved afresh to bring pressure to bear on the latter.[6] On November 12 it was reported that yesterday, the

4. See 288 n. 129.
5. CO 21, 215.
6. Ibid., 216.

11th, the recalcitrant had been summoned to take the reformation oath (as it was now called for the first time) and that some had done so but others not, and that not a single person from one street, the Rue des Allemands, had done so. Again the choice was put before them, either to swear or to leave the city.[7] Things were still the same on November 15,[8] thought this time only the threat was issued, and understandably the more this was repeated the less seriously it was taken.

On November 26 something more specific was said about the reasons for resistance. Farel and Calvin had come before the council to defend themselves against other charges that were being brought against them in the form of rumors. It was being said (by outsiders) that the people of Geneva were guilty of perjury. The preachers used the argument familiar to us from the preface to Calvin's Catechism, namely, that if regard is had to the contents of the confession, this is not so, and plainly the Confession is in keeping with the will of God and the example of Nehemiah and Jeremiah (as the council secretary, who was not so well versed in the Bible, recorded it). What we have sworn is to keep faith in God and believe his commandments.[9] This was obviously the dialectical interpretation of the demand that we were recalling earlier. But even worse, it was definitely stated by the other side that some officials from Bern visiting Geneva had said during (or more likely after) a meal in the house of a syndic that those who had taken the oath were in fact guilty of perjury.

This was one of the first clear shots in the war that now commenced between Calvin and Bern. There was great excitement, for here was an important point in favor of the minority that refused to take the oath. The pastors declared that they were ready to show that the matter was in fact in keeping with the divine will and biblical,[10] and the issue was regarded as important enough to send the two on an official mission to Bern to state their case before the council there. They returned on December 10 and reported that they had been well received by Bern and that an embassy would be sent to Geneva to disown officially the slanderous statements of those officials.[11] But possibly, as often happens, Calvin had too readily assumed that what Bern had said to him was favorable, for

---

7. Ibid.
8. Ibid., 217.
9. Ibid.
10. Ibid.
11. Ibid., 218.

instead of an embassy a letter arrived from Bern on December 13 denying that report.[12] It was then resolved to send Farel alone back to Bern.[13] On the 14th Farel and Calvin asked that the council be summoned to hear the results of their first visit. This was resolved, but Farel, along with other envoys, still had to go again to Bern.[14] Farel and Calvin thus came before the Council of Two Hundred, gave a report on the first journey, and declared that there must have been machinations to prevent Bern from sending the embassy with an apology.[15] They had heard in Bern that they were being slandered from Geneva, the charge being that they had preached that all bad things come from Germany. Farel was thus told again to go to Bern and to find out who had said these things.[16] On December 30 the envoys from Geneva returned.[17] And on January 3 a missive came from Bern at last, but held out little comfort and did little to settle the matter, stating merely that reports had come to Bern that because of the confession there were rebels in Geneva, and urging Geneva to take steps to reach agreement.[18] (It was in this style that German Switzerland, especially Bern, would often intervene in conflicts in Geneva. When these were for him a matter of "to be or not to be," Calvin understandably hated the general admonitions to seek peace that came to him from the German Swiss.)

From this point on the pastors found the question of the confession inextricably linked to the other difficulties with which they had to contend and which finally resulted in their expulsion. We simply have to see now how in this matter, too, their position increasingly worsened, and how the resolution that the council and people had passed the previous summer should obviously have to give rise to another serious crisis before vacillation would give way to that inevitable historical result. Several times again demands were made on those who resisted the oath, but with no further

---

12. Letter from Bern Council to Geneva Council, 12.9.1537, CO 10/II, 133 (no. 84).

13. CO 21, 218.

14. Ibid.

15. Ibid., 218f. In the margin Barth put: "Cf. *Briefe* no. 82-85, 87, ref. to CO 10/II, 130ff.: Bern to Geneva; Bern embassy instructions; Bern to Geneva; Calvin to Bucer." The instructions favored Farel and Calvin, and Geneva had resolved not to send the second envoys, but then came Bern's further declaration (12.28) and the exhortation to seek peace that swayed Geneva on 1.3.1538; cf. CO 21, 220.

16. CO 21, 218.

17. Ibid., 219.

18. Ibid., 220; text in 10/II, 134.

threats of banishing them. It was now agreed with Bern that the matter should be regarded and handled with pacification in view.[19] When the preachers for their part threatened to invoke church discipline and to refuse communion to those who would not take the oath, they were repulsed, and it was resolved that communion should be denied to no one.[20] Clearly the council, the council that had ordered the oath, was not so certain about the matter as not to capitulate when opposition both within and without became too strong. The pastors, of course, had not the slightest thought of yielding. Hence this issue contributed to the catastrophe of April 1538.

3. The prospect was now dim for the third point in the Reformation program, church discipline and the order of the Lord's Supper. Here again the council had at first been fairly favorable as regards adopting at least the spirit of the memorandum of the pastors. It was a fatal sign, however, that the very first resolution regarding it on January 16, 1537, greatly altered what Calvin was seeking. He had asked that there be communion every month, but the council decided for four times a year. An interesting point is the introduction of a primitive form of civil marriage, notice being given before an appointed prominent citizen prior to the threefold calling of banns in church and the ensuing wedding. As regards impediments there was agreement with the preachers that everything must be according to God's Word. Midwives were not to baptize. On Calvin's view, which was followed here, baptism is also and essentially an act of confession, and therefore it can be given only in the context of congregational worship.

Then we read that the remaining articles were passed as written.[21] This means that the council was accepting the main point: church discipline with excommunication. In truth we have here the first expression of the willingness of the council, never wholly abandoned even in the time of conflict, to accept as generally right the strict understanding of the holiness of the community that the preachers were advancing. A series of sharp resolutions and some detailed decisions along these lines make this plain, though the council was not agreeing expressly that the church itself should be in charge of the discipline, or that a special body should be set up to screen those who came to communion, as the memorandum was asking.[22] All shops and places of work were to be strictly shut during hours

19. CO 21, 220.
20. Ibid.
21. Ibid., 206.
22. Ibid., 207.

of worship, images of saints were to be diligently sought out, all dubious customs were to be suppressed, some popular songs in particular were prohibited, and so were games of chance, of which the people have remained fond even up to our own day.[23] Bakers' apprentices were not to cry their justly famous pastries on the streets during times of worship. It may be noted that neither in the memorandum nor in the council resolutions does the much debated Puritan Sunday play any part. Calvin and Geneva wanted to protect worship rather than to sanctify Sunday by enforcing rest. Two syndics — the answer to the demand for a consistory — were appointed to see to the observance of rules of this kind.

On January 29 some private schools whose Protestant character was suspect were closed down.[24] On March 13 it was again resolved to accept fully ("en plein") the articles of Farel and Calvin regarding the Lord's Supper and other things.[25] New clergy appointments, especially in the rural areas, were approved without hesitation as Farel and Calvin, the two leading pastors, proposed.[26] On June 4 strong penalties were resolved for those who were still celebrating former feast days as holidays; Sunday was now to be the only feast day.[27] On July 3 the preachers were instructed to report moral lapses on the part of individuals in writing to the council.[28] It will be seen that the council had no intention of handing over competence in this matter to a special consistory. It wanted oversight and strict rules, but it would itself be the consistory. On July 13 we find for the first time a complaint against a pastor who was close to Calvin, the aged Courault, a former Augustinian monk from France, who, though blind, was one of the most zealous adherents and warriors of Calvin's reformation. He was told not to assign blame for things that do not exist.[29] On July 27 Farel and Calvin strongly urged the need for moral exhortation. This was resolved upon, and complaints were to be made to the "seigneurs."[30]

---

23. At the end of his ministry in Geneva (1911) Barth wrote two articles on this subject, "Pour la dignité de Genève" and "Wir wollen nicht, dass dieser über uns herrsche"; cf. *Vorträge und kleine Arbeiten 1909-1914,* ed. H. A. Drews and H. Stoevesandt, part III of *Gesamtausgabe* (Zurich, 1992), 312ff., 320ff.

24. CO 21, 207.
25. Ibid., 208.
26. E.g., ibid., 208, 211, 214, 221.
27. Ibid., 211.
28. Ibid., 212.
29. Ibid.
30. Ibid., 213.

On October 30 there was still talk of papist schools that had not been visited, though these might well have been on territories in neighboring Savoy. On the same day a pastor was brought to order who was still a laggard and preached papal doctrine. A woman hairdresser had also to spend some days in prison because she had done a young woman's hair in unfitting fashion for her wedding. The same penalty was imposed on several other women who were involved.[31]

Police regulations such as that just mentioned, or the putting in the pillory of a cardplayer with the cards round his neck,[32] were obviously translations and applications of what Calvin really wanted, whether or not he agreed with them. We should not link Calvinism too tightly to this type of justice, but also, of course, not too loosely. In the first instance it was the community that acted thus, and many another community has acted in the same way, and even more strictly, for the same if less sharply defined motives. The only distinctive Calvinistic feature in Geneva is the parallelism between the eucharistic community and the civil community. The demand for the holiness of the former fell like a monstrous shadow over the latter. If it was to show itself worthy of the glory of its transcendent basis, it had to be serious about moral sobriety and could not shrink back from strict and sharp rules. If the secular power was spurred on in this direction by a desire not to let ecclesiastical power have a place alongside it, but to display itself the ecclesiastical zeal required, it need hardly surprise us that among cities with these kinds of regulations Geneva stood out by reason of its strictness, which was acceptable to some, painful to others. It needed two full decades to slip into the role that was assigned to them by Calvin's concept of the church.

We need not be surprised that at first they resisted it strongly. What people would not have resisted strongly being made the subject of an experiment of this kind? The Genevans were restless. They were always prepared for opposition. They loved freedom. They were thus less ready for the experiment rather than more. Hence the conflict with Calvinism was unavoidable in the city of Calvin. The governmental decrees regarding moral discipline, the ruthless purging out from public and private life of all papal remnants, and the strictly meant, though not thoroughly executed, resolution that required the confessional oath of all residents, opened the eyes of the Genevans relatively early to what it would mean

31. Ibid., 216.
32. Kampschulte, I, 291.

for them to live according to God's will.[33] They had enthusiastically accepted this, but without really knowing what the preachers had meant by the term, without realizing that what the preachers meant would be an unacceptable encroachment on the freedom they cherished above all else. For this reason the story of the church order proposed by Farel and Calvin became a tragic one from the middle of 1537 onward, no less so than that of the parallel story of the oath into which it would finally and fatally merge. The history of a laborious attempt to enforce the new outlook became in fact the history of increasingly bold and powerful opposition.

The first truly fatal day for the cause of Calvin's reformation was November 25, 1537, when a general assembly was held at which opponents complained hotly of disregard for the rights and freedoms of the citizens.[34] The assault was not really made upon the preachers themselves but upon their secular supporters, and especially upon the council majority, which within limits gave their approval. At the same time there were bitter complaints against the sharp and offensive terms used in the pulpit. The preachers were told that they wished the people ill, and it did not help much when Farel told them that this was so little true that he was ready to shed his blood for them.[35] No one wanted the blood of the reformers. The general desire, even among adherents, was to be left in peace. The year 1538 began with the prosecution at the first session of the council of someone who had said that Farel was a wicked man.[36] On January 16 we read of drunkards who by night in the streets and taverns had vilified one another with the insult: You also belong to the brothers in Christ![37] Very quietly between all the reports of this kind it is noted that on January 22 the surgeons of the city asked for permission to study anatomy, and this was granted insofar as it was necessary for the human body.[38]

It was a bad sign for the cause of the Reformation when in January Louis du Tillet, the friend of Calvin who had once gone with him from France to Basel and then to Ferrara, and who had finally come with him to Geneva, began to doubt the goodness of the whole enterprise in view of the unhappy conflicts that he saw, and returned to France,[39] where he

33. CO 21, 199, also 203.
34. Kampschulte, I, 301.
35. CO 21, 217.
36. Ibid., 219.
37. Ibid., 220.
38. Ibid., 221.
39. Ibid., 220.

became a Roman Catholic again. Calvin wrote him a letter full of sorrow but also resolve. There is not the slightest evidence that he himself was tempted to relapse by such a disaster so close to him. He had thought that his friend was firmer than that, he wrote. He, Calvin, would prefer the Jewish synagogue to the Roman church, for though the latter knows the name of Jesus, it helps it little, since the power of it has been lost, and at least the synagogue has less idolatry.[40] He finally judged the step taken by his friend to be a dangerous venture. It is tempting God to go back so willingly to prison. The damp sacks with which we are accustomed to cover ourselves before others cannot stand up to the heat of God's judgment.[41] "May the Lord not let you fall on the slippery path you are treading until he has granted you full liberty" (*Briefe*, no. 90, 10/II, 147ff.).[42]

How the situation came to a head in Geneva in February 1538 we see from a letter of Grynaeus to Farel and Calvin that begins: "I have read your letter with sorrow. I see the storm, I see the assaults. Satan rages and pushes and pursues you on all sides."[43] Grynaeus consoles them with an image that Calvin himself would often use later: Christ the Lord is himself a spectator of the tragedy; no one in this theater does anything to no purpose.[44] Calvin himself writes calmly to Bullinger: "We will not have a strong church unless the ancient apostolic discipline is restored as we desire in many connections. But thus far we have not been able to succeed in introducing a pure and holy order relating to excommunication." Even the demand of the preachers that the city should be divided into parishes for pastoral care had thus far been frustrated (*Briefe*, 92f.).[45]

Calvin, then, was unbowed, and he constantly came up with new ideas in the final phase of the conflict about his church order. On February 3 there were elections for a new council and syndics. In vain the day before Calvin and Courault tried to promote their cause by admonition.[46] Those who previously had been relatively favorable to them were not reelected, but were replaced by those of the opposition party. The change soon began to make itself felt. On March 2 Farel had to answer to the council for a rumor that he had said in Bern that in Geneva some wanted the mass and

---

40. Letter dated 1.31.1538; CO 10/II, 149 (no. 90).
41. CO 10/II, 150.
42. Ibid.
43. 2.13.1538, CO 10/II, 152f. (no. 92).
44. Loc. cit.
45. 2.21.1538; CO 10/II, 153f. (no. 93).
46. CO 21, 221.

others the gospel.[47] On March 12 a complaint was lodged that Calvin in a sermon had called the council the devil's council. Significantly on the same day Farel and Calvin were forbidden to interfere with the government.[48] On April 8 the aged Courault received a reprimand for attacking the regime from the pulpit.[49] In his parting address to the pastors on his deathbed Calvin tells them that at this time, to frighten him, shots were fired from arquebuses in front of his door, as many as 50 or 60 (9, 892).[50] He was naturally not the man to be taught in this way. From this time on error and confusion regarding the church order merged into the stream of general discontent with the preachers, discontent that reached a peak between April 19 and 23 and ended with the banishment of the preachers.

Nevertheless, we have a mistaken view of things if we think that conflicts were the only result of the momentous memorandum of November 1536. Even Kampschulte has to state (I, 292f.)[51] that the labor had not been in vain, that public conditions had gradually improved, and that the churches were zealously attended. The council, even in part the new one of 1538, was not really unwilling except when it came to the pastors' severest demands. So far as possible it tried to meet their wishes and support their work in church and school with all the resources available. For example, it even seems to have dealt favorably with the not unimportant issue of stipends. Even in the difficult month of February 1538, just after the anti-Calvinist elections, it adopted a recommendation of the pastors and on one day found positions and support for no fewer than three French refugees as rural pastors.[52] As regards church discipline, though it did not follow Calvin's pattern and treated it more as policing, Calvin himself later had to say that the worst enemies of our religion were forced to give God the glory (10/II, 207).[53] Geneva was beginning to achieve renown as a Protestant city, as we see from a letter of Bullinger to Calvin on November 1, 1537, written on behalf of three devout, scholarly, and wealthy Englishmen, Eliottus, Buttlerus, and Partrigius, who in the well-known Anglo-Saxon manner were going from one place to another

47. Ibid., 222.
48. Ibid.
49. Ibid., 223.
50. OS II, 402, 1ff.
51. Loc. cit.
52. CO 21, 221.
53. Farel and Calvin to the Zurich pastors, June 1538; CO 10/II, 207 (no. 121).

to get to know famous people. They had already achieved their aim in Zurich, and now they wanted to visit Geneva to listen to Farel and Calvin and to observe their piety.[54] Referring to their ability to pay, Bullinger asked Calvin to provide them with lodging.

All in all, this was a time in Geneva when things must have been strangely balanced, yes and no, for and against, very strong influence and very stern resistance, radicalism on the side of the preachers, no less unbroken vitality on that of the Genevans, and seen from outside, holy and audacious willing and venturing on the one side, the opposition of ancient carnality and the obtuse world on the other; or, seen in another way, on the one side, spiritual impelling and compelling that had already come to be described as a new papalism,[55] on the other side, the not unjustified claims of free citizens, indeed, the threat to freedom of conscience and conviction. Why should we not conclude that there was present on both sides something of what was thought to be perceived? The picture was a colorful and lively and significant one, but by no means unequivocal. Students to this day can make of it what they will. After the many things that we have already said about Calvin's general position and orientation, and especially his view of God and the world, I will now refrain from indicating in what direction these things point us.

We are now at the end of our discussion of the first Genevan program of reform. As regards both the ideal and the reality it offers us a good and in its own way complete picture of what Calvin was and wanted and achieved as a churchman. In the later periods of his work, for which unfortunately we will not now have time, everything became more complicated both as a program and as its execution. Like the 1536 *Institutes,* the catechism and the articles concerning the organs of the church and cultus[56] were only the first links in a chain of ever richer and more comprehensive constructs. But as we can find the spirit of the *Institutes* already in the first edition, especially when we have some knowledge of the last, so it is with the documents of church reform. Calvin would rearrange, enrich, sharpen, and less frequently excise, but substantially his work remained the same. The results were similar, too. The battle of 1536-38 was only a prelude to the much greater and longer war that occupied him lifelong, and the symptoms of his impact were also similar,

54. CO 10/II, 128 (no. 80).
55. Kampschulte, I, 307.
56. See above, 264ff.

a strange mixture of some love, much respect, much fear, and some hate, a mixture, too, of success and failure, although with time success began decisively to predominate. If we have let the picture of church reform in 1536-38 gain our attention and speak to us, then we must have acquired a fairly definite idea of what Calvin's reformation was all about. But the man himself as an individual, and the universal problematic that impelled him, and that alone enables us to see in any meaningful way what he wanted and did, are truly unsearchable. We thus have every reason to go further with him in the hope of gaining a better understanding of this central point from which all the details radiate.

§15 CONFLICTS

We have seen that the reformation program and its execution in Geneva led to a crisis in Calvin's relation to those outside. It might seem to us that the knot had been tied tightly enough already to bring on disaster. But in reality we have as yet learned to know only one of the lines that led to the fatal end and the happy new beginning. Apart from the program of reform three great concerns filled and occupied Calvin at this time and finally produced, like clouds, that great storm. First, he was engaged in conflict with the Anabaptists, second with Dr. Peter Caroli, and finally with the leaders of church and state in Bern. The first two of these battles contributed only indirectly to the 1538 disaster, but indirectly they did so very powerfully. The third was decisive in precipitating it. Neither the question of the confession, nor that of the church discipline, nor the agitation of the Anabaptists, nor the accusations of Caroli, nor all of these combined could probably have brought about Calvin's downfall. What actually brought it about was the most uninteresting and earthly or at any rate nontheological intervention of the republic of Bern in his affairs. In a secondary matter Bern obstinately insisted on its bond[1] and opposed both the view and the purpose of Calvin, a second time decisively for Geneva's further history. It was around this event that the other difficulties that beset Calvin crystallized and this period in his life came to a sudden close. There was as a result something almost mathematical in the way all this had to come about as it did, but when it did, it seemed to do so by chance, by surprise, giving us a strange and clear example of the way in which, at turning points in history, that which is absolutely puzzling and unique and irrational will finally speak the decisive word amid all that runs at all points on foreseeable and understandable lines.

Anabaptists

On March 9, 1537, when Farel and Calvin were hard at work on their program, two Dutchmen were brought before the council, Hermann von Lüttich and André Bénoit, with the request that they might be allowed to dispute with the preachers. They came to be known as Catabaptists,[2] probably more in perplexity than because there was any exact knowledge of their purpose. From what took place we gain little clarity concerning their teaching. The only certain thing seems to be that they were mystics who toned down all church dogma and reshaped it into a comprehensive theory of a natural deification of humanity and a realistically conceived redemption through the implanting of the Spirit of God released in Christ's death and resurrection.[3] That at least was the kind of mystical doctrine then proceeding from the Netherlands. It could come in two forms and might do so even in the same advocates, the one form ascetic, the other libertinistic. Those who combated it in the church might at will regard it as a serious teaching that, however, erroneously rejected culture, state, and church, and so on, or as a frivolous teaching that fanatics who preached the liberty of the flesh espoused. At a later date, in the 1540s, when he ran into this type of influence again, Calvin opted for the second possibility, and by using the label Libertines for the Enthusiasts was able to hit at two enemies at the same time, the foreign preachers on the one hand and on the other hand his foes at home, who were not, of course, mystics, but who for obvious reasons supported in part the doctrine of the liberty of the flesh.[4] Calvin's right to use the term "Libertines" for the Dutchmen has recently (*ZKG* 40, 83ff.) been contested by K. Müller on the basis of a thorough investigation of their writings.[5] Probably his objection to the Catabaptists in 1537 was not of that type. From the popularity of that

1. Cf. Shakespeare's *Merchant of Venice,* act 4, scene 1: "I would have my bond."
2. CO 21, 208f.
3. Cf. K. Müller, "Calvin und die Libertiner," *ZKG* 40 (1922), 83ff., esp. 85, also 97 with reference to the theology of the mystic Antoine Pocque.
4. Cf. the two works of Calvin in 1544 and 1545, CO 7, 49f. and 149ff.
5. See above, n. 3.

argument we may almost conclude that it might be found in some degree in the records. Yet there is no evidence for it, and we are left with the impression that the authorities followed the two-day disputation without much understanding of it.[6] Yet we also have no evidence of ascetic teaching.

We may thus suppose that the issue was instead the basic theological view of the foreigners, which, as is possible, they might well have asserted provisionally as such without working out the implications either the one way or the other. It is the great beauty of mysticism that we can always leave it open whether we turn to seriousness or frivolity. We remember, of course, that this basic mystical view was an old acquaintance of Calvin's from the days of his *Psychopannychia,* which still lay unpublished on his desk.[7] Since Calvin published this work in 1542 in the same form in which he had written it in 1534, might it not be that the form in which he met the Anabaptist opponents was the same as he had in view then, so that it was for this reason that he would now publish the older work that Capito had earlier called inopportune? And since his foe in this work was Quietist mysticism, might we not conclude that the people who were now trespassing in his not yet fully laid out garden were Quietists of the same kind? It need hardly be said that they were an unwelcome disruption at the very moment when Calvin was engaged in establishing the quite nonmystical parallelism between the national community and the eucharistic community.

The conduct of the council gives us the impression that they were definitely hostile to the alien prophets, though not without some fear of them. The foreigners had obviously gained a following in the city and were told to put forward articles for disputation. Nevertheless, the council thought it dangerous to hold the disputation publicly, and it was not to deal with all their articles but only with the question of the priesthood ("l'affaire des prêtres").[8] Farel in particular did not agree to the exclusion of the public from the disputation, and so, contrary to the real view of the council, a two-day disputation took place in the Cours de Rive church. Thus we read that on March 16 there was disputing all day at the Rive with two Catabaptists, and then disputing all day again on the 17th.[9] The

6. CO 21, 209f.
7. See 146ff. above.
8. CO 21, 208.
9. Ibid., 209.

council minutes tell us no more. The disputation must have been either too scholarly for the scribe, or too odd for him. Writing to Capito Farel says that the opponents were simple and ignorant.[10]

On Sunday, March 18, the Council of Two Hundred convened and resolved (1) that the disputation should be broken off, since only diverse opinions were coming to light, the faith was coming out only flickeringly, and the attackers had not advanced sufficient reasons for their cause; (2) that all Anabaptist writings should be called in; (3) that Farel should be admonished not in the future to enter into any disputations with such people; and (4) that the Catabaptists should be told they had been refuted and should recant. But the latter were not of this view and replied to the council that they were subject to the will of God and would not recant. "Note," added the council minutes touchingly, "that we first called them brothers, but since they did not agree with our church and would not pray with us, we no longer do so."[11] The following day, the 19th, it was resolved that if they refused to recant they should be permanently banned from the city. They again refused, appealing to conscience, and banishment ensued.[12] In spite of the assurances in Beza's biography,[13] however, the reformers had not won a true or decisive victory, not merely because they had not convinced their opponents, but because an irritating number of followers still remained and even the clergy had been exposed to some slight infection. Whether there was an underground link to similar outbreaks with which Calvin had to contend in the 1540s we cannot say. The one sure thing is that the prestige of the reformers had suffered a blow through this affair, since it had been shown that people could have a form of piety different from that set forth in the official teaching of the church.

Caroli[14]

Briefe, 10, nos. 48-78, 193; *Adversus Petri Caroli Calumnias Defensio Nicolae Gallasii 1545;* E. Bähler, "Petrus Caroli und J. Calvin," *Jahrbuch für*

10. Letter dated 5.5.1537 (no. 59), CO 10/II, 99.
11. CO 21, 209f.
12. Ibid., 210.
13. Ibid., 22f., 126.
14. In the margin the MS has here some headings for greeting Prof. E. Geismar of Copenhagen, who visited the class 7.6.1922 during a summer tour in Germany. See the Swiss edition, 420 n. 1, for details.

Schweizerische Geschichte 1904; F. Trechsel, *Die protestantischen Antitrini-tarier vor Faustus Socin,* 2 vols. (Heidelberg, 1839 and 1844); Hunde-shagen, *Die Conflikte des Zwinglianismus, Luthertums und Calvinismus in der Bernischen Landeskirche* (Bern, 1842).[15]

The Caroli affair was one of the threads in the web that finally resulted in Calvin's downfall in Geneva and in the closing of this second period of his life. Its main significance for us, however, is that it sets a specific aspect of Calvin's theology, namely, his relation to the dogma of the early church, in a sharp light. Along with the biographical result of the affair is the historical result that it gave to Calvin a fuller awareness that the Reformation was not an innovation but a new understanding and comprehending of ancient catholic truth. As we have seen from time to time, he was already conscious of this and had stated it. But the Caroli affair made this insight an important and urgent one. Instinctively he had always held aloof from the sectarianism that thinks the world begins today with its own knowledge of the truth, that thinks that with its better knowledge it can rush heedlessly past the thinking of those who were wise before us.[16] The Caroli affair gave Calvin the unpleasant experience of hearing from a strange Protestant crank what all his Roman Catholic opponents were naturally thinking and stating, namely, that he, Calvin, was himself just an innovator and sectarian who had fallen away from the center of the church's tradition, namely, the dogma of the Trinity, to the heresy of Arius, to Unitarianism. It was a charge without foundation. The first edition of the *Institutes,* in chapter II on faith, contains already an express confession of the trinitarian dogma.[17] Article 31 of the 1536 Catechism also stated the doctrine in a way that is free from objection.[18] Calvin had only to give prominence to these two passages, to put them in more emphatic and lively terms, and the charge of heresy, which he could not allow to go undefended when made by Roman Catholics as well, since if not refuted it made all his theology heretical, would be left hanging in the air.

Whether we take it favorably to Calvin or unfavorably, we must at

15. On *Briefe* see CO 10/II, 81ff., 408ff. On *Defensio Gallasii* see CO 7, 289ff. E. Bähler, "Petrus Caroli und Johann Calvin," *Jahrbuch für Schweizerische Geschichte* 29 (Zurich, 1904), 41ff. On Hundeshagen see above, 97 n. 10.

16. Goethe's *Faust,* I, 572f.: "Zu schauen, wie vor uns ein weiser Mann gedacht."

17. OS I, 70-75.

18. OS I, 396.

any rate adopt as a motto for our account of the Caroli affair the words: "Something sticks."[19] There was something about the charge, and it has symbolical significance inasmuch as its occurrence helped to bring about the break in the course of Calvin's reforming work. In a singular way it was the great question mark that we have to put against Calvin's whole reforming position and work if we are to evaluate them properly. In the best sense Calvin's theology rested on a rationalistic and monotheistic premise, and therefore it presented a window to antitrinitarianism that was not absolutely closed. Those who move far in any one direction in theology need not be surprised or annoyed if they are confused sometimes with undesirable neighbors who move a little further in the same direction, even though they may have a perfectly good conscience that they do not think as these neighbors do.

Calvin did venture far afield either in stressing a final link between faith and knowledge or in stressing the strict unity of God. Both emphases had a necessary basis in his historical and systematic position. He could have a good conscience in this regard because he did in fact lift up knowledge on to the step of faith rather than bringing faith down to that of knowledge, and because Christ was clearly the heart and axis of his monotheism. Nevertheless, like all the contrasts in his theology, the knowledge of God and faith in revelation, the unity of God and the deity of Christ, were linked in an extremely sharp and even paradoxical way. It could easily happen that less dialectical thinking than his would seize on one side of the contrast, ignore the other side, make some inference or other, and either espouse or accuse it, in a way that was the more difficult for him because he could not easily show dialectically less gifted minds how unjustified it was but had to be content simply to affirm in a more or less successful way how abhorrent it was to him. Self-evidently Calvin did at times make it possible for others to exaggerate some aspect of his teaching. No theology can be so careful as to make it totally impossible for others at times to seize on its own words and twist what it says, and especially what it has not said, into a cord that it finds hard to unravel.

This is how it is with the relation between Calvinism and Unitarianism. It was naturally no accident that the latter enjoyed particular success in the Anglo-Saxon world. We cannot deny that in the history of dogma Calvinism's neighbor on the left is Socinianism. That Calvin did in fact

19. Cf. Plutarch, *De adulatore et amico* 24: "Audacter calumniare, semper aliquid haeret."

initially open the door to this neighbor and to the charges that resulted for himself may be seen from the strangely unemphatic and "loveless" position that the doctrine of the Trinity occupies in the *Institutes* and the catechism. It has an honorary place, but we cannot possibly maintain that his heart beat faster when he dealt with it. It began to do so only when there were those who dared to question his orthodoxy. He had in fact transposed the core of his trinitarian and christological dogma into the doctrine of the appropriation of salvation. It was there that the questions arose for him and the decisions were made. He could very well have done without the dogma if it were not there, not because he was against it but because its content was not for him an urgent concern. The same applied, of course, to all the reformers. Luther, for example, essentially honored the lofty mystery of the Triunity, tipped his cap to it in his own words,[20] but then went back to his own questions. In Luther, however, great reverence for the church's past acted as a cover, and Calvin definitely did not have any such reverence. In this regard, then, Luther never left any opening, any occasion for a charge such as that of Caroli.

As an authority or formula, the early church confessions meant little to Calvin, as he would say more than once in the Caroli controversy. Perhaps, as in *Institutes,* ch. II, he would find in the terms *ousia* and *hypostasis,* in which the dogma of the mystery of the deity was expressed, a useful and necessary clarification and definition of biblical truth, so that we are not to reject them,[21] but he definitely did not have what we can call a real relation to these venerable teachings. He had this only from the moment when he was brought to awareness by Caroli's accusation that it might almost seem as though he had something against them. He could say with a good conscience that he did not, but that he saw little in their favor is clear from the fact that he did not object when Farel's confession of faith, after devoting only six lines to christology and not touching on the decisive points in the ancient dogma, was content merely to quote the Apostles' Creed.[22] This attitude of Calvin shows us that the questions and answers of the early church were for the Reformation only ballast in the sense that it had to work at first on its own new questions.

20. WA 37, 40, 16ff. Barth was using the rather different EA (2nd ed.), 9, 1 version, as in Loofs, *Leitfaden,* 4th ed., 751, and he seems to have followed Loofs in seeing disinterest in the Trinity in Luther.

21. OS I, 72f.

22. OS I, 420.

That could not mean, however, that the reformers wanted to separate themselves from the Christianity of past centuries and begin a new church history. Fundamentally they were much too strongly convinced that for all the differences of times and people there can ultimately be only one truth, only one question and answer, to be able rather arbitrarily, like the antitrinitarians, to sever the link with the dearly won classical results of the theological battles of the past even though they might not see at once in these results their own results won on a very different field. When the issue was put to them, they were naturally able and obliged to affirm these results, for severing the link that related their own enterprise to the church of the past would not only have compromised that enterprise outwardly — the reformers did not really fear this even though they took precautions against it — but above all would have made the enterprise meaningless in their own eyes because it would have entailed losing the connection with the real world to which the church belonged. The moment the dogma came into question as an expression of the truth-content of the catholic church, the Reformation had to abandon its indifference to it and affirm it. How far it was able truly to demonstrate the unity of old and new questions and answers, to build early theology into its own Reformation theology, was another matter. It was a difficult matter that gave rise to a full-scale scholasticism with whose emergence a dividing post was set up marking the end of reformation and the resumption of church history. In any case, however, the response had to be a positive one if the whole breadth of the Reformation conception as a relating of conservatism to Radicalism were to be preserved and the Reformation were not to go the way of the Enthusiasts.

That is the point of this moment in the life of Calvin. Here he plainly took on the feature in his physiognomy that made him the last reformer, the Hippocratic feature in the face of the man who closed the cycle that Luther had begun and ended it on a higher level than at the start. Yet it was not blind chance, as Doumergue thought, that even outwardly the picture of the aging Calvin with its unbearably sharply etched lines impressed itself upon the recollection of the nations rather than one of the more expressive portraits from the earlier years.[23] What is that Calvin to us? No doubt he lived at one time. But the historical Calvin is the man with the uplifted finger, half teaching and half threatening, the man who laid hold of his racing spirit, checked it, and forced

23. E. Doumergue, *Iconographie Calvinienne* (Lausanne, 1909), 10.

313

it backward, the man who on the far side of the antithesis of enthusiasm and traditionalism subjected himself to the law of historical continuity, and who now demands the same iron obedience of others. This Calvin — the Calvin who had Servetus burned — begins to emerge in the Caroli affair. It is not for nothing that in his letters on this affair he brings to light for the most part the less pleasant side of his character. It is not for nothing that this affair caused him to write his most crushing and from a human standpoint his most questionable polemical work, the *Defensio Gallasii.*[24] The doctrine of the Trinity was the issue here as it would be sixteen years later in the Servetus trial. But then the accused became the accuser. Changes of that kind do not usually go unpunished.

Dr. Peter Caroli had become the first pastor in Lausanne in the fall of 1536. Like Farel he came intellectually from the Faber Stapulensis circle. He was born in 1480. He was thus almost thirty years older than Calvin and could easily have been his father.[25] It is not without importance to note that two generations of the evangelical movement in France were here confronting one another. An older man, who might have been the father, had to understand and agree with and perhaps indeed follow a younger. Farel did that. But it is not the norm. If the younger are understood by the older, it is by their grandfathers rather than their fathers. When it is by the fathers, as it may often be, that is grace.

Caroli was a French evangelical like Bishop Roussel, with whom Calvin had crossed swords in the second open letter of his Italian journey. He belonged to the school whose conscience had been awakened by Luther but whose heart was still in the beautiful medieval liturgy, the school that was judicious but had no sharpness of insight, that was gentle and patient with others but especially with itself, trying to veil the antithesis of the old and the new ages rather than to grasp their unity, trying to glue them together and merge them by compromises and combinations. If people of his kind could be hostile, it had to be against a man like Calvin, who so coldly and unlovingly rejected their dearest concept, that of an evangelical Catholicism. As a rule they showed no hostility. They left anger and fury to those who would hate them for their many-sidedness.

It was the special individuality of Caroli, however, that he was a sharp proponent of what was basically not sharp. He was a recognized

24. See above, 310 n. 15.
25. Bähler, 44.

scholar of his day. In 1529 he had published a fresh edition of Faber's translation of the NT.[26] He would undoubtedly have made an even greater name for himself in this direction if the Reformation had not partly deflected him and made him a church agitator. I say "partly" because for all the instability that gives him the stamp of a restless spirit, we never see in him any real or deep unsettlement or disturbance. He had the posture and fervor to make him a reformer, but not the discipline or humility. I say, too, a "church agitator" because in what he undertook, apart from an overly strong interest in his own person, his obvious concern is the church, the visible church, which he seeks now in one place and now in another. What he did in these later years of his life makes this plain. For all his gruff individuality and self-will, he was more an exponent than a cipher, that is, an exponent of the instability with which innumerable scholars, even theological scholars, faced the questions that were put to them for decision at that time. No less than three times he turned his back officially on the Roman Catholic church and its theology, and no less than three times he returned to them. According to the accounts of his adversaries, in early years he had pandered both gladly and generously to both Bacchus and Venus. He certainly had a strongly developed vitality, a worldly streak, which might also manifest itself as a business sense. Yet although the reformers knew all this and could not stop it, they took him seriously. His youthful sins and instability of character first came to be portrayed and emphasized only when they had to defend themselves against him on other grounds. The age was familiar with two approaches. It could quietly and nonpharisaically overlook human failings but it could no less mercilessly attack the person publicly when occasion seemed to demand. At any rate, one would do well not to engage the man polemically from that angle.

He had his second departure from the church behind him when he came to Geneva in the spring of 1535 and in his own strange and ambivalent way took part in the decisive religious discussion of the time. To no obvious end he sought to mediate and would not sign the minutes of the disputation. He then went to Basel, where he became friendly with Erasmus and Karlstadt and especially Grynaeus and Myconius. It must have been then that the idea came to him that would bring him historical fame, the shabby idea that he would declare the stout Farel under suspicion of Arianism because in his *Sommaire* he had described Triunity as an incomprehensible mystery which he did not propose to deal with in this work that had practical piety as its

26. Ibid., 48f.

aim.[27] Caroli thus set Basel in an uproar and caused a question to be put to Farel, though we do not know what answer he sent.[28] In May 1536 Caroli became pastor in Neuenburg, and as such, having first married, he took part in the Lausanne Disputation. His appearance there must have made a good impression, at least among the Bernese who were present, and even the Genevans would later have no reason to complain of his conduct on this occasion, which they would certainly have done had there been any grounds. The result was that he was called to be the first pastor of Lausanne along with Pierre Viret, Calvin's intimate friend.[29]

But now strange signs began to appear. He seems to have viewed his position as first pastor in the Vaud capital as a kind of episcopate, and to have allowed himself to address his colleagues as though they were under his charge (Bähler, 59). Much more offensive was a further step that he took in January 1537 when his colleague Viret was in Geneva. To the great astonishment of the congregation he then read from the pulpit a number of theses defending prayers for the dead.[30] He was not proposing a revival of the medieval idea of purgatory or of intercessions that would earn merit on behalf of its residents. But his position was certainly not in line with the customary caution of the reformers regarding anything to do with death or the dead. If my view is correct, Caroli (7, 328)[31] had generally in mind a stressing of the neglected eschatological complex of ideas in the NT. If he had really taken this in bitter earnest, he would truly have made contact with Calvin on this issue. In the background of his plea for prayers for the dead stood the thought of the coming of God's kingdom that would put an end to death. In expectation of this coming redemption all creation sighs and Christ intercedes for his community as high priest before God. Trusting in the divine promise, the community living on earth must stand in for the departed and beseech the Lord that he will soon cause the day of judgment and resurrection to dawn.[32] But Caroli was not enough of a serious and disciplined religious thinker to realize that in no way may we send an intuition of such breadth flashing and sparkling forth only

27. Ibid., 71, quoting Farel's 1537 or 1538 preface to a new edition of his *Sommaire*.
28. Bähler, 56.
29. Ibid., 56-58.
30. Ibid., 60f. For the text of the theses cf. CO 7, 328f.; and cf. Farel to Calvin, 10.21.1539, CO 10/II, 408f. (no. 193).
31. CO 7, 328.
32. Barth summarizes here Caroli's eight conclusions; cf. theses 5 and 8 in CO 7, 329.

aphoristically and even with very worldly secondary purposes. What he himself put to the fore, to the jubilation of the people of Vaud who had only just been forced out of their traditional beliefs and practices, and to the irritation of all honest Protestants, especially his colleague Viret, was the curious, futile, and noxious dogma, as Calvin called it,[33] of a renewal of an active relation of piety, such as we find in Romanism, between living believers and those that have gone before them.

On hearing the news, Viret hastened back as fast as possible to Lausanne.[34] Who knows, there might have been a peaceful and profitable discussion if Caroli had been a little greater than he was. There was in fact a real lacuna in Reformation thinking at this point, as we are now well aware for many reasons, more so than was the case then. But Caroli was Caroli, and he was ill-advised enough, in lively conversation with Viret but in some context unknown to us, to question again the trinitarian orthodoxy not now of Farel alone, but also of Viret and Calvin.

With the putting of this new question the eschatological question at once lost its prominence. Viret took the accusation seriously, reported it at once to Geneva, and in mid-February 1537 Calvin, no less aroused than Viret, went to Lausanne. We learn about the course and content of the discussions that now began mostly from Calvin's own records. Apart from their biographical and theological interest, which engaged us yesterday, these offer us a welcome insight into Calvin as a fighter according to his own depiction of himself. He would often be in similar situations later. It will repay us to give close attention to this first instance because it is typical of all that would follow (*Defensio Gallasii*, 7, 289ff.). Those who do not know how Calvin could conduct a quarrel do not know him at all. According to his own statement he saw in Caroli's thrust (*Briefe*, 50)[35] a threat to the foundations he had laid in his work thus far. He viewed the calumny as an intolerable stain that would bring shame on the gospel as a whole if not removed.

Lausanne Disputation, 2.17.1537[36]   On February 17 an official disputation took place between Calvin, Viret, and Caroli in the presence of

---

33. Cf. CO 10/II, 82 (no. 49), Genevan to Bernese pastors, February, 1537; also 7, 333; 10/II, 85.

34. Barth has here the marginal reference 7, 314, but this cannot be CO 7, 314. Calvin tells of Viret's return in CO 7, 334. For details see the Swiss edition.

35. CO 10/II, 85-87, Calvin to a Bern pastor, February, 1537.

36. In the MS this heading was in the margin.

Bernese envoys then in Lausanne under the leadership of the city secretary Zyro (cf. *Briefe,* 49, 50, 74).[37] The proceedings seem to have opened with the reading by Caroli of eight theses on prayers for the dead.[38] Then Zyro asked him to listen to what his colleagues had to say about them. Caroli replied rather pompously that he would give an account of them to the Bern council and clergy (*Briefe,* 49). Calvin then spoke, and according to his own record he argued so victoriously that Caroli could make no response and suddenly switched to his real theme, furiously and without cause assailing Calvin and his followers with the charge of Arianism.[39] The main point made, at least according to Calvin, was that in their writings Caroli's opponents avoided the terms "Trinity" and "person."[40] In answer Calvin quoted two passages from his catechism, articles 31 and 33, which, as he saw it, gave material expression to an orthodox confession of the Triunity.[41] It is true that the terms Caroli was asking for were not used. Calvin might justly have appealed to ch. 2 of the *Institutes* in which they were.[42] He did not do this. Perhaps in Lausanne he had to maintain solidarity with Farel, who was especially severely attacked and threatened. Or perhaps he realized that the point of that passage in the *Institutes* was that the trinitarian confession, though possible and necessary, has no literal basis in scripture, and cannot be shown to be necessary in the context of the Reformation doctrine of salvation.[43] Even less could he adduce the passage in the Genevan Confession, which was the main object of the attack. He did not occupy, then, a wholly favorable position.

Caroli, however, did not enter into a discussion of the passages in the catechism that Calvin quoted, but simply declared that we must ignore all new confessions and subscribe to the three early church symbols. Calvin

37. CO 10/II, 82-84, 85-87, 119-23.

38. See above, 316 nn. 31f.

39. CO 10/II, 83 (no. 49).

40. CO 7, 316, 318.

41. CO 10/II, 83 (no. 49).

42. See above, 310 n. 17.

43. The MS originally had a further sentence to the effect that Calvin probably realized that the two terms did not occur in the passage, but Barth struck this out and added the marginal note that this suggestion did not fit in view of 7, 316; he then struck this note out as well, adding instead that the terms are in the *Institutes* at 7, 316. In fact Calvin used "person" in his account of the doctrine of the Trinity (OS I, 72ff.) but used "Trinity" only in the short treatment of the Holy Spirit (85). The term is, of course, implicit in the passage I, 72. Barth's marginal reference is to a passage in *Adversus Petri Caroli calumnias,* CO 7, 316f. (Note: BI 65 has "trinity of persons.")

and his followers were under suspicion in his eyes because they did not accept in particular the Athanasian Creed, which Calvin claimed not to have the support of any legitimate church (*Briefe,* 49), and in relation to which he stated that he was not accustomed to recognize anything as God's Word, which he had not thoroughly tested (*Briefe,* 50).[44] Caroli then made the dramatic declaration that Calvin was not worthy to be called a Christian (*Briefe,* 50).[45]

Calvin had clearly spoken somewhat audaciously to evoke this angry cry from Caroli. In a letter of justification to the Zurich clergy in August 1537 (*Briefe,* 74) he left out that utterance of his and contented himself with the offering of material reasons why he would not subscribe. As he put it, the only ground on which they avoided the use of "person" was that as Caroli put his demand its acceptance would have amounted to a confession of guilt. Requiring subscription to the symbols would have meant not only casting doubt on what they had built up with their ministry but actually overthrowing it radically. They did not want an example to be given in the church of the kind of tyranny that declares people heretics because they will not subscribe to what others put before them.[46]

But in the *Defensio Gallasii,* which was published in 1545 and addressed to a wider European public, we find no mention of this first Lausanne disputation even though a broad and explicit account of the affair as a whole is given. Calvin had "forgotten," then, his own much too extreme sayings, and even the whole gathering, proof enough that he did not look back on them with any feelings of pleasure. The two letters from which I have quoted (49 and 50), which he obviously wrote immediately on his return from Lausanne, the one to the Bernese clergy, the other to a single unnamed Bernese minister, almost certainly Megander (the note in CR on 50 rests on a confusion!),[47] show that he had two aims in view: first to gain support for himself in Bern against Caroli, and second to arrange if possible for a synod before Easter to settle the dispute once and for all. For no settlement had been reached at Lausanne. Calvin himself tells us that the envoys from Bern could see no outcome in view of the

44. CO 10/II, 83f., 86.
45. Ibid.
46. CO 10/II, 120f.
47. The editors of CO 10/II (85, n. 1) thought Megander was at the disputation and refer to a letter he wrote to Bullinger (88f.) containing an account of it. Barth, however, argued on the basis of Calvin's account in CO 7, 310, that Megander was not in Lausanne until May 14. He believed the reference in 88f. was to the Bern Disputation on 2.28.1537.

controversy regarding the authority of the Athanasian Creed, and he stated that a theological convention would have to decide the matter.

Bern Disputation, 2.28.1537[48]   For the time being the convention was not held, but a second preliminary confrontation between the two parties took place on February 28, 1537, two weeks later, before the body that exercised spiritual jurisdiction in Bern, and that Calvin had asked to convene a synod (cf. *Briefe,* 59, Farel to Capito; and *Defensio Gallasii, 7,* 308ff.; also on this *Briefe,* 660, Viret to Calvin, 7.14.1545!).[49] Things must have gone much the same in Bern as in Lausanne, but were much more dramatic. Caroli expanded on his view of prayers for the dead. Viret and Calvin refuted him, and they seem to have succeeded in getting a ruling that Caroli should in the future stop teaching his theory. But Viret and Calvin were also told not to boast of their triumph, that is, to say nothing about it. That was a typical Bern decision.

The disputation seemed to be at an end. In reality it had only just begun. For hardly had Caroli recovered from the way in which the judgment shook him — as Farel and Calvin tell the story he even shed tears — before he asked permission to make an announcement. For the glory of God and the honor of the government of Bern, he said, to promote the purity of the faith, the unity of the church, and public peace, and to fulfill his duty of venerating God, he had to tell them something on which he had for a long time kept silence and secrecy — after this invocation of all the gods some decisive novelty was naturally expected, but it turned out to be the same old thing: many preachers in Geneva and in Bern as well were tainted with the ungodliness of Arianism.[50] To the general consternation a list was then produced and read of those whom Caroli had in mind. He offered no proofs, says Calvin, but was content to have spread abroad his poison and taken his revenge. It was a genuine stroke of the theater on Caroli's part.

But then Calvin spoke, and he told the assembly, according to his own account, that Caroli had recently invited him to a meal since he was a beloved brother. He had also told him to send friendly greetings to Farel. He thus regarded all those whom he now called heretics as brothers, and said that he had always tried to cultivate fraternal fellowship with us.

48. In the MS the heading is in the margin.
49. CO 10/II, 97-106.
50. CO 7, 308.

"There was never any word about Arianism. Where, then, was the glory of God and the honor of the government of Bern? Where was the purity of the faith? Where the unity of the church? Either you are now making it clear that you lied to God and men and are a culpable traitor to the truth, or it is evident to all of us that you have other reasons for your accusation than those you give. For with what kind of conscience could you twice celebrate the Lord's Supper with your Arian colleagues? If you had even a single spark of true faith and zeal, would you have been able to tolerate it that your brothers and colleagues were denying the Son of God? How could you have dealings with those who were infected with so great ungodliness? But let us assume that your own zeal is not the issue. I ask you how you know that I am an Arian heretic. I recall that I have given open testimony to my faith and you will not easily find anyone who is more zealous than I am in upholding the deity of Christ. My works are in the hands of the people, and I have found that all orthodox churches approve of me and my beliefs. But you, have you ever documented your own faith except in drinking and tippling? That has been thus far the warfare in which you have engaged. With what right, then, do you accuse me of Arianism? I will purge myself of this insult and will not tolerate it that such unworthy suspicion should rest upon me."[51]

Note the refined technique that Calvin displays in this address. The old attorney has reawakened in the reformer. How cutting he is, how self-conscious, how sharply prepared to be in the right at any price, how ready not only to smash his foe intellectually but also to destroy him morally! And this was how Calvin portrayed himself eight years later, when the battles were long since over and another might perhaps have looked back on the stormy time with gentle irony. But Calvin at 36 was not prepared to take Calvin at 27 any the less seriously or to refrain even one jot or tittle from justifying him.

Caroli in response was forced to some extent to withdraw. He was not attacking Calvin's writings, which were in fact orthodox, but Calvin had made common cause with Farel, of whom the same could not be said. But at once Calvin and Viret replied that they were prepared to vouch for the absentee's innocence. The affair ended with fear and trembling for Caroli, said Calvin.[52] The disputation concluded at this point. Calvin attained his wish in that Bern resolved to convene a synod, but against

51. Ibid., 309.
52. Ibid.

his[53] desire it was put off until after Easter. For the rest it was clear that he did not meet with favor in Bern. We have a remarkable letter from Megander, one who soon enough would have to suffer much from Bern, addressed to Bullinger and dated March 8, 1537 (*Briefe*, 52), which is definitely not friendly at all to Calvin. Megander briefly describes the collision on the eschatological issue and writes that some of the French in the newly occupied territory (Vaud) are under suspicion of unorthodox teaching about Christ and the Trinity of persons. For this reason Calvin came to Bern and obstinately asked for a synod, which was denied him until after Easter. Be on the watch for how much work these bigoted and refractory Frenchmen *(Galli illi superstitiosi ne dicam seditiosi)* will still cause us.[54]

Crisis[55]   At this same period Farel received a most ungracious letter from the Bern council (Bähler, 69).[56] The offense was that during the absence of Viret and Caroli he had gone from Geneva to Lausanne. It was surmised that he had done this to stir up feeling against Caroli. This greatly displeased Bern, and he was told to desist at once. His church was Geneva, and he should not meddle in the affairs of others. At the time relations between Bern and Caroli seem to have become increasingly friendly and the latter still had unbroken confidence in his cause. We can well understand why Calvin was pressing for further and clearer decisions.

Meanwhile the situation was made more complicated by the compromising emergence of a real antitrinitarian close to Calvin. This came in the person of a certain Claudius of Savoy (Trechsel, 56;[57] Bähler, 73). Claudius was an unstable and volatile advocate of a mere humanity of Christ, the son of God naturally and in time, but not the eternal Son. He had been driven out of Bernese territory and went to Luther and Melanchthon at Wittenberg by way of Basel. Nowhere finding a welcome, he returned to his own home territory of Thonon, formerly in Savoy but now part of Bern. There he was trustingly received by the local pastor Fabri, a close friend of Calvin and Viret. On fresh instructions from Bern he went to Geneva to await the return of Calvin with a view to a disputation with

---

53. The MS had *ihren* ("their") here for *seinen* ("his").
54. CO 10/II, 89.
55. In the MS this heading is in the margin.
56. Bähler, 69 n. 1, prints an extract from the letter.
57. Trechsel, vol. I.

him. In the interval Farel and the other pastors who had stayed behind worked on him so thoroughly that they succeeded in securing an orthodox confession of faith from him.

But these dealings of the Genevans with a suspected heretic, even though they led to his conversion, were obviously not calculated to make a favorable impression abroad. It all seemed to indicate that things were not well with the triumvirate Farel, Calvin, and Viret. I will quote two letters to prove this. On May 20 Myconius of Basel wrote to Bullinger to the effect that something would have to be done by learned men if these Genevans were trying to bring back the Arian heresy, as he had heard, or even worse the evil error of the Spaniard Servetus (*Briefe,* 60).[58] During this whole period Myconius was a definite friend of Caroli and his cause. Even in July (*Briefe,* 72), when Caroli had become a Roman Catholic again, he could still write that he would have sworn that Caroli was a good man, whereas it was in a dissident spirit that those in Geneva and Lausanne refused to subscribe to the Athanasian Creed and thus seemed to cast doubt on belief in the Trinity (*Briefe,* 69).[59] What those at a greater distance, with no knowledge of the details, thought of the way things were going in western Switzerland may be seen from a letter sent by Melanchthon to V. Dietrich on August 5, 1537, in which he said he had heard that an associate of Servetus was scattering the seed of samosatanic error and that frivolous people were paying so much attention to this new delirium as to hold a synod already to deal with it.[60] Naturally there is here a confusion or intermingling of the causes of Caroli and Claudius, but we can still see that the reputation of the author of the *Institutes* was damaged if he could be spoken of in that way. We must take all these considerations into account if we are to explain Calvin's attitude. If we do so, we can at least understand, if not condone, his more than energetic response to Caroli. His life's work was at stake when he defended himself so strongly against the attack of this man.

Lausanne Synod, 5.14.1537[61]   On May 14, 1537, the synod that Calvin had wanted for so long finally met in Lausanne. To know how it went we are almost totally dependent on Calvin's own account in his *Defensio*

---

58. CO 10/II, 103.
59. CO 10/II, 117f., 113f.
60. CR 3, 400 (no. 1599); cf. also Bähler, 91.
61. In the MS this heading is in the margin.

Gallasii (7, 310ff.). The synod convened in the Franciscan church and consisted of over one hundred pastors from the Vaud territories conquered by Bern and twenty from Neuenburg. The two pastors from the city of Bern, Megander and Kunz, presided, and the Bern government was represented by two council members, Rudolf von Graffenried and Nikolaus Zurkinden. The synod had the character of an inner Bern affair, with the Genevans Farel, Calvin, and Courault present only as guests. The antitrinitarian Claudius seems to have been there as well.

After the reading of a formal complaint drawn up by Caroli, Viret was asked to respond first. This type of opening shows something we might gather from Megander's letter of March 8, namely, that in the trinitarian dispute the situation of Calvin's party was not a favorable one subsequent to the February colloquies. The tension of the months in which Calvin and his friends were under formal complaint helps to explain the crushing force with which Calvin proceeded to reply to Caroli now, then to reply again eight years later, and then to attack Servetus later still. In no circumstances did he wish to see his life's work exposed again to the peril under which it stood in the spring of 1537, when people were linking his name to that of Claudius of Savoy, and indeed confusing the two, as we learn from Melanchthon's letter.

Viret made the following declaration in answer to Caroli's charge: "When we confess the one God, then in the essence of the one Godhead we associate the Father with his eternal Word and the Spirit. We thus name God the Father in such a way that we proclaim the Son and his Spirit with the Father as the true and eternal God, but without confusing the Father with the Word or the Word with the Spirit. For we believe that the Son is other than the Father and the Spirit other than the Son, though there is only one divine essence. For this reason we say only of the Son, not of the Father or of the Spirit, that he became flesh, and thus that Christ is very God and very man. For at the time appointed for our redemption he took our flesh, and became participant in our humanity, in two natures that are united but not mingled."[62]

We see from this statement that good care was taken to retain the content of both the Nicene Creed and the Chalcedonian definition, to avoid Arianism on the one side and Sabellianism on the other, yet not to use — for reasons we saw last time — the terms that Caroli was demanding, namely, "Trinity" and "person." The statement was a real work of

62. CO 7, 310.

theological craftsmanship. Caroli called the confession sparse and thin, too short, ambivalent, and scanty, and for his part he began to recite the Nicene Creed and then the Athanasian Creed, and to do so with such strange twisting of the body and shaking of the head, and in such a bellowing voice, that general laughter broke out. By an unhappy chance he also got stuck after the third clause of the Athanasian Creed, so that he was abruptly forced to abandon his declaiming of it.[63] His obvious purpose was again to demand of Calvin's party subscription to these ancient symbols, or express confession of them.

This moment of comedy turned the tide against Caroli. Calvin's moment had come. On the principle that attack is the best form of defense he opened a strong point-blank attack on the devilish and envious rage with which Caroli was daring to confuse the church, to halt the progress of the kingdom of Christ, and to tear down worthy men. Caroli, he said, has kindled strife regarding the nature of God and the distinction of persons in God. He himself would begin further back. He would ask Caroli whether he believed in one God at all. For he would maintain before God and men that there was no more faith in him than in a dog or a swine. The proof was that he was an Epicurean in lifestyle, as they all knew.[64]

After this pithy introduction, which reminds us of the insults with which Homer's heroes usually opened their battles, Calvin read an express confession upon which he had reached an agreement with his Genevan colleagues, since they could not afford to let this kind of affront rest upon them. As he put it, a confession of faith must be based on respect for the mystery of the divine majesty and therefore on the Word of God. It must not be affected in any way by what is pleasing to others. It must state the very truth of scripture itself, not according to the words but according to the sense.[65] God is eternal, infinite, spiritual essence. As the one God he has his being of himself, and he has conferred being on his creatures. In this one essence of God we recognize Father, Son, and Spirit, not as three gods, nor as mere terms for his operations, but as three hypostases, subsistences, or modes of being that are not to be mixed with one another and that all lie in his essence. Thus in scripture the Son, too, is called Jehovah (Heb. 1 [vv. 7ff.]), our life, light, salvation, righteousness, and sanctification, in whom we put our trust and on whom we set our hope.

63. Ibid., 310f.
64. Ibid., 311.
65. Ibid., 311f.

But this is practical knowledge, not idle speculation. That it has to do with being quickened and enlightened and saved and justified and sanctified makes it certain knowledge, a viewing and grasping of God very present to us. Similarly, the deity of the Spirit follows from the manner of his working on us, which we see to be divine.[66] It is in this context, Calvin is saying, that the doctrine of God as Father, Son, and Spirit is scriptural and that we accept it. (He again stubbornly and in opposition to Caroli leaves out the terms "Trinity" and "person.")

These concepts of Calvin that I have just presented throw great light on the whole situation. Calvin was inclined to regard the Greek dogma as idle speculation in contrast to the practical knowledge that he himself thought he could gain from scripture, and it was only to the extent that the doctrine of the Trinity could be understood as practical knowledge that it seemed to him to be scriptural and acceptable. This evaluation of the Greek dogma, which was then original and necessary, has now become, especially under the influence of the view of dogmatic history inspired by Ritschl, one of the theological things that sparrows trill from the rooftops.[67] I would advise you to treat it with great caution. When an age regards the statements of a previous age as idle speculation, in the first instance this is just an indication that it now has different problems, or rather the same problems in another form. Calvin might permit himself to suspect the serious religious thinking of the 4th century of being idle speculation, but this evaluation was no more correct than if we, as we might easily be tempted to do, were to permit ourselves to reject the contention that the Reformation doctrine of justification or predestination is practical knowledge. The contrast that Calvin made simply shows us how great was the curve in the path that came with the Reformation, so great that the stretch behind the reformers was no longer visible to them and they could no longer adjudge the thinking of that earlier period to be practical knowledge. Caroli had not gone round this curve. Insofar as he did any vital thinking at all, he did so on the path of the older problems, and what Calvin had to say about the God who is so present to us seemed to him to be idle speculation, a modern discovery, as one might say today.

66. Ibid., 312f.

67. Barth obviously has in mind Harnack's thesis that early church dogma was a Hellenizing of Christianity (*History of Dogma,* I [New York, 1962], 47ff.), where the argument is that in the light of historical research we must see in the development of dogmatic Christianity a work of the Greek spirit on the soil of the gospel.

In the last analysis not merely two different minds but two different dogmatic epochs were speaking past one another here.

Calvin upholds then — and as in the *Institutes* his scriptural proof lies chiefly in the baptismal formula — the belief that there is distinction in the Godhead, but he argues that this does not abolish the most simple unity, so that the Son is one God with the Father because he is in harmony with the Father in one Spirit, and the Spirit is in no way different from the Father and the Son because he is the Spirit of the Father and the Son.[68] Arius is expressly repudiated for contesting the eternal deity of the Son. Macedonius, the bishop of Constantinople who was deposed in 360, is repudiated because in Calvin's eyes he was responsible for the heresy of the Pneumatomachi, who sought to subordinate the Spirit to the Son. Finally, Sabellius is repudiated for abolishing the distinction between Father, Son, and Spirit.[69]

It should be noted in this regard that had Caroli been more acute he would have had to accuse Calvin and his party of Sabellianism rather than Arianism. On this front his offensive would have been more promising, for Calvin himself later found the equation of Christ and Jehovah, in spite of its biblical basis, rather surprising, and for this reason, in a way that is not entirely free from objection precisely in the most striking passages of his Lausanne confession, he omitted it in the *Defensio Gallasii* (7, 322; cf. 9, 708!).[70] The reformers undoubtedly tended to stress the unity rather than the distinction in God, as we see plainly in Calvin. You probably are aware that on the last pages of his *Christian Faith* Schleiermacher counsels a serious weighing of the Sabellian solution in contrast to the Athanasian.[71] Calvin did not go that far, but a more perspicacious adversary who advocated the Greek dogma could certainly have found it necessary to attack him on this side. Calvin himself could rightly feel immune to the charge of Arianism, for the Reformation approach, like that of the early church, found the deity of Christ to be self-evident, no matter what one might think of the authority of Athanasius. Just because so much depended for Calvin on the true and eternal deity of the Son

---

68. CO 7, 313.

69. Ibid.

70. For the 1537 text cf. CO 9, 708; for the 1545 text, 7, 322.

71. *The Christian Faith*, §172, where Schleiermacher finds the NT unclear, views the Athanasian and Sabellian concepts as both valid and serving the same purpose, and asks whether the latter does not do so without entangling us in insoluble difficulties.

(and not simply on rational grounds here!), he felt that he had to stress the unity more than the distinction. If he was an antitrinitarian — and if there are any who feel confident enough to take this view in spite of his assurances, let them do so! — then it was certainly not as an Arian. Caroli's accusing him of being both an Arian and a Sabellian at the same time was, of course, nonsensical. (In almost all the controversies of this kind Calvin had the good fortune to fight with opponents who put their case with astonishing ineptitude.)

A further section of the confession deals with the two natures in Christ. Calvin calls Christ prior to his incarnation the eternal Word before all time, begotten of the Father, true God, of one essence, power, and majesty with the Father, and therefore himself Jehovah, that is, the self-existent one.[72] For if he is God, everything that is true of God is true of him, too. There can be no God of a second ranking for Calvin in spite of all the difficulties that arose for him here and in spite of the proximity to Sabellianism into which he brought himself. In calling Christ the Word, he adds, he does not have in mind the fleeting and dying voice of the oracles and prophecies given to the fathers, but, as he puts it with admirable clarity, the perpetual wisdom resident with God from which all oracles and prophecies derive. For the ancient prophets and others who imparted the truth of God to us spoke no less by the Spirit of Christ than the apostles.[73] As the incarnate Word Christ is both true God and true Man. The natures remain distinct, but are in mutual communication, so that we can predicate the qualities pertaining to each of the other. The church is redeemed by the blood of God, the Son of Man is in heaven.[74] This is the familiar doctrine of the *idiomata* ("attributes"), and it was the part of the early teaching that Calvin found it necessary to appeal to most. He rejected the Marcionites, who in his view substituted a specter for Christ's body; the Manichees, who spoke of a heavenly flesh of Christ; Apollinarius, who accorded to Christ only a half humanity; and Nestorius, who taught both a human and a divine Christ.[75]

It may be noted again that if he was really determined to find a heresy Caroli might have seized perhaps on the last name, the name of Nestorius, with more success. The Lutherans later knew how to raise

72. CO 7, 313f.
73. Ibid., 314.
74. Ibid.
75. Ibid.

serious objections against the Nestorianism of Reformed christology.[76] But Caroli let his best chances slip at every point. In so doing he showed that he no longer lived in the spirit of the ancient dogma but was a real man of a later generation who, unable to grasp the spirit of the new age, had to content himself with brandishing a few extracts from an earlier age against his adversaries. He was not in truth the dragon slayer of his posturing. Breaking off his report of the Lausanne colloquy at this point, Calvin asked who could not be satisfied with so clear a confession. What could a judge who was not wholly unjust miss in it?[77]

Calvin concluded his address with an explanation of the strange fact that he and his friends refused to meet Caroli's demand for subscription to the early confessions. Why not? Simply because Caroli was demanding it. Yielding would have compromised their work thus far, and Farel in particular would have been left unprotected. They could not set a precedent by allowing the tyranny of an individual over the church or an obstinate insistence on words.[78] I cannot wholly avoid the impression that Calvin was glad to be able to use this defiant argument, which is so right. It really is the case that we must not yield to people like Caroli even though their cause is the very best. Nevertheless, why had not the Genevans themselves thought of honoring or at least mentioning the early creeds somewhere in their reformation program as the Augsburg Confession and the Schmalkald Articles do, and even Zwingli in the first article of his 1530 *Fidei ratio*?[79] It was really a good thing for them that the admonition regarding this omission came from a man to whom they could reply: "We cannot!" with pride and with no taint of suspicion. Calvin could even permit himself to jest about this argument, as he himself tells us (*iocatus*, 7, 315). Jocularly he pointed out to Caroli that he had recited the first lines (of the Athanasian Creed), stating that those who do not keep this faith cannot be saved, but he then observed that Caroli himself did not keep it, for with all his efforts he had reached only the fourth clause. Supposing death had overtaken him and the devil had come to fetch him after he had expressly consigned himself to the everlasting perdition that

---

76. This criticism arose in connection with the so-called Calvinistic extra; cf. A. Calov, *Systema locorum theologicorum*, vol. VII (Wittenberg, 1677), 225; J. Gerhard, *Loci theologici*, vol. I (Leipzig, 1885), 506.

77. CO 7, 315.

78. Ibid.

79. BSLK 55, 8f.; 414, 25f.; Z 6/II, 15ff.

is certain without the protection of this confession.[80] Those who can joke in this way about the rather pompous introduction to the *Quicumque* can hardly be called ardent in their respect for the church's tradition.

And the continuation is even better, for Calvin asks: What if he should deny that the statement that Caroli wants to thrust upon him really was the work of the Council of Nicea? Can we believe that the holy fathers, who surely wanted to put everything necessary in as brief a formula as possible, would have played around with such a superfluity of words? Is there not repetition in such clauses as "God of God, light of light, true God of true God"? Why this repetition? Or does it have some real point or meaning? What we have here is obviously more a hymn for singing than a confession, in which one syllable too many is absurd.[81] This is a genuine Calvinist objection, but the astonishing thing is that it was raised at all. Historical criticism based on a judgment of taste! Those who go so far afield show that they have no direct relation to the object of criticism. It would have been better for the matter under discussion if that had been rather more apparent at the time. But we cannot dictate to history its tempo. And there was wisdom in the way in which Calvin made it clear how free he was regarding earlier authorities, did so better than any other reformer, yet did not come right out and say that these were not authorities for him. Something of that sort had taken place at the first Lausanne disputation.[82] This time Calvin was content to put a few question marks after agreeing materially with the confessions. These observations brought his address to a close.

Caroli then spoke again, and again, providentially, he made himself an object of general ridicule. He thought he should reprove his youthful antagonist by bidding him respect his white beard, but instead of *canus,* meaning "white," he used *calvus,* meaning "baldheaded"; and even though general laughter broke out, with his usual boldness, says Calvin, he repeated his statement three times, always with the same result. People then knew Latin better than they do now, and the mistake, along with the unintended pun *calvus-Calvinus,* was enough to make him once and for all a figure of fun. He had nothing new or cogent to add, and he certainly could not make any impression.

The president Megander tells us the result of the colloquy in a letter

---

80. CO 7, 315.
81. Ibid.
82. See above, 319.

to Bullinger dated May 22, 1537 (*Briefe*, 61).[83] Here he says that the synod of Vaud brethren met under his presidency on May 14 and came to a happy conclusion. Claudius of Savoy recanted his Arianism. (This was one matter the synod did take care of, though Calvin for obvious reasons does not mention it.) Farel, Calvin, and many other brethren, pious and learned men, were wrongly accused of heresy. Caroli, who was responsible for this tragedy, was on account of it, and of other ungodly, vain, and odd acts, deprived of his office by the brethren, and Megander had no doubt but that the council would support the judgment of the synod.[84] Calvin, too, records the deposition, but also states that the synod recognized the Genevan confession.[85] This was naturally more important for him than the ousting of Caroli, especially as there were other reasons for the latter apart from his calumniating of the Genevans.

It seems possible that here again Calvin later saw the actual proceedings in rather a different light. At any rate, he and Farel received an unfriendly letter from the Bern council on August 13 to the effect that it had been reported that Calvin had written to a Frenchman in Basel saying the synod had accepted and "approved" the Genevan confession. The exact opposite was the truth. He and Farel had expressed their readiness to subscribe to the Basel confession, which held sway in Bern. (Calvin himself mentions in passing that at Lausanne he did in fact endorse this confession.)[86] There was surprise in Bern, then, that he should write the way he did, and he was told to desist, and that if he did not Bern would be forced to resort to other measures.[87] Obviously if Calvin had secured from the synod he so much wanted all that he had desired, namely, a full and unequivocal clearing of his name, Bern would not have dared to address him in this manner. Clearly the situation was that although his opponent Caroli had been defeated, this was not because he and his accusation had been totally routed, but because he had succeeded in making himself impossible quite apart from his relation to Calvin.

Bern Synod, 5.31.1537[88]   The next and last stage in the controversy, in which outwardly Calvin achieved rather more than at Lausanne, was also

83. CO 7, 317.
84. CO 10/II, 104.
85. CO 7, 317.
86. Ibid., 319.
87. CO 10/II, 118f. (no. 73).
88. In the MS the heading is in the margin.

a Pyrrhic victory for him, the true and profoundest outcome of the whole affair being that although nothing could be made to stick against him, he was not really trusted, so that occasion was sought to prevent this uncannily zealous man from Geneva from growing trees that would reach to heaven. Caroli saw fit to appeal from the French-speaking part of Bern canton and its decision to the German-speaking part, which came together on May 31 to deal with another dispute between the two city pastors Kunz and Megander.[89] Calvin welcomed the opportunity to vanquish his adversary more completely. Here the situation proved to be different from the very outset, for Caroli was now the one who stood accused. Calvin and his companions were asked to bring their charges against him, and after he had tried in vain to anticipate them by frankly confessing some dark blots in his past, Farel and Viret gave a very full and most unedifying account of his moral weaknesses both past and present.[90] It was not a happy occasion, since the final victory over Caroli was won simply with the help of a flood of old and new anecdotes, and the unfortunate man still had the audacity to compare himself to that great champion of the faith Athanasius, who had had to suffer so much for the truth.[91] On June 5 the Genevans were rehabilitated in Bern as well, the judgment on Caroli was confirmed, and banishment sharpened it.[92]

For reasons that are not clear there was a sequel to the decisive action of the synod, this time in the ecclesiastical court of Bern (7, 336). It seems that in spite of everything Caroli had friends in Bern, especially in the Lutheran faction among the clergy, and by turning to these friends he sought a last chance to come to terms with his opponents.[93] But again he conducted himself in such a way that he did not achieve his end, and Farel, Calvin, and Viret now went over to the offensive, visited the mayor, who had attended the synod along with the whole council, and asked that Caroli not be allowed to leave the city until he had cleared them as the synod demanded. Naturally this was not because he (Calvin)[94] thought it necessary that his orthodoxy should be acknowledged by Caroli — which he had persistently and sharply refused to do — but because this public

---

89. Peter Kunz belonged to the Lutheran party in Bern, Megander to the Zwinglian; cf. Hundeshagen, 64ff., 157ff.; and above, 97 n. 10.

90. CO 7, 325-27, 335.

91. Ibid., 335.

92. Ibid., 336.

93. Ibid., 336f.

94. The MS simply has *er* = Calvin.

humiliation of their adversary would give force to the somewhat cool declaration of the synod. Their request was granted, and it was to be formally satisfied on June 6. But Caroli did not show up at the time appointed by the mayor, and when a servant went to fetch him, it seems that the missing man had left the city before daybreak.[95] He went to Solothurn, where the French ambassador resided, and from there, on June 16, he sent a remarkably shameless letter to the Lausanne council (*Briefe*, 660) saying that he thanked God for being freed by his grace from bonds that had irked him so long. The foes of the Holy Trinity would not be able to enjoy their triumph for long. He believed that all he had said was true, and he would uphold it before the forum of the whole church.[96]

What he meant by the last statement became clear at the end of the same month when we find him at Lyons with Cardinal Bishop Tournon, who would arrange for his (second) return to the Roman Catholic church. From Lyons he sent a no less astounding letter to Pope Paul III (Bähler, 8f.)[97] saying that for thirteen years he had championed, spread, and preached the theses of Luther that were for the most part rejected, that finally for seven months he had led and taught the Lausanne congregation according to the new doctrine, although not in all points, and that in keeping with the accepted custom there he had taken a wife, but appealing to the holy father as a suppliant, he stated that he had seen others spread a dreadful heresy among these people and perceived a relapse into terrible ungodliness as he saw clergy and theologians who styled themselves preachers adopt the errors of Arius, Sabellius, Paul of Samosata, Nestorius, and Basilides, and even go so far as to ridicule, disparage, and tread under foot the symbols of the Council of Nicea and Athanasius, and to deny that these had ever been recognized by the true church, so that he, Caroli, could no longer tolerate such abhorrent apostasy and error and such dreadful blasphemy. At synods and disputations in Lausanne and Bern he had zealously made every effort to oppose such ungodly errors and to break the horns of the heretics above mentioned, and by God's help he had become ever stronger and more victorious in this fight, but for that reason he had been the more hated and finally expelled. He had had to save his life by swift flight last of all from the city of Bern. In deep penitence for outwardly rather than inwardly leaving the bosom of holy mother church,

95. See n. 104 below.
96. CO 10/II, 110f.
97. Ibid.; see n. 3 on 310.

he now wished to return to its fellowship, to renounce all heresies, and to do penance for his sin. He begged that he might do this, and to that end he begged this his marriage might be annulled, and that he might be restored to his doctor's degree, his ordained status, his ministry at the altar, and his qualification to receive a stipend.[98]

Two years later, in July 1539, Caroli turned up again in Neuenburg, then Basel, then Strassburg, and for the third time he went over from Rome to Protestantism.[99] He thus began a second and no less tumultuous period of relations with Calvin into which we cannot go here. Rightly to assess his letter to the pope, however, we must say that in Strassburg he signed the Augsburg Confession, and when asked how he had been able to go back to Christ's enemies, he replied that he had taken this step out of weakness and error, but that in spirit he had never really left his former companions in the faith.[100] In him the relation between what is inward and what is outward, between the spirit and the flesh, must have been a complicated one. In 1543, after various switches, we find him in the role of a polemical Roman Catholic preacher at Metz,[101] and it was as such, in virtue of his attacks especially on Farel, that he became the target of Calvin's polemical work in 1545 to which we owe the most detailed and vivid account of the whole affair.

In what I have told you about the matter I have used this account with caution, with hints at various times why this is so. Controversy, with its terrible urge to be right and to win on both sides, and of which we have just seen a striking example, offers a good deal of smoke as well as fire. It was the dust cloud of the Reformation and not its marching column. We recall the tragic ambivalence of Calvin's whole historical position. He stood at the point where the flame was becoming smoke. Someone had to stand there. When we realize that, we will be on guard against disliking Calvin because he wanted to be right and he had to win after the manner of his day, but more fiercely, consistently, and brilliantly than perhaps any of his contemporaries. But we will also use great caution in viewing the testimonies of his lively spirit as sources by which to evaluate others.

It cannot be maintained that much can be said to redeem Caroli. Nevertheless, we cannot say anything final in evaluation of him because

98. Bähler, 84ff.
99. Ibid., 96ff.
100. Ibid., 112, 115.
101. Ibid., 122f.

we have too little of his own sayings and writings. To engage in a thorough investigation of his life and his relation to the Reformation from a broader and deeper standpoint than we find in Bähler would be a rewarding task in the course of which it would perhaps emerge that this virtuoso of switching back and forth might have been an example at least of a little regarded but much stronger and more widespread middle movement between the Reformation and the Middle Ages, the type of movement which, with no feeling for the either-or that the epoch posed, tried to hold the balance and thus had a certain characteristic significance of its own. Was it not inevitable that most people of the time, though unable to switch back and forth as Caroli did, should still be basically undecided in exactly the same way? In the long run being a classical representative of those who do not see that the hour has struck counts for something. Caroli finally died in a hospital in Rome, naturally, as Calvinists would have it, as a result of his excesses.[102]

But let us go back to his opponent who triumphed in 1537, to Calvin. At his insistence the Bern council gave him a testimony to his innocence, as he called it, on the day after Caroli's flight, June 7. It is worth noting that he was able to steel himself to request this from the neither very spiritual nor very intellectual men of the Bern regime, he who had so scrupulously argued that he was under no suspicion and that he would not regard Caroli's approval as even remotely necessary. But so seriously did he take his view that secular governments have a vocation to watch over the orthodoxy of what the church preaches that he was willing to do this. Since the synod had acknowledged that he was right, the council could not refuse to make this officially known. The council accepted the logic of this. The remarkable official document is now in the Geneva Library with the seal of the republic of Bern on it, showing the bear that is slowly but surely inclining upward, an eloquent symbol of what Bern has always wanted and not wanted. In religious matters Bern wanted order, precision, comprehensibility, not intellectual ferment of any kind, not unfathomable depth or freedom of thought, especially not what was arbitrary and strange, and might disturb the peaceful course of administration.

The unhappy Caroli now came to feel the severity of this bear's claws, but Calvin and his party did not wholly escape. The people of Bern gladly made use of the occasion to say that it was they who had the say in their territories, not merely in judicial and military matters but in those per-

102. Ibid., 165.

taining to the Holy Trinity as well. Not for a moment, however, did they think of confirming turbulent Jehan Chauvin, who for them was basically on the same level as Caroli, in what had become his somewhat doubtful seat in the saddle at Geneva. Hence the testimony to Calvin's innocence did not mean much (*Briefe*, 63).[103] Caroli had not been able to make good his charge of Arianism. The accused were innocent. The charge had no merit. At the request of Farel and Calvin the ecclesiastical court had been ready to arrange a declaration of innocence. The flight of Caroli had blocked this. At the further request of Farel and Calvin the government had declared them innocent, having no good reason not to. It thus ordered all its officials, if necessary, to see to it that right was done to Farel and his fellows against Caroli and his supporters.[104] But if the tone of this document is not enough to show us how unfavorable things really were in Bern for Calvin and his friends, we should read the singular letter, already mentioned, that Bern sent to Farel and Calvin on August 13 (*Briefe*, 73), which tells the learned, modest, loyal, and good friends that they were reported to have tried to convince the preachers in neighboring Gex that the terms "Trinity" and "person" were empty terms, and to seduce them from their allegiance to the customary way of speaking of the Trinity that they had inherited from the catholic church. There is then added the complaint about Calvin's untrue account of the Lausanne Synod, which made out that Bern had accepted his confession rather than he himself accepting that of Bern, with the threat of other measures should this warning not suffice.[105]

Reading this crude missive might well have given Calvin cause to consider the shadow side of his concept of church and state. He departed from his own path, of course, as little as Bern did from its path. But the lords of Bern were not the only ones for whom the palpable result of the Caroli affair was in fact a distrust of Calvin that was hard to remove. Read the letters that passed between Myconius, Bullinger, and Grynaeus that summer (*Briefe*, 60, 65, 69, 71, 72),[106] and you will be convinced what shaking of heads there then was after Calvin's victory over Caroli even

---

103. CO 7, 337.
104. CO 10/II, 105f.
105. Ibid., 118.
106. Ibid., 103f. (no. 60), Myconius to Bullinger, 5.20.1537; 109f. (no. 65), Grynaeus to Calvin, June 1537; 113f. (no. 69), Myconius to Bullinger, 7.9.1537; 116f. (no. 71), Bullinger to Myconius, 7.23.1537; 117f. (no. 72), Myconius to Bullinger, 7.26.1537.

among stout Protestants, and even, indeed, in leading Reformation circles from the shores of Lake Geneva to the unruly and riotous people of the Allobrogi. Any letters addressed to the author of the *Institutes* were always respectful and restrained, but there was no decisive shunning of Caroli, at least not until his return to Rome was complete, and the letters were not without a tone of quiet avuncular admonition to Calvin, with some anxiety about all the things that might be possible in Geneva, and joy at any report that seemed to indicate that things were not as bad with this good friend as had at first been assumed. When the disaster took place in Geneva a year later, the admonitory tone became more pronounced, as usually occurs when something bad happens. In Bern, as later events would show, Calvin had made a definite and conscious enemy of the Lutheran Kunz.

Bern Synod, 9.22.1537[107]   The last act in the Caroli affair, mainly unfavorable to Calvin, took place in the presence of Bucer, Capito, Myconius, and Grynaeus. It was the Synod of Bern on September 22, 1537,[108] and centered on the agreement with the German Lutherans concerning the Lord's Supper. This synod, fully in line with the wishes of the Bern Council and under the dominant impress of Bucer's personality, would establish the preponderance of a Lutheranizing trend in Bern. But the aim was also to settle in this broader Reformed circle the question of the Trinity that had not yet been wholly laid to rest. The letter sent by the Bern Council to Farel and Calvin requesting their presence (*Briefe*, 77) does not mention either item on the agenda but simply says that the synod will deal with certain matters concerning the catholic faith. Capito and Bucer had expressed a wish that, being of like mind, Farel and Calvin should take part in the discussions. To advance the "true truth" ("vraie verité") and to please them this wish was granted.[109] But basically the attitude of Bern to the Genevans was equivocal. On the one side they were doing the Strassburg leaders the favor of according them the like-minded helpers they wanted in the eucharistic controversy (at that time Calvin was thus regarded as anti-Zwinglian at least). On the other side the Genevans were being called to account before this forum in the matter of the Trinity, in relation to which the attitude of Bern was naturally one of caution if not of actual mistrust. And we have to say that for these statesmen, who knew so well

107. In the MS this heading is in the margin.
108. On the course of the synod cf. Hundeshagen, 79ff., 114; also Trechsel, I, 163f.
109. CO 10/II, 125f.

how to direct the play put on by the unsuspecting theologians, everything went astonishingly very much as they desired.

Our present interest, of course, is in the part that Calvin played in the proceedings. As regards the Lord's Supper he had the undoubtedly important task of presenting in the name of the Swiss churches a statement that the Strassburgers, of whose sincerity there was at first some mistrust, could sign as a proof of their agreement with the Swiss at the points at which they were particularly opposed to Luther. This statement, the *Confessio Fidei de Eucharistia* (9, 711f.),[110] is brief, but it is a little masterpiece for which a Calvin was needed. It sets out with extraordinary sharpness the essence of the Lutheran view and that of the Zwinglian view (as Calvin understood it!) and makes no attempt to mediate between them. Instead, precisely by harshly opposing them to one another, it aims at a paradoxical but as such illuminating unity, and says nothing whatever about the points that are not essential on either side (i.e., not essential for Calvin).

The spiritual life that Christ gives us, says Calvin, is not just vivification by his Spirit but also participation in his flesh; it is an imparting of the whole Christ. No words can worthily describe the mystery of our fellowship with the body of Christ.[111] There we have Luther. Calvin adds, however, that all this in no way contradicts the fact that our Lord is exalted to heaven, that he has withdrawn from us the spatial presence of his body, which is not needed for the purpose. For though we pilgrims in our mortality cannot be with him in the place where he is, nevertheless the efficacy of his Spirit is no less surely not restricted by any limits, as though the Spirit could not bring together and unite into one that which is separated in space.[112] There we have Zwingli. We thus read in conclusion that we find in the Spirit of Christ the order or bond of our fellowship with Christ, but in such a way that the Spirit truly nourishes us to immortality by the substance of his body and blood, and imparts life to us by the fellowship of this body and blood. Christ, however, proffers us this fellowship of his body and blood under the symbols of bread and wine in the most sacred supper, and he gives *(exhibet)* it to all who celebrate the supper rightly according to its institution.[113] There we have Calvin.

For purely technical reasons, quite apart from the force and depth

---

110. OS I, 435f.
111. Ibid.
112. Ibid.
113. Ibid.

of the underlying conception, those who know a little of what the eucharistic controversy of the time was all about will rejoice at the quality of what Calvin did here. From this lofty height how tedious the battle about the *est* ("is") seems, how scholastic the Lutheran inference that the wicked also partake, and how rationalistic Zwingli's eternal insistence that the flesh profits nothing. But how unnecessary, too, seems the attacking of either left or right now that the two are brought together in this unity as equivalent ways of describing the same thing, comprehended in the cardinal concept of the Spirit of Christ by whose power the impossible becomes possible, the distant near, the heavenly earthly, though not for a moment losing its own worth or significance and becoming an immediate actuality. Here we have a mediating theology that is not a mediating theology because no room is left in it for either party as such.

The Strassburgers signed without demur, though Bucer at least appended a brief statement to the effect that he had never believed that Christ was locally in the elements or diffused everywhere, but also that we cannot allow the wine and the bread to be called naked and empty symbols.[114] If we want to study the difference between good theology and average theology, superior theology and untalented theology, we should compare the two brief statements made by Calvin and Bucer on the Lord's Supper. From the standpoint of Calvin's statement the controversies regarding ubiquity on the one side and the purely symbolical character of the elements on the other are now meaningless in virtue of the strong reference to the miracle of the Spirit, who is himself the Lord. But Bucer, according to his appended statement, seems to have had little comprehension of this point. Be that as it may, Bucer and Capito, who were present in Bern as go-betweens for the great zealot of Wittenberg, signed Calvin's statement, and if as a result concord between Luther and the Swiss was closer to achievement than it has ever been before and would ever be again, this was due not least of all to Calvin. It was not his fault if the peace proved to be of short duration.

Naturally, however, the domestic problems of the Reformation movement were too serious to be set aside by one good formula. Calvin would derive no pleasure from what he did. He had built for the Strassburgers a golden bridge to the hearts of the Swiss, but the result historically was not to lift up the debate to the higher level of the statement. Instead, against Calvin's intentions, the crude and banal outcome was a strengthening of

114. Ibid., 436.

the Lutheran influence as opposed to that of the Zwinglian in Bern. The one who came out on top in Bern was now Kunz, and the one who soon after had to give ground was Megander.[115] The Bern regime had in fact triumphed. It preferred Lutheranism to Zwinglianism, for Lutheran teaching suited the government, giving free rein to the state, much better than Zwinglian teaching, in which the church with its threats and actions claimed that it should at least have a say in determining the course of the state. In fact the obstinacy of Luther had also triumphed when, to the annoyance of Calvin, his[116] statement was at once openly given a Lutheran interpretation. After the deposing of Megander in Bern, Calvin wrote a letter to Bucer on January 12, 1538, in which he openly expressed his displeasure at the situation created by what he called Bucer's craftiness (*Briefe*, 87; Schwarz, 15).[117]

I will give you as a sample a passage dealing with Luther, since it shows us instructively what was Calvin's image of Luther — and there are bothersome passages — when he became annoyed at him. He did not take it kindly, he said, that Luther would accept them with this confession, for Luther was not the only person worthy of note in the church of God. We would have to be thrice-dreadful barbarians if we did not take into account the many thousands who would be terribly insulted by a union of that kind. What Calvin ought to think of Luther, he said, he did not know, though he was firmly convinced of his true piety. If only it were not true what even most of those who would not allow any injustice to be done to him still maintain, namely, that there is a good deal of stubbornness mixed in with his staunchness for the faith. Luther himself is not the least responsible for this suspicion. If it was true, as Calvin had recently heard, that there was a rumor going about in all the Wittenberg congregations that they had now brought almost all the churches to a recognition of their error, what vanity that would be! Would that there were no such unhealthy arrogance among us, that it were enough that *Christ* alone be held to be true, and that *his* truth shine in human hearts! Truly I see how it will be, said Calvin. There can be no health among us so long as the fury of arrogance is at work. Both sides, then, must bury all recollection of the past if they want lasting peace. The battle was too sharp and too

---

115. Cf. Hundeshagen, 94-96.

116. I.e., Calvin's.

117. CO 10/II, 137-44; R. Schwarz, *Johannes Calvins Lebenswerk in seinen Briefen* . . ., vol. I (Tübingen, 1909), 26-31 (1961 ed., Neukirchen, vol. I, 58-64).

bitter to be remembered without at least some sparks reigniting, and if Luther wants so much the glory of victory, no true union in the truth of God can prosper. For this reason, if there is a desire to do anything for Luther as a favor or out of respect, we must see to it that he subject his former opponent in the unholy dispute to Christ and not to himself, and that he himself be ready to welcome the truth even where he is in contradiction with it.[118]

This, then, was Calvin's part in the first item on the agenda of the Bern Synod. The second affected him more closely, and here the result brought him less regard and was much more unpleasant for him. The aim was to settle two outstanding matters that arose for Protestant circles out of the Caroli affair. First, why did not the Genevans use the terms "Trinity" and "person"? Second, what did they mean by equating Christ with Jehovah? They now had to explain themselves on these issues in the presence of the Strassburg leaders. We see how different the situation was even outwardly. As regards the Eucharist, Calvin in his statement was representing the Swiss churches to Strassburg. Now, however, the Strassburg leaders were witnesses, if not judges, in questions addressed to Calvin himself. The second point seems to have caused no difficulty. The Genevans explained that calling Christ Jehovah summed up his deity, which pertains to the Father, Son, and Spirit equally, and that it does not imply any denial of the Son's begetting from the Father even according to his eternal essence.[119] No one apparently offered any opposition to this explanation. Here Calvin had logic if not custom on his side. Yet he never liked his views to be regarded as peculiar to Geneva even when they were recognized to be such, and so, as we have noted already, in his later account he took steps to conceal the fact that this issue was a point of controversy. We have here one of the few cases where Calvin, though officially justified, showed by his later silence that he was not ready to insist on his view.

The situation was not such a good one for the Genevans on the other issue, the question of the terms "Trinity" and "person." Calvin's view, and the advice of the Strassburgers, was that no one should be compelled against his or her conscience to use these doubtful terms.[120] For Calvin, who had to protect his friend Farel in this regard, this meant that the use

---

118. CO 10/II, 138ff. Barth uses the translation (with a correction) given in Schwarz, 26f. (59).

119. CO 9, 708.

120. Trechsel, I, 163f.

of the terms should be wholly voluntary, but for the Strassburgers it meant that in time fear of the words would and should evaporate, though there should be no enforcement of them. The formula upon which agreement was finally reached[121] can only be described as unfavorable to Geneva. The Genevans had to allow that they saw that in the churches of Christ these terms were calculated to suppress unhappy controversies and that therefore they would not refuse to accept them, to hear them from others, and to use them themselves. They had to recognize that as they had been used previously, so their use should not be stopped in their churches. They would not avoid them and they would teach others not to be afraid of them. If there were any who in mistaken zeal would not use them, they would not approve of this and would make every effort to correct them. But since such zeal is no reason for rejecting those of true faith, they would tolerate their lack of insight on this matter and not excommunicate them or regard them as heretical. They would not take it amiss, however, if the Bern pastors would not admit to the ministry of the Word any who would not accept the terms (9, 707f.).

If it had only been a matter of Calvin's own position, this formula, apart from the final provision sponsored by Bern, would not have been so bad. Calvin had said this much in ch. II of his *Institutes,* that since the terms "Trinity" and "person" had come in with good reason, it would be wrong to reject them.[122] But things were different for Farel, against whom, as we saw, Caroli's attack was chiefly directed. Farel's intentional avoidance of the terms in his *Sommaire,*[123] even though he himself was not mentioned by name, was now branded as superstitious and preposterous. It might be tolerated but it could not be sanctioned, and Bern would not even tolerate it.[124] The last point was a slap in the face for Calvin in his solidarity with Farel. The whole conclusion meant no more and no less than that the Genevans had to fall back on their repeated declaration that they refused to use the required terms only for tactical reasons (i.e., not to yield to Caroli), but that fundamentally they had nothing against them. In my view this was tantamount to admitting that the charge was legitimate except as Caroli's, to promising amendment, and also to promising not to take it amiss if Bern adopted toward them the same attitude as that of Caroli.

121. CO 9, 707f.
122. See above, 312 n. 21 and 318 n. 43.
123. See above, 316 n. 27.
124. CO 9, 708 (cf. above, n. 121).

So the last act of the Caroli affair ended with the ignominious retreat of its true hero. Unquestionably Calvin and his party had not gained a victory but suffered a defeat. Calvin's contemporaries saw it that way in spite of the reassuring manner in which they told Calvin how glad they were to be convinced now that he was innocent.[125] This came to light later in 1539 in Strassburg when Caroli resurfaced and all the proceedings of 1537 came under fresh scrutiny.[126] The impression left in Bern, Basel, and Strassburg, perhaps least of all in Zurich, and despite all Calvin's efforts to counteract it, was that in this matter he had gone too far and made a mistake.[127] The general view of Calvin as he emerged from his first period in Geneva was that he was a learned and zealous man who could not be rated too highly as such, but that he was still too young and hasty and rather unpredictable — who really knew what he might do next? Certainly nothing could have been more galling to Calvin than the half-distrustful and half-paternal tenderness with which people usually greeted him from now on and well into his Strassburg days. That it was the skill of the Bern government that had been able to bring him into this situation in 1537, and with his theological help in the matter of the Eucharist to put the Bernese Lutherans in the saddle, was one of the humiliations at the hands of these men on the banks of the Aare that the reformer could never forget. We will not try to examine how far the quiet anger that he would cherish from this point on was on account of his cause or on account of his own reputation and person. All his life it had on a big scale, as with most of us on a small scale, both sides to it.

We may remark that Calvin was perhaps right, when giving his account of the affair in 1545, to refer to the fatal second synod of Bern in September 1537 only incidentally, unobtrusively, and without saying anything about the solemnity of the occasion. Strictly speaking, it was no longer a real part of the Caroli affair that he was seeking to report. But he was hardly justified in ending the work by quoting the testimony to his innocence that at his insistence the Bern Council had provided, thus giving the impression that this was the end of the matter and that the same council had not, shortly afterward, sent that very different letter,[128]

---

125. Barth has in view Bullinger's letter to Farel and Calvin, 11.1.1537, CO 10/II 128 (no. 80).

126. Bähler, 112-20.

127. Ibid., 116f.

128. CO 7, 335. See above, 336 n. 103, 331 n. 87.

quite apart from the autumn synod. Nor was he right innocuously to present the declaration that he and his friends had had to make concerning the terms "Trinity" and "person" as though it were a testimony to his goodwill offered to an intimate circle of Bern pastors, and to leave out the final and decisive caveat of Bern, so that the declaration closes with the statement that those who do not use the terms are not to be excommunicated or regarded as heretics.[129] That was an amending of the sources after the manner of the Ems dispatch and a well-known example of our own day.[130] There is no excuse here except perhaps to claim that in the spheres into which Calvin believed he had to move energetically on the basis of his own view of Christianity, he could not operate without ambiguities of this type.

It is not without penalty that we push on as forcefully as Calvin sought to do to the glory of God. Normally and gladly we find in the Jesuits the dangers of doing all to the greater glory of God. But honestly we have to see the same dangers in the reformers as well. Nor is it any wonder if in their different ways we find the dangers especially clearly in Zwingli and Calvin. They arose for these two, as they did not for Luther, just because of the temptations to which they were exposed in virtue of their distinctive tendency to engage in decisive action in the world. It has always been the feature precisely of an ethically oriented Christianity that it does not safeguard its best and most zealous champions from the ethical ambiguity of all human action but has often made them embodiments of the warning to play the man and not follow them![131] That is part of the tragedy of the life and work of Calvin to which we have often alluded and which rightly, as it should, arouses fear and pity[132] in us but should not cause us not to see how necessary and relatively justified is the reformation type that he represents.

---

129. CO 7, 319.

130. Barth alludes first to Bismarck's emending of the Ems dispatch in July 1870 that whipped up Prussian opinion against France and prepared the way for the Franco-Prussian war. Regarding the second allusion, in the typed copy of the MS Barth puts the name Eisner here, referring to Kurt Eisner (1867-1919), a Bavarian politician, and possibly to his making public some documents on the question of German guilt for the war of 1914-18 in the hope of gaining Allied support for his plans.

131. Barth quotes from the last line of Goethe's poem *On the Sorrows of the Young Werther:* "sei ein Mann, und folge mir nicht nach," which was the motto of the novel in the 2nd ed., 1775.

132. Cf. Aristotle's *Poetics* 7.1449b, on the purpose of tragedy.

We know little or nothing of the direct repercussions of the Caroli affair in relations in Geneva. Indirectly it contributed more strongly than anything else to a thickening of the atmosphere of mistrust under which the preachers were living there. It could not be concealed from the people of Geneva that abroad, especially in their highly regarded and indispensable neighbor Bern, their strict reformers did not enjoy the unconditional respect that they demanded at home, if not for themselves, at least for their teaching. It must have made a remarkable impression when it could be told that the authors of the new confession, to which all residents had to swear on pain of banishment, were refusing to sign the venerable, ancient, and fundamental creeds of Christianity (A. Lang, 41).[133]

When Farel and Calvin returned to Geneva from the fifth and last of all the disputations and synods, at a session of the Council of Two Hundred on September 27, they did, of course, refer finely and plainly enough to the constitutional powers of these representatives of the people and to their duty to admonish the people to live according to the law and commandments of the Lord, to act justly in relation to all, both rich and poor, and to live in harmony with the lords of Bern (words no doubt taken from a concluding address at the Bern Synod and specifically directed at the delegates from Geneva). They also reported that the lords of Bern had paid their expenses and given them each another two ducats for the journey, and that after all the proposals and speeches had been heard agreement had been reached at last on the question of Christ's presence at the supper.[134]

This account was undoubtedly calculated to give a favorable impression of the acts and experiences of the reformers abroad, but the impression did not last long. Shortly thereafter the dispute concerning the Genevan confession began to come to a head. It made the whole winter a period of unrest. With the spring there came from outside the great wave of resentment that the Caroli affair had intensified. In Geneva itself other charges against the preachers combined with this to produce the flood that finally engulfed them.

133. Lang, *Johannes Calvin.*
134. CO 21, 215.

Bern Ceremonies

A look at this third and decisive controverted issue and the related disputes will lead on directly to an account of the disastrous outcome that had been in course of preparation for so long. What was the issue? At the beginning of December 1537 the Bern Council dealt for the first time with some differences in church practices between the churches of Bern and Geneva that Bern regarded as disruptive and wished to set aside, naturally by the submission of Geneva to Bern's judgment. There were four main differences.[135] (1) In Bern Christmas, New Year, the Annunciation, and the Ascension were still kept as feasts, a modest remnant of the medieval calendar. In Geneva, however, all such feasts were done away with on strict biblical grounds, and only Sundays were observed. (Later, when Calvin's system triumphed, even keeping Christmas at home could be punished,[136] and on Good Friday street work is still done in Geneva today as needed.) (2) Bern churches retained the font, Geneva discarded it along with other medieval furnishings. (3) Bern used wafers at the Lord's Supper, Geneva ordinary bread. (4) At church weddings Bern had brides wear hair adornment, Geneva forbade this on the basis of 1 Pet. 3:3: "Whose adorning let it not be that outward adorning of plaiting the hair, and of wearing of gold, and of putting on of apparel, but let it be the hidden man of the heart."

All of us would probably agree with Hermelink when he calls these differences mere trifles.[137] But the *i* in *homoiousios* and Luther's *est* ("is") at Marburg and many another strange jot and tittle in the history of the Christian church were also mere trifles, and it is a distressing truth that very decisive things may hinge precisely on such trifles. It so happened in this case that on the matter of these four differences all the combustible material that had gathered around what Calvin was doing caught fire, and that in connection with them the event took place which would for the time being bring the work that he had begun to an end, although, as would be seen, it had more vitality than was supposed, and would only establish itself on more solid foundations, because by its very nature it did not allow of any turning back.

135. On what follows cf. Hundeshagen, 129.

136. Cf. Kampschulte, II, 290.

137. Hermelink, 161, sees a question of principle — whether church or state should have final ecclesiastical authority — behind the trifling issue of wafers.

The Calvin who was expelled from Geneva in 1538 seemed there to be someone they had done with altogether. But the Calvin who had been expelled and who had to be recalled in 1541 was one they could not do without as things then were. When wrong and hurt have been done to a person, but then it is seen that we cannot do without this person, that we are tied to this person, then the injury that has been done is all the more serious and severe. Without the painful event of the spring of 1538 Calvin would not be the Calvin who later fought and won. That event was the secret accolade that made him invincible. For this reason it will repay us to deal with the trifles that led to the event. Why did it come about that this question of the Bern ceremonies acted at once like leaven in Geneva? What did Bern want in demanding that Geneva accept them? What did Geneva want when at once a majority voted in favor of compliance? And finally, looking at the third actor in the drama, what did Calvin not want when he stubbornly, and ultimately at the cost of his career and work in Geneva, resisted the demand?

Bern View[138] We begin with the first question. Why did the Bern government insist on these trifles? The first answer, if we adopt a theological approach, is undoubtedly that Bern, as we have seen, was then inclining to the Lutheran side. The results of the September synod had far-reaching ramifications along these lines. The catechism of the Zwinglian Kaspar Megander, which had thus far been the standard of instruction throughout the canton, was subjected to a thorough revision by Bucer without Megander's knowledge or consent. Understandably Megander opposed this, and as a consequence he was dismissed by the regime.[139] Heading the clergy in his place were Sebastian Meyer, a native of Bavaria, who was a committed follower of Bucer, and Peter Kunz, a more passionate and coarser man, who had studied for some years at Wittenberg, then made his name as the reformer of his native Simmental in the Bernese Oberland, and come out as a decided Lutheran.[140] It was Kunz who now became normatively responsible for the theological character of Bern's ecclesiastical policy.

When Bern made strenuous efforts to counteract the biblicist purism of Geneva, it was first undoubtedly in an application to externals of the

138. In the MS the heading is in the margin.
139. Hundeshagen, 93-95.
140. Ibid., 69f.

well-known Lutheran conservatism that might also be called liberalism.
Above all no legalism! "Destroy it not, for a blessing is in it!" [Isa. 65:8].
Reverence for what has come into being and is now present! No understanding for the synthesis of OT and NT approaches, of antipagan fervor
and moral earnestness, that characterized the reformation in Geneva. More
instinctively than intellectually, with something of hostile peasant cunning,
Kunz sensed clearly from the very first that Calvin was the adversary they
had to fight in every possible way. During the whole of the Caroli affair
he tenaciously took Caroli's part, different though the two were. Then as
the ecclesiastical leader he began attacking Geneva long before the Bern
authorities determined on any definite steps. It was hardly without his
knowledge that in December 1537 the Bernese areas near Geneva forbade
their pastors to invite the Genevans to their discussions or to attend
discussions in Geneva, or that Farel, who had so many contacts in all
western Switzerland, and who had done so much to promote the Reformation there, was forbidden to preach on Bernese soil. Certainly it was
his doing that pastors who had been admitted or accepted in Geneva were
no longer given free access to the territory of Bern and that pastors who
inclined to Geneva were brought under severe pressure.[141] Calvin complained strongly about this in a letter to Bucer (January 12, 1538) to which
I have referred already. Notorious Anabaptists, known thieves, people
worthy to be hanged on the gallows, were now appointed pastors in Bern
territories, while even the best who had proved themselves in Geneva were
not accepted.[142]

It might well be that what Kunz was doing along these lines was
seen by him as an executing of the Bern caveat at the end of the agreement
on the question of the Trinity. But his opposition to Geneva on that issue
rested simply on the all-consuming hostility of Lutheran theology to this
new and alien body that had arisen in the west after Zwinglianism had
been set aside. Here then, in a narrow section of western Switzerland,
especially in the extreme corner of Vaud where it borders on Geneva, and
in the poor heads of rural pastors who only a short time ago had read
their last mass, the two great waves of Lutheranism and Calvinism broke
upon one another for the first time. We would do much to know more
about what this involved in detail. It is unfortunate at any rate that the
young master in Geneva had no worthy opponent on the other side. The

141. Ibid., 130f.
142. CO 10/II, 141f. (no. 87).

spirit of Kunz did not permit any large-scale engagement. Kunz dragged Calvin into a petty strife of whose meanness we have sad glimpses in more than one letter that Calvin wrote that winter and the following spring.

But the fine eyes of Peter Kunz or even regard for the theology of his teacher Luther were naturally not the only reason for the intervention of Bern in church matters in Geneva. We know that the government of Bern had political plans for Geneva. Reformation in Geneva, indeed, radical reformation, formed part of these plans. Because of the difference in language, Bernese theologians, or theologians from any part of German-speaking Switzerland, could not bring about reformation there. It was a pity, but unavoidable, that the reformers would have to be French. It was intolerable, however, that these Frenchmen should champion, and champion so energetically, a theology and ethics that were as alien to Bern lifestyle and sentiment as Calvin's were; that Geneva should thus experience a different, non-Bernese, strangely abstract, radical, and international type of reformation; that a new and alien world of thought should arise precisely at what was meant to be the key bastion of a revived Burgundian kingdom. It may be that Bern saw in this theology and ethics something that was simply French, and that they feared Calvin and fought him as an emissary of the French spirit and even of French politics.

In February 1538 came another intrigue on the part of Francis I, who himself had not given up his own designs on Geneva, and who had made alliance with some of the citizens of Geneva who, not wholly by accident, were also friends of Calvin.[143] The powerful French immigration (and occupying of clergy positions)[144] was also a factor that had to be dealt with. The equation of Calvin with what was western and of Luther with what was Germanic was already playing a role at that time. It is testimony to the undeniable sharpness of vision of the Bern rulers that on the one hand they treated Calvin with great respect, and sometimes supported him in his position, for example, in his difficulties with the confession, as we saw, and even later, on the occasion of his expulsion from Geneva and recall to it, when they saw that a strong man was indispensable to their own interests; but that on the other hand they did not cease whistling him back, as it were, humiliating him a little, throwing a few rocks in his path,[145] in order that his work in Geneva should not be too

143. Kampschulte, I, 308f.
144. CO 21, 221 (council minutes, 3.15.1538).
145. But cf. the feeble support given by Bern to Farel and Calvin, above 297ff. On

successful after its own Calvinist manner, since, if that were to happen, if a distinct spiritual kingdom were actually to be set up, then the hope of a political unification of Geneva and Bern, and indeed the political assimilation of the newly conquered neighboring Vaud, would be severely jeopardized.

For all its original unpopularity in Geneva, the Genevan view of the church had great revolutionary, missionary, and infectious force. It produced great agitation. The rulers of Bern did not fail to see this. We have here a good example of Christianity being such a real and vital factor in social life that a clever and farsighted government could not be indifferent to the question what kind of Christianity its subjects and even its neighbors were cultivating. It was realized, and feared, that if it were truly different, then something would come of it. It would have political ramifications. It would have to be watched and checked no less than Bolshevism has to be in our day. But for what denomination or trend would a modern state have the same kind of respect as Bern then had for Calvinism? What modern denomination or trend today would the state work to counter?

Bern worked thus against Geneva, as we have seen, by means of the attitude it adopted in the Caroli affair. It then continued its opposition by treating the divergent biblicist ceremonies of the Genevan church as exponents of the Genevan view of the church, and by taking offense at this view as the champion of, shall we say, an antinational or anational view of life and the world that Bern could not use as a suitable basis for its attitude to the state. That Bern did not treat these obvious trifles as trifles, but as symbols which as such had more real significance than many a great and apparently serious controversy, is yet another sign that the Bern rulers had good eyes in their heads.

Geneva View[146]   At a first glance it is much less easy to understand why the Genevans, especially the council newly elected in February 1538, acceded to the Bern demands. With surprising certainty and force, once the question had been put precisely, they decided to yield, that is, to accept the Bern ceremonies.[147] Undoubtedly an explanation in terms of Calvin versus Bern, or Calvinism versus Lutheranism, or solely in terms of Ger-

---

Calvin's expulsion and recall, see below, 368f., 379ff. See also Hundeshagen, chs. 6 and 7 (253ff.), which reflect the tensions between Geneva and Bern, 1549-1559.

146. In the MS the heading is in the margin.

147. CO 21, 223f.; and Kampschulte, I, 310.

many versus France, such as we find indirectly in the recent depiction of Calvin by H. Bauke,[148] will not hold water. This antithesis played a part, no doubt, but if it were decisive, why did not the decision go in favor of the conational Calvin and not in favor of his German Swiss opponents? We should also note how unlikely it really was that a city which had only recently secured its freedom would let itself become entangled with another city, passionately adapting itself to ordinances that came to it from a power that had, of course, just before given it strong support, but of whose selfish purposes, threatening to its own independence, it had undeniable proof? There had to be some strong reason why, against their French nationalism and their civic pride, the Genevans came to the decision they did.

Even when we look at the theological antithesis, we would really have expected that the rigorist standpoint of the preachers in Geneva would have won greater applause than the Lutheran tendency that lay behind the demands of Bern. For rationalistic, if not biblicist, reasons, the radicalism with which Calvin and his party were purging out the papist leaven from every obscure part of the cultus would seem to be more in keeping with the character of the people. In Geneva there could certainly be no question of the Lutheran motives that lay behind what Peter Kunz was doing in Bern.

It has often been suggested[149] that for the council a decision was being made in the battle of the secular against the spiritual power that it was now hoped to win with the help of the Bern demands. Considerations of this kind, which are stupid and muddled vis-à-vis the real situation, might well have motivated some members of the anti-Calvinist trend in Geneva, especially among the most radical of those who had fought for freedom. But I have the impression that we are making too much of them if we see here the real reason for the Genevan attitude. Calvin's theory did give the state an almost incomparable dignity and majesty, and even in practice a conflict between council and clergy could have taken place only insofar as the council did not wish to be left behind by the clergy in zeal for church affairs, and would thus be unwilling to hand over the decision in church practices to a special consistory,[150] a position that on the basis of his concept of church and state, even though he might have serious practical doubts, Calvin could hardly oppose. How could the clergy object

148. Bauke, *Probleme;* cf. 114 n. 44.
149. Kampschulte, I, 306f.
150. See above, 351.

if the secular power proved so willing to undertake the necessary regulating in the spiritual field as well? The *Institutes* had anticipated this.[151] And how could the council object if the clergy commonly and repeatedly claimed its support along these lines? The council had itself asked the clergy to do so, and up to the spring of 1538 it had helped to push through all the proposals of the clergy to the best of its ability.

In my view the conflict of church and state in Geneva was not primary but secondary, just as in the *Institutes* the possibility of revolt against the government is viewed as final and inescapable only when it is seen that God must be obeyed first [Acts 5:29].[152] Conflict between church and state could not arise here primarily or in principle, but only when the chosen representatives on the two sides no longer wanted the same thing as the theory presupposed and as had at first been the practice. Only then, by reason of the different desires of their representatives, could the two factors emerge as warring forces. It was a sign of prudence, if not of distrust, when Calvin asked for a consistory in addition to the council. In case the council were to use its assumed consistorial power in a way that did not suit the church, Calvin wanted to give the church a means by which it could protect its rights within certain limits. The situation was like that of swimmer across the English Channel who for the sake of safety arranges for a boat always to be present at a certain distance.

The demand for a consistory and the refusal of this demand did not cause the break as they would have done if the issue had been that of church and state. The real problem was that the council in a particular matter showed that it was exercising its ecclesiastical function in a way which made it clear that it wanted something different from the clergy. The state as Calvin envisioned it in the *Institutes* would not be in any sense subordinate to the church or the clergy, nor the church ranked above the state. What Calvin had in view was a perfect parallelism of the two forces, both of which had to serve the same end of the glory of God on earth, but with different means, the church with preaching, the state with regulatory measures. Like a lightning flash, it seemed for a moment in the fall of 1536 as though this parallelism had been achieved. But in fact it could only be for a moment in the midst of the reality of secular history in which such miracles usually manifest themselves only to vanish again. Then the question had to arise, not the question of the relation of church

---

151. See above, 209.
152. OS I, 279f.; BI 310f. Cf. also above, 225 with nn. 239f.

and state as such, but the question whether this church and this state really meant the same thing when they were serving God's glory, the one with its preaching, the other with its regulatory measures. Was the council really acting according to the law of God in its decisions, the clergy began to ask more or less clearly in their sermons. And on the other side it was asked whether what the clergy were preaching and demanding was really the law of God. During the whole of 1537 this double question remained latent. The only complaints were that the council was too dilatory, the clergy too zealous, though both basically wanting the same thing.

But when the new council was elected in February 1538 and Calvin's opponents were in a majority, these issues had to become acute, for now it was obvious that the council and the clergy did not understand the same thing by the glory of God. And because there had been no success in 1537 in setting up an emergency church authority with its own special ecclesiastical rights, there was no chance to do this now that the parallelism had broken down. It was not unimportant that the council had a different view of the glory of God from that of the clergy, for the council could now put this different view directly into practice in the field of the church. The question whether God should be obeyed first was thus put. (This issue arose much faster than Calvin could have foreseen at the end of the *Institutes!*) The conflict between church and state had come. But as we have said, it was not primary but secondary, not the cause but the effect of the much deeper conflict between what Calvin really wanted and what the Genevans really wanted.

In this latter conflict of approaches, of viewpoints, of concepts of God's glory, the question of the Bern ceremonies took on symbolical significance just as for Bern itself the ceremonies were the exponent and symbol of its opposition to Calvin's system, which did not fit in with Bern's political calculations. In their own way the Genevans were in the same basic conflict with what Calvin wanted. So long as no issue arose to give living expression to this, the parallelism did not fall apart, though all the signs, as we have seen, pointed to its actual disruption. When the issue arose with the demand of Bern that there should be adaptation to the practices of neighboring churches, the Genevans realized and stated plainly that they wanted something different from what Calvin wanted. They were not ready to be a testing ground for Calvin's theology. They did not want to be different from neighboring communities. They did not want something distinctive of which there was talk all around, with much shaking of the head for the most part. They did not want to have to be the people of God with all the claims that this involved. If not without religion, and indeed in harmony with the basic principles of the Reformation, they simply wanted to live as free citizens as best they could. What Calvin wanted, the parallelism of faith and life, the paradoxical relation of otherworldly truth and this-worldly reality, the understanding of life as a pilgrimage with one's gaze steadily fixed on the heavenly home, a visible holy community of men and women who before God, however, can only confess their total unworthiness, the total anchoring of existence in ground at an infinite depth so that in our little boats on the surface we constantly feel the tug on the chain that holds us fast below — how could the Genevans want all that? What city, village, or hamlet could ever have wanted it? For them serving the glory of God simply meant something much more harmless and much less threatening and demanding, a half-friendly and half-serious commitment to life, not this determination of all life that posed such a threat, made such a claim, and involved such everlasting unsettlement.

We must add, of course, that naturally they did also want what Calvin wanted. How could they wholly escape the force of the truth that spoke to them out of what Calvin wanted? It was no empty self-deception when at first they gladly forced themselves to take the oath that was demanded, nor again when finally in 1541 they recalled Calvin, only to make life more difficult for him than it had been before, yet to go along with him for a considerable stretch on the way. Yes indeed, just as the people of any city or village want in some way that which to their great surprise was then presented to citizens in the form of the Calvinist way of life. Nevertheless, they also did not want it. It was the not wanting that characterized the situation and had come to the fore early in 1538. Being in contradiction,[153] we still have a strong inclination not to want. The individualism of our old nature rises up and prattles about tutelage, bondage, arbitrary rule. Is it totally wrong to do so?

In this reaction did not nemesis lurk for Calvin's overly bold wishes: for the dramatic gesture we have seen, for example, in his daring to demand a confessional oath; for his overly precise knowledge of what was at issue, so precise that it almost seemed to involve forgetfulness; for the severity that is bound up with any overly ethical outlook and position, and that

---

153. "Mensch mit seinem Widerspruch" occurs in the last verse of the poem *Homo sum,* from *Huttens letzte Tage: Eine Dichtung,* by C. F. Meyer. It is also the motto of the whole work.

often, as I said yesterday, leads those who take such a position most strongly far afield from the sphere of true ethics? What Calvin with his ideal of life was setting over against the old nature in Geneva was not the new nature as such and in its purity, nor was it Jesus Christ himself. Let us say it for once, it was Calvin's Christ, but it was also Calvin *himself*, Calvin causing offense. Calvinism is not the gospel pure and simple. Like all isms it stands under the judgment of the gospel. Hence we cannot deny that the not willing of the Genevans was relatively right, and why, indeed, should the actions that the Bern politicians and Lutherans took against Calvin have been contrary to the divine will *(sine numine)?*[154] I am not saying this to excuse them, but simply to make clear that I cannot with confidence one-sidedly condemn those who then thought they had to oppose their no to Calvin. In face of actions of this kind both excusing and blaming can have only limited worth. Better than both is understanding. In the context of the Reformation Calvin's great attempt had to be made as the fiery sign of a possibility that then came within the compass of human willing and achieving, but only at once to show yet again that this is a divine possibility that is impossible for us [cf. Mk. 10:27 par.]. For that reason it was inevitable that there should be the massive opposition that Calvin encountered and that erupted — we are on earth — over a trifling cause.

From the point of view of Geneva, too, the issue was a minor one, a mere conflict about feasts, fonts, wafers, and bridal attire. But in these minor matters the people of Geneva found a way of expressing their not willing. They did not want compulsion, biblical purism, a radical alteration of custom. They saw this refusal plainly exemplified in the matter of the Bern ceremonies. More was being asked of them than of others. Living according to God[155] did not have to mean such a harsh destruction of every bridge as they were experiencing. The few church ceremonies that the Bernese had retained, more conservative and Lutheran as they were than Calvin, became a banner for what the Genevans understood by Christian liberty, namely, the rejection of all that was of the OT, terrifying and all-penetrating. That it was only a matter of opposing Calvin on ceremonies made it easier to offer resistance at this point. If what would have been much more oppressive moral and religious demands had been

---

154. *Sine numine*, constructed on ancient models, is a common expression in Zwingli; cf. his *Sermon on Providence*, ch. 5, Z 4, III, 143, 4-6.

155. CO 21, 199; see above, 257 n. 37.

at issue the opposition would have been much weaker and with a more uneasy conscience. Just because the issue was a trifling one, they hoped for victory. Victory here might lead to victory later in more important matters. The Genevans had as little understanding of the theological motives of the Lutheran Peter Kunz as Calvin himself had, and they would naturally have rejected the underlying political aims of the Bern government. But they could understand and welcome the reaction against Calvin's program as such, and that is why they acted at once without any lengthy consideration of the matter. It was for the same reasons that they had elected an anti-Calvinist council in February 1538, and this council acted according to the wishes of those who elected it when it decided to accede to the demands of Bern.

Calvin's Attitude (Easter 1538 in Geneva) Of most interest, of course, is the third question: What was the inner reason for the attitude of Calvin that the people of both Bern and Geneva opposed? But before we try to answer that question, let us first look simply at the facts. It was on March 11, 1538, that the council in Geneva basically decided to adopt the Bern order, that is, to live according to the Word of God and the ordinances of the rulers of Bern.[156] That was the anti-Calvinist interpretation of the law of God! It was certainly no accident that the following day a letter came from the Bern council politely stating that a synod would be held at Lausanne on March 31 to which Farel and Calvin should be sent.[157] Plainly they were to be sent there only to receive sentence. That this was Bern's intention may be seen from a second letter from the Bern council dated March 20 which states clearly that the business of the synod was to achieve unity on the basis of the Bern ceremonies. The Genevan preachers were invited to attend on the understanding that they would agree. If they were not ready to do so, Bern and Vaud would come to an agreement and then enter later into separate negotiations with Geneva.[158]

On both sides, then, Farel and Calvin faced a fait accompli when at the end of March they went to Lausanne accompanied by one of the negotiating syndics. In Lausanne, to which they had gone only at the command of the council, they held aloof from the real proceedings; and

156. Barth quotes according to n. 1 on letter 101, CO 10/II, 179f.; cf. CO 21, 222.

157. CO 10/II, 178f. (no. 100).

158. Ibid., 179 (no. 101).

when the synod voted to adopt the Bern ceremonies, the theologians of Geneva refused to recognize this result. They stated that they had less against the ceremonies as such than against the way they were forced upon them, and they demanded a reconsideration of the whole issue at a general synod. They unconditionally rejected adoption of the four feasts that Bern was supporting. Thus they returned to Geneva unbowed, but with nothing settled.[159]

Three uneasy weeks now had to follow with both parties resolutely refusing to give ground and both waiting for a chance to make this clear. On April 19 two new letters came from the Bern council to Geneva, the one addressed to the Geneva council communicating the results of the Lausanne synod, and in a friendly way asking that its decisions be observed in Geneva,[160] the other addressed to the preachers with the courteous request that they should accept what had happened, since the two churches were at one in the fundamentals of the faith. What they should now do was proclaim this externally by unity in the ceremonies, thus taking away any reason for calumny on the part of enemies of the gospel. They were asked to consider that the differences were of little significance and that no harm could be done to the truth if the Genevans accepted the articles — a consideration that Bern was obviously inclined to put forward one-sidedly in its own favor. The preachers were also implored to reach agreement and therefore not to wait for the general council that was being planned for Zurich.[161]

Farel and Calvin were next invited to attend a meeting of the council at which these two letters were read to them. It was Good Friday. Easter was at hand. The council made a peremptory demand that the Lord's Supper should then be administered according to the Bern rite. Farel and Calvin replied with a request that the innovation be postponed until Pentecost and that in the meantime they should await a decision by a general synod. They also asked for time to consider, and then withdrew. In their absence the council resolved in any case to forbid the pulpit to the aged Courault. How far this move was directly connected to the Bern issue is not wholly clear. On Sunday Courault had preached from the pulpit that there was no longer any righteousness in Geneva and that what was right was being trodden under foot by the syndics. He had compared Geneva to a state of frogs and called the citizens rats who lived in the

159. Kampschulte, I, 310.
160. CO 10/II, 184f. (no. 106).
161. Ibid., 185 (no. 107).

straw, a wild and unruly horde. He was thus forbidden to preach on pain of imprisonment. At the same time the council decided to stand by its demand that at Easter the Lord's Supper should be administered for the first time with wafers as at Bern. It also seems to have negotiated separately with one pastor who, as would be seen later, did not go along unconditionally with Calvin, Henry de la Mare, trying to arrange that if necessary he would take the place of the others. But this pastor refused, so that in the minutes we read that all three protested, Farel, Calvin, and Henry.[162] Obviously the council was determined but did not know quite what to do. When the bailiff was then sent to Farel and Calvin requesting a definitive answer, the unequivocal response was that they would neither preach nor give communion if the Bern ceremonies were adopted.

Who, then, did preach on the Saturday before Easter and was at once thrown into prison? The aged Courault! The battle had begun. Farel and Calvin, accompanied by all their secular supporters, at once came forward to protest the imprisonment of Courault and to call for the summoning of the Council of Two Hundred. The minutes said of the secular supporters that they had many strong things to say. One of them even declared that their friends would preach regardless, and an angry Farel, recalling his decisive role in the Reformation, went so far as to remind the rulers that without him they would not be sitting there at all! An attempt was made to make clear to the complainants that the arrest of Courault was not related to the eucharistic issue but had taken place because he had held the council in contempt. But the presence of the participants provided an opportunity to ask them again whether they would comply. They replied that they would do nothing but what God ordered them to do. The proceedings closed with a lively discussion whether bail would be accepted for the imprisoned Courault. The request was finally rejected on the ground that Courault was not a citizen of Geneva, and after one of the supporters of the preachers had stated threateningly that there were traitors in the city and that they were well known, the complainants left.[163] Strangely the council thought it advisable to send the bailiff a second time to the preachers with a further demand that they comply, and only when he naturally did not meet with any success did he tell Farel and Calvin that they were forbidden to preach the next day.[164]

162. CO 21, 224.
163. Ibid., 224f.
164. Ibid., 225.

It was a strange Easter Day for the people of Geneva and their pastors in 1538. During the night arquebus shots had again been repeatedly fired in front of Calvin's door and the cry went up through the streets: Into the Rhone with the preachers! a sure sign that the government and the people were at one on this issue. At the last hour the Bernese envoy von Diesbach tried to persuade Calvin to yield. But it was too late. Both sides were now more sharply and intransigeantly determined than could have been intended or foreseen at Bern when the stone had first been set rolling. What had now happened had not, in fact, been what Bern had planned.

When the morning of Easter came, without any flinching, as though there were no official prohibition, as though one part of the *Institutes* had never been written, or rather, as though the last resort for which it finally provided had come, Farel and Calvin went to church with their supporters, prudently armed for the occasion, Calvin to St. Pierre cathedral, Farel to St. Gervais on the right bank of the Rhone. They mounted the pulpits and told the large crowds that assembled that for the time being they would no longer administer the Lord's Supper in Geneva, not out of dislike for the disputed Bern rite, but because the situation in Geneva was obviously such that the sacred mystery could only be profaned and the supper eaten only to judgment. There followed a description of the then state of the city and its inhabitants that must have been extremely colorful, and in conclusion the preachers declared that never and nowhere could they recognize such a people as Christian or cast at their feet the supreme graces of Christianity. Growing murmuring on the part of the assembled congregations greeted this not very Easter message. Finally, the voices of the preachers threatened to be drowned out by the furious clamor, swords were drawn, and it was at the peril of their lives that the preachers had to be escorted back through the inflamed mobs to their own homes.[165]

I have told you already how we are to explain such incidents in Calvin's life. He had a flair for the dramatic. When he wanted or did not want something, he loved to press things to a climax, signifying not merely by words but by meaningful actions what the issue was in a way that was quite unmistakable. We need not be surprised that the less the situation was in keeping with the NT the more forceful was the purpose and the more dramatic the action. That was Calvin.

The council was told what had happened. Its first concern was the

---

165. For this account cf. Kampschulte, I, 312f.; Stähelin, I, 134ff.; CO 10/II, 190 (no. 110) and 205 (no. 121).

remarkable one of making arrangements to replace the Lord's Supper that had not been administered. It decided to hold it the next Sunday. Calvin's outlook had already made such an impact that in the last resort the eucharistic community was now the basis of the civic community. Even without Calvin, or in opposition to him, this basis of the state had to be secured. It was also decided to summon the Council of Two Hundred and the *Conseil général* and to leave any further decisions to them. Finally, Pastor Henry de la Mare, who, it was confidently thought, would not stand by Calvin through thick and thin, was asked to preach in the afternoon. From him, however, the council received the weak answer that Farel and Calvin had forbidden him to do so under pain of excommunication.[166] He did not dare as yet to act as a strikebreaker.

The next day, April 22, the Council of Two Hundred was asked whether it would accept the Bern ceremonies and what should be done about the disobedience of Farel and Calvin. Should they be put in prison? the council asked, obviously uncertain because of the protest in the case of Courault. The Council of Two Hundred resolved to accept the ceremonies and to banish Farel and Calvin.[167] The *Conseil général* agreed the following day but made the sentence of expulsion even more severe by stating that they must leave the city within three days. The bailiff who communicated the decision to the pastors came back with the report that Calvin had replied: "Well and good, if we were serving men, we would be poorly rewarded, but we serve a great Master who will reward us."[168]

The two did not wait for the three days to expire but, no doubt in order to make a demonstration, packed and left at once the same day (April 23). The exalted mood in which they did so finds expression in Calvin's later preface to his commentary on the Psalms (31, 25): "On being violently ejected, I was more joyful than was fitting." Due to his more timorous nature he was not really a match for events of that kind and he viewed the disaster as deliverance from a calling that did not suit him and as permission to retire to a life of private scholarship. Everything points to the fact that his conduct during those days was a kind of outbreak of enthusiasm.

But the rejoicing on the other side was just as great. A popular feast was celebrated, and Farel in particular was exposed to the city's ridicule in

166. CO 21, 225f.
167. Ibid., 226.
168. Ibid., 226f.

a kind of shrovetide masquerade.[169] On April 25 the aged Courault was released from prison and expelled like his colleagues. On the 26th a first hearing took place for the remaining pastors Jacques Bernard and Henry de la Mare. The council asked them whether it was not really according to God *(selon Dieu)* if brides were adorned on their wedding day, and they received the satisfactory answer that it was not against God *(contre Dieu)* but that the way their hair was done was a totally indifferent matter *(tout égal).*[170] The new era of a more moderate Christianity had begun in Geneva.

We are now in a position to put our last question: What did Calvin have in mind when he consciously allowed his work to be wrecked over this question of the Bern ceremonies? In Lang's biography of Calvin (p. 45) I find the judgment that the reformers' attitude in this matter was both stupid and morally dubious, stupid since an unimportant practical issue of this kind was no proper occasion for the battle for great principles that in practical life always have to be brought to recognition in struggles about detailed requirements, and morally dubious because fidelity to principle does not rule out yielding in small and detailed matters.[171] There is some basis for this verdict in that Calvin later did not try to justify his attitude at this time.[172] This was right, for who would not be able to put against it all kinds of question marks regarding its wisdom or moral soundness? Nevertheless, I for my part would not make this kind of judgment. We might well ask whether unimportant practical matters do not often provide in fact the occasion for the battle for great principles, and whether, in so doing, they do not cease to be unimportant. We might also point out that even if fidelity to principle does not rule out yielding in matters of detail, it does not at any rate necessarily include it.

As regards the specific issue, we may also say that the whole question of the Bern ceremonies no doubt seems petty and unimportant to us because we no longer appreciate the power of symbolical thinking. In our thinking forms constantly detach themselves from content, images from things, appearances from essence, and in so doing form a second kingdom of truth that we like to call petty and unimportant. But I regard that not as progress but as a bad sign that we are perhaps approaching, as Spengler

---

169. Kampschulte, I, 313.
170. CO 21, 227.
171. Lang, 192 n. 9.
172. See below, 382 nn. 53f.

would have it, the fellaheen stage of culture that is characterized by insipid abstraction.[173] Calvin and his contemporaries thought in more full-blooded terms.

In trying to look at the conflict from the standpoint of Bern and Geneva, we have noted already that in Calvin's deviation from the Lutheran ceremonies of Bern his opponents had to see signs of a champion of a whole system of life that they found strange and suspect. When the Bern council wrote to Farel and Calvin on April 15, 1538, that the matter was not of such great importance that it would damage the truth if the pastors were to yield, that was an effective rhetorical flourish; materially there stood behind it, however, a consideration that the people of Bern (and not just the Bern theologians) did not relate to their own standpoint.[174] No one ventured to argue this point seriously against Farel and Calvin because no one really thought that it had any cogency. Those who blame them today on the ground that the issue was small and unimportant take their stand on a reason that was then a mere flourish.

For Calvin, in fact, all these forms, without ceasing to be such, or ruling out the freedom that he fully recognized, represented content with an urgency that made it impossible for him to separate the two. How this was so, of course, we can gather only tentatively from his thinking elsewhere. As regards the four feasts, which were the main point at issue, his chief objection was biblical, but apart from that he must have seen the triumphant way in which the Middle Ages were always on the point of going too far toward making weekdays Sundays and the next world this world. Sunday is Sunday and heaven is heaven, and by God's ordinance and command they are set at a fitting distance from us. Anything more comes of evil! [cf. Matt. 5:37]. His insight into the relation between God and the world shows us this. Again, in Calvin's eyes, and from the standpoint of his sacramental teaching, the baptismal font and eucharistic wafers of Bern looked like attempts to detach the matter of the sacrament from the earthly sphere of the sign, to come to the help of faith with direct vision, to weaken the paradox of the presence of the risen Lord by the Spirit with the bridge of things that quicken the imagination, to transform pilgrimage and promise into the bold depiction, however modest, of arrival and possession. Calvin did not want that, nor could he want it. Finally, the strange offense that he took at the Bern wedding adornment that the

173. Barth refers to O. Spengler's *Decline of the West* (New York, 1926), 107ff.
174. See above, 357 and n. 161.

362

ladies of Geneva so much coveted, apart from the rather amusing biblical reason,[175] was surely due, was it not, to his dislike for anything that might be seen as a demonstration of vivacity. Vivacity urgently needed to be disciplined, checked, held back. In no case must it be solemnly affirmed. In no case must it be linked to a religious and ecclesiastical action.

Naturally, different decisions in such matters might well be reached in all good faith, and Calvin himself declared that except on the subject of the feasts he *could* at a pinch yield. But with what wisdom or morality did he *have* to yield? Indeed, we might well ask finally whether he *ought* to yield when the demands of Bern were presented to him so plainly as the expression of a basic outlook that was opposed to his own, when he could see so plainly reasons of principle on his adversaries' side. Mutatis mutandis, was the decision for him so different from that for Luther at Worms even if the fact that it was now a problem of ethics or conduct — those whom it suits may add an "only" here — meant that his gesture could not be such a magnificent one as that of Luther.

We cannot accuse Calvin of mere obstinacy. He was not just insisting on his own will *(sic volo, sic iubeo)*.[176] He constantly insisted that the dispute ought to be settled by a general Swiss synod, that is, on an informed basis achieved by way of dialogue, not by self-will on the other side. In this respect he was unquestionably right. If he was obstinate it was only because he was given no reasons, or only the inadequate reason that he should yield because of a desire for external conformity. In the long run, however, this obstinacy was the proof of a greater freedom than would have been shown by a conciliatory approach. In people who know what they want and have the right to want what they know, conciliatoriness of that kind for no good reason is not usually what wisdom dictates.

But no matter how we look at all that in detail, we certainly cannot view Calvin's attitude in those critical days as a fixed and intrinsically meaningless proof of character. When he said that he served a great Master who would reward him,[177] he did not mean a fad that he was promoting or a system to which, once it was set up, he was feverishly attached, but a well-considered position in a living situation in which, taking into account all that might be said either way, he could not in the long run just as well say yes as no, but finally had to say no in spite of everything.

175. See above, 346f.
176. "Sic volo, sic jubeo; sit pro ratione voluntas," Juvenal *Satire* 6.223.
177. See above, 360 n. 168.

One other thing that we must add is that often in explanation of Calvin's attitude there has been appeal to the struggle for the formal principle of the church's independence of the state. Calvin, it is stated, wanted to show the state plainly that the church would not allow interference of that kind.[178] I cannot accept this explanation. As I argued last time, Calvin's opponents in Geneva, too, were not trying to establish the state's authority over the church. To think that way is to introduce modern issues, I think, into a situation that knew nothing of a dispute of that kind. By his conduct Calvin did indeed offer a dramatic proof of the need for the church's autonomy; but for him, like the authority of the state for his adversaries, this was a secondary issue and not the primary issue, an emergency measure when the parallelism of church and state that he envisioned in the *Institutes* was painfully denied. It would not have occurred to Calvin to violate the majesty of the state even in matters of church policy, which included the ceremonies. Later, indeed, he showed that for him even the subtle questions involved in the doctrines of predestination and the Trinity were matters for the state as well as the church, to be referred to the council as well as the consistory.

If a conflict could arise between church and state, it was not because one or the other was going beyond its competence. What external affairs in Geneva were not within the competence of the church, what internal affairs were not within that of the state? The eucharistic community there constituted the civic community, and the civic community had to remind itself again and again that from the very first it was the eucharistic community. If conflict arose, it could be only because representatives of the one party or the other lost sight of the common orientation. That in a given case this would be the civic community, the representatives of the state, was naturally the determinative insight for Calvin. But he did not make of this insight, in a kind of papal whim, an a priori normative one, as is alleged against him. Instead, when serious controversies arose, as in the cases of Bolsec and Servetus,[179] he urged that before deciding opinions should be sought from

---

178. Lang, 45; and see above, 351 n. 149.

179. The physician Hieronymys Bolsec (died ca. 1584/5) publicly criticized Calvin's doctrine of predestination and after debating with Calvin was expelled from Geneva in 1551. The magistrates sought the views of other Swiss churches during the course of the trial. Michael Servetus (1511?-1553) was prosecuted at Calvin's request on account of his antitrinitarian views. Opinions were sought from the other Protestant cantons. He was burned for heresy in 1553. Melanchthon expressly approved of the city's action in a letter to Calvin, CO 14, 268f.

other Reformed and even Lutheran spiritual and secular bodies. He appealed neither to his own intellect nor to his own exposition of scripture, but to the consensus of mind and exposition in Geneva on the one side and in Basel, Bern, Zurich, Strassburg, and even at times Wittenberg on the other, and always on the assumption that he would find in these places not only a church but also a state serving the same ends as the church.

In this first and most severe of all his conflicts he called for a general synod that would be an organ for the participating states as well as churches. His call meant that now that the parallelism between one church and state had been fatally disrupted restoration could be achieved by means of the intact parallelism of all the churches and all the states. It was not Calvin who acted violently and arbitrarily but the people of Bern and Geneva when they did not follow up this call, and in this regard the Genevans heedlessly went much further than Bern (and would be at once disowned by the latter, as we shall see) by thinking they could unilaterally restore the broken parallelism by simply expelling the obstinate preachers and sending them packing when they did not yield as Bern had obviously hoped they finally would.

On Bern's view the council should no more enforce its own will than should Calvin. The prohibiting of the pastors from preaching was already an infringement, and Calvin and Farel were right not to dispense the Eucharist in either the Bern form or their own, but to withhold it, even if they did this provocatively. The situation that arose when the council banished those who resisted it and put strikebreakers in their place was from the outset an untenable one, for a church on this basis could not be regarded as a complete church by the other churches, nor was it thus regarded, so that the council had to reap what it had itself sown. It could not evade the consequences. Desperate though everything must have seemed at first, the rehabilitation of Calvin was from the very first inevitable unless the consensus of the national Protestant communities, which found such arbitrary actions intolerable, was to be totally rejected.

§16 April to September 1538[1]

Let us go back to what took place. Our theme is the period between Calvin's expulsion from Geneva and his arrival in Strassburg. Naturally the enthusi-

---

1. In the MS the heading is in the margin.

asm with which the reformers and the Genevans parted company was only one side of the matter. The other side was that the reformers had lost a battle. Calvin, who had a better view of things, understandably was the first to see that they could not leave it at that. First of all then, and more painfully than his opponents, he had to discover that it is easier to run a ship aground than to refloat it. He tells us in the commentary on the Psalms that he returned to his private studies with joy when he turned his back on Geneva.[2] Nevertheless, the broadly undertaken reformation of the faith and life of fifteen thousand people that he had initiated in Geneva, and that for the time being had been brought to a halt, had become so much a part of his own being, at least as much a part of him as his academic achievements and plans for the future, that he could not simply break free from it when he shook off from his feet the dust of this city that was so hard of hearing. Perhaps he thought of what he was now doing as a kind of mopping up and concluding of what lay in the past, but at any rate his next steps were not at all directed to the finding of a place somewhere to study, but rather, astonishingly enough, to the opening again of the gates of Geneva, which he had just left so dramatically and with such satisfaction.

Calvin in Bern[3]

He and Farel went — who would have expected it? — directly to the place which had set the stone rolling that caused the landslide, namely, to Bern. Here again we have proof of Calvin's sure political instinct. The rulers and pastors of Bern were not his friends. He knew that, as we have seen. But he guessed rightly that the way things had turned out could not be what Bern had planned or wanted if it had any grasp of the situation at all. If he, Calvin, aroused no sympathy in Bern due to what was seen there simply as his restless French radicalism, in the eyes of the people of Bern his adversaries had shown themselves equally at fault by their turbulent proceedings. No matter what ecclesiastical aims the people of Bern might have, they certainly could have no liking for crude and one-sided swing movements, and what one might expect from them would be an attempt to restore the equilibrium that had been disturbed. The Protestant cause in Geneva, where it was still so new, had clearly been severely compromised

2. CO 31, 26.
3. In the MS the heading is in the margin.

by the ejection of the reformers, and it was now under threat again from Roman Catholicism. But on this cause, even though they would have preferred that it be prosecuted along different lines from those adopted by Calvin, there hung the interests of Bern in Vaud, and again the political status of Bern in the west, which was by no means finally secure against either France or Savoy, quite apart from the rather far-ranging plans that might well have been in the minds of the imperialists of Bern. Hence Calvin's strange plan of appealing to Bern for help was in the first instance the most perspicacious, even though things might finally turn out a little differently from what he had thought.

Immediately after their arrival in Bern Farel and Calvin presented a written complaint to the council there (*Briefe*, 110).[4] In this complaint we see signs of the feverish indignation that they felt after the experiences of the past few days. They first complained of the imprisonment and treatment of the aged Courault. Then they tackled the charge made against them that they had acted like rebels and were opponents of ecclesiastical conformity with Bern. Both charges were false. They had never simply rejected this conformity but had merely insisted that consideration must be given to the way in which to achieve a true upbuilding of the church. An unworthy compromise had been proposed to them that involved the deposing of their colleague Courault in exchange for the council's leaving the issue of the ceremonies to the synod. This would have meant for them acting against an express command of scripture, and conflict had thus ensued. According to their explicit declaration from the pulpits, their refusal to give communion was not because the Bern rite was to be used but because administering the mystery would have profaned it in view of the obvious moral and religious state of the city at the time. The Geneva council had never given them the chance to present their reasons either to it, to the Council of Two Hundred, or to the people; it had simply passed resolutions and acted. The council's aim was not to establish the Bern ceremonies but to expel the preachers.

The Geneva council would later complain that this document of the preachers contains many lies.[5] It may well be that in matters of detail (Courault? hatred?)[6] there are exaggerations and omissions. But in spite

---

4. CO 10/II, 188-90.

5. Ibid., 194f. (no. 113), dated 4.30.1538. The letter charges that what Farel and Calvin have said in their complaint is *contre vérité*.

6. The word given here as "hate" is hard to decipher. If correct, Barth must have had in mind CO 10/II, 189f. (no. 110).

of the fact that they were so incensed they were right in the main. On both sides the issue of the ceremonies was only the occasion for bringing to light more deep-seated differences.

I must now lead you through a period in Calvin's life that was very active but that has little to offer the student by way of reward. One reason for this was that in keeping with the situation Calvin was less concerned with the future planning and promoting of his cause than with looking back at himself. It must have surprised Geneva when even before a week had passed after the ousting of the pastors a letter came from the Bern council that against all expectation, if it did not strenuously favor the banished preachers, did in fact criticize the attitude of Geneva. A copy of the complaint that Farel and Calvin had made the previous day was enclosed. The letter made three decisive points (*Briefe*, 109).[7] Bern states (1) that the whole process of expelling the preachers was a scandal and detrimental to the Christian religion (referring, of course, to the Protestant cause in the west); (2) that Bern's demand in the matter of the ceremonies has been meant as an affectionate recommendation (*de bonne affection*) and not as an attempt to use force and pressure in things in which there has to be liberty (Bern had in fact categorical desires about how this liberty was to be exercised, and at the time of the banishment the envoy in Geneva, von Diesbach, had surprisingly taken no steps to tell the Genevans that they were misinterpreting what Bern wanted, though they were not then so exposed as not to be able honorably to retreat); and (3) that Bern found very disorderly and displeasing the harsh way in which Geneva had dealt with the preachers. Bern acted just as Calvin had expected. It took into account the fatal consequences abroad of what had been done, it adopted a broad view of the theological aspect, which meant disapproval of the lack of perspicacity in Geneva, and it strongly disliked the unruliness that the Genevans had displayed. The letter made no demands except that poor blind Courault be released from prison, and, as we know, this had already been done. Bern also requested that it be given the pleasure of seeing its points considered. Calvin could be well content with this result. It had now been insisted, as he expected, that there be a radical cooling down in Geneva.

Both Calvin and the Bern council were mistaken, however, if they thought that would happen. The letter certainly created astonishment in Geneva, for it was not what was expected, but it quickly became apparent

7. CO 10/II, 187f.

that compliance with the wishes of Bern had not by a long way been the driving force behind the ousting of the preachers. The reply from the Geneva council, written at once the day the letter from Bern was received (April 30), is characterized above all by a total and by no means unintentional failure to understand what Bern was trying to do (*Briefe*, 113).[8] The reply does not go into the precise points made by Bern but acts as though it were a matter of refuting Calvin's complaint; as though the fact of the violent breach between the council and the preachers were not the matter on which Bern wished to guide further reflection in Geneva; as though the concern of Bern were to make sure that the Lord's Supper would now be administered according to the Bern rite and that there was a determination to live according to the Bern ceremonies. The main content of the reply, namely, a vivid description of the obstinacy with which Farel and Calvin had simply refused to accept the Bern ceremonies even though they had been lovingly *(charitablement)* asked to do so once, twice, three times, and more,[9] completely misses the point because it forgot to answer Calvin's charge that the preachers had been confronted with a fait accompli, to which they should say either yes or no, with no chance at all to state their case or to appeal to the synod. This omission can hardly be due to bungling or misunderstanding, for the Bern letter and Calvin's complaint were written in good French and were clear enough. Geneva was clearly bent on going its own way either with or without Bern. Its will was stronger than the rulers of Bern had assumed. It had now to be seen whether these rulers were prepared to take further statesmanlike actions in the matter.

Zurich Synod, 4.28.1538[10]

For the time being the reply from Geneva was tabled. The court had primarily to be allowed to speak for whose decision Calvin had again and again appealed in Geneva, that is, the Swiss synod, which had assembled in Zurich on April 28. Once this decision had been reached specific demands could be made of Geneva that Bern had not made in its first letter. The complicated interplay of individual and general church and state authorities made this necessary. The synod, which was composed of

8. Ibid., 194f.
9. Ibid., 194.
10. In the MS the heading is in the margin.

both spiritual and secular delegates, had met in the presence of Bucer and Capito once again to discuss an answer to an extremely friendly and hopeful letter that Luther had sent to the Reformed Swiss cantons on the matter of the Concordat.[11] Once that was dealt with the Geneva affair was taken up.

Two documents in particular give us information about the proceedings (*Briefe,* 111f.).[12] First we have the fourteen articles in which Calvin stated his position, then we have the part of the minutes of the synod that states the position of the German Swiss churches. In the articles Calvin lists — I do not know what we should call them, whether the concessions he is inclined to make or the conditions he must insist on if he is to have any further part in the reformation in Geneva. The articles are a remarkable testimony to his complete inner constancy at that time. In spite of the external humiliations that it involved, the disaster had had no real effect on him inwardly. He speaks with the same considered but unhesitating singleness of mind and sense of purpose, with the same willingness to yield wherever he would and could, but also the same readiness to gain his way by hook or by crook where he would not and could not, as he had already shown before every court in the Caroli affair and as he had also shown in this conflict from the very first. Not incorrectly Kampschulte (316)[13] thinks that the articles must have aroused strange feelings in the assembly. What he was demanding after his defeat was more, he says, than the spiritual authority in any of the Swiss churches could give. At that time and later they could back Calvin, but they could not give him the help he wanted and expected until finally he knew best how in some way to help himself. In any case, there was no way to cause him any confusion as to what he thought he had to desire. He desired it the most strongly when he saw that he could least count on any help. But let us look more closely at these articles that lay at the heart of the discussion at the Zurich synod and that would also play an important role after it.

In article 1 Calvin declared himself ready to yield in the matter of the font if there were no other changes in the rite of baptism, that is, if it were to be administered during public worship and proper instruction on its significance were to be given each time from the pulpit. In my view, Calvin yields in order to stress the more forcefully in another way

11. WA B 8, 149-53, no. 3191, dated 12.1.1537.
12. CO 10/II, 190-93.
13. Kampschulte, vol. I.

the opposition to sacramentalism that really lay behind his initial obstinacy.

In article 2 he accepts the wafer required by Bern but adds that he does so on the condition that Bern will accept the Genevan custom of breaking the bread. Again, while on the one side apparently abandoning his antisacramentalism, on the other side he underlines the more forcefully his familiar understanding of the Lord's Supper as a proclamation of the death of Christ that awakens and strengthens faith.

In article 3 he again yields a little regarding the four feasts. So be it, we will accept them, but those who wish to do so must be free to work as on a working day after hearing the sermon. It seems to me, then, that the command to work six days [Exod. 20:9] remains unbroken but that four of these working days each year begin with a festal sermon, after which individuals may work or not work as seems best to them.

Article 4 deals with the way in which the concessions are to be made. Through its envoys Bern must state that the customs in use in Geneva are not in the least displeasing to it and that it does not wish to see any change in them that might not be in accordance with biblical purity, but that its sole concern is for the unity and concord that might be better achieved with a uniformity of rite. The preachers for their part are to preach on the freedom of ceremonies but then to give detailed reasons to the people for accepting uniformity. The church must be allowed its full freedom of judgment. With good reasons the state may express its own desires, but must not seek to overthrow that freedom. In the freedom that is retained for it, the church on its own judgment will accept the state's desires when good reasons are advanced for them. Once again we have a masterly combination of concession and firmness.

Article 5 is typical of Calvin. It was an intolerable act of "barbarism and inhumanity" that in Geneva they were not given the chance to explain and justify their attitude. As a result they are now covered with opprobrium. Calvin could never tolerate having what he regarded as calumny heaped upon him without replying. He had an almost demonic need to explain and justify himself. He would usually track down any accusation that was made against him until he had dug it out by the roots. It was this need that brought such monstrous expansion to the later *Institutes* and that made it a book we find hard to enjoy in many passages. What can we say about this need? We are confronted here by a strange phenomenon of his nature that primarily defies explanation. We suspect perhaps that between this need and the need to proclaim as loudly and consistently[14] as possible the total unworthiness and culpability of humanity there is some odd relationship of complementarity that we cannot explain in *purely* psychological terms. Here, then, was the first condition of a return to his charge at Geneva. He had to have the opportunity of saying all that he was unable to say before the break because he was not permitted to do so.

Article 6 shows more plainly than those that precede that Calvin's mood was more one of offense than defense. If he was to go back to Geneva, then the discipline — the greatest rock of offense, as we know, that he had put in the way of the Genevans — had to be confirmed. If it were not, then all that had been achieved would be lost. He undoubtedly had in mind more than he was as yet prepared to say. What was absolutely essential was stated next.

According to article 7 the city must be divided into parishes, pastoral districts that would be assigned to the individual pastors. Article 8 then called for more pastors to match the population. Article 9 demanded a consistory to deal properly with excommunication. Article 10 dealt with the ecclesiastical institution of pastors by the laying on of hands and the need not to replace this totally by secular induction. (We see here provisions made for the emergency situation that experiences had already shown to be possible.) Article 11 asked Bern for its part to adjust to Calvin's Geneva in the two points raised in the next two articles: in more frequent communion (article 12), at least once a month if the custom of the early church could not be restored, and in the singing of the Psalms at worship (article 13). Finally (article 14), certain obscene songs and their tunes were to be forbidden so that in this matter the people of Geneva could no longer appeal to the liberty enjoyed at Bern.

In evaluating these articles note that although they are an appeal to the Swiss synod they are really a program that had been tested only in a few points in Geneva itself and that would be in the main points an unheard-of innovation in the places represented at Zurich. The situation was obviously this, that after Calvin's expulsion, although no one had spoken of restoring him to Geneva, the synod had to decide whether something should be done along these lines. He himself acts as though his return were a foregone conclusion. He would in fact return, and it was only a matter of fixing the conditions on both sides. His position is subject to criticism at Geneva but first and foremost at Bern, and whether anything

14. Editorial emendation: The MS read *anderen, nicht laut und beharrlich genug.*

can be done for him obviously depends finally on whether and how far he can and will yield. But he for his part seeks above all to make a defense, and in reality it is only incidentally that he refers to his concessions, and not without at once making his counterdemands, proposing once again a consistory and monthly communion that Geneva had either tacitly or openly rejected, and finally putting to Bern four demands exactly equal in number to Bern's own demands: breaking the eucharistic bread, monthly communion, singing of the Psalms, and the forbidding of immoral songs. Truly a most unusual course of events! We can really explain it only if we assume that Calvin was aiming in part to secure his return to Geneva in this way, but chiefly that he wanted to set up a sign again, that he wanted to give a demonstration of himself and his whole idea, even at the risk of setting himself in a strange light and achieving nothing, as did in fact happen in the first instance.

The impression he made on the German Swiss is best summed up in what their leader Bullinger said a few days later in a letter to von Wattenwil of Bern in which he was commending the cause of Farel and Calvin to him: "They are overzealous, but they are holy and learned men and much, I think, should be given them" (*Briefe,* 114).[15] This evaluation of the two zealots could clearly be reversed: They are holy and learned men, but overzealous! Nor is it wholly clear which way the synod read the judgment. So far as we can tell, they read it for the most part in the second way. The minutes strikingly do not go along at all with the fourteen articles. They state that as a result of the division and unrest the church at "Jhännf" (Geneva) is in danger of perishing. The pastors had perhaps been too strict and the churches are now despoiled. We must have sympathy both with the pastors and with the church and in Christian love see to it that good-hearted Christians are not left destitute. Whether or not the pastors were formerly at fault or too strict, they were now ready to be directed.[16]

The minutes report all this as coming from Calvin and Farel. I cannot think that they did in fact talk that way. What we find there is obviously the view that the synod majority took of the matter and communicated to them. The statement is in too little keeping with what we know authentically of Calvin's position at the time from the fourteen articles. And it fits in too well with the discussions and decisions of the synod itself. It was not only a matter of the church and preachers, the majority

---

15. CO 10/II, 195 (5.4.1538).
16. Ibid., 193 (no. 112).

said, but of many other good-hearted people in Geneva who might profit from these excellent men. It was thus resolved that a friendly recommendation be made to the council at Geneva that it have patience with them, and that Bern be requested to send envoys to Geneva to urge this, and above all to make excuse for any errors on the part of the preachers, since the synod was convinced that their desire was to promote good Christian things. The synod also resolved that some of its own delegates should earnestly counsel the preachers to restrain their in some sense unfitting severity and cultivate Christian gentleness among this people that was as yet unedified.[17]

All that sounds amicable and clearly expresses the intention of actually restoring the preachers to Geneva. But in no circumstances did Calvin himself think of going back there half-justified, but also in humility half-confessing his faults. The findings were more an instrument of peace than a real account of the way in which peace could be achieved. The actual proceedings seem to have involved an effort to console and praise the two pastors on the one side but to tell them on the other that they must be more gentle. They, too, had made mistakes and were thus in part responsible for the disaster. Calvin can hardly have heard all these mild pronouncements without the most vigorous inward protest. How differently, of course, the situation can be interpreted may be seen from the fact that Kampschulte, correctly, I believe, at this point, writes that Farel and Calvin went back to Bern discontented, their hopes having been dashed (316), whereas Stähelin can say on the basis of the same material that with glad and thankful hearts the two preachers left the assembly with this decision and returned to Bern (160).[18] In any case, and at the latest at Bern, it must have become wholly clear to them that their situation was not good, that the fourteen articles in particular had not improved the opinion that the German Swiss had of them, and that Calvin had erred when he thought that on this occasion the German Swiss could perhaps endorse his wrathful enthusiasm (read *Briefe*, 121 = 22 in Schwarz).[19]

17. Ibid.
18. Kampschulte, vol. I; Stähelin, vol. I.
19. CO 10/II, 202ff.; R. Schwarz, *Johannes Calvins Lebenswerk in seinen Briefen*, vol. I (Tübingen, 1909), 35ff. (new ed. Neukirchen, 1961, 70ff.).

Summer 1538

The man they now had to learn to know in Bern was Peter Kunz of Simmenthal. From the letters of Calvin and Farel we see that Kunz must have played the part of a truly furious Roland. Calvin tells us how, when they came to Bern, they were exposed to his downright crudities, insults, complaints, and outbreaks of anger, so that the other pastors and finally the council had at last to protect them almost bodily from his wildness. Especially dramatic is the account of a visit to Kunz in his manse at which they were kept waiting in an antechamber for almost two hours because the pastors were at work on ecclesiastical court matters, and then they were given a most unfriendly and ultimately stormy reception.[20]

From all this we gather that in these tense moments a confrontation took place between two men of different races, the one from Noyon in Picardy, the other from the valley between the Stockhorn and Niesen. It is most unlikely that either of them could think quietly or rightly about the way they each expressed themselves. One thing at least is certain, namely, that on the basis of what he had learned at Zurich Kunz was quietly and firmly resolved for his part to oppose to the hilt all that Calvin was wanting and trying to achieve, and that on their return to Bern, even when Geneva was ready to put into effect the Zurich resolutions, he set out at once very openly to do this. What Calvin saw as fury was more an obstinate tenacity that almost drove Calvin and the like-minded Farel to despair. Kunz seems to have complained to the Genevans that with their reckless striving for innovation they were disturbing the German Swiss churches that had hitherto been so peaceful. He saw intolerable cunning in the fact that the articles were full of exceptions. The synod at Zurich had not approved of these articles in any sense.[21] All such opinions were undoubtedly more than Calvin and Farel could find justified or accept. Sebastian Meyer, the other leading Lutheran in Bern, also held visibly aloof from the Genevans; and Erasmus Ritter, the one Zwinglian who remained after Megander's departure, did not have enough influence to give them effective support. Finally, they had to find that the council was formally demanding that they renounce the fourteen articles and accept the fact that steps would be taken to restore them to Geneva only if they would unconditionally accept conformity.[22]

20. CO 10/II, 203f.; Schwarz, 36 (71).
21. CO 10/II, 204.
22. Ibid., 205f.; Schwarz, 37 (73).

It is one of the riddles of Calvin's life and character that in May 1538 he clung so tenaciously to the idea of a return to the Geneva that he had left so dramatically, but that then only a little while later he took up again his first view of the expulsion and consoled himself with the thought that things were best as they were, and that he neither wanted to return nor should do so. Remember his strong statement: "Well and good!" when the council bailiff came to tell him of his ejection.[23] Remember his description of his mood that day as one of more joy than was seemly.[24] That was on April 23. But on May 20, at the conclusion of negotiations with the Bern council, he wrote that it seemed better to them to agree to any conditions rather than leave unexplored any way to further the cause of the church (*Briefe*, 119).[25] Then two months later on July 10 he wrote to Louis du Tillet that as it was a divine vocation that had kept him there and consoled him, so now he felt that he would be tempting God if he were to take up again a burden that he had found to be too heavy (*Briefe*, 127).[26]

What did he really want, we might ask, when we see how energetically and even with an appeal to the supreme court he now took the one view of the matter and now the other, and always in a way that makes it hard for onlookers to follow him or to see why it has now to be the one way and now the other. We are perhaps forced up against Calvin's concept of God if we are to explain, even if we cannot answer, the psychological question. In the later editions of the *Institutes,* in remarkable parallelism with Thomas Aquinas, Calvin developed the distinctive theory that divine providence constantly uses second causes, including the human will, to achieve its ends.[27] Though he avoided mechanistic thinking, Calvin viewed the decisions of the will, whether his own or that of others, as guided, driven, and motivated by God, to whom we must constantly pay inner heed and whom we must always be ready to follow, so that we do not so much as lift a finger without a nod from him (Rom. 14 [v. 5]).[28] Ideas of this kind — and his actual conduct both here and in many other cases was in keeping with them — show us that Calvin was not so strictly doctrinaire as we often like to depict him, but that in daily life he would

23. CO 21, 226; see above, 360 n. 168.
24. CO 31, 25; see above, 360.
25. CO 10/II, 201, to Bullinger.
26. Ibid., 221.
27. *Inst.* I, 17, 9; OS III, 213; cf. *S. Th.* I, qu. 22 a. 3 i.c.
28. CO 49, 259f. *(Romans Commentary)*.

constantly decide and act in accordance with the situation, which included his own shall we say volatile disposition, naturally within definite ethical limits, yet in detail with an extraordinary and incalculable freedom that we today — who knows? — might regard as romantic caprice, but that for him had the significance of supreme divine necessity. We may perhaps think here of the Socratic daemon[29] that stands in a similar half-light. We do not have here a solution to the riddle but a pointer to the direction in which to look if we are not content to remain standing blindly before the facts as such.

We were describing those days in the middle of May 1538 when Calvin's desire and will was still to go back to Geneva. The reason that he gave was always the welfare of the church, which he regarded as imperiled by the disorderly interruption of his tenure and the resultant situation. Better do and accept anything than let devout people be able to think we were to blame if things were not put right, he once wrote.[30] It seems that he was not the only one to expect his restoration on the basis of the decisions at Zurich. A letter from Capito to Vadian (*Briefe,* 115) contains the noteworthy report that no less a figure than Martin Bucer of Strassburg had a mind to go personally to Geneva to reinstate Farel and Calvin.[31] Could this man who was so skilled a negotiator have succeeded in doing what even the powerful voice of Bern later failed to do? In fact the journey never took place. During the same period we have a letter from Grynaeus of Basel to Calvin and Farel (*Briefe,* 116) in which he seems to have thought that their return was certain, and with the gentle Christian friendliness that Basel in particular was showing to these friends who had come to grief in Geneva, he urged them to overcome all their adversaries with Christian mildness and humility and to take away from them any opportunity of blaspheming the gospel. The letter, which has this admonitory tone throughout, closes with the reminder how great a service it will be, and how true and solid will be their renown, if they can look only to Christ and totally forget themselves in this cause[32] — a most appropriate wish at a time when both of them were very preoccupied with themselves and the rightness of what they had done.

They would not be given, however, the chance to act along such

---

29. Plato *Apologia* 31d; *Phaedr.* 242b + c.
30. CO 10/II, 205 (no. 121).
31. Ibid., 196.
32. Ibid., 197.

lines. As we have seen, the theologians of Bern treated them badly when they asked for support in carrying out the decisions of Zurich. They had better success with the council, which did not have the theological and personal objections against them that alienated a Peter Kunz, but had good political reasons for trying to do as they desired. The result of negotiations with this body was the appointment of envoys to go back with them to Geneva and to see to their reinstatement into office. If Calvin's eagerness to return is puzzling,[33] no less astonishing is the diligence and civility with which the Bern council now acted. It went so far as to abandon its objection to the fourteen more than audacious articles that Calvin had presented as peace proposals at Zurich. The envoys were to put these before the Geneva council in the presence of Calvin and Farel, who would thus have a chance to explain them.

Did the council really read and understand them properly? When we consider that on account of them the furious controversy with Kunz had arisen, and that later everything would founder in Geneva because of them, we may well doubt this. Or was it that Bern knew the mood in Geneva so poorly that it seriously thought it could offer the city this solution? Hundeshagen (139) and Staehelin (161)[34] write that the Bern government was denying itself at this point. I myself would hardly venture to say that; I suspect that Bern for its part had reason to evaluate the political peril in which Geneva then stood in a way that we cannot, and yet at the same time had illusions about the significance of the articles and the mood at Geneva that would quickly avenge themselves. At one point the council refused to give ground. It demanded that the two should return on the tacit understanding that the Bern ceremonies should be definitively adopted. Calvin wanted an authoritative resolution on the matter, since conformity had been violently imposed by the very people who had been as yet only ready to throw the preachers in the Rhone. Yielding here was obviously the extreme condition to which Calvin alludes in several letters.[35] On this occasion he had no cause for complaint against the Bern politicians. The more surprising, then, was the blow that was finally received and the lesson that the help that Bern was ready to give had its limits.

The party left Bern on May 18. Erasmus Ritter, the last Bern Zwing-

---

33. Barth has *Zurückkehrte,* a possible slip for *Zurückstrebte.*

34. Stähelin, vol. I.

35. See n. 30 above; also CO 10/II, 201 (no. 119).

lian, who was well disposed to Calvin and was to act as the theological expert, went with Farel and Calvin, to be joined by Viret at Lausanne, and accompanied also by Hans Huber and Hans Ludwig Ammann as secular delegates from Bern. Directly before starting Calvin wrote to Bullinger: "We are now setting out on our way, may Christ prosper us. For we look to him in taking this path and lay the outcome in his hands."[36] Originally the Bern council had prudently arranged that the preachers should go only as far as the fourth milestone before the city, let the envoys go ahead to negotiate with Geneva, and wait until they came back to conduct them in. Calvin, however, had called this shameful "deprecation," and at his urgent desire the program was changed. The envoys would lead them at once to the city and arrange an opportunity for them to speak (we remember how important this was for Calvin), so that when they had explained matters and been found without fault, and Calvin took this for granted, they would be reinstated.[37]

Things did not go at all as planned, however, for one of Calvin's main foes in Geneva, Peter Vandel, who was often in Bern, had been there and secured secretly a copy of the fourteen articles. Calvin definitely asserted that it was the Bern pastor Peter Kunz who gave them to him. If that was so, it was a perfidious act on the part of this man from the Bernese Oberland. At any rate Vandel was right when he openly boasted that he carried "mortal poison" for the preachers in his pocket and that he did not fear in the least the arrival of the envoys from Bern.[38] He must have succeeded by his talk in fixing the mood in advance. When the company was still a mile away from the city on May 22 a messenger from the council met them with the strict order that they should not bring Farel and Calvin in with them until the city had decided what to do. In this way scandal could be averted.[39] The two wanted to defy the order but were finally persuaded by the others to stay behind and await the result of their mission. Calvin later maintained that this decision saved their lives, since there had been an ambush close to the city gate and twenty gladiators were stationed at it.[40] It is not impossible that

36. CO 10/II, 201 (no. 119). Barth's date for this letter is wrong (it should be May 20); he was perhaps following Kampschulte, I, 317, though he (later?) corrected the error in his copy of Kampschulte.

37. Ibid., 205f. (no. 121).

38. Ibid., 207 (no. 121).

39. The MS has *und* here.

40. CO 10/II, 206 (no. 121).

in this regard an excited imagination depicted the situation as much worse than it really was.

Active negotiations now took place between the envoys and the council, the Council of Two Hundred, and finally the *Conseil général*. The climax came in a meeting with the *Conseil général* on May 26. It would seem that here Ammann and Viret in particular made some impression by what they said in favor of the ousted pastors on the basis of the Zurich decisions. But then Peter Vandel's mortal poison was injected into the discussion. He drew the fourteen articles, which thus far the envoys had wisely left unmentioned, out of his pocket and read them publicly, arousing great ill-will. There were many outcries as he read, all kinds of spiteful comments were made on the individual points, the church discipline was called a tyranny, and some said they would rather die than have to listen to the speech of self-justification by Calvin that was being sought.[41] When the envoys had been brought back in again and a vote was taken in their presence, it was seen that an impressive majority of the people favored upholding the expulsion. It was in vain that one zealous supporter of Calvin, as the minutes tell us, held up both hands in his favor. He and those like-minded with him were in a negligible minority. When the envoys saw this, they said they would tell their rulers and masters and asked that what they had tried to accomplish should not be held against them, since their rulers and masters had only sought to do what was best for an allied city. They were then thanked.[42] That was the end of the matter. The envoys had no instructions to do more and they thus left. Noisy festivities marked the final winning of the victory.[43] All the reformers could now do was to go back to where they had come from, to Bern. It seems that Calvin was offered a pastorate there. One has to ask again how things might have turned out if he had grasped this opportunity. But this time he had no mind to agree to coming under the leadership of Peter Kunz. He made use of a pretext, viewed by him as coming from the Lord, to leave Bern, and even to do so without saying farewell to the council.[44]

Provisionally the two went first to Basel. On the way by horse they had to cross the swollen Aare and were nearly drowned. But, said Calvin, they received more mercy from this river than from their own people. For the latter

41. Ibid.
42. Ibid., 231.
43. Stähelin, I, 162.
44. See n. 45 below; also Stähelin, I, 163.

wanted to destroy them contrary to all right and justice, but the river had to obey the grace of God to their deliverance. Very wet and tired they arrived at Basel.[45] From this city, where they were welcomed by Grynaeus, Calvin sent in both their names the detailed letter to the Zurich clergy to which we owe the most thorough account of this whole episode, including a dramatic description of Peter Kunz and a terrible portrait of the three pastors who succeeded them in Geneva.[46] If we want to study Calvin's creatureliness, we should read this letter. After seven weeks Farel went to Neuenburg (Neuchâtel), where he would find his definitive sphere of work. (The aged Courault had become the pastor of Orbe, but died in the fall of this year.) The joint life of the two such different friends had thus come to an end, and from more than one passage in letters we learn that their other friends were glad of this, for they were convinced that the two sharpened and spurred on one another, and plunged one another into ill-considered actions.[47] Indeed, it is perhaps no accident that from this point onward more calm and stability came into Calvin's life. But by means of letters and reciprocal visits the friendship remained as strong as ever right up to Calvin's death.

A letter of August 4 mentions for the first time an invitation that Bucer sent to Calvin to come to Strassburg (*Briefe*, 132).[48] Bucer's desire and readiness to draw him into the circle in that city had developed at once after the ejection from Geneva. Bucer had written to Calvin saying that if no other sphere of useful work were open to him, it had been an early desire of his people to have him in Strassburg. The congregation to which he would be able to minister was small (i.e., the French congregation), but it was a promising and needy one, and it might well be good for the situation in Geneva, too, if this call were accepted for the time being. Calvin's participation in approaching religious discussions in Germany could also be very useful, but he could obviously play a part only if he were connected with a German church. For the rest, he must not bury his great talents in a napkin but use them to the advantage of those who both needed them so much and were so urgently asking for them.[49]

45. CO 10/II, 201f. (no. 120, Farel and Calvin to Viret and Courault).

46. See nn. 19ff., 35, 37f., 40f. On Kunz see above, 375 n. 20. For the new pastors at Geneva, see CO 10/II, 208.

47. See the postscript of Calvin to Farel 8.4.1538, CO 10/II, 230 (no. 132). Cf. ibid., 227 (no. 131), 236 (no. 136); also Stähelin, I, 166.

48. CO 10/II, 228-30.

49. Ibid., 219 (no. 126). Barth follows Stähelin closely here (I, 166), but cf. CO 10/II, 219.

At first Calvin treated this invitation with the same timid reluctance as that with which he had at first responded to Farel's effort to woo him to Geneva. He asked whether, being French, he would really feel at home in a German city, also whether he could with a good conscience accept responsibility for the specific relations there.[50] But finally, as we see from the Psalms commentary, he saw himself again in the situation of Jonah,[51] gave in, and made haste to Strassburg without even putting his affairs in order. He preached there for the first time on the second Sunday in September.[52]

Before we discuss this third great episode in Calvin's life I would like to share with you some passages from his letters at the period that help to illustrate the rather mixed mood in which Calvin looked back on what had taken place. At Basel on August 4 he wrote that when they saw that it was not without the Lord's will that the people had cursed them, they did not doubt that God had his will for them. They were thus ready to humble themselves lest they should be in conflict with the will of God that purposed their humiliation. In the meantime they would await his day. For soon the crown of the drunkards in Ephraim would lose its luster (*Briefe,* 132).[53] In Strassburg in September he wrote that they certainly had to admit before God and his people that it was partly through their own inexperience, neglect, carelessness, and errors that the church that had been entrusted to them had become so sick. Nevertheless, it was their duty to uphold their innocence and purity against the church by whose deceit, malice, wickedness, and hostility the breach had come. Calvin would gladly admit, then, before God and all the pious that their ignorance and thoughtlessness deserved exemplary punishment. But he would never admit that it was their fault that the church had come to grief. For before God their conscience told them something different. Hence there could never be the acknowledgment of guilt that was asked of them with a view to reconciliation. It should be seen that everything could be had from them if only they were reinstated. But the Lord would, he hoped, open up for them a better way (*Briefe,* 140).[54] Calvin was right. We might question in endless ways what he did in those years in Geneva. We have

---

50. Stähelin, I, 165.
51. CO 31, 26/28.
52. Stähelin, I, 166; CO 10/II, 246 (no. 140).
53. CO 10/II, 229, to Farel.
54. Ibid., 246f., to Farel.

to agree that his friends in Basel, Zurich, and Strassburg were right to object to his actions. We have even to admit that occasionally the Genevans were right to reject so bitterly and frivolously what he was doing. Nevertheless, we cannot fail to see that basically what the accused on all sides was wanting to do also had right on its side in a way that the accusers never suspected. Aware of this higher right, he could seek a new home with a good if afflicted conscience.

5

Strassburg Stay, 1538-1541

In the short space of time now left we must speed things up by no longer following events chronologically but freely selecting various points in the period that were important and that characterize the whole life and theology of the reformer. (I would ask you not to be upset that in discussing the previous period I went into more detail than you expected of me. You will recall that at the beginning of the semester I painted with a larger brush. But I think I would have failed to fulfill my purpose of presenting Calvin to you if I had not studied at least one period more closely and thoroughly in order to show you what manner of man he was in the great problems of his historical existence that have often enough caught at least my breath. We may now treat ourselves to a few leaps in conclusion.)

For our purpose there is not a great deal in the Strassburg years that calls for notice. Outwardly they were a turning point in Calvin's life, the translation from young manhood to maturity, from a tentative effort to the true establishment of his life's work. We might turn once again to the *Institutes,* which he published in a much altered edition in 1539.[1] We might learn to know Calvin as a poet in his *Epinicion* [song of victory] *Christo cantatum* of 1541.[2] We might analyze his work on the Lord's Supper written in the same year,[3] and I would remind you that nowhere can you perhaps study the distinctiveness of Calvin so well as in his

1. CO 1, 255-1152.
2. OS I, 495-98.
3. OS I, 503-30.

385

eucharistic teaching. We might perhaps look at his efforts in Strassburg to give shape to the liturgy and to congregational life, which later found expression in the *Forme des prières et chants ecclésiastique avec la manière d'administrer les sacraments et consacrer le mariage selon le coutume de l'Eglise ancienne* that he published after returning to Geneva in 1542.[4] To give depth to our psychological understanding of Calvin we might take a little glance at the strange way in which he became a married man in Strassburg. All this, and his growing contacts with all kinds of contemporaries both in person and by letter, are things that unfortunately we can only mention and greet from afar. (For material cf. vols. 1, 5, 6, 10/II, 11). The three matters that I want to select for further study out of the abundant topics are the exposition of Romans in 1539, the part played by Calvin in the German religious conversations, and the exchange of letters with Cardinal Sadolet, which would be not the least occasion for the calling of Calvin back to Geneva.

§17 COMMENTARY ON ROMANS[5]

This commentary will give us the opportunity to take note of the essentials of one of the most important sides of Calvin's theology that thus far we have only touched on in passing, namely, his quality as an expositor of the Bible. Scripture did not play quite the same part in Reformed Protestantism as in Lutheran. Its dignity here was one of principle as it never was in Lutheranism, no matter how highly the latter regarded it.[6] Introducing reformation now meant establishing the Word of God in the Bible as the norm of faith and life. The Reformed church is first of all the school in which we learn and then the institution in which we are brought up. The right attitude is first one of docility, then of obedience.[7] Scripture is the guide and teacher (*Inst.* I, 6, title).[8]

All this may sound terribly legalistic. It is not meant that way. But the priority of the scripture principle in Reformed Protestantism, the lesser

---

4. OS II, 11-18.
5. CO 49, 1-292. New ed. Leiden, 1981 (ed. T. H. L. Parker).
6. Editorial emendation.
7. Cf. *Inst.* I, 6, 2; OS III, 2-9, 11f.; cf. CO 31, 21.
8. OS III, 60, 9f.

prominence given to the content, which was the starting point for Luther and Lutheranism, is undeniably beset by ambiguity. This is the ambiguity of the whole Reformed turn given to the Reformation of which we spoke earlier. It was unavoidably linked to the attempt to relate eternity to time, the forgiveness of sins to the life of the sinner, spirit to existence in the flesh, incomparable love to more humdrum obedience. Those who see themselves set the task of recognizing these relations and putting them into effect cannot fail to give the false impression, the more zealously they do it, of losing the whole freedom that comes with the positing of what is incomparable, replacing it by a dreadful tutelage such as we often think we should connect with the OT and that we therefore describe as legalism. Lutheranism, too, was in its own way an attempt, an attempt to let eternity, forgiveness, spirit, and love stand as entities in their own right, making them the cone at the head as it were, maintaining indeed the relation but leaving it to the good Lord to establish it. The bad impression that was made in this case was not one of tutelage but of a great and blessed laissez-faire.

Both attempts gave ample cause for these bad impressions. We will not try to decide here which of the two compromises took Christianity more seriously or which promoted and proclaimed it the more vehemently in spite of every compromise. We can only emphasize constantly the inner necessity of both and their inner relationship. If the Reformed effort is ventured, then the special importance of holy scripture arises out of the quest for a norm by which to regulate the relations, the quest for a rule of faith and life, of knowledge and action. This becomes the primary and vital question. The relation to time to which this concern is linked makes it essential that there be a temporal form and order for us. The real relation is certainly to eternity, but since this is now related to time, form and order are required.

Reformed Protestantism began everywhere as a rejection and contesting of forms and orders that were only apparently and ostensibly the required form and order, that is, of Roman Catholicism, which seemed to be a bringing down of the eternal to the temporal, to which there cannot be accorded the dignity of the form and order in which the relation finds true fulfillment. Reformed Protestantism began by establishing biblical authority. The burning issue for it was how to give God, the true God, the glory, how to do it here and now. In this question it lifted its gaze above the carefully erected steplike structure of medieval authorities until it came to rest on the canonical writings of the primitive Christian era.

There, and there for the first time, and there alone, it found the expression of a dignity, form, and order that imposed themselves and that it could and should respect, the norm with which it could make its venture to the glory of God without falling victim to an illusion. We have to understand the free and revolutionary forward pressure behind this establishment of the Reformed scripture principle and we will then be able to handle at least more cautiously the concept of legalism.

There were inner reasons, then, why the Zurich reformation should begin in such a banal way with a series of sermons on Matthew's Gospel,[9] and we have seen that Calvin had hardly arrived in Geneva before he began at once, not to preach, but to lecture on the Epistle to the Romans. Wherever, as with the Reformed, it is a matter of acting *with* God and *for* God, knowledge *of* God has to come first. And wherever it is a matter of knowledge of God, what else calls for consideration but the Bible, the Epistle to the Romans? That we have to handle the concept of legalism cautiously, as I have said, emerges already from the fact that Calvin took Romans as the first subject of his practical proclamation, also as the first subject of his scholarly work. The way things go is remarkable enough: ethical concern for the glorifying of God on earth leads to the question of the intellectual norm and then to the classical record of Paulinism. If we take note of this, we cannot fail to see what is the root of the ethical fervor of Reformed Protestantism. Truly it was not any lack of understanding for that which was so important for Luther as the pure and simple gospel of forgiveness and faith, but the very desire to understand this gospel. The ethical turn did not imply any abandonment of this gospel but was meant to lead back the more forcefully to it. Knowledge of God engenders a desire to act. A desire to act engenders a new seeking of God. The new quest for God engenders new knowledge of God. That is the way that Reformed thinking goes.

Against this background the task of exposition was important. The relation to the Bible is a living one. The spring does not flow of itself. It has to be tapped. Its waters have to be drawn. The answer is not already there; we have to ask what it is. The Bible calls for objective study. What is in it is, of course, known already insofar as it is a matter of the relation about which we cannot ask without first knowing it, but because it is a matter of the form and order of this relation in time, we do not yet know what is in the Bible, and, as is unavoidable in time, we have to seek and

9. See above, 258f.

find this by work. The Bible is thus opened and listened to with a readiness to receive what is not yet known, not for the purpose of finding again what is known already. In exposition it is a matter of opening up the mind of scripture, as Calvin says in the commentary's dedicatory epistle to Grynaeus.[10]

To this we must add at once, of course, that according to Calvin's express view in *Inst.* I, 7, God himself must bear witness concerning himself to those who would receive and pass on the witness of the biblical author. God is not just the theme but also the Lord of biblical truth. A purely historical understanding of the mind of scripture would be for Calvin no understanding at all. The mind of scripture cannot be merely the object of exposition but has to be its subject as well. "The same Spirit, therefore, who has spoken through the mouths of the prophets must penetrate into our hearts to persuade us that they faithfully proclaimed what had been divinely commanded."[11] Nevertheless, that does not alter the fact that the mind of scripture is *also* an object that deserves and demands objective study. Exegesis has to be a conversation in which the one speaks and the other listens. Listening, even if on the premise of secret identity with the one who speaks, is the task of the exegete.

This is what gives Calvin's expository skill its first distinctive feature: its extraordinary objectivity. We can learn from Calvin what it means to stay close to the text, to focus with tense attention on what is actually there. Everything else *derives* from this. But it has to derive from *this*. If it does not, then the expounding is not real questioning and readiness to listen. Calvin once wrote of Luther's exegesis that he was not too much concerned about the literal wording or the historical circumstances of the text but was content to derive fruitful doctrine from it (*Briefe*, 217).[12] We see gentle criticism here. Calvin wanted to derive fruitful doctrine *from* the actual wording and historical circumstances, not by ignoring them. This is a feature of the way he goes about his task. Thus he engaged in textual criticism insofar as he was able with the tools available and without having the philological skill of an Erasmus. Nor did he shrink from higher criticism, seriously questioning the authenticity of 2 Peter and Jude, and definitely contesting Paul's authorship of Hebrews.[13]

10. CO 10/II, 403 (no. 191).
11. *Inst.* I, 7, 4; OS III, 70, 2-8.
12. CO 11, 36, letter to Viret, 5.19.1540.
13. On the former see CO 55, 441 and 485; on the latter, 55, 5.

The actual exposition follows the text word for word. Only rarely does Calvin allow himself brief digressions. Naturally he does engage in what we call eisegesis, and rightly so, for if we read nothing into the Bible we will also read nothing out of it. But whichever he is doing he keeps his eye firmly on the actual text. He proceeds methodically and steadfastly, seeking diligently to follow the text in all its twists and turns. His aim is to do justice to everything in it. He displays extraordinary freedom relative to the exegetical tradition even at points where, as in the messianic prophecies of the OT, he likes to see what tradition thought it had seen before him. He stays close to what is there because what is there is enough for him, because the one biblical truth is dear and important to him precisely in the form and passage in which it is communicated and not in some other. There is, for example, remarkable tension between his well-known basic view that Christ speaks already in the OT[14] and the great caution with which he critically tests each individual OT passage to see whether and to what extent, either more closely or more remotely, it can carry a reference to Christ. To get a clear picture of this compare Luther's exposition of Psalm 2 in his *Operationes* with that of Calvin.[15]

It is self-evident that Calvin would make only the most cautious use of what is called allegorizing even where NT parallels seem to call for it directly by their *hina plērōthē* ("that it might be fulfilled"). It was naturally no accident that of all the NT books he did not write a commentary only on Revelation. He hated what he called on one occasion the pleasurable playing about[16] with every possible interpretation of the text that we can hardly avoid when it comes to Revelation, and wherever he could he avoided leaving us with two or more meanings. This is perhaps connected with the fact that he seldom engages in the adducing of parallel passages that plays so big a role in many commentaries both old and new (Luther's merry chasing after deer).[17] Each passage has its own truth. Each is self-grounded. Each must be expounded in its own context. The harmony of the whole will emerge of itself without having to be more or less questionably documented in detail. What he still reads into the Bible at every point, in contrast to more recent historical study with which his approach must not, of course, be confused, is the unity of truth, the

---

14. *Inst.* II, 9 and 10; OS III, 398ff., 403ff.
15. WA 5, 47-74; CO 31, 41ff.
16. CO 10/II, 405 (no. 191).
17. Cf. WA 5, 34, 8-12 (on Ps. 28:8).

assumption that though there are many voices, in the last resort they are all seeking to say the same thing. This did not prevent him, however, from seeing what was distinctive as such, from finding the reason for it, and from emphasizing it and establishing its validity in its own place.

This leads us to the second distinctive feature of his method. I might call this its uniformity. We see this even outwardly in his commentaries in the equal way in which each word and chapter is taken up and exploited. He does not give special prominence to Romans 1–8 because these chapters are the biblical basis of Reformation soteriology. He expounds the whole epistle with the same care and attention. Nor does he stop at Romans and some other leading and central writings. Romans is for him, as he says, an entrance that has been opened up to an understanding of all scripture.[18] In gentle criticism he complained that Melanchthon expounded only a few particularly essential chapters and because he was occupied with these he neglected many others that ought not to be neglected.[19] If in principle it is seen to be right to listen to the Bible, then we should listen to the whole Bible.

Calvin too, of course, did allow himself some tacit exceptions. I have already mentioned Revelation. In the OT he omitted especially the works attributed to Solomon. The feeling of being engaged in battle on a long and extended front enabled him to deal with detailed passages in a relaxed and sober manner. He had his eye on the whole, and therefore he did not need to break out and win victories at every point which could be in his view only sham victories. The whole of a single book and the whole of all the books speaks for itself. I do not think that we should view the doctrine of verbal inspiration, which is obviously in the background here, in the rigid and mythological way in which people usually see it.[20] What does it amount to in practice but the hypothesis that in some sense the text is trustworthy, the premise that there has to be a meaning in it, a meaning, indeed, in its wording? This premise did not prevent Calvin in fact from closely examining that trustworthiness any more than his doctrine of predestination prevented him from taking our human responsibility in bitter earnest. But it gave him also a consistent zeal to track down the content of the whole Bible, a zeal that incidentally would also stand historical investigation of the Bible in good stead.

18. CO 10/II, 405.

19. Ibid., 404.

20. For examples in works used by Barth cf. Loofs, *Leitfaden*, 882f.; Seeberg, *Lehrbuch*, IV/2, 566ff.; Lang, 74f.; Bauke, 47-52.

We now come to the third distinctive feature of Calvin's exegesis. I would call this its relevance. This is the more striking in Calvin because his objectivity often borders on what we call historicism. At this point we see again one of the tensions in which his theology is so rich. Like no other Reformation exegete, he gives free play to what is unique in each passage. He really emerges above all the others as a true biblical investigator and scholar. But then he can handle the material in such a way that we do not have the impression with him any more than with others that all we have here is mere history. History is indeed being studied, but it is also being made. It did not simply need such common expressions as "Hence we say" and "Hence we recall," or the occasional attacks on papists, monks, and schoolmen,[21] to make clear to us that the commentary has a purpose, that something is happening in it, that a fruitful and living dialogue is in fact taking place here across the cleft of the centuries. We are in the 1st century but we are equally in the 16th. We hear Paul, and we also hear Calvin. The voices merge into one another so that we can hardly distinguish them, and we get some sense of the truth of the saying that the Spirit who spoke by the prophets must penetrate into our hearts.[22] This relevance of Calvin's exposition, quite apart from specific applications, means that it still speaks and teaches and persuades today. We believe Calvin the more readily because he is not deliberately trying to make us believe but simply setting out what he finds in Paul, yet not, of course, without being able or even trying to hide the fact that he himself believes it. This quiet kinship between the apostle and the exegete speaks for itself.

We have to read Calvin attentively, of course, if we are to profit from him. At a first glance most of us might find him rather tedious. Initially his thoroughness, restraint, and uniformity seem overdone. But finally, especially when we compare him enough with others, we are grateful for these qualities and rejoice to see how here and there between the lines of the commentaries there can be just as powerful lightning flashes as in Luther, but with the advantage that we never lose sight of the primary goal of exposition as we often do in Luther. Whenever I have myself consulted Calvin's commentaries for my own use, I have found pleasure in his distinctive combination of historical and pneumatic exegesis even[23]

21. Barth seems to have the commentaries in general in mind here, since these expressions are not at all common in Calvin's *Romans*. See below, 393.

22. See above, 389 n. 11.

23. The form of this statement rests on a pencil correction Barth made in the

when I have permitted myself to go my own way. His work not only provided an external model for my own special study of Romans but also laid a firm foundation for its content.[24] The exegetical virtue that Calvin held up for himself was "perspicuous brevity."[25] He advocated this in contrast to Bucer, who, he said, had hardly laid hold of the content before the incredible fruitfulness of his mind poured out such a fullness that he could no longer hold it in or reach an end.[26] But why brevity? Does the answer lie in his own character, in the relation to his system, the boundaries here being fluid, since the *Institutes* is a web of exegesis? Exegesis as part of the work of laying the foundations of truth stands in need of brevity. It is in its relation to the practical goal of systematics, though without prejudice to its own significance, that the importance of Calvin's exegesis finally lies.[27]

§18 PARTICIPATION IN GERMAN COLLOQUIES

This side of Calvin's stay in Strassburg is important because here for the first time we have external evidence of the European place occupied by Calvin as man and thinker. You can read in more than one book of the pedagogical significance of his experiences at this point.[1] They supposedly widened his outlook and horizon and directed his attention to the general European situation of Protestantism. I do not think this reading is right. Calvin was from the first a good European who did not take national boundaries seriously and never gave proof of any distinctively French or Genevan way of looking at things; who even in his student days had learned to know the German way; who then on his first visit to Strassburg, and especially in the vital dealings of Geneva with Bern, Basel, and Zurich,

---

MS. He originally wrote: "As one who for years has never preached without consulting Calvin's commentaries I can finally do no more than bear witness that I have always found pleasure in this distinctive combination of historical and pneumatic exegesis even when. . . ."

24. Cf. Barth on Calvin as a model in the 1921 preface to his own *Romans,* and cf. above, 260 n. 10.

25. CO 10/II, 402f.

26. Ibid., 404. Barth follows the translation of Stähelin, I, 187 n**.

27. Barth had obviously not finished preparing his lecture here and simply sketched the outline in the MS. Cf. above, 241 n. 71.

1. Stähelin, I, 171; cf. Kampschulte, I, 323; and Lang, 49.

which were then regarded as Upper German cities, had long ago gained a better sense of this; who in his contacts with the cosmopolitan Bucer had long since come to be immersed in the complicated tangle of the Reformation movement as a whole; and who by the synthetic character of his first theological essay — we have seen how he tried to look at all sides and to bring all possibilities within his purview — had plainly enough manifested the religio-political universality of his purpose.

The plainest proof that he did have such a broad horizon seems to me to lie in the letters he wrote about the first colloquy to Farel,[2] for these are rich in acute comments on men and things and show that he was no novice on this stage. Kampschulte says about these letters that a native could not have given a better evaluation than this Frenchman who was not an expert on the Germans.[3] His later accounts again do not sound like those of one who was gaining experience and learning new things. He judges too quickly for that. He almost sounds the charge. He understands only too well. He has to be there. He sees the importance of the matter, initially more so than later. He is zealous for the cause. But there is no sign of the industrious commitment of one who is a dilettante abroad and in affairs. On the contrary, he has seen through the magic. As a genuine cosmopolitan he realizes that people are the same everywhere, in Regensburg, Strassburg, or Geneva, and that it is no more important or worthwhile to head large or even the largest companies, since everything depends on how this is done.

True universalists do not have to have their horizons broadened, and Calvin was such. He showed this by his participation in the German colloquies. For him the practical result of these was that he went back from the broader arena to the narrower, from Regensburg and Charles V to Geneva and the proximity of Peter Kunz of Bern. If he learned anything from the talks, it was by way of disillusionment, that is, something negative, the fact that European policies and religious policies that he himself would later distinctively pursue would move along different tracks from those in which he was participating there as a critical observer and reporter. After that he would not travel a great deal. He would not expect much from the conferences that were then so popular with their mass pronounce-

---

2. CO 10/II, 322-29 (no. 162) and 330-32 (no. 164). These letters to Farel tell of the experiences at Frankfurt February to April 1539, with Bucer from the middle of March. Cf. also Kampschulte, I, 329.

3. Kampschulte, I, 330: Barth puts *geschah* for Kampschulte's *geschiet*.

ments. He would seldom make any effort to work with princes and other secular powers, or indeed with any others among whom he would simply be one among the rest and compromise would be the only goal or the only means of making headway. Instead, without losing sight of the whole picture, indeed, just because he kept it in view so firmly and without any illusions, he would form a center. He would position himself in relation to this center, which means essentially to himself, and from it he would radiate his influence, preferably indirectly by his writings, by the summons that he and Geneva issued, by his letters that he sent to influential people, so that the impact would be simply his own, which was as yet the case only to a small extent in Germany. Calvin's participation in the German colloquies was indeed important as regards his European relation, not as regards its origin, but as regards the way in which he would put it into effect.

We will first let the facts speak for themselves. Calvin's stay in Strassburg coincided with the time when Charles V, harassed by Francis I on the one side and the Turks on the other, had to try to come to an agreement with the Protestants in the empire. This was the final moment when things favored, humanly speaking, the Protestant cause in Germany. No less was at issue than behind the back of Rome, as it were, which was constantly postponing the promised general council, the achieving of a religious peace in Germany. Under pressure the emperor himself had made the overture, so that no matter what the form of the agreement might be, it would be a basic victory for the Reformation. Typical was a scene at the Worms colloquy in December 1540, of which Calvin reports in triumph that the papal nuncio was not allowed a place of privilege but was seated with all the rest of the delegates; that even Roman Catholics avoided making mention of the pope; and that the nuncio had to suffer the defeat of alone baring his head when he himself referred to the holy father, whereas all the delegates did so when the name of the emperor was mentioned.[4]

Calvin knew how to stress and exploit this angle of Germany versus Rome in a work against Cardinal Farnese published anonymously in March 1541, in which, addressing the Germans in such terms as "we Germans" and "our Germany"[5] — terms, Kampschulte feels, that the German nation had not heard since the days of Hutten (I, 335) — he

4. CO 11, 138 (no. 268), Dec. 1540.
5. CO 5, 461-508; for the terms, see CO 5, 507.

issued a warning to the papal mercenaries among them who were traitors to the fatherland, and defended the right of the Germans not to wait any longer for the council but to protect themselves by their own peaceful negotiations. This was perhaps one of the rare cases when a Frenchman could speak along the lines of German nationalism. Calvin's own true aim was naturally not to be found along such lines, but he did want to strengthen German Protestantism and therefore indirectly the whole Protestant cause. He had proved this the previous summer at Hagenau, where he had zealously appealed for an alliance between the German Protestants and Francis I against the emperor, and for this reason was the recipient of many compliments from Margaret of Angoulême, the king's sister, in a letter she sent him.[6] Nevertheless, the strengthening of German Protestantism was primary for Calvin, and nowhere in his letters had he more bitter complaints than when he spoke about the indecisiveness and disunity of the German princes and yet the skill with which they could handle the papal legates and assert themselves,[7] two factors that together were finally hampering the formation of a national outlook. We need not be incensed as Kampschulte was that Calvin's plan was to play off Germany against Rome and France against Germany, or at least against the emperor.[8] His true cause was neither the French nor the German cause, but the Protestant cause, and it was so to a degree of impartiality found in hardly any other theologian, corresponding exactly to the policy that the internationally oriented adversary in Rome was following. If the aim was to advance the Protestant cause on the stage of global politics, no way of doing it was more shrewd that that which Calvin had in view.

But I will now take things as they come. The series of discussions began in Frankfurt at the end of February 1539 with a conference of Protestant delegates alone.[9] Calvin had an unofficial role as a companion of Bucer. Incredibly quickly, as we have said, and without knowing German, he gained detailed information about the new world into which he had now stepped, and in conversations with the statesmen and theologians present he tried to work chiefly in two directions, first, to unite Protestants, to concentrate their forces, and to play down their differences, then to secure help for the oppressed Protestants in France. He first advocated an

---

6. CO 11, 62 (no. 226).
7. Cf. ibid., 178f. (no. 290).
8. Kampschulte, I, 331-35.
9. CO 10/II, 322, 9 (no. 162); also Stähelin, I, 230ff.; and Kampschulte, I, 328ff.

alliance between the German Protestants and Francis I by which he hoped to gain a breathing space for those who were under persecution in his own country. But he found no great hearing for this proposal. He thus worked the more energetically at first to achieve the primary goal. He wrote with obvious irritation about the Duke of Württemberg, who at that time preferred to go hunting instead of attending meetings that might decide what would happen to his state and perhaps to his own head.[10] Everything that seemed to give material or moral strength to the Schmalkald League interested Calvin and gave him pleasure. If he had had there the influence that Luther had and did not use, things might have turned out very differently! In Frankfurt — and this was a subsidiary aim of his going there — he met Melanchthon for the first time, and although he saw his weaknesses, he quickly came to a remarkably good understanding with him. There thus arose the friendship between the two, cultivated though it was more diligently by Calvin than by Melanchthon, that would last until the death of the latter.[11] It was undoubtedly their common origin in Humanism that linked them at first, but also perhaps the need to complement one another that two very different people so often have. As we know, Melanchthon before his death became almost a martyr to his crypto-Calvinism. It would be a worthwhile study to examine the relation between the two more closely.

The commencement of the more polemical colloquies had to wait a year, but at last in June and July 1540 a conference took place at Hagenau. The Roman Catholic delegation was so weak, however, that no really important decisions could be reached. The Roman party was clearly trying to gain time so as to prevent the achieving of any agreement, or even the discussion of essential questions, without papal participation. Here again Calvin called for vigorous action on the part of the Protestant states with the cooperation of Francis I. The pope and the emperor were simply biding their time until they could attack with force.[12] The result of Hagenau was the calling of a fresh conference at Worms, which was opened in October 1540 and lasted until January 1541. Calvin now took part officially as the representative of the dukes of Lüneburg,[13] at first gladly, but quickly

10. CO 10/II, 326.
11. Stähelin, I, 230ff., 237ff.
12. CO 11, 50ff. (no. 221) to Farel, 6.21.1540; and 64-67 (no. 228) to du Tailly, 7.28.1540; cf. also Kampschulte, I, 330f.
13. Kampschulte, I, 332.

enough disillusioned by the delaying tactics of the Roman party, which endlessly raised questions of form and procedure. From this time onward Calvin's letters to Farel become increasingly morose. On the only decisive issue discussed, that of original sin, the Roman Catholics were ready to compromise, for in this matter they were not agreed among themselves — "it was remarkable how noisily they wrangled among themselves over it" — [14] but they were victorious as regards their main objective of obstructing any kind of binding agreement. It is not surprising that Calvin, who almost died of impatience, had no great desire to take part any further when it was resolved to continue the talks in connection with the Diet of Regensburg. At first he refused to go there, but Melanchthon in particular summoned him to do so, and thus, most unwillingly, he went *(invitissime Ratisponam trahor)*.[15]

The proceedings began on March 10, 1541. In the short intervening time Calvin had written the polemical work against Farnese under the name of Eusebius Pamphilius (5, 461ff.).[16] This work simply shows how different would have been the caliber and tempo of the action he favored from what he was now — a Prometheus bound — permitted to do. At the very beginning of the Diet Calvin, along with the other Protestants, had had to sign the Augsburg Confession, for the Roman Catholics would hold conversations only with its adherents.[17] The version was the *Invariata,* that is, that which was least favorable to Calvin's view of the Lord's Supper.[18] But how could he not sign? He had already persuaded himself at Frankfurt that its author thought in the main essentially as he himself did. The anti-Calvinist reading that the relevant article would be given later was not as yet to hand. For Calvin only the existence of the *Variata* made the *Invariata* the shibboleth of an exclusive Lutheranism that it became.

At last in Regensburg serious discussions began between the Roman

14. CO 11, 138 (no. 268).

15. Ibid., 156 (no. 277) to Farel. Following Kampschulte, I, 334 n. 1, Barth has *invitissime* for *invitissimus.*

16. See above, 395 n. 5.

17. Stähelin, I, 234.

18. See above, 182 n. 88. We cannot say for certain which version Calvin signed. In favor of the *Invariata* cf. CO 15, 336; in favor of the *Variata,* 16, 430. Stähelin calls the question one we cannot answer for sure, and three years later Barth himself opted for the *Variata;* see *Theology and Church* (1st German ed. Munich, 1928; ET New York, 1962), 121.

Catholics Eck, Gropper, and Julius of Pflug on the one side and the Protestants Bucer, Melanchthon, and Pistorius on the other.[19] Calvin's initial pleasure was dampened by the admission, in spite of every protest, of the papal legates Contarini and Morone and by the presence of the emperor, which from the outset weighed down the scales decisively in favor of the adversaries.[20] Nor could he be pleased that the Evangelicals were much too conciliatory and in this way, as he saw it, showed their weakness. On the basis of Augustine an agreed formula was reached on original sin and even on justification.[21] But when an attempt was made to take up the questions of the church and especially transubstantiation, the talks collapsed, to Calvin's no little satisfaction.[22] For a long time he had been listening skeptically. And when Eck, to his sorrow, did not die as the result of an assault ("the world does not yet deserve to be rid of this brute"),[23] and things threatened to drag on forever, the patience he had been showing finally gave out, and he left prematurely on June 15. Undoubtedly negotiations for his return to Geneva played a part in his departure. But it was also in keeping with the mood and viewpoint that had increasingly become his relative to the whole business. He no longer expected anything to be achieved by these efforts.

In this affair, we may quietly admit, Calvin was totally isolated. This must be our starting point, I think, if we are to arrive at any understanding. The way in which he constantly felt himself impelled to open his heart in long and detailed letters to Farel, all of them full of irony and concern, tells us that more than any other theologian there he found himself a stranger who stood alone. Nor was that simply because he was French. I can think of no instance when, as he might so easily have done, he broke out in sighs or scorn at the foreign way things were done. It was what he wanted and was pursuing that isolated him even from his German friends, even from Bucer and Melanchthon. He was isolated in his aims and also in his assessment of things. At the first, and on all sides, the Protestant faction valued him and respected him, but they saw things with different eyes and they were thus separated from him as by a glass partition. This is what irritated him at certain times, as though he would like to ask them why they wanted him in their game when their aims were quite different.

19. Cf. CO 11, 203 (no. 302) to Farel, 4.24.1541.
20. Kampschulte, I, 334-36.
21. CO 11, 215 (no. 308) to Farel, 5.11.1541.
22. Ibid.
23. Ibid., 217f. (no. 309) to Farel, 5.12.1541.

The second related fact was what we might quietly call his total lack of success or influence. He entered into the discussions with his renowned conceptual sharpness — we have already referred to what he had to say about justification and sanctification at Regensburg[24] — and he participated strongly in private talks, some of them with Roman Catholics. In general, however, the course of the whole colloquy would hardly have been different at any point if this stranger, who would later be so influential, had not been there. The only palpable impact he made that calls for mention is that he did perhaps do something to check Melanchthon's tendency to yield and Bucer's to compromise, that is, to rein in the far too conciliatory spirit that the two showed in their different ways.[25]

In both his isolation and his lack of influence Calvin may be compared only with the one Protestant contemporary who held aloof from the whole affair and who in his own way also viewed it critically, namely, Luther. Typically, of course, Calvin wanted precisely what Luther wanted least, namely, the promotion of Protestantism with the help of political combinations. One can hardly imagine any sharper antithesis to Luther's style than the game Calvin wanted to play with France, Rome, and Germany. But the extremes met. In spite of his greater independence and distinctiveness, or perhaps because of them, Calvin was a more faithful theological disciple of Luther than Bucer or Melanchthon, and for that reason his political stance was in its result (i.e., in that isolation and lack of influence) much closer to that of Luther than the stances of the other two, who, without Calvin's resolve upon political action, but with a zeal for compromise, actually did much more to politicize the gospel than did Calvin, who with all his grandiose political schemes had so consistent a concern for the purity of the cause that he damaged his influence.

Then as later we may perhaps describe Calvin's attitude in world politics as one of soberness or objectivity. We saw earlier that his tendency to keep the distance between heaven and earth gave him an inner freedom to tread the more surely and resolutely on earth. He did not act politically as an enthusiast. He was not swayed by religious feelings. As he saw it, he simply acted in obedience. The kingdom of Christ has also an earthly side that we must differentiate from the heavenly. We have to proceed realistically on this side. A game of chess is in order in relation to it. The total lack of any confusion between the visible and the invisible enabled Calvin

24. Cf. 246 n. 4, though the reference is to Worms.
25. Cf. Kampschulte, I, 337.

to look calmly at the visible as such in all its distinctiveness, to see the Protestant cause as a related complex with its own needs face-to-face with the Roman Catholic adversary and the states involved. He wanted to be a champion of this cause, or, if he was that already, he wanted to be it more truly and zealously. Here is the explanation of the earnestness with which he gave himself to the task and the skill that he showed in doing so. His very lack of success, and the subsequent need to develop his own political style, showed that his soberness had less of an earthly origin that it might seem to have at first glance.

We see Calvin's soberness and objectivity especially in the three motifs that finally characterize all that he had to say on this subject. First, he sees European Protestantism as a whole, more so than any of the German Protestants. If there was to be Protestant political action, then, following the example of the adversary, it could be only from a universal and not a German standpoint, the national standpoint being only a means to the end. We may lament when we find the national standpoint primary for someone, but we then have to consider what we are really after. Calvin at least knew that. Second, Calvin had an emphatic and active concern to promote Protestant unity. At all costs he wanted to stay above the Protestant split in Germany. This is why he inclined so strongly to Melanchthon. But his letters to Switzerland also show how zealously concerned he was to urge his friends there to steer clear of Swiss eccentricity, to reconcile themselves to the styles of Bucer and Luther, to stop making so much of Zwingli.[26] Calvin was not aiming to set up any Calvinism, though he might easily have done so. Third, we see an aversion to the zeal of others to reach a modus vivendi. The aim must be not to make peace with Roman Catholics but to clear the way for the cause of Protestantism. Calvin was surely in no sense a middleman when he could dryly write that the first principle of Roman Catholic theology is that there is no God and the second that Christianity is a swindle, from which two all the rest follow.[27] Precisely at this point we see that Calvin's realism, though it took its own path, was no different from that of Luther but totally different from the weak bartering of Bucer and Melanchthon.

The result for Calvin, as we have said, was disillusionment. Protestants as they *were* were not for now any use on the field of world politics. They were no match for the opponent. They were good people, but they

26. CO 11, 24 (no. 211) to Farel, 2.26.1540.
27. CO 5, 654; cf. Kampschulte, I, 336.

had too little knowledge of what they wanted, they vacillated too weakly between different standpoints, they were not outstanding people. A secondary result of this whole period was that Calvin gained information about the conditions of German Protestantism in particular. He objected to three specific things in it: its lack of religious discipline, its form of worship, which had been too little purified and was too Judaizing, and its dependence on the different leaders.[28] At all these points something better had to be done. An active and superior shock force was needed. It was with that resolve that Calvin left Regensburg and went for the second time to Geneva. The confirmation of his own most inward view that the German colloquies gave him was no mean thing. We may thus say that this episode was of decisive significance for him in his life.

§19 CORRESPONDENCE WITH SADOLET

I have chosen this exchange as our third and last topic because in it the whole Calvin was again moving on particularly to the inner structure of his Christianity and because today, at our final session, it brings us back to our starting point, to the contrast between the Middle Ages and the Reformation. When we study the correspondence we have to listen once again to the spirit of medieval Catholicism in the person of an extremely fine and sympathetic advocate — such was Sadolet — and then in antithesis to Calvin's response, and this will give us yet another chance to see what not just Calvin but the Reformation in general both was and is as opposed to the finest and most sympathetic form in which that Catholicism might encounter it. I hope that you have still retained enough of the impression made by the first lecture to realize that our aim is not to attack that Catholicism by contrasting its perversions with a relatively perfect Protestantism. I also hope that you noticed that I did not earlier make that Catholicism responsible for a figure like Caroli. Relatively perfect forms confront one another on both sides in the exchange that we must now discuss. Remember *this* antithesis when you again have occasion to clarify what really separates us confessionally from Rome if we are genuine Protestants.

28. Cf. Kampschulte, I, 339; CO 10/II, 331 (no. 164) to Farel, March 1539; and 340 (no. 169) to Farel, April 1539.

Jakobus Sadoletus (1477-1547), bishop of Carpentras in the district of Avignon and cardinal presbyter of St. Calixtus at Rome, was a man who was as it were on the left wing of the papal camp. Himself deriving from Humanism, he had formed an independent and distinctive view of Catholic Christianity. In the papacy he contended constantly, and not without criticism, for church reforms, and he had his windows open here, as we might say, toward Protestantism. He, too, had written an exposition of Romans that aroused much opposition.[1] In 1537 he had also written a friendly letter to Melanchthon with an invitation to return to Rome.[2] It is in the same role that we shall learn to know him now.

A confused situation had followed the departure of Farel and Calvin from Geneva. The pastors who were appointed in their place were of little significance and the council followed no fixed course, trying to steer between Bern's earnest desire for a full reformation of faith and life and a popular laissez-faire that would acquiesce in almost anything. A party favoring Calvin made things difficult for both the pastors and the council, and only admonitory letters from Calvin[3] stopped this party from making things even more difficult. But the secret friends of Roman Catholicism both in the city and outside, along with those whom the Reformation had driven abroad, also began quietly to raise their heads again, thinking their hour had perhaps come. The situation aroused much interest outside as well, so much so that early in 1539 a bishops' conference at Lyons attended by the former bishop of Geneva, Pierre de la Baume, could seriously plan steps that would win back this important city.

The result was a charge to Cardinal Sadolet, who had the skill to carry out the plan if anyone could, and in execution of this charge he sent a letter on March 18, 1539, to his dear brethren the council and citizens of Geneva.[4] This letter rather surprised Geneva, but it was politely received and a provisional acknowledgment was sent. One of the preachers was deputed to make the real response in the name of the city.[5] The friends of Romanism saw to it that the letter was sent round and read from house

---

1. This was published in 1534 but censored in 1535 because of its semi-Pelagianism and its being too far from Augustine. With the help of Contarini, however, Sadolet managed to get the ban removed. Cf. K. Benrath, "Sadoleto, Jacopo," *RE,* 3rd ed., 17, 329f.

2. CR 3, 379-83 (no. 1587).

3. CO 10/II, 250-55 (no. 143, 10.1.1538) and 350-55 (no. 175, 6.25.1539).

4. Cf. Kampschulte, I, 352; OS I, 441ff.

5. Stähelin, I, 295; Doumergue, II, 679.

to house. Those who favored the Reformation in Geneva, and the people of Bern in particular, were worried as to what might come of it. Since the pastors of Geneva showed no resoluteness in grasping the nettle, no other than Peter Kunz finally advised that they should turn to Calvin as the proper man to do so.

Calvin, once a swift messenger had brought him a copy and he had digested the contents, had no hesitation in meeting the request, and in six days he wrote his reply, dated September 1. The reception of this reply in Geneva restored the shaky situation there almost at once, and even Kampschulte agrees with the general verdict that the reply brilliantly disposed of the adversary.[6] Of all Calvin's shorter works it is in fact the most incisive and powerful, and it evoked express praise from Luther, so that Melanchthon could tell his friend at that time that he stood for the moment high in Luther's graces.[7] The reply helped at least intellectually to prepare the way for the recall of Calvin to Geneva. Other more forceful events would be needed, however, before that could happen. Let us now turn to the two works themselves (5, 369ff.).[8]

Sadolet's letter is a masterpiece of its kind, and not only because formally it was composed with such skill and charm. It sounds like an Italian adagio. It avoids anything offensive. It is content to issue a pious admonition to the readers and to point out to them quite dispassionately how much finer and better it would be for them if. . . . Yet it also has a serious dignity that could not and did not fail to have its effect. The contents are also very good. The letter firmly plays down what is hierarchical and superstitious in Roman Catholicism. It openly admits the partial corruption of the church. What remains is a refined and intelligent Christianity whose warmth one can hardly escape even if one does not have sharp ears. The words "love" and "peace" recur again and again, words which were not really the most used in the vocabulary of the Reformation and for which even today many churchgoers have an instinctive longing. In this letter Roman Catholicism seems to be such a natural and a given thing. How could they resist it? Nor are some more profound passages lacking for the more thoughtful. There is thus something for everyone.

---

6. Kampschulte, I, 354: "in truth one of the most brilliant polemical works ever to flow from his pen, and even those who do not share his views must accord him the palm in this controversy."

7. Ibid., 355; and CO 10/II, 432 (no. 197), to Farel, 11.20.1539; cf. 402 (no. 190); and WA B 8, 569, 29-32, Luther to Bucer, 10.14.1539.

8. OS I, 441ff.

The familiar road from earth to heaven is opened up. A cardinal who is both friendly and accomplished stands at the entrance and recommends that we take it.

If we look more closely we find that in fact what he says might have a place in what are at least supposedly good Protestant sermons. Why should we not accept his invitation? And over the whole there arches a blue and cloudless heaven that compares favorably with the gray north of Germany and Gaul. The cardinal tells the people of Geneva that as their neighbor he has always had their interests at heart and has heard with sorrow that certain cunning men have brought them into confusion and apostasy. Mother church weeps over the desolate, and they can see by the result what kind of seed was then sown. Thorny and subtle investigations, a useless philosophy, and an obscure interpretation of the Bible have directed them on to this path. The cardinal will talk to them humbly and simply and clearly. Why do we become Christians? Well, clearly and simply, to be saved and to go to heaven. Christ rose again, and did so for all, in order to open up for them this way. This matter was so important for God that he sent his own Son for us in the flesh.[9] We thus believe in Christ in order that through him we may find salvation for our souls, that is, our own life. If we are dear to ourselves, the salvation of our souls has to be important to us.[10]

What is faith? Not just trust in God without love? That would not be possible. No, faith includes an inner readiness to do good and to live for God. God is himself love. Hence faith and love are the cause *(causa)* of our salvation.[11] For the salvation of their souls many martyrs have shed their blood and many learned fathers have poured out sweat. Should they not be an example for us? They form and constitute the church, which is surely worth pious consideration as an authority. The church it is which with its institutions shows us the way of faith and love[12] that we cannot and should not leave if we are to be humble and to remain humble. And how important humility is before God! How dangerous for the salvation of our souls, and therefore for ourselves, is its opposite, a wrong and arbitrary worship of God![13] Let us assume that it is not certain that the

9. Ibid., 442-45.
10. Ibid., 445.
11. Ibid., 446.
12. Ibid., 447.
13. Ibid., 447ff.

Catholic church does have true and humble worship of God; is it not at least more probable that it does so with its fifteen hundred years of past history than that the new church only twenty-five years old should have it? Is it not more advisable, then, to be in agreement with this church than the latter?[14]

The Genevans must tell themselves that they are now at a crossroads. Let us imagine two persons at the last judgment.[15] The first one says: I received my faith from my parents. I resolved to be faithful to it. I heard some new people who had scripture often on their lips and who tried to seduce me away from obedience to the church. But I did not listen to them. Even their reference to the defective lives of many of the princes and priests of the church could not lead me astray. I remembered the saying that what the latter told us, we should do, and I obeyed them and committed myself to the judgment of God. I now stand before thee, God, and invoke thy mercy.[16] The second says: I saw the wicked lives of those who ruled the church and burned with righteous indignation. I had applied myself diligently to theology and literature and learned a great deal, and I saw unworthy people taking the posts of supreme dignity ahead of me. I then made up my mind to attack those whom the Lord also hates, and I stirred up the people to break the laws of the church, I called the papacy a tyranny, I preached righteousness by faith alone, so that people can live as they like, and I studied the Bible particularly to make polemical use of it. I thus achieved renown and recognition, and if I could not wholly overthrow the authority of the church, I caused a great commotion.[17] Then, the cardinal goes on in his summary of the Protestant confession at the last judgment, this person makes no mention of the involved vainglory, self-seeking, craving for popularity, and hidden deception known only to the self.[18] Even if, inconceivably, the church should be wrong, will not the first person be justified in virtue of the humility displayed and for the sake of pious ancestors?[19] But who will stand by the arrogant second person? The one who in opinionatedness scorned the church, the bride of Christ, and not only cut but tore to pieces the seamless robe that even the soldiers spared?

14. Ibid., 450.
15. Ibid., 451.
16. Ibid., 451f.
17. Ibid., 452f.
18. Ibid., 453.
19. Ibid., 453.

Look at your sects and parties! The truth is one, but among them are many truths. What does Christ command us? That we should all be one in him. The Christian religion is peace with God and concord with others. Everything, absolutely everything, depends on unity.[20] It is this unity that the Catholic church is seeking. I pray for the seducers. I do not curse them. May God bring them to knowledge. But you Genevans, I admonish you, now that the mists have been cleared away from your eyes, return to concord and give new obedience to our mother church. Do not be put off by the lives we live. You may hate us personally if the gospel permits you to do so, but you surely cannot hate our teaching and our faith.[21] These things could hardly be expressed in a more illuminating, skillful, or mischievous manner. Note the contrast that is made, namely, between the Roman Catholic laity and the Protestant preachers.

What would Calvin say in reply? He stated that he would come forward as one of the cardinal's supposed seducers of the city, not renouncing solidarity with them even though no longer resident in Geneva. If this had been just a personal attack, he could have kept silent. But it would be disloyalty to do so when the attack was on his office and ministry.[22] If ambition had driven him, he, with Farel, would have done better to remain in the Roman Catholic ministry. Did he really have to have the charge of ambition flung at him by a Roman cardinal?[23]

But to the point. What about Sadolet's long disquisition on the salvation of souls? Certainly it is good to be reminded of future eternal life, to have this reminder sounded in our ears day and night. In our own sermons we do little else than refer to spiritual fellowship with God in the hope of a blessed eternity.[24] But our primary concern should not be for ourselves but for the glory of God.[25] From him and in him and to him are all things. Only in order that we might truly glorify his name has he linked to this the achieving of our own salvation. It befits a Christian to aim at something higher than simply seeking and achieving the soul's salvation. I cannot regard people as truly devout if they do not find such an insistent reference to heavenly blessedness superfluous, if they leave

20. Ibid., 454.
21. Ibid., 455.
22. Ibid., 457, 486.
23. Ibid., 459-61.
24. Ibid., 463f.
25. Ibid., 463.

people to themselves, if they do not help them with a single word, if they do not incline them to hallowing the name of God.[26] (This passage is clearly the heart of the whole work. The naive desire to get to heaven, with a crass appeal to human self-love, was the foundation stone of Sadolet's structure and also its weakest point. By making here his familiar reversal — we live for God, not God for us — Calvin robbed his opponent's whole train of thought of its point. We also see here once again that Calvin's belief in the hereafter is not to be confused with what we usually call this. It is fellowship with God in hope, and serious people cannot primarily seek what is just in their own interest. We achieve our own salvation because God in his wisdom and goodness has linked this to his own glorifying, but it comes second, not first.)

Calvin then attacks Sadolet's view of the church. Sadolet seems not to know that the Spirit *and the Word* together constitute the church. He has thus no standard by which to know the true church.[27] Papal theology has it in common with Anabaptist theology that it speaks constantly of the Spirit but forgets the Word.[28] We do not seek to erect a new church but specifically to set up again the oldest and true church that is now almost destroyed. Does the opposite party, scholastic theology, really have the recklessness to call the study of holy scripture thorny and subtle?[29] Calvin then gives an express account of the doctrine of justification that Sadolet had totally misunderstood.[30] He could honestly reject the complaint that he preached license for the flesh, and he could quietly repeat something he often said, namely, that where Christ is, there is the Spirit of sanctification, even though always with a backward glance at the gratuitous righteousness of God that brings salvation.[31] Again, what is humility? Is it really reverence for the church, for human beings? Certainly a true humility will accord to all people their due at the appropriate level, but basically it relates to the head of the church, to Christ. Certainly we are to offer obedience to those above us, but only according to the rule of God's Word. Certainly the church is important, but its sole concern must be for God's Word and nothing else.[32] Things must not be left to scholars,

---

26. Ibid., 463f.
27. Ibid., 464f.
28. Ibid., 465.
29. Ibid., 466-68.
30. Ibid., 469-71.
31. Ibid., 470f.
32. Ibid., 475f.

but even the simplest must be armed in the hard fight they have against the devil so that they may fight with assurance.[33]

In conclusion, Calvin places two persona before the judgment seat, but this time it is not a Roman Catholic and a Protestant, as in Sadolet. (He calls that a game on Sadolet's part to enable him to give his own picture of a Protestant.)[34] Instead we have two Evangelicals, the one a preacher, the other a believer (a good answer!). The first says: Thou, Lord, art the truth. Judge whether I did right to turn aside from human precepts, the veneration of saints, and works righteousness. I did not think I went too far by thus doing what I saw all your servants have done. Is it arrogance to seize the standard when others flee and to rally the scattered to their posts? Was the standard anyone else's but thine? Could I serve unity at the cost of truth? Did not the prophets contend with the priests of their day?[35] The second says: Before, I blindly obeyed the church and I had a bad conscience. Not without resistance I then saw its authority to be arrogance, and I wanted to obey thee alone. A reference to the faith of ancestors could equally well justify the religion of Jews, Turks, and Saracens.[36]

Calvin came back to the foolish charge of vainglory and self-seeking and then at the end to the accusation that the Reformation caused strife and division. The truth is that it seeks peace for the kingdom of Christ, but no other peace. If we seek any other peace we simultaneously tear the Christian religion out of human hearts. May Sadolet and his like come to realize that the only bond of church unity is for Christ the Lord, reconciles us to God the Father, to unite us in the fellowship of his body, so that by his Word and Spirit we grow to be one heart and one soul.[37]

33. Ibid., 477.
34. Ibid., 480.
35. Ibid., 480-84.
36. Ibid., 484-86.
37. Ibid., 487-89.

Index of Subjects

Index of Names

Index of Scripture References